Education in a Single Europe
Second Edition

D0147350

This book brings together contributors from the fifteen member states of the European Union in order to understand the different degrees of commitment to the concept of Europe and the role education plays in such a process. This second edition includes the new countries which have become part of the Union and also considers recent developments in policy and practice.

The introduction considers the main issues involved in education across contemporary Europe, while subsequent chapters provide individual case studies for nations. The countries covered are: **Austria; Belgium; Denmark; Finland; France; Germany; Greece; Ireland; Italy; Luxembourg; the Netherlands; Portugal; Spain; Sweden** and **the United Kingdom**. All sectors of education are dealt with in each case and the central theme of 'the European dimension' is examined throughout. Contributors also explore any matters of special relevance within their particular countries.

What emerges is a picture of a Europe very much in development, with the European identity being reinforced throughout the various education systems and supported by the success of link schemes. The material presented here will make a significant contribution to the literature in this field of research and study.

Colin Brock is Lecturer in Comparative and International Education at Oxford University. **Professor Witold Tulasiewicz** is a fellow of Wolfson College, University of Cambridge.

Education in a Single Europe

Second Edition

Edited by
Colin Brock and Witold Tulasiewicz

London and New York

First edition published in 1994 by Routledge
This edition published in 2000 by Routledge
11 New Fetter Lane, London EC4P 4EE

Simultaneously published in the USA and Canada
by Routledge
29 West 35th Street, New York, NY 10001

Routledge is an imprint of the Taylor & Francis Group

© 1994, 2000 selection and editorial matter Colin Brock and Witold Tulasiewicz and
© individual chapters the contributors

Typeset in Goudy by Keystroke, Jacaranda Lodge, Wolverhampton
Printed and bound in Great Britain by Biddles Ltd, Guildford and King's Lynn

British Library Cataloguing in Publication Data
A catalogue record for this book is available from the British Library

Library of Congress Cataloging in Publication Data
Education in a single Europe / [edited by] Colin Brock and Witold
   Tulasiewicz. — 2nd ed.
       p.   cm.
   Includes bibliographical references and index.
   (pbk. : alk. paper)
     1. Education—European Union countries. 2. Europe—Study and
teaching. I. Brock, Colin. II. Tulasiewicz, Witold.
LA622.E3814 1999
370'.94—dc21   99–26322
                                                         CIP

ISBN 0-415-16440-0 (hbk)
ISBN 0-415-16441-9 (pbk)

Contents

Contributors

Margarida Belard is Counsellor at the Ministry and Head of the Coordinating Unit of the *Clubes Europeus* of the Portuguese Ministry of Education

Sylvia van de Bunt-Kokhuis is an International Educational Consultant and was formerly Director of the Office for International Relations at Tilburg University

Kieran Byrne is Vice-President: Academic Affairs at the University of Limerick and President of the Education Studies Association of Ireland

Andrew Convey is Honorary Research Fellow in the School of Geography, University of Leeds

Françoise Convey is Head of Studies in French at Trinity and All Saints College, University of Leeds

Peadar Cremin is President of Mary Immaculate College, University of Limerick

Germain Dondelinger is Professeur Attaché and Head of the Department of International Relations in the Ministry of Education Luxembourg

Nathalie Druine is Assistant in Comparative Education Research: Department of Educational Sciences of the Catholic University of Leuven

Antonia Ruiz Esturla was Coordinator of Spanish Mother Tongue Teaching at the Spanish Embassy in London. She is currently Director of Studies at the Fray Luis de Granada Institute of Secondary Education

Rosarii Griffin is an Educational Researcher at the University of Oxford Department of Educational Studies

Luusi Hendriks is Programme Manager at the Netherlands Centre for Innovation of Education and Training

Michael Kassotakis is Professor in the Education Section of the School of Philosophy: University of Athens

Friedrich W. Kron is Professor at the Institute for Education: Johannes Gutenberg Universität Mainz

Josef Leidenfrost is Director of the Austrian Socrates National Agency and Deputy Secretary General of the Austrian Academic Exchange Service in Vienna

Attilio Monasta is Lecturer in Experimental Education at the University of Florence and Coordinator of the European Union Network of Inter-University Cooperation Programmes in Educational Studies

Anthony Merritt is Principal Lecturer in Education, Trinity and All Saints College, University of Leeds

Reijo Raivola is Professor and Dean in the Department of Education at Tampere University

Josien Roelands is Assistant in Research at the Educational Policy and Analysis Department of the Catholic University of Leuven

Sven Salin is Head of the Department for Educational Policy: the National Union of Teachers in Sweden

Nicole Vigouroux-Frey is Professeur des Universités: at the University of Rennes II

Chris Waterman is Education and Arts Officer for the Association of London Government

Thyge Winther-Jensen is Professor in the Department of Education, Philosophy and Rhetoric at the University of Copenhagen

Foreword

Since the first edition of *Education in a Single Europe*, the European Union has progressed still further on its long journey towards becoming a truly united continent. In 1995 Austria, Sweden and Finland completed the European Union's fourth successful enlargement and in 1996 the Intergovernmental Conference was concluded at the European Council meeting in Amsterdam. The European Union now faces another critical juncture in its history. The deadline for Economic and Monetary Union has been passed, and there are currently twelve membership applications on the table from states who have – for various reasons – been excluded thus far from the greatest success story this century.

The exchange of students between member states of the European Union facilitates the movement towards greater European unity. When Chancellor Adenauer of Germany met President de Gaulle of France in their great reconciliation at Rheims in January 1963, one of the foremost practical measures which emerged was their agreement about exchanges between the young people of both countries. The two Heads of Government agreed to make provision for tens of thousands of young people to visit each other's country each year. Generations of young French and Germans now fluently speak each other's language, have a better understanding of each other's way of life and share a wider knowledge of the traditions and treasures of each other's countries.

If we look back to the eighteenth and nineteenth centuries it was customary for the British to make the grand tour of the countries of Europe before they settled down to their life at home. I know from my own experiences in the 1930s that this will have led to a deeper appreciation of our common European culture and civilisation. That is why I am glad that British universities in particular are now very active in EU schemes such as Socrates, Erasmus, Comenius and Leonardo.

I constantly found in government negotiations that it was a considerable advantage to be able to speak the language of the other person as well as one's own. The quality and extent of language training teaching should be of concern for us all. The European Union's Lingua programme points the way forward.

I said in my foreword to the first edition of *Education in a Single Europe* that education is a vital means of building up the international trust that was shattered during the first half of this century. I would like to reiterate this point. There are currently more than 60 million young people in the European Union aged between 15 and 25, and we must look to these youngsters to provide the next generation of European leadership. We must ensure that the educational systems across the European Union provide the right skills and training so that we and our children can look to the future with confidence.

The UK Presidency of the European Union, which commenced on 1 January 1998, illustrated the commitment of the UK. There is now a huge majority of MPs at Westminster who want the United Kingdom to be at the forefront of making the European Union work better, and more closely, together. The Conservative Party made a terrible mistake in thinking that a sceptical shift on Europe would prove popular amongst the voters in the last general election. The new leadership must not make the same mistakes that the Labour Party did in the 1980s with their short-sighted and immensely damaging views on the then European Community. The polling evidence of the last 25 years should destroy the idea that attacking the EU unfairly makes either political or economic sense. I believe that we must remain constructive, positive members, which will help the rest of the Union develop in a way that best suits the interests of the Union and the British people.

I was delighted to be asked to give my support for the second edition of *Education in a Single Europe*. This edition has been completely revised and redesigned to take into account the changes that have taken place within the educational systems of the European Union over the last few years. I warmly commend it to you all.

The Rt Hon. Sir Edward Heath, KG, MBE, MP
House of Commons

Preface

This second edition of *Education in a Single Europe* has arisen not only from demand for the first, but particularly in respect of the enlargement of the European Union. The book now comprises fifteen country chapters in addition to the introduction. In the meantime, the Community has developed significantly in terms of the degree of consolidation achieved, especially the start of monetary union. The overall effect of these movements has been towards a union of states based on the principle of subsidiarity, bringing 'Europe' closer to the people.

In planning and preparing this new edition, the editors have been able to secure the continuing support of most of the original contributors and to welcome the collaboration of several new colleagues. As with the first edition, we accepted from the outset the authors' of the fifteen chapters own interpretation of the brief provided. This in itself is instructive in enabling of a comparative overview of the situation of education in the European Union. Of particular interest is the degree in which the European dimension in each national system is evident in the text. In this way, the diversity of responses to the European reality given by the authors, within an overall framework, is a source of strength.

We are particularly grateful to Sir Edward Heath for his continuing interest in the project and for providing an illuminating Foreword to this edition. We are also indebted to Bill Musk, Deputy Director of the Central Bureau for Educational Visits and Exchanges, and Dan Taverner OBE, formerly Chief Inspector of Schools in the London Borough of Newham, for reading the drafts and for making helpful comments.

Both editors acknowledge with thanks stimulating discussions of the European issue with Sir David Williams, formerly President of Wolfson College, Cambridge; Wolfgang Mitter, Director of Research at the German Institute for International Educational Research in Frankfurt; and Erhardt Schulte, Senior Executive of DG XII of the European Commission.

Particular thanks must go to Shirley Brock for compiling the index, to Phil Hill, technical officer at the University of Cambridge School of Education, for valuable computing assistance, to Jennifer Webster for typing much of the text, to Audrey Bamber for copy-editing, and to Sally Carter of Routledge for being a most helpful and innovative desk editor.

Colin Brock
Witold Tulasiewicz

Introduction

The place of education in a united Europe

Witold Tulasiewicz with Colin Brock

The context

Introductory comments

The two principal policy objectives of the European Community, the goal of monetary union and 'concrete progress to European unity' reiterated in the Maastricht Treaty, are on course to being achieved by the start of the new century. The adoption of measures such as the working rules for the European Central Banks System and 'European Political Cooperation' are evidence of this. Implementing the principle of subsidiarity with 'decisions taken as openly as possible and as closely as possible to the citizen' in the words of Article A of the Treaty of Amsterdam, and involving the regional structures of the European Community, the subject of Part Five of Maastricht, are intended to smooth out the functioning of its administrative machinery. Considering the diversity of languages, cultures, religions and political traditions to be found in Europe, the setting in motion of a further enlargement of the Community confirms its dynamic growth.

In the context of this chapter, the specific mention of education in Title VIII of the Treaty on European Union (Maastricht) and in the Recital in the Preamble to the new Treaty for Europe (Amsterdam) promoting 'wide access to education and its continuous updating' deserve special mention.

The 'Single Europe' in the title is intended to highlight the aim of the Single European Treaty to accelerate progress by activating the integrating measures of free movement and right of establishment as an essential precondition to successful economic and political cooperation. A study of the vocational and educational articles and preamble of the post-Single Europe treaties is to reveal the close link between the economic and educational activities of the European Union.

At the same time the formulation of the detailed policies of the new treaties also illustrates the progress made since the immediate post-war impetus for uniting Europe in the 1952 Schuman Plan, whose aims of preserving peace were agreed upon by statesmen at a time when acutely felt threats coming from outside the Community in the east and fears of the danger of disunity in the west emphasised economic sufficiency and protective political objectives.

By the 1990s the threats and fears had largely disappeared, slowing down the original global imperative to unite and giving way to specific European Union policies, on human and civic rights, equality of men and women, ethnic and racial respect, high employment, environmental and social protection, of a broadly socio-educational nature and written into the Amsterdam Treaty, in addition to the political machinery facilitating agreement in the fields of foreign and security policy (Title V) and police and judicial cooperation (Title VI).

Indeed, the unequivocal 'contribution to education and training of quality and to the flowering of cultures of the Member States' as part of the Principles in Title II of the Maastricht Treaty, spells out the important role of education.

Each of the fifteen specialist chapters which follow examines the state of education in one of the member states of the European Union after the coming into force of the Single European Act (1987), the Maastricht Treaty (1993), the Amsterdam Treaty (1997) and the Intergovernmental Conferences of that time when decisions on relevant Union programmes, including research and technology, were made, and all on the eve of negotiations for a wider Europe in 1998 and 1999.

These critical accounts give an interpretation of the problems arising and the priorities for solutions necessary to face the challenge of the Single Europe and affect matters such as the programmes implemented and the socio-economic expectations associated with the educational reforms introduced within the context of the fifteen nation states, guardians of diverse linguistic, cultural and socio-political identities.

They feature 'readiness for Europe' on the part of their populations and their reception of elements of what is known as the European Dimension both in the wider socio-political practices of each member state as well as in parts of its school curriculum.

The chapters document national initiatives with an international interest, such as raising the status of vocational training to that of general education in France; citizenship and international friendship education through play projects, such as the Portuguese school-based *clubes europeus*; and networks on a primary school teachers' curriculum, such as the Irish *meitheal*. Because of the educational sovereignty of member states, details of the school curriculum and day-to-day portraits of classroom life are bound to be dramatically different in the fifteen countries.

Not all the economic, social and political objectives which prompted the original six member states to create the European Communities and attracted nine other nation states to join later have been accepted. The character and pace of introduction of some policies led to their abandonment. The European Defence Community was defeated early on in Paris, while the reference to a 'federal' Union was deleted in Article 'A' of the EEC Treaty. Indeed, attempts to forge a political 'union of the peoples' are not entirely clear to many Europeans.

It is frequently assumed that prosperous countries near the heart of Europe, such as Luxembourg, seemingly preoccupied with the priorities of European government, are more typically representative of the European Union than are later members such as the United Kingdom or Denmark. This is not so: the Grand Duchy has problems with the cultural and linguistic diversities within its borders which are similar to those of other European Union countries, and like them has maintained an individual approach in search of solutions, retaining its own distinctive educational structures to achieve its political and economic goals.

With Union membership expectations confined to economic and socio-political advantages, it may be that educational initiatives would not feature largely when compared with measures to improve production methods or to tighten up asylum policies. The most striking examples – the introduction of far-reaching Spanish educational reforms which coincided with Spain's joining the European Community in 1986, and Portugal's insistence in the same year on 'lining up with the rest of the European Union' in the preparation of new educational structures to raise educational standards – happened not only without much comment in the rest of Europe, but went unnoticed by most Spaniards and Portuguese.

Indeed, educational measures, when introduced, are often less likely to be seen as a direct response to the opportunities of the Single Europe than as an initiative of the nation state. After years of isolation under Franco the 'return to Europe' was particularly welcomed in Spain; Danish educational reforms are first and foremost an expression of Denmark's own two ideologies and Danish nationhood, matched with the need to compete in the production market. 'Testing educational performance' was introduced as a key component of British socio-economic policies without direct reference to the European Union, although comparisons with other countries' better pupil performance in science and mathematics are made particularly frequently in the United Kingdom. Swedish decentralisation and democratisation coupled with regular nation-wide performance testing to ensure educational quality may in part be paralleled by what goes on in the United Kingdom; however, it is not a case of imitating British practice but of national policy to secure Swedish relations with countries within as well as outside Europe in the conditions created by the free market. In Germany the structures of the former Democratic Republic have largely disappeared and the federal, selective system of education, which includes the once praised but since often criticised early vocational training, the so-called 'dual' system, has taken over, despite the fact that the compulsory education system is nearly everywhere else in Europe based on the non-selective comprehensive school.

National priorities are also evident in the far-reaching changes in vocational training and higher education, including privatisation, happening in Greece, indicative that the oldest nation in the European Union is becoming concerned with the implications for its identity among the fifteen as one of its more 'distant' and poorer relations. To be sure, no industry–university research schemes existed in Greece before the adoption of European Community programmes.

National positions can be found in other policy areas, such as the negative attitude to the European Monetary Union in the United Kingdom and in Denmark, despite the fact that the absence of a single currency has been calculated to cost the European Union 2 per cent in lost growth and 1.5 million jobs.

Overt educational commitment in member states' legislation on Europe is usually regarded as stemming from their own national historical development within Europe rather than from membership of the European Union. Even so, initiatives such as the consultation on aspects of teacher preparation which were carried out by the *Réseau d'institutions de formation* (RIF) network,[1] and which stem from most European states' current involvement in reforming teacher preparation and raising standards in the lower secondary–higher primary school sectors, are distinctly European.

The physical dimensions of the Single Europe are dictated by political and socio-economic parameters rather than by geographical or indeed cultural factors. Economic advancement and participation in decision making in areas extending beyond the nation state, such as wider access to Irish goods or a voice in European decision making for Finland, were in these two cases strong motivating factors for European collaboration. However, these moves can as easily be taken as a wish for socio-economic emancipation and the expectation of economic help to be given to the poorer regions of the same countries from the Structural Funds under the provisions of EU economic and social cohesion policies.

More especially, economic factors are binding the European Economic Area (EEA) countries, Iceland and Norway but also Liechtenstein, closely to the fifteen; they may be said to be enjoying the mobility and citizenship rights of the Union without taking on members' political obligations. In the case of the Nordic countries, historical links have been responsible for including EEA countries in the agreements on the abolition of passport controls. Factors of cultural and historical affinity can be added to economic cooperation in the case of the Benelux area. The Federal Republic of Germany sees its political future firmly within Europe, a policy which has much to do with the early French espousal of the partnership for defence and peace.

More urgent in the present political perspectives are the circumstances which have brought the countries of Central and Eastern Europe to the threshold of the European Union.[2] The collapse of the former Soviet Union has led to a number of contacts, especially as far as the oil trade and measures to improve the environment are concerned, with member states of the Commonwealth of Independent States.

This seemingly consolidating situation is undergoing almost continuous change caused by new constellations forming and reforming. Smaller European nations, like the Catalans or the Welsh, have been able to synchronise their cultural policies protected by European legislation, the Bureau for the Lesser

Used European Languages in Dublin being an example. The cracks which are appearing as a result of devolution do not affect the state of the economy of the Union so much as demonstrate the status of national identities which, as the Spanish example proves, need not damage the economic integrity of the macro-state unit. Italy and Spain with their autonomous regions are two member states which can reconcile the implications for their plural cultural identities with an enthusiastic acceptance of economic union. Belgium is an even more classic example. Countries with a traditionally centralised form of government, such as the United Kingdom, are beginning to accept the prospect of devolution for some of their territories, the trend nearly everywhere being towards a 'Europe of the Regions'.

The aim behind the move to establish a Committee of the Regions during the negotiations of the Maastricht Treaty was to bring the European Union closer to the people, involving locals in the development and implementation of EU policies at regional level. It was not intended to devolve EU economic powers to member states. One of the specific aims of the economic and social cohesion policies is to improve the infrastructure of those regions that require it, with ECU141 billion allocated for this purpose in the period 1994–9.

This development demonstrates the existence of a variety of national and regional dimensions in the Single Europe where prioritising one dimension must not be seen as deliberately neglecting the others.

It is not the aim here to present statistics relating to commitment to Europe. Sampling figures taken at intervals can contradict each other; however, in the matter of attitudes of Europeans to European unification, a 1995 Eurobarometer registering an average 70 per cent as 'a good thing' showed that at the time of the poll a majority favoured some sort of unification. Social class, age and experience account for significant differences in attitudes to European integration in all member states.

The informed stance adopted by many Europeans indicates that they have had to take account of the historical and geographical European commonality and its cultural and political diversity, a combination that has registered triumphs, in the shape of scientific discoveries and humanitarian works, as well as tragedies, in the shape of wars and persecution. Both the older and the younger generations of Europeans seem to have been learning by adjusting to new experiences which are the outcome of the diversity inherent in the European commonality. In matters such as peace and social justice, this population of millions of citizens of sovereign nation states reacts more in concert than does the smaller population of the federal entity of the United States.

Perhaps because as sovereign nationals they have to live together as Europeans, these millions are more aware of their joint responsibilities, more careful to avoid extremes and anxious to secure negotiated solutions, in that they have to reconcile their individual positions with those of others, as shown in popular responses to international crises in the Middle East or the former Yugoslavia: a role performed perhaps less satisfactorily by their governments.

Democratic traditions make Europeans prefer to decide things at a more local level, requiring the application of subsidiarity and regional structures.

National upbringing with international insights is a factor which has played a significant role in the formation of the attitudes described. Significantly, 'Education and training' is one of the eight standing commissions of the Committee of the Regions.

Intra- and inter-European cooperation initiatives resulting from the need to promote unity while respecting diversity are in stark contrast to unification imposed from above and a departure from the 'Fortress Europe' mentality, where the installation of new external ramparts used to replace those of old; such criteria are crucial in any discussion of education in the Single Europe.

Educational change in member states of the European Union has to do with:

- the economic challenge which highlights the need for preparation for skilled work of school pupils and professionals through wide access to technological innovation, the socio-political skills of citizenship and the creation of opportunities for life-long learning.

In view of the virtually unrestricted mobility it has also to do with:

- the existence of the 'European machinery' concerned with European economic prosperity, such as access to international research and innovation, and the ability to respond to the different cultural and linguistic identities in the nation states, which requires making adjustments in their situation if people wish to live harmonious personal and productive working lives as citizens of the new Europe.

These challenges require the acquisition of common trans-national European items of knowledge, skills – such as languages, and attitudes referred to as the European dimension in the Resolution of the Council and the Ministers meeting within the Council (*The European Dimension in Education* (1988) OJ (1988) CL 177/02) and a sharing of national experiences through exchanges.

The seemingly obvious European educational objectives may well be in conflict with the existing educational diversity. The different populations and authorities of the fifteen member states are by no means equally enthusiastic about the prospect of European unity, whether in cooperation or in competition, and this presents problems with plans to achieve a European future in a context of nation states.

Socio-economics: political and legal backgrounds

Against the background of socio-political upheaval the policies of the European Economic Community have focused firmly on the aims of 'an ever closer union among the peoples of Europe'. With the emphasis, in the words of the Treaty of

Amsterdam, on 'social and economic progress for peoples', should be mentioned first of all:

- the institution of a European citizenship giving entitlement to European consular protection and political activity, including voting for and petitioning the European Parliament; together with
- commitment to a high level of employment and raising the standard of living, indicated by the insertion in Article 109N of the Treaty of the line 'coordinated strategy for employment . . . promoting a skilled, trained and adaptable workforce and labour markets responsive to economic change', with a view to achieving (as per Article 2): 'a high level of employment and social protection . . . raising the standard of living and quality of life'.

Unemployment in the European Union having risen to over eighteen million, the chapter on employment of the Treaty of Amsterdam is a timely reminder of the measures necessary to ease the problem. The European Social Fund distributes monies for vocational retraining and resettlement.

'Promoting a harmonious, balanced and sustainable development of economic policies' has absolute priority in all of the European Union's undertakings. The aim of economic integration moulds member states into a community which takes in every sector of the economy, the movement of money, goods and workers, consumer rights, citizens' freedom of establishment, with the ultimate objective of economic convergence and monetary union. The freedom to provide services as part of occupational mobility and the freedom of abode have, since 1991, included the mutual recognition of many higher education diplomas (Article 57.1) and, since 1992, of non-academic qualifications, such as those of crafts and trades, after a tentative start was made with plumbers and hairdressers in 1964.

The principle of solidarity and coherence which supports regional development (the richest European regions meanwhile being six times more wealthy than the poorest), is to ensure that the economic benefits of the Union are fairly distributed and that citizens' basic rights are fully respected. The social clauses follow on from the 1989 Community Charter of Fundamental Social Rights of Workers guaranteeing agreed workplace conditions, health, social and employment protection.

Cooperation in the fields of justice and home affairs has led to enabling legislation which allows for intergovernmental police and judicial measures regulating the movement and protection of peoples, such as asylum policies. The jurisdiction of the Court of Justice includes observance by the European Union of the provisions of the European Convention on Human Rights.

European political cooperation assumes a Community foreign and security policy intended to 'safeguard the common values . . . , strengthen the security of the Union . . . preserve peace and strengthen international security' (Treaty of Amsterdam, Article J.1). This includes the 'eventual framing of a common defence policy, which might . . . lead to a common defence' (Article J.7). Integrating the Western European Union (WEU) into the EU has managed to include the neutral member states in the common foreign and defence policy, with the European Council deciding the principles and general guidelines and cooperating with the Commission. Member states' freedom to keep their Transatlantic and European bilateral commitments within the general framework of the WEU and the Atlantic Alliance strengthens intergovernmental cooperation and prevents NATO being able to sign a treaty which ignores the European Union.

The successful achievement of its objectives requires an efficient EU administrative apparatus. In an important move, subsidiarity, defined as a social organisation, was elevated to a constitutional principle in the internal political transactions of the Union, bringing more decision making closer to member states. Though seen as a federal gesture, the decision making capacity of the Union has been strengthened by the direct and indirect post-Maastricht co-decision powers of the European Parliament in Community legislation which member states are obliged to introduce. Extending 'qualified majority voting' by member states and the stipulation that action by the Community 'shall not go beyond what is necessary to achieve the objectives of the Treaty' indicate the sensitivity of the entire process.

The revision of existing Community and Union treaties, which has been conducted since 1996 with full public participation, has improved the procedural politics of the activities of the Union and enabled increased initiatives in the socio-economic sectors. These qualifications make it possible to speak of the European identity which is resolved in the Preamble of the Maastricht Treaty.

Agriculture, transport, social provisions, trade, industry, the environment and aid figure prominently in all accounts of the work of the Union. The Common Agricultural Policy seeks to guarantee a livelihood to European farmers while preventing the accumulation of production surpluses. European Transport Policy recognises the goal of an open transport market centred on free and fair competition, essential for implementing EU agricultural, industrial, environmental and commercial objectives. The Common Commercial and Industrial Policies are concerned with the fixing and adjustment of customs tariffs, the resolution of trade conflicts, the dispensing of funding and the observation of the principles of fair competition. In the new treaties all these have assumed a more distinctive formulation than in the provisions of the Rome Treaties which established the original Communities.

The political implication of the European Union's economic objectives can be seen in the trading and training relations which the EU, as the largest single economic bloc in the world, maintains with close and distant neighbours. They range from common policies and practices within the Union, including the

European Economic Area, to agreements with individual countries or groups of countries outside the Union, which protect European markets from being flooded with imports while curbing European exports.

The European Union has economic agreements with Turkey, Cyprus and Malta as well as with countries of Central and Eastern Europe, several of which have been given association status in preparation for joining the Union.

A comprehensive range of economic and financial aid and cooperation packages, plus social and cultural dialogue programmes, such as Phare (originally with Poland and Hungary) and Tacis (with the Commonwealth of Independent States) are available to facilitate the process of socio-political and economic transformation. The former aid and education collaboration Tempus Programme has been phased out, with eligible countries becoming part of the all-European Union Socrates and Comenius Programmes in and after 1998–9. There is also participation in European Environmental Education (Envers) Programmes. In Africa, cooperation agreements have been concluded with the Maghreb and Mashreq countries. The Mediterranean area is scheduled to become a free trade area by the year 2010, the process being accelerated for important socio-political developments in order to prevent unrest on the southern flank of Europe.

The Treaty of Union imposes a special responsibility on the Union for development cooperation to help the poorest countries to become integrated in the world economy. Trade concessions and the abolition of customs duties for former European colonies are a part of the successive Lomé Conventions (the fourth covers the years 1990–2000), the generous commercial trade policy also used to relieve humanitarian crises. Seventy ACP countries in Africa, the Caribbean and the Pacific enjoy duty-free access for their industrial goods to the European Union. There is, moreover, no discrimination as regards the right of establishment and the provision of services. The European Development Fund, maintained by some 9 per cent of the EU's budget, has been used to benefit countries throughout the world, the European Union being the biggest provider of aid, including educational assistance in the form of bursary schemes, for students in developing countries.

The capacity of the Community as a whole is assumed to transcend that of the individual member states combined. Common interests involve countries within and outside the Union in pursuits such as nuclear research while the achievement of an EU–US 'Transatlantic Market Place' includes the liberalisation of services in an overseas context which extends earlier contacts among students and professionals.

It has been argued that the assumption by the European Union of a significant political role in the world has not received the same priority as the achievement of economic objectives. There is no general will perceived among member states for a closer political union and a more proactive role in world affairs, in contrast to the somewhat protective priorities of the clauses establishing the original Communities and identifying European economic concerns. This is despite the EU's commitment to the UN Charter and the principles of the Helsinki Final

Act and elsewhere in the world. To become a political force the European Union must be able to speak with one voice, forging its own European political identity. Full political integration is not an immediate prospect.

According to Joseph Weiler[3] the institutional machinery of the Union points in the direction of a European supra-statehood. However, particularly because of the flexibility in justice and home affairs permitted by the cooperation clauses by member states, the combined policy priorities have been pulling away from decisive steps taken towards political 'integration'.

Intervention in the political problems of other nations is more likely to be undertaken as a bilateral initiative. Thus, although the European Union has become involved in several parts of the world, action, such as that in east and west Africa involving former European colonies or whatever concerted progress can be made in the Balkans, has been the product of *ad hoc* arrangements under NATO, principally by Britain and France. Arguably, the Amsterdam Treaty may have done less to sharpen the Common Foreign and Security Policy than the Maastricht conferences.[4]

As against that, fulfilment of the EU objective of contributing to European growth for creating wealth by strengthening its scientific and technological bases through encouraging research and technological development is gathering pace. To achieve the policies listed in the treaties, their protocols and declarations require an implementation apparatus, in particular, for raising productivity and improving services and for managing the economic union by enabling the free movement of persons, goods, services and capital and administering the bureaucracy of the Union itself. The governments of member states and the institutions of the European Union have comprehensive policies for the training and education of the personnel needed for these tasks.

Significantly for the history of European development, about the time of the Single Europe the global economy was becoming dependent on the interaction between fewer and larger units in an internationalisation process. This situation requires the use of new types of skills acquired under different learning conditions as patterns of economic geography change. Though the demand for new initiatives comes from member states and their industrial enterprises, much of it is Union-mediated, the Union being involved in the coordination, support and execution of many of the projects.

To achieve full economic and monetary union in the EU on time, full convergence, for example in taxation, incomes and pricing policies, will be required, involving an explicit centrally orchestrated regulations framework in the form of direct agreement by member states. Such a framework is not available to date. As is shown by the outcomes of recent referendums, for example in Denmark, and the reservations of individual member states illustrated by the protocols and declarations attached to the treaties, for example concerning the Schengen Agreement, there is opposition to giving too much power to the Union.

This prompts the question: what precisely is the status of Union help given to joint activities undertaken by member states which involve EU economic relations outside the EU?

Access is necessary to information about Community activities and responsibilities, such as priorities of Union legislation over national law on, for example, flexibility over traditional immigration movement patterns into Europe. Education and training facilities which brought about economic and political success must be available to scrutiny and comment. There is a gap between the undoubted economic success and the profits achieved by the Union and the failure by the public to understand how this success is being achieved. A criticism made of the legislation contained in the recent treaties is that it is opaque,[5] and that its inaccessibility prevents ordinary Europeans from playing a more committed and proactive role.

The path to Europe

National and legal constraints

Political and institutional homogeneity in Europe tended to be achieved by conquest and influence exercised by a few powerful states. The unity imposed, such as that identified with Rome and its successors or with the Church, was broken at intervals by a power conflict started in the parts of Europe excluded from the original political links or by the breakup of philosophical and religious certainties leading to new upheavals. This situation prompted individuals to attempt to construct a unity by rational and peaceful means on the basis of socio-humanitarian principles. The concept of the *République très chrétienne* of Maximilien de Bethune Sully is one example of what continued in later centuries to combine in producing Republican, Socialist, Religious and Romantic thought on European unity. Nationalist aggression, much of it originating in Europe, succeeded in preventing the full realisation of plans which had begun to assume concrete political form in the League of Nations. Happily, after the Second World War, new attempts would include wider humanitarian, health and educational concerns.

The fact that the European Communities were founded on a smaller and more clearly circumscribed territory and were committed to achieving economic as well as defence objectives which strengthened their political status enabled the Community to act more decisively in its realistic pursuit of peace and international cooperation.

Even so, nation state attitudes which had prevented an earlier enlargement of the Community continued in the failure to realise the potential of the Common European Market to transform itself into an economic and political structure in which 'member states would not lose their individual identity but gain more by combining together'.[6] British reluctance to accept the implications of the political principles arising from an internationalisation of interest was illustrated by the pursuit of British-centred political priorities in the run up to the United

Kingdom application to join the Common Market clashing with the strength of French national interests determined to retain France's leading role in an essentially European construct.[7] The Nordic countries are an example of a smaller union of states which do not readily share all their affinities with the larger European Union.

Indeed, the intricacies of the unique grouping of fifteen states prepared to relinquish some of their sovereign competencies in favour of creating a community prompted by the prospect of economic growth in an international context conducive to promoting such growth make it difficult to expect equally lasting commitments from all member states in a rapidly changing socio-economic climate.

The Union is the outcome of compromise between the conflicting interests of Community and nation state priorities which affect its internal (such as interpretations of social democracy) and external (for example, defence policy) commitments, Anglo-Saxon liberal social policies clashing with more protective continental European ones. This is demonstrated by nation state governments, divided on more or less federalist or functionalist integration lines, trying to obtain acceptance of policies that meet with their approval.

Close links with non-European partners – for example, the UK often on the side of the USA – may cause resentment among member states which prefer to promote a European identity by, for example, access to the media for European culture. The recently proposed council of deputy prime ministers, it was feared, would turn out to be another European centralising fixture.

A particularly contentious issue requiring legal advice concerns the three so-called Pillars of the Community which determine centre and periphery responsibilities. Asylum, visa and immigration were moved to the First Pillar (Community) from the Third (Intergovernmental Matters) where Police and Judicial Cooperation still remain. With the First Pillar there is no need for ratification of measures by national governments although unanimity in the Council, which is being questioned, is required. In the Third Pillar no assent to legislation by the European Parliament is needed, enabling closer or looser intergovernmental cooperation.

Acknowledging the supranational remit of the European Court of Justice has been made part of the Treaty of Union despite the objections of individual member states, notably the United Kingdom. Many areas of activity are shared, for example employment is mainly a member state concern, but the Community is expected to introduce remedying measures. In foreign and defence policy the responsibilities are more evenly divided.

Citizens' expectations are an important factor to consider. In the words of the British Prime Minister at the end of the 1998 British presidency of the European Council: 'it is necessary to feel safe in your national identity while reaching out to European partnership'. Many Europeans see European Monetary Union as a blow to this cherished identity. Consulting the regions may have the effect of activating new policy makers representing transnational parties, expert professionals and lay partners, instead of national party interests.

Committed Europeans regret the inability of ordinary citizens to find their way in the European Union, an ignorance which politicians representing the different Community or member state priorities tend to exploit. The exact meaning of terms such as 'subsidiarity' when linked with 'qualified majority voting' and the need for Community 'intervention in competitive trading policies' has been the subject of extensive debate. Whether national sovereignty is compatible with economic interdependence is a topical question as the last regulations on monetary union have been put in place.

The acknowledgement of the existence of such problems triggers demands for opening up EU internal organisations and institutions, a right of freedom of information and open government. A citizenry directly affected by the macro-level economic integration and political cooperation processes in the European Union will be more likely to support initiatives expected to bring prosperity to Europe if it is informed about their implications for national sovereignty. New policies will require individual member states, preoccupied with economic and training cooperation, to find more room in their education programmes for spreading the European knowledge essential for maintaining the political will to progress, since 'a single currency cannot be constructed in a political desert'.[8]

Unity in diversity

The historical, expansionist or retreating, attacking or defending policies of the fifteen member states are part of their national experiences and as such have affected the structures and practices of their systems of government and administration. Even so, they have gained from centuries of parallel efforts to respond to social, political, economic, cultural and religious developments of a broadly comparable though asynchronic nature.

The social care work of Western (Catholic and Protestant) Christianity blossoming in the nineteenth century, which contrasts with its virtual absence in Orthodox (Russian and Greek) Christianity in the same period, is an example of religions shaped by different spiritual concepts and political realities.[9] Similarly, the socio-economic and political structures affecting the ownership of land and the emergence of democratic systems of government in the European west developed from different concepts of authority to those in the European east, which, because of the rise of Communism after the outbreak of the First World War, were modified less fundamentally between the wars.

Such developments had taken root within parameters in the form of frontiers secured in part by national systems of education which supported the processes of consolidation, cohesion and expansion inherent in the operation of the nation state as the highest order of regulation of human societies expressed in their identities.[10] The move to a united Europe is often in danger of facing new barriers set up to protect interests tried out in one society working against reforms which require convergence.

The European Union growing organically from common pursuits, especially in the economic sectors already well in place which have agreed convergence in a number of areas, has a wider, global remit in which common aims and training and the availability of information have created new practices which are different from individual national initiatives. The question 'Which Europe?' which arises in this context can only be answered by allowing not just for the existing cultural and linguistic varieties and distinctive socio-political traditions of member states of the European Union, but also for the emerging new economic and political commonalities. Account must be taken of the contribution of variety brought in by non-territorial immigrants, citizens of member states whose often non-European origins confirm Europe's growing global dimensions.

The confrontations which arise have to be resolved. The number of Europeans freely seeking work in other member states or settling there, no more than 1.5 per cent of the total population of the European Union, is small. It would be unfortunate if dissatisfaction resulted in a two-tier Europe of a minority fully committed to the Union and of a majority who prefer to stay out.

Implications for European education

With economic multinationalism as the driving force pointing to convergence in an intercultural context and the growing practice of enterprise-based training in world-wide undertakings, a case has to be made out for a distinctive European education which does not assume the emergence of a European super-state. Indeed, since the dismantling of member states' national systems of education is unlikely, a European dimension with global perspectives may have to be placed beside each national and regional education system, enabling it to assume the supra-national features necessary for more efficient joint economic and political activity and as a sign of international understanding in the multilingual, European and global reality. In the areas of vocational training and research, collaboration and convergence schemes, involving both EU member states and countries which are not, are increasingly frequent.

The following scenario is there for consideration: the evolution of the European nation states over centuries and the role of education in that; the effect of the relatively recent migration to member states of significant numbers of peoples from extra-European cultural zones; the economic trend towards globalisation and the role of political associations of states. Together they combine in creating a complex mixture within the existing diversity in which the role of education has been rather less conspicuous.

In the context of the European Union the implications of a European education are bound to create difficulties for the educational sovereignty of member states, differences in the structure of school systems, school government as well as rituals, being especially manifest. Even assuming full commitment to the European idea, the creation of a European awareness through curriculum development is still in need of definition. Curricular priorities may create problems with school mobility if certain subjects or subject combinations are given a different rating in different member states and are an indicator of the neglect of a European identity in education. Synchronizing procedural practice alone, for example releasing time for attending European meetings and participating in collaborative programmes, is not sufficient.

The components of a European education have to reconcile the already practised vocational training collaboration with the need for an education necessary for the provision of European services and the national education components, usually organised with little reference to Europe. This is because increasingly skilled people, with the combination of good local knowledge and of the wider European context and in possession of a caring attitude to that environment, will be managing the 'new Europe'. The 'People's Europe' will enable those who wish to do so actively to participate in designing the socio-political and economic construct of the European Union.

Experiences of collaboration involve an interdisciplinary approach (for example, social studies and engineering, French and legal studies), which suggests professional and vocational training programmes in which Community involvement is to coordinate and support national and regional initiatives, enriched by an educational value-added component.

A European education, in the form of an upbringing as well as of instruction, is to enable Europeans to rethink their futures. The components of such an education must show Europeans that they can work more efficiently and live more comfortably together because of mediating educational and professional procedures and training patterns agreed in the Union as part of the economic goals. Extra-curricular activities as much as traditional school curriculum subjects are involved. Pursuits dealing with freedom and liberty, justice and equality, peace and environmental protection will be the new priorities of a European and global education in which the importance of traditional subject matter handed down in national school curricula will decline, giving way to an international interest which is becoming available already.

A policy of facing up to the existing unity in diversity, emphasising the advantages of both unity and diversity, has been suggested by the Council of Europe as a policy for the European Union. It accepts diversity as an asset resource which, after a critical examination of their needs by EU member states, would enable the most appropriate models, a unifying move, to be adopted. Creating an intercultural process by exploiting the multicultural character of Europe in training and education initiatives which demonstrate the commonality of effort and the contribution made by the diverse elements involved must be a 'doing things together' approach. This recognises that European unity is not so much the result of a common legacy which is a static element, but that it is agreed common actions which are the catalyst to future developments – the dynamic stimulus to the pursuit of social, cultural and environmental as well as economic goals uniting the participants in their endeavours.

The implications of membership of the Single Europe of which Europeans must be aware can be summed up as:

- *economic*: the internal market leading to closer fiscal policies and monetary union;
- *social*: the reduction of disparities leading to an improvement in the human and physical environments;
- *legal and political*: the democratically controlled powers of European institutions, leading to intensified cooperation involving citizens at all transactional levels;
- *educational and technological*: the essentially enabling instrument, having led to relevant socio-political and economic Community action, has moved beyond the acknowledgement of a common tradition to the achievement of future common goals.

The parameters of European education

General curricular considerations

Since the volume and variety of activity generated in the European Union requires the services of a qualified as well as an educated workforce, the omission of 'education' from the original EEC Treaty has been the subject of comment.

General education, professional and vocational training, and research to improve the quality of production and increase its quantity traditionally provided by nation states is increasingly becoming an international concern. Unlike workers confined to their nation states, those going to work in the European Union in the production, service and administrative sectors will have to be able to make the best use of their professional training as well as their mobility rights as workers and as citizens alongside fellow workers from other member states in what is a European undertaking. The success of the Union depends not only on the ability to keep up in the technology race but to do so in a multicultural and multilingual environment in which the relevant skills can be deployed most effectively. The link between education and vocational training and the expansion of the economy has to be fully established in the context of the European Union.

The route which, as with the predecessors of the European Union such as the Coal and Steel Community, has taken education to economic convergence is accepted as the most suitable way for educational collaboration in the Union in the future. Many good examples of innovative European education-vocational training and research collaboration can be found in the regions, such as the three-nation Alfa Vocational College Consortium.[11] It is encouraging that the take-up of cooperation contacts, such as the vocational Leonardo

Programme, is catching up with the more school and university orientated Socrates Programmes.

Using the wider connotations of the English and American term 'education' to include the contexts of upbringing and instruction it is possible to name the following five components of the education of citizens of EU member states.

National education

Mother tongue, national culture and history are the key elements of compulsory schooling, the responsibility for school programmes being vested in national education authorities. The content in some curriculum areas, such as mathematics and science, may begin to reflect increasing European collaboration on quality leading to the use of Europe-wide teaching materials. In subject areas such as history and geography there has been harmonisation of syllabuses in order to deliver a more Europe-orientated programme. The growth of foreign language education is encouraging the development of more efficient teaching approaches for both national and foreign languages, in which the role of a European or international language of communication will require consideration.[12]

National curricula are likely to continue to emphasise national achievements and an upbringing in national values, a task made easy with the curriculum delivered in schools where the methods and practices are predominantly national. Claude Thélot, Director of the INSEE CREST Institute in Paris, is confident that the national curriculum will remain, although it may be reduced to the distinctive 'national' cultural elements in school programmes, emphasising 'national pride and consciousness', for example by encouraging workers in their member state to outperform those of partner states in economic output. Astonishing is the quantity of similar curricular priorities but different teaching approaches and methods of assessment adopted in member states' schools.

With considerable variety in the assimilationist policies of individual member states, such as opportunities for first language maintenance,[13] the European Union, unlike the classic countries of immigration, is not a 'melting pot'. European identity is not being constructed by abolishing national differences, their existence guaranteed by the independent member states.

European education

European education which consists of items of European knowledge and foreign language skills to inform pupils about their continent and to enable them to live and work anywhere in the European Union is bound to grow and will encroach on curricular areas such as social and personal education, including citizenship, to facilitate communication. In the words of the UK National Curriculum Council Citizenship Group: 'young people should be able to live and work in Europe comfortably but not uncritically',[14] easily adjusting to the conditions found abroad.

The form of European education accepted in principle by all member states, in school curricula and teacher preparation courses without being made a compulsory part of the curriculum, has become known as the European dimension and identified with exchange visits and collaborative activities. Cross-disciplinary programmes such as environmental education and skills such as European citizenship, will be delivered through transnational projects which are beginning to be seen as the most important element of a European education. Details of the European dimension in education originally proposed by the European Commission, published in 1988, and being further defined can be found in Bell[15] and in Tulasiewicz.[16]

The European dimension

In addition to the above, this also comprises twinning and cooperation programmes in which educational institutions in at least three EU countries have to take part to prevent a bilateral partnership developing. Common projects and curriculum development initiatives, for example extending modern foreign language teaching or environmental education, enable this activity to be classed as an active education element distinct from the more cognitive learning approaches of European knowledge.

In particularly well thought through examples, pro-European attitudes and the acquisition of 'European cooperative' skills, such as travel, hosting and guiding, can be formed which enable young people to plan and execute activities together in a region they share as Europeans. 'Doing things together' can activate European values through pursuits which promote youth concerns, health and sport as well as civic education as a cross-curricular initiative. Young Europeans develop a spirit of European collaboration and comradeship which may include European competitiveness in contradistinction to the predominant cultivation of national 'one-upmanship'.

Vocational preparation

This involves, in addition to the preparation for employment, technological and research collaboration and 'work experience', which encompasses the skills and attitudes required of a well-adjusted member of a working team as well as of an efficient specialist. Work placement abroad can secure multinational experience.

Vocational training is an area in which the Community has always been involved since it is directly concerned with its central aim of economic development, 'a policy capable of contributing to the harmonious development both of the national economies and of the common market'. Arguably, the concomitant activities to vocational training can constitute an education.

Research and development

R&D at advanced and applied levels uses cooperation to improve products, production methods and their marketing. As such it is the concern of the Community, which under the new Article 127 'implements a vocational training policy', to strengthen the Community's economic base while 'respecting the responsibility of the Member States for content and organization'. Facilitating adaptation to industrial change through vocational training and retraining and encouraging mobility of instructors and trainees, stimulating cooperation on training and exchanges of information and experience are areas of EU involvement. Research and technological development (R&TD) conducted in Joint Central Research centres and elsewhere is financed by member states via the Union out of direct contributions and indirect levies to support the funds responsible.

The Union is involved in the 'development of the highest possible level of education . . . through a wide access to education and its continuous updating' (New Recital in the Preamble to the Amsterdam Treaty). This allows the Union to enact enabling measures to improve access to education for disadvantaged and disabled minorities through the application of directives under the social policy areas of Title VIII (Maastricht).

An imaginative approach in the five areas discussed may result in education becoming not simply an aid to building a socio-economic and political construct but as an integrated upbringing enabling Europeans to begin to think of themselves as Europeans, much as other heterogenous communities have developed a common American or Australian identity.

European considerations

To deliver a European education consisting of the dimensions discussed involves the removal of actual and perceived bias in curriculum areas such as geography, economics, social studies and language. Though no longer a problem in the EU, intergovernmental commissions as well as academic experts working on the revision of textbooks and teaching materials, notably members of the Eckart Institut in Braunschweig,[17] have been examining ways of achieving a homogeneous interpretation of episodes of European history. British geography textbooks have undergone a radical change with the departure of the British Commonwealth as the centre of study.

European history and geography textbooks are becoming available to those teachers who will use them, to enable children to learn about their common roots and environment, to study the phenomenon of prejudice and to encourage using the opportunities for travel and exchange visits. Reading texts are beginning to include European as well as national material. Even so, member states' cultural autonomy encourages differences in the acceptance and reception of innovations by existing national systems. The extent of EU responsibility is left to the interpretation of its member states.

As part of the general school curriculum, attention will focus on common upbringing and instruction elements, in order to instil 'European values' and attitudes while studying a diversity of school subjects. Social and personal studies, predominantly part of national education delivered as an enhancement of the individual as a person and as a member of society, are being exploited for the European curriculum.

In the European education sector school pupils as well as adult populations are becoming part of the rationale of the notion of European citizenship and European responsibility.[18] The concept of European citizenship has been receiving attention, not least in the United Kingdom where citizenship education has been a relatively late curriculum arrival. Citizenship education involves acquainting people of their rights, duties and responsibilities, making sure at the same time that they understand those of others.[19] The art of nego-tiation and so-called procedural awareness are important components of civic education. Political education can be acquired through studying the difference between participating in voting and in political pressure groups.[20]

A European education must consider the needs of the 'new Europeans', whose origins are outside the traditional boundaries of Europe, requiring schools to adapt their programmes to their intellectual and cultural priorities. Quantitatively and qualitatively, different minority groups of extra-European origin show considerable variation.

Since the 1960s the European Community has been promulgating agreed guidelines concerning the educational expectations and rights of minority groups, including the important Council Directive of 25 July 1977, but they pertain in the main to the equality of access to mainstream provision and the maintenance of territorial minorities' home cultures in line with their economic roles. Although important, the guidelines do not address the implications of the enlargement of the concept of 'European' to include the socio-cultural and political contribution of the non-territorial 'new European' minority groups or the potential for further migration within the European Union.

As a result, nationality–citizenship problems and rights associated with a two-way traffic, implying settlement, perhaps only temporary (unlike the one-way traffic of the traditional immigration pattern), have led to little more than a European Union travel and work permit for those eligible.

Learning from Europe

The similarities of educational structures and practices in European Union member states, the result of the application of explicit EU directives, cooperation and exchanges, have encouraged a pooling of resources and the joint organisation of parallel European courses in individual European institutions using the European Credit Transfer Scheme (ECTS) and other schemes. Similarity of broad educational objectives and practices has to do with countries pursuing similar socio-economic policies in similar socio-political and economic circumstances requiring similar measures, for example seeking private investment in education or the involvement of customers of education in the choice of curriculum facilities. Notwithstanding, member states tend to work from their own conditions and traditions which do not encourage direct transfer of policies and practices.

The question whether Britain has anything to learn from Europe appears every now and again as when a quality problem arising from British membership of the Union has to be confronted. In cases of a negative trade balance in the competitive international market conditions, government and people tend to put the blame for the production of poor-quality goods on Britain's falling educational standards and to make comparisons with the situation elsewhere.

These actions have the effect of drawing attention to existing practices, such as the criticism made by Prais of the emphasis given to law and banking careers in the United Kingdom[21] instead of concentrating on a sound scientific education. Education for productivity is likely to figure prominently in outlines of education in Europe, with practice in such matters as the introduction of a central curriculum (as in France), the regular testing of pupils' performance (as in Sweden) or the provision of curricular guidance (as in Germany) being given out as models. Teaching mathematics for application in industry rather than for the 'intellectual stimulation of school pupils' is a curriculum example originating in Britain.

A comment on the nature of such comparative studies is appropriate. The fifteen chapters which follow can be said to attempt an idiographic approach which sets out to deliver an educational portrait of the European Union as a whole by providing individual educational portraits of the fifteen sovereign member states. This is useful in view of the increasing mobility of professionals, practitioners as well as learners, within Europe. Learning from diversity has been one of the stated aims of comparative education.

The approach suggested above would, for example, examine the principle of selective education, such as that found in the tripartite structure of German compulsory schooling which separates vocational preparation from general education, in the wider European context, assessing its impact on more than the equality of access alone. Indeed, a comparative examination of the educational problems found in the tripartite system may demonstrate the economic defects of 'a division between general and vocational education', suggesting phasing out the divisive system in Europe in favour of longer vocational preparation provided alongside general education to deliver an educated, professionally flexible workforce.

Education in the European Union

Status and scope

Education is placed among the socio-economic actions which include health, consumer and environmental protection, certain industrial and research measures as well as 'quality education', 'vocational training' and 'culture of the member states' which were added in the Maastricht Treaty to the other concerns which are the responsibility of the European Union. They represent areas of activity in which the sovereignty of the member states has traditionally been respected.

In the broadly federal-like character of the European Union member state responsibility is based on the principle of subsidiarity (Article 3b) according to which, with the exception of certain economic and political areas exclusive to the Union and the day-to-day running of national governments of the member states, the Community may only take action on condition that the proposed objectives cannot be sufficiently and efficiently achieved by the member states acting alone or jointly. There can be no interference in the structure and content of schooling and no attempt at harmonisation, for which full consultation and agreement among member states and the approval of the European Council, the executive arm of the Union, would be needed.

In matters to do with education policy the action taken will usually be that of a general outline commitment rather than the introduction of detail. Harmonisation in transport policy or consumer protection to enable a more efficient working of the Union by adopting common legislation or joint projects is more likely than in education and vocational concerns where EU support or complementation of member state actions has led rather to European collaboration and exchange initiatives such as Socrates. As an advisory body the Committee of the Regions may give opinions which encourage opening the way for popular and local involvement in educational and cultural programmes in which citizens of Europe will find it easier to be represented.

Collaboration is achieved by the application of decision making procedures, of which two, co-decision and information, were introduced at Maastricht. Vocational Training Policy (Article 127) involves co-decision procedures (following Article 189b) requiring European Parliamentary opinion on a Proposal by the Commission and a Common Position by the Council after a Qualified Majority Vote. Adoption by Council, if amendments are accepted after a further Parliamentary Reading, can happen within a maximum of four months. Education (Article 126) is subject to the same co-decision procedures in which Council Decisions are taken when, after a Qualified Majority Vote, the Council may adopt the Act subject to Parliamentary approval. Failure to obtain approval can prevent legislation from being adopted. In the case of Culture (Article 128), co-decision is further subject to unanimity.

In Research and Technological Development Framework Programmes (Article 130i), the Council also acts according to the provisions of Article 189b.

Maastricht Treaty Competition Clauses, a part of the EU's new competences, may affect the status of research and technological development. Community aid given to projects is only available if they are socially and economically beneficial, for example leading to improved production (Article 85). The Council has rules governing participation in research, of which the form, subject to budget restraints, is left to member states' decision.

The new and extended involvement of the Union in social concerns is important for interpreting the provisions of the Treaty and secondary legislation since it is subject to the same rules, the effect of which is to strengthen the powers of the European Parliament in co-decision procedures, with the result that the entire educational, vocational, cultural and research activity area appears to be lodged firmly as a member state responsibility.

In accordance with Article 189, in the task of fulfilling the provisions of the Treaty the institutions of the European Union shall make Regulations and issue Directives, take Decisions, make Recommendations and deliver Opinions. A Regulation is binding on all member states in every respect. Directives are likewise binding but details of implementation, form and method are left to the member state. A Decision is binding only on those who are addressed by it. Recommendations and Opinions have no binding force.

The application of the principle of subsidiarity is intended to stimulate debate by parties such as trade, business, professional and social associations on activities of a social and environmental concern not necessarily covered by existing legislation under the Treaty, for example the protection of children or the employment position of pregnant women, which could, at a later time, be put into formal channels as part of new EU social policy initiatives. In a way this is made relatively easy, since a legal examination of the obligations presented reveals that they are somewhat imprecise in character, with general phrases such as 'encouraging cooperation' and 'adopting incentive measures', expressly 'excluding harmonization of the laws and regulations of member states', although 'subsequent agreements may be concluded with the "unanimous approval" of member states' for purposes 'other than harmonization'.[22]

Even so, Chapter 3: Education, Vocational Training and Youth considerably expands EU competences to act in developing a European dimension in education, particularly through language teaching and the exchange of personnel, information and experience at all levels and the mutual recognition of diplomas and periods of study (education, Article 126). Improving vocational training policy aims at facilitating adaptation to industrial change and improving social and vocational integration in the labour market, cooperation on training between educational and training establishments and firms (vocational training: Article 127), so as to strengthen industry's competitiveness and ensure a high level of employment.

Like the two previous Articles, Title IX (culture: Article 128) does not allow harmonisation of laws and regulations. Indeed, it may 'give a legal basis for protection against Community action which is harmful to the identity and language of a certain culture', explicitly preserving 'diversity', when allowing the free movement of goods and services (see note 22).

The provisions of Research and Technological Development (Articles 130f–130p, especially 130i) emphasise the importance of securing the scientific and technological bases of Community industry and encouraging it to become more competitive at international level. The mention of 'complementing Member States' activities' and 'coordinating Member State and Community initiatives' again confirms the location of powers. The Council adopts the multi-annual framework programmes by a qualified majority vote.

The wider social policy competences, including education and training, of the European Union have generated media attention focused on interference and loss of national independence, especially in countries where, as in the United Kingdom, economic and social problems tend to be linked with falling educational standards.

Educational initiatives in the European Community

The education of the children of occupational travellers is a good example of the involvement of the EU Commission in education.

The improvement of provision is a socio-educational matter addressing equality of provision and the improvement of educational opportunity. These come under the remit of education and employment. In accordance with Article 126, an examination and sharing of educational information obtained, which leaves the exact curricular arrangements to be made by the member states, does not preclude collaboration but is unlikely to be taken as harmonisation, since the measures adopted do not constitute a general change in policy on school structures or grouping of pupils according to ability.

The statistics collected by national agencies are often incomplete and the measures adopted differ. In this particular case the additional educational provision made for children of occupational travellers to enable the employment of more teaching staff and the scrutiny of suitable reading materials provided under Section 210 of the English Educational Reform Act 1988 is not replicated in the other countries. In France literacy projects are singled out as part of a larger action which includes occupational travellers' children, while circus artists receive special training to help them cope with their profession in Belgium, Germany, Italy and France.

The delay in responding to proposals from the Community which, in the case of the Resolution of the Council and the Ministers of Education Meeting Within the Council of 22 May 1989 (EC Resolution 89/c 153/01 about the Education of Occupational Travellers' Children), led to national responses within five years, the last one being that from Belgium, is not unusual. In fact the EC Resolution of 24 May 1988 (88/c 177/02) on the European Dimension in Education was not formally addressed by the UK Department of Education and Science until three years later, although the National Curriculum Council Citizenship Task Group had prepared its definition of the dimension in 1990.

* * *

Much has been made of the fact that the original text of the Treaty of Rome does not deal with education, although it holds an explicit brief for implementing a common vocational training policy capable of contributing to the harmonious development of national economies and of the common market (Treaty of Rome, original Article 128). This somewhat false distinction has in fact enabled progress in preparing for the appropriate development of human resources for technological requirements, especially in the further and higher sectors of education.

Indeed, taking the wider interpretation of the term 'education', it can be said that the earliest education initiatives of the Community, the resolutions of the Council of the Communities of 9 February and 13 December 1976, and the 'Action Programme' and the Directive of 16 June 1976 which introduced the tentative mutual recognition of diplomas (those of medical doctors) and gave impetus to professional exchanges, confirming the 'European Principle' of cooperation to develop a 'Europe of quality and equal opportunity' through educational measures, predate the Treaty of Maastricht by some twenty years. The Jean Monnet lectures and lectureships providing education on problems of European integration go back to 1977 and 1973 respectively.

To be sure, although this activity was regarded as professional and vocational preparation with advice from higher education on research and development, the main consideration being the preparation of a qualified and mobile workforce, the interpretation of the original Article 128 by the European Court of Justice in a number of early cases in favour of allowing study in another member state (cf. Case 293/83 in 1983) before the full mobility of the Single Europe had been agreed, confirms an earlier than generally accepted emergence of 'education' as a Community concern.

The funding of a number of other initiatives of collaboration in education was enabled by the Court, which in Case 242/87 (*Commission* v. *Council*) deemed Erasmus collaboration eligible for EC funding, allowing the particular course in 1987, although educational in detail, to count as a vocational project.[23]

The Single Europe Act opened up wider opportunities. The then twelve member states could go beyond the purely economic and professional considerations of their collaboration in parallel vocational preparation schemes to look at socio-political circumstances in Europe involving European workers' social, moral, civic and political development, giving rise to the question: Where does training stop and education begin? The poor demarcation had already appeared with Article 128, since educational concerns could find their way into professional and vocational preparation schemes as part of job training unless they constituted national education provision. The provisions of the Maastricht Treaty which envisage developing the non-reserved areas of the European dimension and language teaching, and further promoting mobility and exchanges, can involve a further blurring of boundaries.

In the circumstances, the new social and environmental initiatives (Titles VIII and XVI) enable an educational collaboration of the type suggested, notwithstanding the economic and political priorities allowed by the Treaties, which have led to education in the European Union being understood as an economic facilitator in the service of professional and vocational preparation. Thus, workers' mobility is a vocational necessity rather than a cultural experience; however, migrant workers' children's entitlement to mother tongue instruction and learning their cultures of origin constitutes education, though it is a consequence of the right to free movement of labour (Article 48).

Research and Technological Development, assisted, encouraged and coordinated by the Community and especially the establishment of scientific and technological objectives (Title XV) to strengthen the scientific base of Community industry, not being conducted in a social and political-ideological vacuum, would be linked with the higher and further education sectors.

The origins of educational initiative in the then European Economic Community can be traced back to the 'common cultural heritage' invoked in the Janne Report of 1973.[24] Although it envisaged an agreed vocational training policy only, it considered an Educational and Cultural Committee for the Community. By the time of Maastricht, educational collaboration initiatives had found favour with committed educators in all member states, encouraged by the provision of exchange facilities. The 'European dimension' could easily incorporate double aspect projects where the example of modern foreign language collaboration in the classroom would lead to discussions of computer training syllabuses, as part of vocational training but also to developing Europe-centred educational initiatives using e-mail. The Stuttgart Declaration of 19 June 1983 requested information on European history and culture.

The earliest initiatives concentrated on three areas:

- higher education, which introduced several collaboration and exchange schemes such as Comett (education and action for training in technologies), Eurotecnet (innovations in vocational training) as well as Tempus and Erasmus, which had the effect of revitalising European university and school links. The mutual recognition of diplomas was not intended to create a uniformity of qualifications or to seek legal equality but was based on trust of equivalence and the acceptance of diversity of content;
- equality of opportunity, which applies as much to employment prospects as to the elimination of discrimination against groups such as slow learners or other minorities. European 'democracy cannot allow the schooling of some 25 per cent of young people to be forgotten'. Programmes such as Petra helped young people to prepare for adult working life, updating qualifications through the use of new technologies. Foreign language Lingua programmes could aim at improving employment chances by enabling cultural flexibility;
- democracy and citizenship education, which launched pilot schemes in the 1984 Fontainebleau Declaration of a 'Community for Citizens and the Wider World' and the 1985 adoption by the Milan Council of the Report (*A Citizens' Europe*). The Resolution of 24 May 1988 on the European

dimension in education, which called for an education in European values as well as joint economic development activity sponsored by the Community, gave the strongest impetus to later initatives. These involved the European Parliament with its June 1992 Resolution on the inclusion of the European dimension and European citizenship instruction in schools and the establishment of the Economic and Social Committee with the September 1992 Comments on the 'value added' of studying the European dimension and citizenship. Teacher preparation, particularly as educators in citizenship, led to some 210 actions, bilateral exchanges and partnerships.

The Commission produced three memoranda dealing with:

- easier access to higher education and diversification of courses, with increased collaboration with industry;
- investment in improving teacher education and the recognition of qualifications in the circumstances of the market;
- promoting open and distance education, thus ensuring virtual mobility.

Following the Commission's White Paper of 5 December 1993, *The Challenges and Ways Forward into the 21st Century: growth, competitiveness and employment* (COM(93) 700 final), especially its chapter 7, and the Resolution of the Council on the European dimension, the Commission's Green Paper (COM(93)457 final) stimulated discussions on the initiatives opening up in the wider areas of social cooperation, listed in Titles VIII and XVI of the Maastricht Treaty.

By that time educational programmes could be consolidated in three pilot schemes:

- Youth for Europe III (CL DEC 818/95), which subsumes the previous programmes, Petra and Tempus, and concentrates on retraining links with third world countries;
- Leonardo da Vinci (CL DEC 94/819) which subsumes Petra, Comett, Force and Eurotecnet proposals affecting all partners. Its aim is to improve the quality of all education and promote innovation in the market and the European dimension;
- The Socrates Programme (CL DEC 819/95) which includes Erasmus exchange initiatives, especially the promotion of inter-institutional links in preference to individual contacts. Its remit extends to the mutual recognition of diplomas and to counting time spent studying in another country towards qualifying for a degree. The European Credit Transfer Scheme (ECTS) constitutes Part iii – Socrates Policy Communication 1994 (COM(94)656).

'Europe at School' organises partnerships cooperating on common priorities, such as language education, protecting the cultural heritage and the environment, as well as twinning programmes involving exchanges of head teachers, with the aim of developing an 'intellectual mobility' which constitutes a European flexibility and openness with a sense of community belonging.

Part iii – Socrates emphasises the European preparation of all personnel concerned with education, concentrating on language study and using the new technologies and information, much of it made available through distance learning. Teacher training is the aim of all three schemes, especially in-service programmes, which, more specifically than initial preparation, constitute professional training.[25]

Research and development programmes in 1994–8 were those of a socio-economic nature.

Extended educational and training collaboration resulted in activities of the then European Community in the medium term (1989–92) which promoted the setting of university entrance criteria, improving the mutual recognition of qualifications as well as facilitating mobility.

The dynamic effect of research conducted in joint research and enterprise centres and its potential as an investment in the future was recognised early on by European political leaders. Original Article 128 enabled the European Council to complement training activity at national level by promoting projects involving laboratories in several member states and a mingling of scientists from different disciplines, allowing it to finance a wide range of initiatives. The fourth Research Framework Programme adopted by the European Commission, which ran from 1994 to 1998, concentrated on improving the European Communities' industrial competitiveness as its prime objective, with 3 per cent of the Union's GNP devoted to research and development.

The Commission's full-term programme (1992–5) was more specifically 'educational', taking in secondary education. It led to the production of guides to European education systems for parents and pedagogical subject handbooks for teachers emphasising European and interdisciplinary teaching approaches. The Council of Europe produced packages on the Industrial Revolution, immigrants in Europe and education of the Roma.

Increasingly, the syllabuses of national school leaving certificates include a European dimension. Schools and universities have appointed officers in charge of European cooperation programmes, in some cases overseeing the European Credit Transfer Scheme (ECTS).

Exchanges and common study programmes at school level which bring Europeans together are helping in this process, complementing the traditionally more European higher education sector, whose involvement in professional preparation fitted into the vocational responsibility of the Union.

The learning objectives in a European context advocated in the Commission's White Paper on Education and Training (*Teaching and Learning: Towards a Learning Society*, 1995), which takes forward its 1993 White Paper on growth, reinforce the concept of a life-long European education made up of different but not necessarily incompatible initiatives. It stresses the 'merits of a broad base of knowledge', the ingredients for adjusting to the economic and employment situation and the 'personal fulfilment of citizens', of which the third objective is traditionally at the centre of an education provided by the nation state. Paradoxically, it takes up the Community's concern in Article 126 with developing quality education.

The emphasis on world-wide research into production methods, marketing and technology policy is linked with the educational objective of mobilising and financing Europe's 'true wealth: the creative spirit and energy of its people' to help in the production of an educated, professionally trained workforce which is flexible and interculturally aware to respond to the diversity in Europe. Beside professional preparation, space is found for a European education ranging from human rights and social protection to an awareness of common financial policies and the standardisation of products.

Enabling students and teachers to find time to participate in collaborative programmes as a learning resource may require that member states give up some educational autonomy by relaxing the grip on school timetables, as suggested by the RIF (see note 1).

The priorities of educational outcomes

The wide interpretation of education which includes vocational and upbringing considerations allows the inclusion of literally hundreds of actions covering the entire gamut of pursuits as part of the educational achievements of the European Union. The volume of work produced in the past forty years can be gauged from the pages of Schäfer's *Bibliography of the Education Systems of the European Community*.[26]

An examination of the actions taken reveals that Community priorities are those of a socio-educational nature already suggested such as access to education, equality of opportunity, development of qualifications, training and retraining projects and the mobility of students and professional workers. The emphasis on technology and mobility in the EU accounts for the promotion of education–industry links, such as Leonardo and the study of languages through Lingua.

Increasingly, non-governmental agents, such as business, social and private interests, have been taking the initiative in promoting educational and development activities, some of which are of regional significance, and involving research. The effect of research has been of a cumulative nature, stimulating fresh thought on practices and moves towards encouraging the introduction of innovations in the Union through Council decisions and regulations.

In the ongoing process, teachers, pupils, researchers and the public at large take part in producing and studying ethnic culture, camp together and protect the environment with partners from other European countries or they are involved in expanding the teaching of certain foreign languages, the work having started through exchanges and collaborations under EU programmes such as Socrates or Lingua. In many institutions teaching and training approaches have changed as a consequence of the opportunity provided by the Community to observe practice elsewhere through exchange and collaboration.

* * *

The repeated and updated versions of Council Decisions and Directives reveal the topics of particular interest. Exchange and mobility programmes, such as CL DEC 819/95 establishing the Community action plan Socrates, the Youth for Europe Programme (CL DEC 818/95) as well as a number of directives and decisions which take up previous programmes on the European Community Action Scheme for Mobility of University Students (Erasmus: CL DEC 87/327 and following) and *An Action Programme for the Promotion of Youth Exchanges in the Community* (CL DEC 88/348), come up especially often.

Education of the Children of Migrant Workers (CL DIR 77/486) demonstrates the priority of access to education facilities, while *Establishing an Action Programme to Promote Foreign Language Competence in the EC* (CL DEC 89/489) confirms the importance in the Community of communication. The recent *Adoption of a Multiannual Programme to Promote the Linguistic Diversity of the Community in the Information Society* (CL DEC 96/664) proves the EU's long-term commitment to both diversity and to information technology.

Action Programmes on the Comparability of Vocational Training Qualifications Between the Member States of the EC (CL DEC 85/368) are the prerequisite enabling workers' mobility, while CL DEC 87/569, *Concerning an Action Programme for the Vocational Training of Young People and Their Preparation for Adult and Working Life* is a response to EU vocational preparation commitments under Article 127. Programmes to do with exchanges implementing an EC vocational training policy, continuing vocational training and preparation for adult and working life on a comparative basis are updated, for example, Eurotecnet and Force (CL DEC 89/657) into Leonardo (CL DEC 94/819).

The economic priority is evident in CL DEC 91/504, *Adopting a Specific Research and Technological Development and Demonstration Programme for the EEC in the Field of Agriculture and Agro-Industry Including Fisheries*, while the training and mobility of researchers is the focus of CL DEC 94/916, *Adopting a Specific Programme of Research and Technological Development, Including Demonstration, in the Field of Training and Mobility of Researchers*. Three recent directives on competition show the Union's commitment to a free production and marketing activity in the Common Market.

Many regulations deal with the recognition and status of professional and vocational qualifications, and are indicative of EU concern to ensure the maximum possible mobility and right of establishment. These are the *Action Programmes on the Comparability of Qualifications Between the Member States of the EC.*

The lists in *Butterworths' European Communities Legislation: Current Status*[27] run to many pages, going on to include environmental concerns, machine translation, stimulation plans for economic science and other initiatives, in many of which the distinction between education and vocational priorities is not at all clear.

Member states' compliance with the legislation varies depending on its type. Some states have been arraigned before the Court of Justice for non-compliance with directives on the mutual recognition of diplomas as qualification: for example, Greece, in the case of the *frontistiria* language schools and the exclusion of nationals of other member states from holding jobs in public education. In Germany, the status of teachers as professional civil servants was not relaxed for non-German nationals until 1993. In Italy, non-Italian graduates may still be excluded from permanent teaching posts in universities.

To find direct links between an EC or EU directive and national implementing legislation in the United Kingdom is relatively easy with *Butterworths EC Legislation Implementator*[28] which lists the Directive number (title and *Official Journal* reference), the target date and the corresponding UK legislation (that is, the Statutory Instrument number followed by the relevant acts). There are similar compendia in the other EU languages.

Financing education and training: deciding the priorities

Educational initiatives which merit Community assistance can be said to be financed by member states via the Union out of direct contributions and indirect levies on VAT takings as well as customs, agricultural and other duties which together sustain the European Social and Structural Funds. R&TD research conducted in Joint Research Centres such as that at Ispra in Italy is contracted out, with between 25 and 50 per cent of the total financed by the Community. National and business money is invested in specific research projects.

Transnational projects which can be commercially exploited are prioritised. They are likely to be of an industrial and economic nature, to do with changing employment patterns and vocational retraining, as, for example, in the recent cases of the steel and clothing industries. Funding is available under the *Treatment in Access to Employment* Directive (CL DIR 76/207) or the *Common Vocational Training Policy* Decision (CL DEC 63/266). Information technology and national education initiatives aiming at European identity or European Citizenship are new areas which attract Community support.

'Education' in the wider sense can be assisted by financing certain training and retraining initiatives: 'research, technological development and demonstration programmes' including 'dissemination and optimization of the results' (Article 130g). In addition to the Social Fund, research can be funded by activating the aim of developing and pursuing 'actions leading to the strengthening of . . . economic and social cohesion' (Article 130a). The reduction of disparities between the development levels of the various regions will ensure that better progress is made with the overall economic and political objectives of the Community. The resources of the Structural Funds set up for this purpose, the European Agricultural Guidance and Guarantee Funds and the European Regional Development Fund, redress imbalances and make structural adjustments.

Cooperation and consultation through the 'educational mobility' programmes of the European dimension comes largely out of the budget of the Directorate General (DG XXII) responsible for Education, Training and Youth. Over the years, all Union member states have received assistance from the various sources available.

In 1997 monies available for training, youth policy, culture and audiovisual media information and technology amounted to ECU780 million, which represents 0.9 per cent of the total available expenditure. This compares with research and training expenditure, including R&TD and JRC, of ECU3,160.4 million, representing 3.8 per cent in the same year. The sums received by member states are not in proportion to the payments made by them to the Community but are allocated in accordance with need.

It is significant that in the United Kingdom between the years 1995–6 and (March) 1998, according to statistics relating to actions for which the Central Bureau for Educational Visits and Exchanges is the national agency, the take-up of cooperation contacts of the actions of the Lingua programme, which may have a readier vocational application (especially the 1990–4 programme), has been keeping up with the school and academic orientated Socrates programmes. Lingua Action B: Language In-service Training for Teachers/Trainers increased from 868 to 2,408, compared with Comenius Action 1: Multilateral School Partnerships Teacher Placements and Exchange, which went up from 100 to 688. To be sure, the statistical differences may reflect the different volumes of funding available.

Although in view of the economic objectives of the European Union financing the explicitly cultural and civic aspects of education will be a low priority unless their usefulness to improve productivity can be argued, it is not entirely fanciful to take Union involvement in the 'development of the highest posssible level of education . . . through a wide access to education and its continuous updating' (New Recital in the Preamble to the Treaty of Amsterdam) in the sense of promoting an environment and upbringing that will be conducive to the fullest exploitation of the knowledge and skills acquired, an area in which education as upbringing will have an important part to play. Improving access to education for the disadvantaged and disabled minorities through enabling social policy initiatives indicates the general drift in that direction.

Educational achievements

The European dimension

The 1988 European Community Resolution is generally recognised as the strongest stimulus to the whole range of educational activities, including the so-called European dimension which introduced European knowledge and attitudes into the curriculum of member states' schools. It is identified with collaborative exchange and research programmes mounted within the framework of existing Socrates and Leonardo exchange schemes, which make up its single largest voluntary component fostering a spirit of European cohesion and identity.

In a 1994 interview the former European Union Commissioner Antonio Ruberti said that educational visits and exchanges were an integral part of the

European dimension. As part of the educational achievements of the European Union he listed the take-up of exchanges during his tenure of office as proof of the growth of the European dimension. As voluntary activities, these visits do not impinge on member states' educational autonomy.

Generously funded, they are available at all levels and for all types of education and promote group and individual activities geared to appeal to people at the ages for which they are designed, whether as general education or as vocational guidance for those already at work. Erasmus, Comenius, Lingua and Leonardo exchange sub-networks are available respectively to pupils, students, school and university teachers and researchers, workers in industry; apart from study visits, they include in-service professional development schemes in the form of European 'summer universities' or industry–education partnerships which include training and work placements. Leonardo focuses on education leading to professional qualifications.

The Erasmus schemes, generally considered as the flagship of the programmes, are an important exchange initiative in the influential higher education sector, bringing together as participants not only EU citizens: many are open to nationals of associate members.

Europeans probably already use or are learning to use exchange experience to improve their vocational and professional skills and knowledge. In addition, exchange helps to foster a spirit of European inquiry and adaptability together with the European knowledge used by workers and learners in the economy of an integrated Europe.

Its multiple, cognitive skills and affective character achieved through the medium of cross-curricular 'dimensions' enables it to have a strong influence on all Europeans by reforming the school curriculum and work plans, which encourages an active approach to intercultural and personal development.

Even so, opportunities for the mobility on offer have not been taken up to the fullest extent possible. Relatively few teachers spend part of their preparation period studying in another member state or extending their skills into areas such as health care or careers advice. Indeed, the effects of the exchanges and visits are mixed because they do not necessarily register an enhanced European awareness on the part of participants, many of whom see themselves as citizens of Europe, dedicated to the European ideals of peace and solidarity. An unpublished questionnaire administered to a cohort of British Comenius participants by Adams, Evans and Raffan in 1997–8 in Cambridge revealed ignorance about Europe and a reluctance, especially among boys, to admit to a Europeanness.

Organisations concerned with European education, such as the Central Bureau for Educational Visits and Exchanges in the United Kingdom and its sister organisations in other member states of the Union, have introduced networks of information services, many of them taking on the function of processing applications for European collaborative research and study awards. They also disseminate European literature, such as the magazine *Central Bureau News*, and examples of good practice. The popular series of television programmes *Inside Europe*, compiled by the Central Bureau, was shown and discussed widely in contemporary history lessons in schools in several European countries after its presentation on BBC 2's *The Learning Zone*.

Initiatives such as the European Schools Day and lectures on European events organised by the Central Bureau are part of a network of activities by linked organisations in other member states financed by the European Union. Jean Monnet Community and European Heritage lectures acquaint Europeans with their own home backgrounds and those of fellow Europeans. European dimension programmes at 'home' are an addition to study in institutions of another member state fitted into the regular teaching programmes, enabling a comparative European dimension.

The European schools which provide an education leading to a European or International Baccalaureate for the sons and daughters of expatriate European civil servants and workers in member states present a separate and distinctive way of experiencing the European dimension.

The above programmes are the achievement of the Directorate General of the European Community 'Education Training and Youth' (DG XXII) responsible for the organisation of most of the European education initiatives.

Collaboration in research

The Directorate General Science, 'Research and Development' (DG XII) shares some responsibility for education and vocational training with DG XXII, being concerned mainly with research. Other Directorates, such as Employment and Industrial Relations, may be marginally involved.

Technological and scientific development fits the economic and professional objectives of European Union intervention which is to deliver 'Knowledge and learning through Community and Member States collaboration'. Research pursued by Directorate General XII is in the areas marked as priorities for raising economic standards.

Targeted Socio-economic Research Programme 1995–1998 was awarded ECU105 million for its activities, 3 per cent of the Union's GNP given to R&TD. The Directorate used workmanlike approaches with three separate calls for proposals, ranging from an overview of the whole work programme, followed by a separate examination of the three areas focusing on priority topics encouraging 'Transversal Proposals' and onto 'Highlighting Strategic Orientation'. In the areas covered – information and communication technology (ICT), teacher training, teaching methods and education policies – thirty-eight projects were submitted.

The current (fifth) R&TD Framework Programme, as of May 1998, foresees 'Improving the human research potential and the socio-economic knowledge base' and includes joint Community and member state initiatives on the 'Quality of Life and Management of Living Resources', a 'User Friendly Information

Society', and 'Competitive and Sustainable Growth and Preserving the Eco-system'.

This Key Action encompasses four main blocks:

- societal trends and structural changes;
- technology, society and employment;
- governance and citizenship;
- new development models fostering growth and employment;

closely linked with Maastricht Treaty provisions on employment and citizenship.

Each of the four blocks is divided into what are educational issues of inter-national concern which can be translated into school curriculum programmes, for the detailed framing of which member states alone are responsible. Their industrial application, for example in production, has to be negotiated in a different context.

Phenomena of xenophobia, racism and migration, changing patterns of work and organisation of time (Key Action 1), the impact of technologies in socio-economic, territorial, institutional, political and structural contexts or the role of the public sector in the innovation process (Key Action 2) can be incorporated into syllabuses or lead to rethinking on the roles of the state (public) and private (business) sectors in educational change. The concept of citizenship across Europe or the influence of the various components of culture and of educational models on the development of values (Key Action 3) are topics for inquiry by qualified representatives of member states for promoting national curriculum development in member states. Findings resulting from innovations in socio-economic partners' cooperation or organisational patterns, new types of work and employment (Key Action 4) are matters for economists and work-efficiency experts.

In the programmes, school education–upbringing concerns, including the need for different teaching and learning processes, such as integrating multimedia pedagogic material or safety at school, share pride of place with vocational training. Despite the widely proclaimed differences in national educational systems and practices in European Union member states, the advantages of a common approach are acknowledged as contributing to the achievement of a more efficient, just and prosperous Europe. The demarcation line between education and training indeed looks blurred when the topics being researched are compared. However, the economic objective of the Community is never lost sight of, while the actual introduction of new programmes in national curricula is devolved to the member states, which leaves the provisions of the Maastricht and Amsterdam Treaties unviolated.

Languages in a multilingual context: language awareness

The eleven official, national or main mother tongues plus the dozen or more regional languages of the European Union of fifteen states are one of the most readily perceived features of diversity. To a varying but increasing degree, since the start of the European Communities all official languages have been taught not only in their countries of origin, but have been available in the other member states as school subjects. The regional 'territorial' languages of France are now officially admitted, which they were not in 1952.

Exact policies and regulations for teaching the first or 'official' language in school vary in the member states but it is the core subject of the curriculum. The main language, for example Castilian, will be available throughout Spain, but the regional languages, for example Catalan, will be used and taught in Catalonia, identified with their territory. Their status is left to individual member states, which in addition, for example in Spain, have to provide Portuguese and French as foreign or migrants' languages.

Foreign languages, in particular the other languages of the European Union, are supposed to be available in schools. In practice, some languages, especially English, have achieved the status of an additional language of instruction, for example in the Netherlands. This may result in competition with the regional languages. Several member states, notably France, have introduced foreign languages in their primary schools. Educational autonomy determines the details of teaching policies and methods. Unlike the Scots, the English teach hardly any foreign languages in primary schools.

There is a distinction between the prestigious languages which are part of the prescribed curriculum and the smaller languages which include territorial or non-European immigrants' home languages which, like dialects, do not enjoy the same status as languages. In this case also, individual policies are applied, for example on the position of 'standard' language in the United Kingdom.

All approaches can be justified, whether indicative of the government's responsibility for promoting the country's first language for historical and national–political reasons, as in Greece, or giving school leavers the advantage of qualifying for a wider variety of jobs because of their linguistic facility, especially with English. In the Netherlands minority languages can not only be taught as a subject but some are used as the medium of instruction in special schools financed by the state. The second approach is in response to the spread of Anglo-American influence through information technology.[29]

The status of minority languages depends on their users' attitude to maintaining them. Immigrant users of Castilian are more likely to resort to the language of their host country than are the Portuguese. The former find it easier to secure jobs without seeking the help of their own compatriots already in a job and are less worried if they cannot address them in their mother tongue when approaching them.[30]

The Lingua programme, which expands language instruction, first, second or foreign, at all levels, was created not only to facilitate communication but also in order to protect the identity of different language groupings in multilingual Europe. The actual policies differ in accordance with the status and popularity of the country with immigrants, asylum seekers and refugees.

Integrating immigrant minorities may be a problem in the case of those non-EU immigrants whose languages and cultures do not enjoy the same degree of protection given to the territorial languages, although many can be used as the languages of school instruction. The gap between the parity of status of the territorial languages and of the 'new' languages is as wide as the related social problems. European Union provision for these minority interests is not necessarily reciprocal, as is the case of the official languages of EU member states.

Literature reading lists are national, while foreign language teaching emphasises the communicative skills in preference to the study of literature. Not much 'European' literature is taught in first-language lessons to encourage multiculturalism. However, the practice of reading texts and short works in the original or in translation is growing; while making use of more European texts in translation in literature classes in England, which used to rely exclusively on texts written by Commonwealth authors, marks a changed emphasis in the 'foreign' experience.

Making reference to foreign languages in general classroom transactions, as opposed to foreign language lessons, is left largely to the teachers. Member states' teaching methods and teaching traditions may allow more or less account to be taken of language structures and comparison made with other languages and dialects in lessons.[31]

The policy of encouraging the spoken language means that, as a rule, an approach which does not have much recourse to grammar teaching is preferred. In the 1980s a movement known in England as Language Awareness advocated the use of a language education which encouraged reflection on the language acquisition process in the case of both the mother tongue and modern foreign languages. This introduced a cognitive dimension to language learning[32] which broke up the routine of repetitions.

Language Awareness, which meanwhile is taken to include affective (sensitivity to other speakers and their languages) and somatic (pronunciation and listening skills) as well as cognitive (learning about language) approaches in language study, have found interest in a number of European Union countries.[33]

Awareness of language not only enables pupils to 'learn' more about their first language, making them more skilful, emancipated users of it, but can also give them an insight into how language is acquired in the first place. This allows them to use the experience also as a reference in the process of language acquisition made while learning a foreign language, expediting the undertaking by encouraging awareness of similarities as well as differences and distinguishing between regular and irregular occurrences.

Learners who are aware of how they acquire or learn a language are more likely to take an interest in learning other languages, and in their users and their cultures, language being recognised as part of a nation's culture.[34] In the European Union where languages enjoy a priority the use of a Language Awareness approach may improve learning motivation and encourage the finding of suitable ways of learning them.[35]

Since Language Awareness is an intercultural curriculum dimension sensitising learners to language functions, its structures and varieties, it has a role to play in the intercultural considerations of a European education in a multilingual Europe, encouraging tolerance and an involvement in the acquisition of language and a willing acceptance of language users[36] (see also note 32).

Salvadori's suggestions[37] for a thriving European partnership exploiting the technological and economic dimensions could be linked with the suggested language study as cultural diversity becomes a goal worthy of pursuit.

Intercultural education and European pedagogy

It will most likely always be possible to distinguish teachers' different nationalities by their general national 'mannerisms' as well as their professional preference for pupil-centred or teacher-dominated teaching approaches. The class teachers' role in a multiethnic situation must be that of an expert intercultural practitioner who can act for the whole multicultural group, requiring both a systematic theoretical and a practical preparation.

Interdependence, a two-way traffic from group to group and group to teacher in a classroom of pupils with an equal claim to time and resources, is the key to intercultural pedagogy. Personal experience acquired through participation in exchanges enables intercultural expertise to develop.[38]

The curricular elements suggested in the European dimension defined earlier must be practised by the teachers themselves. They will be expected to have a global outlook and to teach across European borders. At least an acquaintance with some European languages or linguistic facts and a language awareness, are essential.

The acquisition of a multicultural and multilingual view of Europe is an integral part of factual knowledge of the continent, which includes one's own member state. Quoting official documentation, Convey[39] gives details of the skills and knowledge necessary to work in other member states. Intercultural teaching is cooperative teaching free of bias and prejudice, giving pupils the opportunity to study ethnic materials and to learn about the cultures around them[40] and to acquire indispensable European travel skills.

The European Association of Teachers (AEDE), the Association for Teacher Education in Europe (ATEE) and the European Secondary Heads Association have taken initiatives to develop practical approaches to intercultural teaching. The European skills suggested above are part of a European pedagogy to be used by the growing numbers of what will be ethnic teachers teaching in multiethnic classrooms. So far, research conducted on European topics has not included an explicit European pedagogy.

Mario Reguzzoni[41] sees European pedagogy (*pédagogie européenne*) as addressing European super-values, helping to overcome the reluctance to acknowledge one's European identity. He develops his concept by suggesting a shift of the Community's general 'European dimension' towards promoting specific Europe-orientated project initiatives, with the users of education exploiting the opportunities of Socrates and Leonardo for this purpose, and developing a sense of pride in European achievements.

'The principle of subsidiarity [which] will become a pedagogic medium' appropriates the socio-economic priorities of the Community for creating a new identity for Europe, not in the sense of one nation stronger than the others but 'as an economic and political space shedding hidebound national traditions and prejudices in which distinct, original initiatives can be developed by Europeans for the benefit of the European Union as a whole', with the help of available European Union facilities.

The new pedagogy assumes starting with the providers and recipients of education and training. Reguzzoni warns of the danger of a European super-state which would destroy the equilibrium between central and peripheral responsibility; this may arise despite restrictions placed on excessive Community involvement.

Unifying European super-values subsumes those of individual member states, the new component being the adoption of an autonomous, overarching supra-national position which supplants the outdated, national forms of thinking and doing.

Reguzzoni pleads for the Community to promote the development of the European dimension in the direction of discarding member state government initiatives in favour of fresh European ones by practitioners at below-government level. This would involve social workers, voluntary groups and others, drawn from the wider range of European citizens acting as agents, professional and non-professional parties, teachers and experts, as well as pupils, parents and business, attempting to find solutions to problems of health, environment, employment and safety as well as education besetting Europe being dealt with as a part of the economic and political priorities of the Union. Poor linguistic ability which inhibits students in making full use of exchange programmes is also responsible for the lack of interest in a European pedagogy.

Global and regional education perspectives

An entire section of European dimension syllabuses is given over to extra academic aspects of the curriculum such as human rights and environmental and citizenship education, which are global concerns that cannot be limited to Europe or the European Union. The European knowledge, skills and attitudes acquired as a European 'literacy' must address wider world issues to keep pace with economic developments, through the contacts which the European Union maintains with the rest of the world.

National curricular procedures and suggestions such as those of the Commission on Citizenship (see note 19) can be used for the efficient teaching of regional schemes through linking with national ones that confront the same problems but concentrating on their local implications. Working on such parallel projects is an example of cooperation by the two sets of interests, combining the satisfaction of regional and local achievement with activities which are necessarily world-wide.

Recognition given to the 'regions' is a feature of the European Union. The Committee of the Regions attempts to bring Europe closer to Europeans by placing decision making in matters of politics, economy, employment and ecology, health and education at the centre of local activity, encouraging a 'bottom-up' collaboration in matters which affect their everyday lives and open to innovatory practice in the region, with regional legislation approving and financing socially and economically valuable projects for regional development.

The educational implications of the rise of regional units are reflected in the revival of local crafts and skills and collaborative efforts for improving employment prospects. In borderland areas there may be provision for teaching a minority territorial language or dialect (see note 11) and the award of regional diplomas.[42]

Several hundred regions can be found within one 'nation state', such as Catalonia in Spain, or they can straddle two or three state borders such as the 'Euregio' links between communities in the Tri Rhena area around Basel or those in the Noord of Holland and North Westphalia. The transborder links are particularly good examples of 'European' areas fought over in the past by different sovereign states and currently administered by different governments but meanwhile sharing economic or ecological concerns and often a common dialect and cultural tradition.

Regional work is seen as enhancing the 'European dimension' in an education concept demonstrating concern for employment, public health, vocational training, transport and social legislation: matters on which the European Council is enjoined to consult the Committee of the Regions. The economic and ecological revival of a number of areas has been particularly successful, the result of joint micro-European effort. It is not an attempt to encourage the growth of exclusivity and separatism because the work is carried out against a multilingual and multicultural background replicated in other regions and on a European level also.

Conclusion

General comments

It has been the aim throughout this chapter to qualify the attempt to claim that education is one of the EU areas of activity for which the sole responsibility has been left with its member states. To be sure, it is in the actual provision of educational services that most of the differences between member states can be found, in a pattern described as a 'mosaic' by Francine Vaniscotte,[43] and in a political system which foresees no powers being available to impose structural or curricular change from outside.[44]

Schools which deliver compulsory education and supply the basic work skills of a country's economy differ most in respect of their structure and content (provision of nursery schooling, the length of compulsory education, pupil admission policies, the 'national' parts of the curriculum) and the details of their management (involvement of parents, teachers, pupils, business interests and the community at large in school administration). Teaching methods and styles which depend on the form that teacher–pupil relations assume can vary from school to school. What may be referred to as school rituals, the minutiae of length of teaching periods, pupils' dress or personal freedom differ most of all. The countless differences which affect pupils, their parents and their teachers are variously determined by local school governors or by central government.

At the same time, the national systems of education have been in receipt of financial assistance through regional aid from the Community, which member states have been able to invest in their own prioritised projects, as shown in the following chapters. They have also been able to benefit from the professional advice forthcoming from the Community through the findings of research and collaboration. Innovatory projects, for example in teacher education to improve the quality of education in Europe, have been eligible for EU funding.

Member states have had to comply with Community legislation on such educational concerns as equality of provision or the mutual recognition of diplomas. The use made of exchange facilities has had the cumulative effect of making educational practice in the European Union more homogeneous.

A helpful way to make a comparative examination of the provision of educational facilities by EU member states is to concentrate on the common problems which confront them and the solutions arrived at. Such an examination reveals differences, for example in the involvement of schools in the professional preparation of teachers as opposed to locating most of it, apart from practical teaching, in institutions of higher education, as well as similarities in tackling a Europe-wide reform of teacher preparation. Differences will continue alongside convergence, for example in the adoption of the European Credit Transfer Scheme and work on curricular schemes towards common European qualifications. They have not managed to supplant the award of national certificates, despite the unique freedom to manoeuvre that mobility has created.

Of the uses that can be made of the knowledge gained from a comparative study of education provision, the most important one is probably the stimulus given to considerations for further improving educational quality. The raising of standards of the first phase of secondary education in the comprehensive school, involving the elimination of the lower-level vocational school, or the greater control of access to tertiary-level education, safeguarded by the scope of national leaving certificates and student fees, are examples of a common tradition and response to economic developments.

The implications of practices such as the existence of a selective school system in Germany and Belgium, even though access to it is administered differently, or of central curriculum planning, while leaving its delivery to the schools, being differently resolved in Belgium from the solutions adopted in England, are matters which are debated not only in the national context but are also the subject of discussions by politicians and professionals meeting in European Union assemblies and conferences.

The involvement of parents, business and community interests in the government of schools is indicative of the status of central and local control of education. Total financial devolution of many schools in England contrasts with the role of central government in controlling the system by its teams of inspectors, indicative of both the speed and extent of the introduction of a market economy in education.[45]

If the outcome of a collaborative and agreed approach to European *vocational preparation* has been the production of better trained and skilled European employees and employers, then the aim of a European *general education* is to produce committed Europeans able to live and work in the European Union. The two are not incompatible, education including:

- schooling at all levels, in which the best practice in conventional curricula would to a large extent be shared in order to promote economic growth;
- professional preparation of a well-educated, trained and skilled workforce which will use shared research facilities to improve practice;
- personal and social education with a European bias to promote an inter-cultural, cooperative approach to learning and the formation of European attitudes;
- political awareness and the skills of European citizenship which include commitment to Europe with a global respect for human rights and the environment;
- knowledge, values and general skills and an open and flexible stance required to operate within the Union, together with adequate language and travel skills, and the European expertise needed to use that mobility beyond the workplace;
- the ability to interpret communication initiated by those using different media and to understand what is being transmitted thanks to the education received.

There are six educational areas where developments, to a varying degree, affect a 'European identity' in the school:

- the curriculum: administration and school governance and parental involvement;
- business and community representation: government control;
- the status of denominational and private education;
- admission policies: responses to minority interests;
- work experience in school;
- restructuring the higher education sector.

The allocation of time to humanities and science education areas may allow for a different emphasis to be given to the study of modern foreign languages and the choice of languages, for example to reduce the dominant position of French in England. Account should be taken of the fact that teaching methods differ, for example in the teaching of reading due to the different length of words and the different syllable structure in different languages.

There are significant differences in 'personal and social' education and the teaching of health and hygiene, partly determined by the denominational character of some schools.

In the administration of schools the position of the head teacher and the independence of teachers as the agents responsible for delivering education play a crucial role. This is handled differently due to practices stemming from developments such as the involvement of the state, the Church or private individuals in the provision of compulsory education and its status.

Although the so-called 'independent' schools have to provide a prescribed core curricular minimum, there is freedom in interpreting ministerial guidelines and the production of an individual school profile in many EU countries. French commitment to transmitting national republican values mitigates undue individualisation and commercialisation of education on the scale happening in Britain.

The representation of teachers and pupils on governing bodies varies; the United Kingdom allows less place to these interests than does France. The role of parents has grown, commensurate with their right to choose their children's school and their newly found status as consumers.[46]

Parents' say in deciding parts of the curriculum has led to involvement in 'personal and social', including sex, education. Assisted denominational and ethnic minority schools may have their own religious components of the curriculum. Socio-political reformers have been promoting tighter control of social science syllabuses to fight hidden misrepresentation and bias.[47]

The influence of business and community interests reflects the application of market principles to financing education.[48]

The involvement of business interests in the provision of education facilities can be seen in the changed vocational preparation sector at secondary and tertiary levels in Greece, in further and higher education in the UK, and the arrival of private universities in Germany. It may result in a different emphasis being given to subjects such as foreign languages, mathematics or the arts. Increasingly, local businesses have become identified as the main employers of school leavers.

The nation state usually has ultimate responsibility for and control of education, extending to deciding the curriculum taught and monitoring the award of certificates. Concern with quality has prompted governments, in Britain and France for example, to create academic centres of excellence. Fear has been expressed that Educational Action Zones may threaten the continuance of innovative curricular practices, such as Sommerhill, whose priorities lie in the areas of personal development and independence.

Control of the teaching syllabus has led to the detailed prescription of daily 'literacy' and 'numeracy hours' in England and Wales ten years after the introduction of the National Curriculum and of central inspections of all schools by the OFSTED (Office for Standards in Education) agency, evidence of a stricter application of government control of 'quality worthiness' leading to the publication of performance 'league tables', a development closely watched elsewhere.

Financial support of denominational schools is practised in EU member states although details of the conditions attached to it differ. Regulations arise from different arrangements made with the Churches to relinquish control of education, as in England, or the introduction of a secular school, as in France.

Historical developments in the provision of compulsory education by the state are responsible for the prestige of 'private' schools as well as the status of Christian schooling in Europe. The Republic of Ireland, with almost total provision of state-maintained Catholic schools, is exceptional, but in the Netherlands some 3.3 per cent, as against 1.7 per cent, of GDP intended for state schools is being allocated to the state-assisted denominational and secular schools. This compares with 0.8 per cent and 5.1 per cent respectively in France in the year 1992. The need to increase provision and improve educational and vocational standards which requires substantial outlay is likely to affect Church involvement in education in Europe, particularly that by the established denominations.

Admission policies according to ability vary. Most state-maintained schooling is non-selective and free. However, there may be links with a system of 'donations' from parent and business interests, documented in England, which can secure admission. Limiting comprehensivisation to the end of the lower secondary stage or the end of compulsory schooling, after which selection takes over,[49] illustrates the different origins of compulsory education and its control.

The introduction of work experience as part of the general education curriculum throughout the European Union is intended to make education less 'academic' by preparing school leavers for employement through giving them an insight into the world of work and the economy. The link between general education and industrial experience is a contribution to school–industry links, work experience placement in another member state being the type of European dimension supported by programmes such as Leonardo.

European vocational schemes include student exchanges and work practice locations under early European Vocational Education (EVE) and the Leonardo and Lingua programmes, as well as schemes run by business firms. Economic priorities prompting change in order to achieve a supply of skilled workers reflect a trend which has led to a shrinking of the academic school sector. The greater permeability between the three parts of the German system is an example of dilution of the strict selective practice of the *Gymnasien*.

Tertiary-level religious academies and universities have shared a common European educational tradition for longer than other institutions, with a travelling population of academics and students having its origins in a culturally united Europe. Though this tradition began to break up as education became more closely identified with the achievements of nation states, features of an international and religious character can still be seen in the management and rituals of the older universities.

The ready exchange of students and research findings, the mutual recognition of degrees and the appointment of teaching staff on an international scale have experienced an upsurge in the European Union, strengthened by prioritisation of professional and vocational study and the greater involvement of higher education in professional preparation.

Contacts among EU institutions, strongly supported by the Union as well as some national governments, notably the UK, Germany, Austria, the Netherlands and France, and professional associations have led to the establishment of degrees and diplomas with a European profile and to courses run jointly by several institutions leading to the award of what are called European qualifications. New degree and diploma courses reflect the high demand for qualifications in science, technology and engineering, business and the law as well as information technology. Though often financed by national or regional governments, their contents are not as a rule government-controlled, although the economic viability of courses is an important factor in their continued existence in those countries where the concept of 'education as an entitlement' is less respected now than it was in the immediate post-war expansion of university education. EU economic and business priorities, including manning the European administrative machinery, have kept up the numbers of applicants.

With education in Europe increasingly being received in more than one country for Europe-wide positions, the possession of 'European' qualifications, such as the International or European Baccalaureate or the European Diploma in Education being instituted in Italy, is likely to be expected not only of new recruits to the Union bureaucracy but of professionals in other specialisms. This area is still being explored.

Especially in the more 'popular' European countries, particularly England, France and Germany, exchange study is very much on the increase. An English language component is particularly valuable despite EU initiatives to expand the knowledge of more than one language and of more than one education system among Europeans (see note 12).

The absence of an agreed European policy on the funding of university education and the payment of tuition fees by students has been known to hold up some ECTS schemes. Students may be reluctant to study where the facilities are inferior because the low funding received in some member states, including fees, does not allow the same scale of improvement as in their home countries, where financial help from industry is more readily forthcoming. The introduction of tuition fees has not been tackled on a Europe-wide scale.

Students from all EU member states can take up available places in the institutions of other member states as if they were studying in their own countries, subject to paying the same fees and with entitlement to the same grants or scholarships provided for member states' own nationals. They are eligible for financial assistance from European Union exchange and collaboration schemes.

* * *

Teacher preparation, of primary teachers in particular, has recently become an integral part of the higher education sector almost throughout the Union, consisting of academic study followed by professional training. This policy has put the theory of education among tertiary-level professional qualifications and is favoured by teachers' professional bodies and unions. The reform of teacher preparation in France involving the introduction of compulsory professional training at university level in the *Instituts Universitaires de Formation des Maîtres* (IUFMs) is particularly noteworthy.

The mutual recognition of foreign qualifications is linked with the eligibility of teachers for employment in other member states. England and Wales (not Scotland) have been in the forefront of recognising teaching qualifications awarded by other states for teaching posts. This practice, its slow growth linked with the civil servant status of teachers in some member states, is being extended in the Union. This is confirmed, for example, by the acceptance of teachers who are nationals of other member states as permanent teachers in Spain and France. In the UK, the Department for Education and Employment in particular is involved in mobility. The influence of teachers' unions on training and remuneration varies from very little in, say, England compared with the major role of unions and professional associations in France or Sweden.

Teachers as the purveyors of a 'national' education, expected to educate their nation's children according to national criteria, have, in many ways, to undergo the most dramatic changes to qualify for their role as European teachers. While perfectly capable of responding to innovations, proved by their enthusiastic espousal of computer pedagogy, they have often shown a conservative, even nationalistic, stance in other areas of professional activity, their loyalty rewarded by their civil servant status, salaries and working conditions.[50]

The division of competences for education and training implied in the definitions found in documents produced by way of commentary on the Maastricht Treaty makes it difficult to agree an explicit joint education programme in member states of the European Union. Without prejudice to actions undertaken by member states, regional and borderland collaboration is probably the best forum for trying out educational collaboration constructed on the unity and diversity experienced by borderland dwellers in the regions and which may lead to more lasting educational institutions throughout the Union.

European educators will continue to share their new findings and their acquired expertise to develop suitable approaches to deliver a qualitatively different education, a European education for the socio-economic and political advancement of member states of the Union and their citizens, respecting diversity without abandoning their individuality, a challenge for the coming years.

Notes

1 Details of RIF activities can be found in A. Adams and W. Tulasiewicz, *The Crisis in Teacher Education*, London: Falmer Press, 1995.

2 M. Shennan, *Teaching about Europe*, London: Cassell, 1991.

3 J.E. Weiler, 'Fin de siècle Europe', in R. Dehousse (ed.), *Europe after Maastricht*, Munich: Law Books in Europe, 1994.

4 A. Duff (ed.), *The Treaty of Amsterdam*, London: Federal Trust, 1997.

5 Dehousse, *Europe after Maastricht*.

6 Lord Gladwyn, *The European Idea*, London: Weidenfeld & Nicolson, 1966.

7 R. Denman, *Missed Chances*, London: Cassell, 1996.

8 Dini Lamberto, 'Foreword', in Duff, *Treaty of Amsterdam*.

9 W. Tulasiewicz and C.Y. To (eds), *World Religions and Educational Practice*, London: Cassell, 1993.

10 V. Mallinson, *The Western European Idea in Education*, Oxford: Oxford University Press, 1980.

11 W. Tulasiewicz, 'Towards a pedagogy of the regions', paper presented in the University of London, mimeo, 1998.

12 F. Coulmas (ed.), *A Language Policy for the European Union*, Berlin: Mouton de Gruyter, 1991.

13 W. Tulasiewicz and A. Adams, *Teaching the Mother Tongue in a Multilingual Europe*, London: Cassell, 1998.

14 National Curriculum Council, *Curriculum Guidance 8: Education for Citizenship*, York: NCC, 1990.

15 G. Bell, *Developing a European Dimension in Primary Schools*, London: Fulton, 1992.

16 W. Tulasiewicz, 'The European dimension and the national curriculum', in A. King and M. Reiss (eds), *The Multicultural Dimension of the National Curriculum*, London: Falmer, 1993.

17 The Eckart Institut in Braunschweig has a distinguished record of examining textbooks and other school publications for bias.

18 W. Tulasiewicz, 'Education for citizenship: school life and society', in W. Tulasiewicz and G. Strowbridge (eds), *Education and the Law*, London: Routledge, 1994.

19 A. Osler, H.F. Rathenow and H. Starkey (eds), *Teaching for Citizenship in Europe*, Stoke-on-Trent: Trentham Books, 1995.

20 D. Heater, *Citizenship*, London: Longman, 1990.

21 S.J. Prais, *Productivity, Education and Training: An International Perspective*, Cambridge: Cambridge University Press, 1998.

22 *Legal and Political Analyses*, Brussels: Belmont European Policy Centre in Brussels, 1992.

23 J.A. McMahon, *Education and Culture in European Community Law*, London: Athlone Press, 1995.

24 Janne Report: *For a Community Policy on Education* in Bulletin of the European Communities, Brussels, European Communities Commission, 1973.

25 A. Adams and W. Tulasiewicz, *The Crisis in Teacher Education*.

26 U. Schäfer, *Die Europäische Gemeinschaft und das Bildungswesen*, Berlin: VWB Verlag für Wissenschaft und Bildung, 1994.

27 *European Communities Legislation: Current Status 1952–1997, Spring Supplement 1998*, London: Butterworth.

28 *Butterworth's EC Legislation Implementator*, London: Butterworth, 1998.

29 A. Adams, 'Language awareness and information technology', *Curriculum and Teaching*, **11**(2) (1996).

30 T. Goldstein, *Two Languages at Work: Bilingual Life on the Production Floor*, Berlin: Mouton de Gruyter, 1997.

31   W. Tulasiewicz, 'Knowledge about language awareness: a new dimension in school language curriculum', *Curriculum and Teaching*, **8**(1) (1993).

32   W. Tulasiewicz, 'Language awareness: a new literacy dimension in school language education', *Teacher Development*, **1** (3) (1997).

33   E. Hawkins, *Awareness of Language*, Cambridge: Cambridge University Press, 1984.

34   W. Tulasiewicz, 'Whither language awareness?' in A. Adams, B. Maylath and L. White (eds), *Language Awareness and Educational Policy*, Amsterdam, Amsterdam University Press, 1999.

35   A. Adams and W. Tulasiewicz, 'Beyond simple skills', *Education*, **186**(7) (1995).

36   B. Cox, *Cox on Cox*, London: Hodder & Stoughton, 1991.

37   E. Salvadori, 'Les partenariats d'établissements scolaires en Europe: analyse d'une experience', *Recherche et Formation*, **18**, 1995.

38   A. Adams, W. Tulasiewicz, K. Turner, A. Convey and D. Taverner, *The Changing European Classroom*, European Community Funded Research Report, Cambridge: University of Cambridge Department of Education.

39   A. Convey, 'The European dimension in teacher training' in D. Phillips (ed.), *Aspects of Education in the European Union*, Oxford, 1996.

40   A. King, 'Introduction', in A. King and M. Reiss, *The Multicultural Dimension of the National Curriculum*, London: Falmer, 1993.

41   M. Reguzzoni, 'Politique de l'education et Union européenne', *Recherche et Formation*, **18** (1995).

42   G. Neave, *The EEC and Education*, Stoke on Trent: Trentham Books, 1984.

43   F. Vaniscotte, *Les Ecoles de l'Europe*, Toulouse: IUFM, 1996.

44   M. MacLean, *Britain and a Single Market Europe*, London: Kogan Page, 1990.

45   W. Tulasiewicz, 'Education for sale', in C. Kodron, V. von Kopp, U. Lauterbach, U. Schäfer and G. Schmidt (eds), *Comparative Education: Challenges – Intermediation – Practice. Essays in Honour of Wolfgang Mitter*, Cologne: Böhlau Verlag, 1997.

46   G. Grace, 'Education: commodity or public good?', *British Journal of Educational Studies*, **37** (1989).

47   C. Brock, 'Formation, diffusion and convergence in European education', *Curriculum* **12**(3) (1991).

48   D. Bridges and T. McLoughlin, *Education in the Market Place*, London: Falmer, 1996.

49   L. Elvin, *The Educational Systems in the European Community: A Guide*, Windsor: NFER/Nelson, 1981.

50   M. Lemosse, 'Le professionnalisme des enseignants: le point de vue anglais', *Recherche et Formation* **6** (1989).

1 Austria

*Josef Leidenfrost**

Introduction

During the last decade or so Austria, like many other European countries, has been confronted with four major challenges: two of them highly political, the consequences of the fall of the Iron Curtain and the accelerating processes of European integration facilitated, in part, by the end of a divided Europe; two of them in the field of education, on the one hand the globalisation of the world economy, and the explosion of the information society on the other.

Austria is a relatively small country (8 million inhabitants, approximately 84,000 sq. km), and it has the rather unique geographical position of common borders with eight neighbouring states: the Czech Republic, the Slovak Republic, Hungary, Slovenia, Italy, Switzerland, Liechtenstein and Germany. In light of its history as an empire up until 1918, it has a rich historical tradition shared as a common heritage with many of its neighbours. For obvious reasons, its cultural-linguistic and economic ties are most intensive with Germany.

During the last three or four decades, Austria has accumulated a considerable amount of experience in accommodating to fluctuating political circumstances – from the Cold War in the 1950s to the advent of the 'new Europe' at the end of the 1980s. An intense debate about the necessity for a closer relationship with the European Community in the late 1980s culminated in the establishment of a domestic political consensus on that issue just as Communism began to collapse in central and eastern Europe. The prospects of accession to the European Union and the end of Communism not only facilitated a dual process of reorientation; they also presented Austria with an unprecedented opportunity to redefine its relationship within the region. In figurative terms, Austria moved west and east at the same time: to the West by joining the European Union, to the East by re-establishing long and historical connections with its immediate neighbours.

* The author wishes to thank Norbert Neumann and his team at the Amtsbibliothek of the Austrian Ministry of Education and Cultural Affairs for the valuable and unbureaucratic support they provided, as well as the following colleagues from the Austrian Socrates National Agencies and the Leonardo National Contact Unit: Rudolf Brandstaetter, Nikolaus Douda, Margit Heissenberger and Friedrich Wittib.

Since the Second World War, the Austrian educational system has participated in the trends that have been characteristic of Western European systems in
general: a widespread reform of higher secondary education in the 1960s provided
the basis for a period of university reform in the 1970s. The demographic
consequences of the 'baby boom' and the liberalisation of access policies to
higher education dramatically increased the numbers of students in upper
secondary and higher education institutions.

To the challenges of the 1990s the Austrian educational system has responded
in a number of different ways. Austria has been receptive to the influx of
European models and ideas as well as to the necessity of orientating its education
to meet the demands that exist in the European Economic Area and a reunited
continent. In the light of the Austrian presidency of the European Union during
the second half of 1998 and the establishment of a new generation of European
educational cooperation programmes for the years after 2000, education is an
issue of national priority, and the role of education in preparing young people to
compete in the European and the global market place is a matter of particular
concern.

The onset: the European dimension in education

The impact of the European dimension in education is crucial for an understanding of the policy concerns which characterise the Austrian educational
system today. Defined in 1988, the main objectives of the European dimension
– as adopted in the Resolution of the Council and the Ministers of Education
Meeting within the Council – are:

> measures which should help to strengthen in young people a sense of
> European identity and make clear to them the value of European civilization
> and of the foundations on which the European peoples intend to base their
> development, in particular the safeguarding of the principles of democracy,
> social justice and respect for human rights, to prepare young people to
> take part in the economic and social development of the Community,
> to make them aware of the advantages which the Community represents . . .
> in opening up an enlarged economic and social area to them, to improve
> their knowledge of the Community and its member states in their historical,
> cultural, economic and social aspects and bring home to them the signi-
> ficance of the cooperation of the member states of the European Community
> with other countries of Europe and the world.

The measures conceived to implement the 'European dimension' in all
member states entail the inclusion of the European dimension explicitly in
school curricula, textbooks and teaching materials and encouraging contact
across borders between pupils and students as well as their teachers, in order to
give them direct experience of European integration and the realities of life
in other European countries.

With the launch of Leonardo – the Community Action Programme in the field of vocational training – in early 1995 and of Socrates – the Community Action Programme in the field of general education – in spring 1995, actors and institutions in the field of education at all levels in Europe (in fifteen member states, in the three remaining EFTA countries and, since 1997–8, also in the countries of central and eastern Europe) have been actively involved in the implementation of the European dimension. The Treaty of Maastricht states emphatically that the Community will support and complement the activities of member states in developing their educational systems as well as in maintaining their linguistic and cultural diversity. The Community does not intend to establish one European educational system; what has been agreed are guidelines for a European educational policy characterised by diversity and cooperation. For Austria, participation in European educational programmes opened up all its educational sectors.

Primary and secondary education

The School Organisation Act 1962

According to the constitution, educational matters in Austria require 'special regulation by federal acts'. Due to the high level of ideological polarisation in the First Republic (1918–38), there was initially a low degree of consensus and a limited degree of reform. Immediately after the Second World War, the two main governing parties – the (Christian Democratic) Austrian People's Party and the Socialist Party of Austria – had sharp differences on educational policy, and they did not reach an agreement on Austria's first major reform in education until 1962: a comprehensive School Organisation Act (*Schulorganisationsgesetz* 1962) which is still the legal foundation for the school system in Austria today.

In light of the fact that the School Organisation Act has the status of a constitutional law, any amendment requires a two-thirds majority in the lower house (*Nationalrat*) of the Austrian Parliament, a provision which is not found in many other states and indicates to what extent a broad political consensus is needed to implement educational reform. The legislative hurdle of a two-thirds majority has provided the Austrian school system with a high degree of stability, on the one hand, but made any educational reform a difficult task, on the other.

According to the School Organisation Act of 25 July 1962:

> it shall be the task of the Austrian school to foster the development of the talents and potential abilities of young persons in accordance with ethical, religious and social values and the appreciation of that which is true, good, and beautiful, by giving them an education corresponding to their respective stages of maturity and to their respective courses of study. It shall give young people the knowledge and skills required for their future lives and occupations and train them to acquire knowledge on their own initiative.

Young people shall be trained to become healthy, capable, conscientious and responsible members of society and citizens of the democratic and federal Republic of Austria. They shall be encouraged to develop an independent judgement and social understanding, to be open-minded to the philosophy and political thinking of others, they shall be enabled to participate in the economic and cultural life of Austria, of Europe, and of the world, and to make their contribution, in love of freedom and peace, to the common tasks of mankind.

Setting new priorities

An OECD report on the status and problems of education in Austria in 1968 instigated an intense debate on educational policy and institutional reform in Austria. There was a considerable amount of experimentation in the 1970s, inspired to a large extent by Social Democratic educational policy, which included the introduction of foreign language instruction at earlier ages, elective subjects and a diversification of branches of specialisation at the upper secondary school level. However, the project of introducing a comprehensive secondary school to replace the prevailing two-track selective system did not materialise.

The mid-1980s represent a 'paradigm change' in the development of the Austrian school system marked by a shift from external, organisational and structural measures to an 'internal reform' conceived to provide educational institutions with more autonomy, improve the quality and increase the level of professionalisation in the institutions themselves. One of the objectives of introducing autonomy was to enable the schools to develop their own profiles – a response to the needs of their constituencies; as a result deregulation has been one of the guiding principles of the Ministry of Education.

European integration provided another important impulse for innovation. The main trends of the 1990s – the acquisition of knowledge and skills that are applicable in any number of European countries and the increasing importance of life-long learning – have contributed to reforming European educational systems and, as a consequence, Austrian institutions have been compelled to address a wide variety of structural issues.

Volksschulen

Compulsory schooling in Austria consists of nine years of education, beginning with four years of primary school (*Volksschule*) and concluding with the mandatory general secondary school (*Hauptschule*) for five more years, or continuing with the eight-year cycle of the upper secondary school (*Allgemeinbildende Höhere Schule*). Compulsory education encompasses all children permanently residing in Austria regardless of their nationality. Parents are obliged to register their children at the appropriate school in their district of residence and are responsible for ensuring that children attend on a regular basis. The main objective of the primary school is to give pupils a common elementary education.

Classes are co-educational, the maximum number of pupils per class is thirty. In 1994–5, there were 3,384 primary schools in Austria, 2.3 per cent of which were private.

Rather than attempting the codification of a fixed amount of educational subject matter, with the content delivered in a defined sequence, the current Austrian primary school curriculum provides a broad framework of objectives, the achievement of which is to a large extent left to the discretion of individual teachers. This provides for the application of a nation-wide curriculum at the primary school level, but at the same time it makes the collection of locally relevant matter and additional content possible. Thus, the number of teaching periods assigned to individual compulsory subjects may be determined, within the limits established regarding the allocation of periods, by the provincial school board. Optional courses on European topics have been offered recently to raise pupils' awareness of developments in public life, for example, the European integration process as such, the introduction of the Euro, the Joint Foreign and Security Policy, and European identity. Schools have established their own initiatives, of which 'Experiencing and Shaping Europe' (*Europa erleben und gestalten*) or 'Cultural Heritage: Youth in Europe' (*Kulturelles Erbe – Jugend in Europa*) may be mentioned as examples.

In line with the target of opening curricula to internationalisation, for several years now 'intercultural learning' has been included in the curriculum of basic schooling and newly defined in the general educational target of primary schools. It is supposed to arouse children's curiosity for and interest in cultural differences and variety. Better mutual understanding and mutual respect, recognition of common characteristics as well as the removal of prejudices are the main issues: issues which sound familiar also from reading the 1988 Resolution on the European Dimension.

Secondary education

Although considerable efforts have gone into increasing opportunities for lateral movement within the school system, Austria still has a fundamentally two-track secondary school system. After primary school, pupils enter either a general secondary school (*Hauptschule*) for five years of mandatory education followed frequently by apprenticeships or medium-level vocational-technical training, or begin at an upper secondary school (*Allgemeinbildende Höhere Schule*). This is divided into a four-year lower stage and a four-year senior stage and concludes with a school-leaving certificate which entitles graduates to study at a university or other institution of higher education.

Neither type of secondary school is organised on a classroom-teacher system, all their pupils being taught by subject teachers. The number of parallel classes and teachers employed vary for regional and demographic reasons. In 1996–7 there were 1,182 general secondary schools, the educational objective of which was to prepare pupils for medium- and upper-level schools. These schools offer compulsory, optional and voluntary extra subjects, the exact educational dimensions of which can be adjusted by the schools themselves by means of distinct, school-autonomous curricula. Thus, general secondary schools tend to develop specific profiles, for example in the field of modern foreign languages, in the arts, in sports, ecology, information technology, and so on.

Completion of compulsory education is the prerequisite for admission to pre-vocational schools, medium/upper-level technical and vocational schools or colleges that cover a large area of general education and initial technical and vocational training, encompassing engineering, business, fashion and clothing, social services, general services, tourism, agriculture and forestry, training for nursery school teachers and non-teaching supervisory staff. In particular, they prepare their students for professional life. At the end of the training there is a school-leaving examination, success in which entitles leavers to exercise their respective occupations. Curricula are drawn up in close cooperation with experts from the school administration services, industry and the business sector as well as representatives of the social partners (trade unions, chambers of trade and industry, chambers of commerce).

Upper secondary schools (Allgemeinbildende Höhere Schulen)

The *AH Schulen* are supposed to provide pupils with a comprehensive and in-depth general education. The number of these schools, at 318, is considerably lower than that of general secondary schools (in 1996–7 pupil numbers were approximately 360,000). At least one foreign language is taught, beginning in the first form.

Upper secondary technical and vocational schools are experiencing a steady increase in numbers. In 1996–7 there were 270 of these schools with some 111,000 pupils. This is partly due to the well-balanced curriculum they offer which comprises general education and technical theory as well as practical and vocational training.

The impact of European educational cooperation

Socrates in primary and secondary education

Ever since the implementation of Socrates and the opening up of the various school strands to completely new activities – Comenius 1 (school partnerships) and Lingua E (joint educational projects for language learning) – an intensive transnational cooperation has started within both these programmes involving Austrian primary and secondary schools at all levels. In fact, the participation rate within Comenius 1 has risen from 45 in the first year of participation to more than 400 projects at present and within Lingua E from 25 to almost 40.

It is very clear from the many reactions received from teachers and parents alike that the European dimension as intended by the 1988 Resolution is capable of playing a key role in both: motivating pupils and improving their learning progress. Teachers frequently comment on the excitement that has accompanied their work in class with partner schools and on the fact that the European dimension has been successful in linking what pupils learn at school and their experiences in the 'outside world'. Transnational work generated by participating in a European education project plays a key part in pupils' motivation and has been influential in raising achievement levels in a range of curriculum areas.

Cooperation with Europe in Austrian primary and secondary education is not a new phenomenon. International curriculum initiatives have been part of the life of a number of schools for several years. What is novel is the growing number of educational institutions where work with partner establishments has become part of the whole school curriculum planning process and is subject to the same monitoring and evaluation processes as other areas.

Schools are being encouraged to become involved in European partnerships and to work together on aspects of the curriculum that link up with school development priorities. With the help of so-called 'regional educational brokerages' (*regionale Bildungsbörsen*), located with the provincial government authorities of all nine Austrian federal provinces (*Länder*), information on educational cooperation is disseminated to schools and institutions in the respective provinces and advice on how to prepare projects is available. Furthermore, the Vienna-based Austrian Socrates National Agency holds special Comenius and Lingua E contact seminars which provide Austrian teachers and their other European colleagues with regular opportunities to get together and develop common ideas for future cooperation.

Leonardo: technical, vocational and further education

Since 1995 Leonardo has provided important impulses for the development and adaptation of vocational training in Austria. The European dimension has become an important aspect in the articulation of national measures that address the development of new teaching methods and curricula leading to qualifications in traditional professions as well as in new fields, such as modern media and ecology. Major objectives of vocational training policy in Austria include enhancing autonomy in order to increase flexibility, the adaptation of the legal framework conditions of vocational training, improving the attractiveness of training programmes, diversifying the opportunities of continuing education for the employed, and developing apprenticeship programmes for emerging professions.

The so-called 'dual system' of apprenticeship training has a very long tradition in Austria. This system is based on the company-based training of apprentices complemented by compulsory attendance at a part-time vocational school; as a result, it provides recognised vocational training and qualifications which otherwise are not available at full-time secondary schools or colleges. Training lasts from two to four years, depending on the vocational specialisms chosen, and some 45,000 companies in Austria are involved in training approximately 130,000 apprentices per year. Within the context of Leonardo, the placement of interns in enterprises is a high priority, especially in view of the fact that the concept of vocational education mobility promoted by the Comett programme has meanwhile been extended to other educational spheres.

Since 1995, 59 pilot projects (survey and analysis projects) and programmes for the mobility of students and young graduates have been executed under the auspices of Leonardo in Austria. There also were 123 placement and exchange projects for apprentices, young workers and pupils, with about 1,500 participants during that period.

Higher education

Three institutional models

Higher education in Austria is dominated by three separate institutional models: universities (*Universitäten*) and universities of the arts (*Universitäten der Künste*); colleges (*Akademien des nicht-universitären Bereichs*) for the training of teachers and social workers; and vocational-technical *Fachhochschule* programmes.

In the past decade, the concept of internationalising study programmes and promoting mobility within 'traditional' higher education (universities, teacher training colleges) has assumed a correspondingly important position in the foreground of the debate about the meaning and function of internationalisation in Austrian institutions of higher education, the European educational cooperation programmes being of the utmost importance to this process. Official government documents, such as coalition agreements and government programmes, reflect how the consciousness and level of awareness of internationalisation in the broader, and for Europeanisation in a narrower sense have developed over the years.

The Austrian debate has been increasingly influenced by several 'hot' topics in the past decade: improving competitive capacity, innovation and quality; enhancing social, political and cultural participation; and developing the ability to act in a multinational setting. These last two points illustrate particularly well to what extent the internationalisation of the Austrian educational system must be seen in the context of European integration: a 'European dimension' that transcends the concerns of economic integration.

Bringing higher education back to Europe

The university is a European institution *par excellence*. As a community of teachers and students, equipped with special rights of self-administration including the articulation of curricula and research objectives, and entitled to award publicly recognised academic degrees, the roots of the European university reach back to the Middle Ages. The University of Vienna, founded in 1365, is among the oldest universities in Central Europe and the German-speaking world. The university's traditional four medieval faculties of theology, law, medicine and philosophy have been subject to considerable changes in the course of time and have been joined by new disciplines, such as the social sciences and engineering. Since the eighteenth century the university, *universitas litterarum*, has been responsible for the cultivation of knowledge in its entirety. To date there are twelve universities and six universities of the arts in Austria.

In post-war Austria, the interest in transnational cooperation in higher education grew rapidly due to the severe setback of its university sector during the first half of the twentieth century. Austria's interest in accession to the European Community (as of 1987) and corresponding interest in participating in the multilateral mobility and research programmes of the EC prompted considerable innovation at all Austrian institutions of higher education. The extension of European Community research and education programmes to the member states of EFTA, including Austria, and the establishment of the European Economic Area as an antechamber to full accession to the EC provided Austrian institutions with a series of unprecedented opportunities and challenges a decade ago. A few Austrian universities began participating as 'silent partners' in Erasmus as early as the beginning of the 1989–90 academic year.

The participation of Austria's institutions of higher education (HEIs) in Erasmus II was officially finalised in autumn 1991, which also was the deadline for the initial applications for participation in this programme by the institutions mentioned. This initial participation in EC programmes marked the beginning of a qualitatively new phase of internationalisation of Austrian higher education characterised by their multilateral and European dimensions, extending also to teacher training colleges and soon to the *Fachhochschulen*.

Post-secondary teacher training colleges

Training for primary and general secondary school teachers in Austria is based on the three-year (six-semester) tertiary programmes at teacher training colleges (*Pädagogische Akademien*), established in the late 1960s and early 1970s. Apart from training future teachers, these colleges are also engaged in research work in the field of pedagogy, and each of them is affiliated with an adjacent school that provides a forum for practical training. Currently the relations with the in-service training centres are being intensified in order to improve the student teacher training programmes before graduation as well as providing guidance during teachers' first year of active teaching. There are twenty-six teacher training colleges in Austria and in-service training centres in each of the nine federal provinces. Post-secondary colleges also exist for training social workers and for the paramedical professions.

Fachhochschulen: *a new response to 'old-fashioned' structures*

This new sector of higher education was established and opened up in the early 1990s. Among the immediate concerns of the Austrian government in those days was the development of vocationally orientated post-secondary programmes that would take into account specifically the needs and expectations of the Austrian private sector, which had to prepare for the competitive challenges of the common European market. These considerations played a considerable role in the Austrian decision to develop the *Fachhochschule* sector.

Since universities have traditionally dominated post-secondary education in Austria, which, unlike many other countries, did not develop a substantial sector of non-university tertiary institutions in the 1960s and 1970s but rather 'opened up' its university sector in order to respond to the demographic and education challenges of the time, in 1993 federal legislation provided the basis for the establishment of a distinct *Fachhochschule* sector which represented the abandonment of the Austrian federal government's traditional monopoly on centrally administered higher education.

The Ministry of Science and Transport is not directly involved in the administration or articulation of *Fachhochschule* programmes. These consist of eight semesters of career-orientated post-secondary vocational-technical training. The operation of these programmes is supervised, accredited and periodically reviewed by an independent agency of experts: the so-called *Fachhochschulrat*. The federal provinces, municipalities, professional associations and private organisations – or 'joint venture' combinations thereof – may found and operate *Fachhochschule* programmes, provided they meet the formal and qualitative criteria established by law. Almost forty programmes have been established to date, and many of them are pursuing ambitious internationalisation programmes in the vocational sector.

New aims and expectations in higher education cooperation

Fostering the European dimension

As already indicated, Austrian institutions of higher education were officially participating in EC programmes even before Austria's accession to the European Union on 1 January 1995. In this respect they functioned as a vanguard of integration. Erasmus, a programme familiar to the twelve 'old' members of the European Community, was fully open to Austria's HEIs at the beginning of the 1992–3 academic year (with an application deadline of October 1991). Eligible institutions included not only Austria's four 'classical' universities, eight specialised universities and the six universities of the arts but also the colleges of the tertiary sector (*Akademien des nicht-universitären Bereichs*) responsible for the education of teachers and social workers.

The most important national political signal that accompanied the beginning of Austrian participation in Erasmus was the decision to top up Erasmus grants with national funding to make them even more attractive and to enhance mobility, a policy still in force. Austrian participation grew exponentially in just a few years. The student flows under the new 'institutional contract' arrangements of Socrates/Erasmus represent an even further increase, as shown below.

During the first round of Socrates applications for the Erasmus Chapter (higher education) under the so-called 'institutional contract' (with the application deadline of 1 July 1996), fifty-three Austrian universities, universities of the arts, teacher training colleges and *Fachhochschulen* submitted applications to the European Commission. In doing so, Austrian HEIs applied for participation in Erasmus Action 1 activities for the promotion of the European dimension in universities for the first time. The official Socrates Guidelines for Applicants define 'universities' as 'all types of higher education institutions which offer qualifications or diplomas at that level, whatever such establishments may be called in the participating countries'.

The requirement of only one application per institution (or a cluster application by several small-sized institutions) needs strategic management. The main objective is to help HEIs develop European cooperation policies by formulating a contextual framework for their proposed activities – such as student mobility, teaching staff mobility, or the development of joint curricula – a relatively new concept for Austria. Another objective is to give students a greater chance to benefit from the European dimension to their education, even if they do not directly take part in an exchange scheme.

New 'Erasmus at home' curriculum development activities have different and separate programme slots: two for comprehensive restructuring of degree programmes or major portions thereof (CDIs and CDAs – curriculum development at initial and at advanced levels), and two for developing certain European components (EM – European modules; ILC – Integrated Language Courses). It is too early to anticipate what Austrian HEIs will achieve by implementing the approved activities. The approval rate of 'Action 1' activities during the 1997–8 round was 55 per cent, with above average figures in several categories. Due partly to low levels of Commission funding made available to institutions which applied, the interest during the second round of Socrates/Erasmus applications (November 1997) decreased at universities and universities of the arts. It rose, however, in the *Fachhochschulen* sector and has remained constant in the teacher training colleges sector.

'Europeanisation' through student mobility

The most successful instrument of European cooperation in higher education since the establishment of the Erasmus Programme in 1987 has been that of student mobility. Today, under the auspices of Socrates/Erasmus and after the introduction of the new centralised administrative system (different from the original ICP – Inter-university Cooperation Programmes – system), the encouragement of student mobility and the financing of student grants under Erasmus Action 2 continues to be an undoubted success story, with numbers still moving up.

According to student reports on record at the Austrian Erasmus National Agency, the student mobility strand of the Socrates Programme has been the one aspect of the programme that has contributed most to the 'Europeanisation' of HEIs in Austria. Returning students consider the degree of their integration into the academic and social life at their host institutions, the achievements of their academic training, their overall educational development as well as their personal growth to be the main advantages of their study abroad periods. Insight into different academic situations, experience with new teaching methods and the improvement of foreign language skills are also frequently cited benefits.

Student exchange figures have risen from 893 during the academic year 1992–3, the first year when Erasmus was fully accessible to Austrian students, to almost 2800 during the 1998–9 academic year. The most frequent destinations for Austrian students were institutions in the United Kingdom, followed by France, Spain, Italy and Germany. The leading courses of study among Austrian Erasmus students abroad were economics and modern languages, followed by legal studies, engineering and social sciences. Teacher training also presents an important segment within outgoing Austrian mobility overall.

Erasmus has had a particularly strong impact on internationalising teacher training colleges, which before the initiation of the programme had fundamentally national interests and curricula. For the *Fachhochschulen* programmes, many of which have included an international dimension in their core curricula, Socrates/Erasmus has been a more than welcome instrument for promoting mobility and international contacts. The Austrian *Fachhochschulen* sector is definitely the fastest-growing sector of educational cooperation within Europe at present.

Administration and supervision of higher education

Traditionally, the Ministry of Education (*Bundesministerium für Unterricht*) was responsible for all forms of education – primary, secondary, post-secondary and university. However, in 1970 a new Ministry for Science and Research (*Bundesministerium für Wissenschaft und Forschung*), which was entrusted with university and research agendas, was established by moving the relevant departments out of the Ministry of Education. In recent years, the Ministry of Science and Research has been reorganised a number of times, primarily due to extraneous political considerations, and gained as well as lost several responsibilities. In 1994 it was renamed the Ministry of Science, Research and the Arts; in 1995 it became the Ministry of Science, Transport and the Arts; and in 1997 it was reorganised as the Ministry of Science and Transport. All agendas concerning primary, secondary and adult education as well as part of tertiary education have remained at the Ministry of Education, which has also been renamed and reorganised on a number of occasions (Ministry of Education; Ministry of Education and the Arts; Ministry of Education, the Arts and Sports; Ministry of Education and Cultural Affairs).

General legislation relating to all educational matters is the responsibility of the Austrian Federal Parliament. Provincial (*Länder*) parliaments can pass only minor ordinances. Their direct competence covers almost all pre-school education and the allocation of funds for the maintenance of a few categories of schools, but no interference with curricular issues. Thus, the organisation of schools, their curricula and the arrangement of all school activities are highly uniform in Austria. General school administration and school inspection are carried out by the Ministry of Education and Cultural Affairs, and there are further supervisory authorities active at the provincial level (*Landesschulrat*) and the district level (*Bezirksschulrat*). These bodies maintain a certain degree of independence from the central administrative structures. Various consultation mechanisms exist which give different social and economic interest groups the possibility to articulate their views during the legislative process.

Austrian participation in EU programmes such as Socrates and Leonardo has led to the establishment of a series of special national advisory boards: for the Socrates programme such boards now exist for Erasmus, Comenius and the Transversal Measures; there is also a corresponding board for the Leonardo programme. The members of these boards come from various educational constituencies: for example, ministries, social partners, regions, and pupil, student and teacher associations. These boards function as policy advisory and supervisory bodies, and their most important tasks are to formulate strategies and articulate priorities, primarily to implement the European dimension in different fields of education in Austria.

Growing autonomy

After some recent changes and reforms in the primary and secondary systems in previous years, as already indicated, all Austrian HEIs have since the late 1980s pursued increasingly autonomous institutional policies, tailored to meet their specific structures, strengths and needs. As a result of Austria's involvement in European educational cooperation new institutional actors and structures have appeared at policy and operational levels at about the same time.

The University Organisation Act 1993

As far as the universities and the universities of the arts are concerned, a new University Organisation Act (UOG, *Universitäts-Organisationsgesetz*), a major piece of reforming legislation conceived in 1993 to promote the decentralisation of university education in Austria and substantially to enhance university autonomy, gave Austrian universities a much greater capacity to implement their own institutional strategies.

The ideas of deregulation and decentralisation are at the heart of the UOG, which has redefined the relationship of the Ministry of Science and Transport to the universities by shifting a substantial number of responsibilities from the central level of government to that of the individual HEIs themselves. The resulting higher degree of autonomy, now in the process of implementation, will contribute to making Austrian HEIs more flexible, dynamic, efficient and internationally competitive. The universities remain state institutions, nevertheless, and the state has retained its responsibility for financing them. The Ministry now assumes a predominantly supervisory function and continues to be responsible for strategic planning.

For their international affairs Austrian universities began to establish Offices for International Relations during the mid-1980s. Since then, all Austrian universities and universities of the arts have established such offices which, in turn, have assumed a growing number of 'autonomous' responsibilities.

All smaller and more centrally organised higher educational institutions, such as the teacher training colleges and social workers training colleges, have made special arrangements for monitoring their international activities. They receive a considerable amount of support for these activities from the Ministry of Education and the Office for European Educational Cooperation in Vienna, which serves as the headquarters for almost all of the Socrates action lines (and the entire Leonardo programme). Just recently another amendment to school legislation was finalised by Parliament which provides tertiary institutions of the non-university sector with a certain amount of corporate autonomy that will allow them to conclude contracts on an independent basis.

Decentralisation and deregulation are two of the main trends in the administration of higher education in Austria in the 1990s. This entails placing funds for 'international relations' in the broadest sense of the word more and more at the discretionary disposal of individual HEIs. Traditions of self-government together with decentralisation will give HEIs more opportunities to establish their own priorities and internationalisation strategies.

The University Studies Act 1997

Whereas the University Organisation Act 1993 fundamentally changed the management structure of universities in Austria and provided them with the autonomy they need to articulate their own strategies, the new University Studies Act (Unist, *Universitätsstudiengesetz*) of 1997 has made an equally profound change in the manner in which degree teaching programmes will be organised at Austrian universities in the future. Whereas the University Organisation Act changed the form of Austrian university education, the adoption and implementation of the University Studies Act will change its content.

This body of legislation represents not only a substantial simplification of the legal regulations guiding curricular design and content, it gives individual institutions a much greater freedom to develop programmes with specific requirements and distinct national and international profiles. It also streamlines the procedures for the recognition of academic work performed abroad.

The University Studies Act also provides for the first time a legal anchor for the Europe-wide launched European Credit Transfer System (ECTS). Since equivalencies and transparency facilitate the recognition of academic work performed abroad and are, as such, the keys to successful academic mobility, Austrian participation in Erasmus initially led to the introduction and promotion of ECTS within an 'inner circle' of five Austrian universities in 1992/3. Additional institutions, including colleges for teacher training, have subsequently joined the ECTS project, enabling it to become legally anchored not only in the university sector but to make advances in the non-university sectors of teacher training colleges and *Fachhochschulen* as well.

Teacher training

Teachers for compulsory schools of general education are trained at teacher training colleges. Prospective primary school teachers are deemed to have acquired the whole range of skills necessary for teaching all subjects and age groups of primary education as a general teaching qualificaton after passing a *Lehramtsprüfung* examination. Teachers for general secondary schools and for pre-vocational schools must be qualified in two teaching subjects and require a teaching accreditation in two subject areas. Teachers at higher secondary schools are trained at universities and required to take a specific course of study for accreditation (*Lehramt*) as teachers in higher secondary schools.

Teachers in state-run schools are awarded the status of tenured civil servants after a certain period of employment, employed by the respective federal provinces, or they are employees according to private contracts. Teachers' training background is a decisive factor for the number of lessons they are required to teach, as well as for their income. The typical workload at a general secondary school is 23 lessons per week.

Current employment regulations impose several obstacles on the transnational mobility intentions of teachers in Austria. For European teachers there are two special regulations in force which are different for EU and EEA citizens.

In-service teacher training colleges provide in-service training and further education for teachers. They also engage in pedagogical research work which aims at a scientific analysis of topics of school life and teacher preparation and adapting the further education and the training of teachers in accordance with research findings. Courses cover organisational, curricular and didactic matters, and meetings of subject teachers or special working groups of teachers are arranged. In-service teacher training colleges have been established in all federal provinces and are financed either by the national government or the provincial governments.

Teacher training in Austria is currently being reviewed in the light of the fact that many European countries have raised all their teacher preparation to higher education level provided by tertiary-level institutions and universities whereas there are still two parallel systems in Austria catering for the different school types. New in-service training facilities are being demanded by teachers to meet the needs to use modern information technologies.

With the implementation of Socrates, there has been a growing interest in transnational projects for the in-service training of educational staff, such as the opportunities offered under Comenius 3. Projects deal with methodologies for implementing the European dimension, areas of national curricula with a European component built in, or '*Qualità nella Scuola*' (Quality at School), or '*La autoevaluacion de los centros educativos del primero y secundo nivel*' (Self-evaluation of primary and secondary schools) joint projects. One ambitious trilateral project currently in its feasibility phase is a joint British–French–Austrian programme with the objective of developing a special curriculum for 'European teachers' (*Europalehrer*): a one-year postgraduate course to be offered in teacher training colleges based on modules to be implemented by the participating institutions.

With language competence becoming more and more important in education, the amount of foreign language instruction for trainee teachers in teacher training colleges is constantly being increased. These efforts are currently being matched by the provision of in-service training centres.

Foreign language teaching

The imperative of working collaboratively with partners abroad highlights the need for improved language competence of teachers and pupils in all European countries. In Austria in the meantime this has led to a concerted action to promote foreign languages (*Fremdsprachenoffensive*). As far as modern foreign language teaching within the Austrian educational system is concerned, compulsory practical exercises totalling two hours a week of preliminary foreign-language instruction as early as grade three (soon to be introduced in the first grade!) in primary schools are possible. The languages that can be learnt at the primary school level, with no formal assessment of pupil performance, are English, French, Italian, Croatian, Slovenian, Hungarian, Czech or Slovak. The large majority of pupils opt for English as it is the first foreign language required in almost all secondary schools. As a matter of principle, general secondary schools teach English as their modern foreign language, although some also offer French and Italian.

In the federal provinces of Burgenland and Carinthia (*Kärnten*), there is special legislation for schools for national minorities or ethnic groups (*Minderheitenschulgesetz*). This means that in a given number of schools elementary instruction is, as a rule, offered in two languages. In Carinthia (which has a Slovene minority) children are taught on the basis of the registration principle: parents can register their children for bilingual instruction. In Burgenland (which has a Croatian minority) bilingual classes were established if there were a certain number of children of the ethnic minority living in the community. Since 1994 children do not have to be registered for bilingual instruction.

Compulsory training in one foreign language is also anchored in the curricula of vocational-technical schools. Two foreign languages, frequently with variable lengths of study, are normally required by higher-level secondary schools, and some of these institutions offer a third foreign language as an elective.

Austrian federal funds are also used to promote the instruction of German as a foreign language outside Austria. A university lector programme (*Institutslektorate*) provides positions for Austrian lecturers at higher educational institutions abroad, whose main task is to teach German language and Austrian literature and culture. Austrian primary and secondary school teachers instruct at Austrian schools in Istanbul, Guatemala, Budapest and Prague, at German-speaking schools in other countries all over the world and at upper secondary-level bilingual schools, especially in the neighbouring countries: the Czech Republic, Slovakia and Hungary.

Since there are eleven official EU languages spoken in Europe, further promotion of foreign language proficiency is one of the main objectives of education at the level of Europe. The initial Lingua programme, launched in 1990 and integrated into Socrates in 1995, testifies to the importance of multilingual competence, fully recognised and supported by the Socrates and Leonardo programmes.

There is considerable interest in Austrian schools and other educational institutions in language projects. As far as the measures for the promotion of language learning under the Lingua strand of the Socrates programme are concerned, Austrian institutions have been quite successful in European Cooperation Projects for Language Teacher Training (Lingua A); course materials have been developed through projects like *EURO-Gruppen als europäische Lehr- und Lernerfahrung, Accréditation Européenne de la Formation en Langages aux Adultes* or *Training Native Speakers for Early Language Teaching*.

Inspired by the concept of the traditional bilateral exchange programmes of language assistants, the European Commission designed its own Lingua support measures for language assistants during the early 1990s. The main difference between the concepts of bi- and multilateral exchange is that the first promotes language teaching by employing native speakers for foreign language teaching, whereas the Lingua C Scheme of Socrates promotes less widely taught and spoken languages and the concept of intensive cultural exchange for all countries involved. The exchanges of participants from all European Union member states (as well as the associated countries in central and eastern Europe) have been designed to promote a truly versatile programme of activities.

As far as in-service language training programmes (Lingua B) are concerned, the mobility of foreign language teachers contributes to an intensive exchange of ideas in the fields of methodology and didactics and the promulgation of good practice. As elsewhere, the demand for openings in Austria far exceeds the positions available for the two action lines.

Participation of Austrian schools in Joint Educational Projects for language learning under Socrates/Lingua E, for example the joint Austrian–British project on 'The Influence of Advertising on Young People', has generated a broad variety of bi- and multilingual products such as brochures, magazines, exhibitions, web sites, theatre plays, videos and CD-ROMs which are used during classes at the schools involved, but which are also available for use by other institutions. Together with the exchange necessary during the project work itself, the extended use of the finished products helps to improve linguistic proficiency as well as knowledge and experience of cultural aspects of the country where the partner school is located. The Austrian hit list of exchange relations is led by the United Kingdom, followed by Italy, France, Finland and Sweden.

At tertiary education level, the new University Studies Law of 1997 provides for instruction at Austrian HEIs through the medium of languages other than

German. Although possible in principle since 1989, subject to certain restrictions, there are now even better opportunities to do so. The curricular commissions at the universities, responsible for the articulation of degree programme requirements, may determine whether or not specific courses are taught through the medium of foreign languages and if written academic work may be submitted in a foreign language. In order to improve the quality and widen the scope of instruction of the languages of Central and Eastern Europe at universities, lecturers from Bulgaria, Croatia, the Czech Republic, Hungary, Poland, Slovakia and Russia are being employed in relevant language departments of HEIs, based on a variety of different agreements.

Adult education: life-long learning

There are various forms of adult education in Austria. Besides school and university education, adult education is the third traditional pillar of Austrian education. Its objectives are the improvement of the qualifications of adults, the requalification of employees and the raising of the general level of education, especially that of adults with low-level initial education. Providers are recruited from a number of state and private institutions, the most important being the so-called social partners: trade unions, syndicates, chambers of trade and industry as well as professional associations. Adult education includes access to a 'second educational chance' which corresponds in content to the curricula of higher secondary schools, opportunities for further vocational training, all programmes of the Public Employment Service (*Arbeitsmarktservice*) and a variety of special training and skill acquisition programmes for those who may encounter problems in the labour market.

Since a 40:30:30 labour market scenario is eminently conceivable – 40 per cent of the labour force with life-long professions; 30 per cent of so-called 'patchwork' carriers of periodic employment in a variety of positions; and 30 per cent threatened by longer periods of unemployment – measures conceived to anticipate this development and combat its consequences are urgently needed. Indeed, with 1996 as the European Year of Life-long Learning, Austrian politicians and actors in the field of education became aware of the problems; however, to date no well-articulated programmes have been implemented.

One field of activity is the further promotion of open and distance learning which, so far, has been rather underdeveloped in Austria. Since the early 1980s, Austrian institutions of higher education have cooperated with the Fernuniversität Hagen (Germany) and in the 1990s they began to work with the Open University (United Kingdom). The Socrates and Leonardo programmes provide new ideas for further European cooperation in the use and development of new media in education that also extend to educational sectors outside higher education. A special advisory board to the two ministries involved in education is developing policy plans and investigating how to focus resources in the field.

Conclusion

At the end of the twentieth century, the Austrian educational system is being confronted with several challenges. There is a growing concern about the adequacy and adaptability of the structure of the system as well as about the quality of education in general to meet the challenges. Budget constraints will undoubtedly restrict the capacity to implement new policies and programmes in the near future, and as a result all sectors of Austrian education are under careful public scrutiny. In debates on education, evaluation is one of the most frequently raised topics today.

Austria has four neighbouring countries that are associated with the European Union and in all probability will join within the next decade. This will have far-reaching consequences for Austria's economy and foreign trade relations. Ever since the fall of the Iron Curtain in 1989, educational and cultural cooperation with these countries has been a top priority for Austria. Yet the structure and the quality of cooperation will change as soon as these countries begin to participate fully in EU educational programmes which, in turn, will lead to a redefinition of the 'European dimension' of education. The Brussels Green Paper *Education, Training, Research: The Obstacles to Transnational Mobility* has pointed out the variety of challenges that cooperation with central and eastern Europe will entail: visa requirements, social security matters, the level of funding of grants, recognition of periods of study, and last but not least, language skills.

Policy makers in the Austrian education community are in the process of establishing national priorities in light of the Europeanisation of education. In the late 1980s, the major concern was to take advantage of the dual opportunities inherent in (West) European integration and the opening of the East, and both of these opportunities became motors for domestic innovation and reform. Deregulation would be another priority. It will only be successful if schools and higher education are able to deal with their new tasks, such as interaction with the wider community in their regions as well as across national borders. Priorities have to continue in the area of modern foreign languages: bilingual schools, a wider range of European languages as additional qualifications, early language learning are additional items on the already long educational agenda.

The decision makers in Austria's educational community are fully aware of the fact that it is of the utmost importance to increase the compatibility of the Austrian system with other European systems and to make it more flexible and competitive; however, there are a number of indigenous obstacles to change. The introduction of new legislation is a long and cumbersome process; many actors in the system have entrenched rights which make innovation difficult; and institutions have to learn to exploit the opportunities inherent in their newly acquired autonomy.

Many Austrian school and university teachers would welcome a more coherent and structured move to finding adequate responses to the challenges on the threshold of the twenty-first century, especially a change in the education process from a teacher-centred to a learner-centred approach, with teachers as facilitators and advisers in life-long learning. They also feel the challenge caused by the rapid expansion of modern information technologies to harness them for the learning processes. For all this an increase of in-service training facilities is needed.

A comprehensive educational policy plan that goes far beyond the statements of intent found in the position papers of the political parties or the Government, which ultimately questions the adequacy of the *status quo*, and which will supply points of orientation for the coordinated development of education in Austria in a unified Europe in the future is sorely needed.

Bibliography

Akademien-Studiengesetz (1999) Vienna, *Bundesgesetzblatt*, Nr 94, 1999.

Altrichter, Herbert and Peter Posch (1995) 'Austria', in T. Neville Postlethwaite (ed.), *International Encyclopedia of National Systems of Education*, Cambridge, UK, 48–58.

Austria: Development of Education 1992–1994 (1994) Vienna, Federal Ministry of Education and the Arts.

The Austrian Education System (1994) Vienna, Federal Ministry of Education, Arts and Sport.

The Austrian University System (1998) Vienna, Federal Ministry of Science and Transport.

Bauer, Fritz, Ortwin Wingert, and Wolfgang Schlöglmann (1996) *Bildungspolitik zwischen Vision und Realität*, Vienna.

'Bildung kennt keine Grenzen. Bildung und Lernen im neuen Europa' (1996) *Sokrates und Leonardo da Vinci – Bilanz und Dokumentation*, Vienna.

Braun, Peter (1995) 'Österreichs Weg zum Aufbau des Fachhochschulbereiches. Bildungsoffensive mit "mittlerem" Entwicklungstempo', *Das Hochschulwesen*, 1: 45–6.

Brünner, Christian, Elsa Hackl and Sigurd Hoellinger (1994) *Fachhochschulstudien – brauchbar und kurz*, Vienna.

Education in Austria: A Concise Presentation (1991) Vienna Federal Ministry of Education, Arts and Sport.

Education, Training, Research: The Obstacles to Transnational Mobility, Green Paper (1996) Luxembourg.

Einem, Caspar (1998) *White Paper on Higher Education in Austria*, Federal Ministry of Science and Transport.

The Erasmus Experience: Major Findings of the Erasmus Evaluation Research Project (1997) Brussels.

'Europa und unsere Bildung' (1992) in *Österreich und die Bildungspolitik der Europäischen Gemeinschaften*, Vienna.

Fachhochschul – Studiengesetz (1993) Vienna, *Bundesgesetzblatt*, Nr 340, 1993.

Field, John (1997) 'The learning society and the European Union: a critical assessment of supranational education policy formation', *International Education*, 1(2): 73–92.

Gruber, Karl Heinz (1996) 'Der Aufbruch der österreichischen Schule in das 21. Jahrhundert', in Trautl Brandstaller (ed.), *Österreich 2 1/2. Anstösse zur Strukturreform*, Vienna, 35–68.

Hilpold, Peter (1995) *Bildung in Europa. Unter besonderer Berücksichtigung der EU-Bildungsprogramme*, Baden-Baden.

Heissenberger, Margit and Manuela Fried (1994) 'Internationale Aufbruchstimmung in der österreichischen Lehrerbildung – Rückblick auf erste Erfahrungen', *Erziehung und Unterricht*, 5/94: 291–6.

Kolonovitz, Dieter (1996) *Minderheitenschulrecht im Burgenland*, Vienna.

Leidenfrost, Josef (ed.) (1994) *Österreichische Hochschulausbildung und die Europäische Union*, Vienna.

Leidenfrost, Josef, Elisabeth Fiorioli and Lonnie Johnson (1997) 'Austria', in Torsten Kaelvemark and Marijk van der Wende (eds), *National Policies for the Internationalisation of Higher Education in Europe*, Stockholm, 42–58.

Leonardo da Vinci-Kompendium 1996/1995 (1996) Vienna Sokrates Büro.

Minderheiten – Schulgesetz für das Burgenland (1994) Vienna, *Bundesgesetzblatt* Nr 641, 1994.

Minderheiten – Schulgesetz für Kärnten (1994) Vienna, *Bundesgesetzblatt* Nr 420, 1990.

Pechar, Hans (1998) *Internationalisierung der österreichischen Hochschulen*, Vienna.

Pechar, Hans and Christian Kerber (1996) *Abschied vom Nulltarif. Argumente für sozial verträgliche Studiengebühren*, Vienna.

Posch, Peter and Herbert Altrichter (1992) *Bildung in Österreich. Analysen und Entwicklungsperspektiven*, Vienna.

Resolution of the Council and the Ministers of Education Meeting within the Council on the European Dimension in Education (1988) *Official Journal of the European Communities* C 177/5 (6 July).

Schulorganisations – Gesetz (1962), Vienna, *Bundesgesetzblatt* Nr 242, 1962.

Schulunterrichts – Gesetz (1974), Vienna, *Bundesgesetzblatt* Nr 139, 1974.

Schulzeit – Gesetz (1985), Vienna, *Bundesgesetzblatt* Nr 77, 1985.

Sokrates in Österreich: 1995/96 und 1996/97. Die ersten beiden Jahre (1998) Vienna, Sokrates Büro.

Sokrates und Leonardo: Perspektiven europäischer Bildungsprogramme bis zur Jahrtausendwende. Beiträge zum Informations-Seminar in Salzburg am 12. und 13. September 1996 (1996) Vienna, Sokrates Büro.

Studieren mit Erasmus, Zehn Jahre Bildungsprogramm der Europäischen Union 1987–1997 (1997) Bonn.

Universitätsorganisations – Gesetz (1993), Vienna, *Bundesgesetzblatt* Nr 805, 1993.

Universitätsstudien – Gesetz (1997), Vienna, *Bundesgesetzblatt* Nr 48, 1997.

White Book of the Austrian Federal Government, *Austria in the European Union* (1995), Vienna, State Secretariat for European Affairs.

White Paper on Education and Training: *Teaching and Learning – Towards the Learning Society* (1996) Luxembourg.

Willmann, Bodo (1991) *Bildungspolitik in Österreich. Vergleichende Daten und Analysen zur Entwicklung in den 80er Jahren*, Munich.

Zweisprachiger Unterricht in Kärnten (1992) Klagenfurt.

2 Belgium

Josien Roelands and Nathalie Druine*

Introduction

In the following the term 'Flanders' will frequently be used when reference is made to the Flemish Community, as the political bodies of the Region of Flanders and the Flemish Community are one. 'Wallonia' is used when writing about both the French- and the German-speaking Communities in that Region.

In 1830, Belgium became an independent state with its own constitution promulgated in 1831. Its structure was based on the principle of unity of legislation and government for the whole country. From 1970 on, the constitution has been reformed in several successive steps (in 1970–1, 1980, 1989 and 1993). As a result, the political, legislative and administrative structures of the state evolved gradually from a unitary centralized system towards a complex federal one. In 1993, Belgium officially became a federal state (article 1 of the new constitution).

Since the recent constitutional reforms, the federal state structure of Belgium has resulted in three distinct government levels, each with legislative as well as executive powers: the Central State, the Communities and the Regions. There is no hierarchy between the three policy levels; they each have their own, clearly defined areas of authority. The Central State is represented by the Federal (formerly 'National') Government and the Federal Parliament (the Chamber and the Senate) and has political power over matters of national importance, such as defence, public safety and public order, foreign affairs and monetary and financial policy, justice, social security and agriculture. The country as a whole is divided into three cultural Communities (the Flemish, the French and a very small German-language Community), which are responsible for maintaining citizens' cultural identity and their personal welfare, for example education, language, culture, social security and health care. In addition, the Constitution has provided for the establishment of three geographic Regions (Flanders, Wallonia and the Capital Region of Brussels), which are responsible (directly or

* The authors wish to thank Professors W. Wielemans and J.L. Vanderhoeven for their advice in the preparation of this chapter.

indirectly) for economic and territorial issues affecting employment, energy, housing, environment, public works and traffic, transport, area planning and scientific research, and four linguistic Regions, the Dutch, French, German and the bilingual region of the capital city of Brussels. The Communities and Regions are political entities within the national system and both have their own directly elected governments and parliaments which are known as Councils. Only the government and parliament of the Flemish Region and the Flemish Community are represented by a single Parliament and one Government of Flanders.

Federal Belgium is subdivided into provinces. Like the municipalities, they are known as lower tiers of government with a certain degree of autonomy, but they also play an administrative role within both the federal and the regional government structures.

Educational policy has been thoroughly affected by these reforms. As a consequence, the authority in educational matters has been transferred from the state to the Communities with effect from 1 January 1989. The educational responsibilities of each Community are vested in the Community Council (legislative power) and the Community Government (executive power). The decrees which the three communities may pass have the same force as national laws within their areas of jurisdiction. Exceptionally, only three educational regulations remain administered at national, central state level: the definition of the beginning and of the end of compulsory schooling, minimum conditions for the award of educational diplomas, and the teachers' pensions scheme. Thus, each of the three Communities has its own educational system, respectively dealing with 57 per cent (the Dutch Community), some 42 per cent (the French Community) and 0.5 per cent (the German-speaking Community) of the total number of pupils attending Belgian schools.

The political reforms mean that, notwithstanding the continuing existence of many similarities between the separate educational systems, the educational policy of Belgium has since 1989 become increasingly differentiated. Indeed, in the past decade, educational policy has undergone a number of significant changes. Especially in Flanders, an extensive range of new decrees has been promulgated which replace the former Belgian legislation regulating educational provision. In the French- and German-speaking Communities, new regulatory initiatives after 1989 have been more limited in scope.

In an interesting counterbalancing act to the growing tendency towards devolution of powers from the centre, in the process of decentralization all member states of the European Union have had to cope with the outflow of powers from their own national centres to transnational agencies brought about by the transfer of a number of decisions affecting educational competences to the said transnational agencies. As a consequence of 'Europeanization', accelerated by the creation of a European internal market with a free flow of goods and persons (1993), the European Union has won powers over the educational policies of the different member states of the Union. Educational policy can no longer be made exclusively within the confines of national boundaries. As supra-national legislation assumes the powers of national legislation, as in the case of European Commission directives and decisions, a not inconsiderable part of educational policy, notwithstanding the contributions made by member states, is beginning to be made by the European Union, the agencies responsible being the Council of Ministers of Education, the Commission of European Communities and the European Parliament. Participation in projects assembled by the European Union, the Organization of Economic Cooperation and Development, the Council of Europe and UNESCO has also increased, albeit at a different pace in the countries concerned. International comparative projects, such as indicators of education, thematical screenings, policy preparation, implementation and renovation have also played a part in the loss of central state influence.

The European influence on Belgian educational policy enacted by the three Communities can be seen in particular in actions concerning the introduction of new media and technologies in education, the promotion of the study of modern foreign languages, the care for and integration of children of immigrants, equality of educational opportunities for girls and boys, the equivalence of diplomas and the broad range of exchange and cooperation programmes for staff and students.

Founding principles of Belgian educational institutions

Freedom of providing education

Since its promulgation in 1831, the Belgian Constitution has guaranteed the principle of freedom of education. This principle is two-sided. First, schools of all types can be established and organized freely without any links with official authorities; however, they must observe stipulations and instructions which have the force of law, regulations concerning the provision of education and the maintenance of standards of quality if they wish to deliver officially acknowledged certificates and diplomas and to be eligible for financial aid from one of the three Communities. The *school-* or *hogeschoolbestuur* which is the organizing and controlling authority of any educational institution, a central concept in the Belgian system, is the government, or the natural or legal person taking the initiative to provide education and remaining responsible for it.

According to the type of organizing and controlling authority, there are three distinct networks of educational provision:

1   Community (also known as 'official') education, which is education set up by the Ministry of Education of each Community and financed in total from its budget. The Constitution requires this education to be neutral, in the sense of respecting all the philosophical, ideological and religious opinions of parents and pupils. In the Flemish Community, a separate Autonomous Council for Community Education (*Autonome Raad voor het Gemeenschapsonderwijs*) has been established as the organizing and maintaining authority on behalf of the Flemish Community, which receives and manages the financial resources required to provide this education. In the

French- and German-speaking Communities, it is the Minister of Education who acts as that authority;

2   assisted ('official') education, which is education provided either by provincial or municipal authorities. Their schools, whilst financially maintained by the Community, can be denominational as well as non-denominational;

3   grant-aided private education, which is also subsidized education but is organized as a private initiative by a private person, association or religious body. It consists of denominational education (mainly Roman Catholic, but also a few Protestant, Jewish and Muslim schools), non-denominational private education subscribing to mainstream educational approaches and independent schools which subscribe to alternative pedagogical initiatives, such as the Steiner and Freinet schools.

Education provided and maintained by the first two networks (the authorities) is part of 'official' education. Official schools are obliged to admit all pupils, irrespective of ideological or philosophical considerations, race, sex, social background or any other. Education provided by the third network is called 'private' education and serves particular ideologies.

In Flanders, a predominant proportion of pupils attend private education (68.9 per cent). Community education and subsidized official education account for 15.9 per cent and 15.1 per cent of the total school population respectively. In Wallonia, which consists of two linguistic Communities, the private schools are fewer (50 per cent). Provincial and municipal education follows with 31.8 per cent, and Community education comprises 18.2 per cent.

The Community Government draws up the general policy framework and structure of the education system, imposes minimum standards of quality and defines the conditions of finance. The various networks have a large degree of autonomy and pedagogic freedom: in terms of school staffing policy, choice of educational methods, curricula, timetables, teaching materials and assessment, on condition that they teach a minimum curriculum timetable and comply with the recently fixed attainment targets and similar details.

The second point of principle is that the federal Constitution guarantees parental freedom of choice regarding the type of education and the specific school parents prefer for their children. Pupils in primary and secondary education are entitled to find a school to their liking within a maximum travelling distance regarded as reasonable. The system is being replaced by freedom of choice within each subregion of the Community.

Compulsory education

Compulsory schooling between the ages of 6 and 14 was first introduced in 1914. In 1983 compulsory education was extended to twelve full years, from age 6 until the end of the school year in which the pupil reaches the age of 18. Compulsory education is full-time right up to the age of 15 or 16 and includes primary education and at least the first two years the lower phase of secondary education. From 15 or 16 years onwards, there is compulsory part-time education (with the possibility of combining a part-time study programme with employment), although most pupils continue in full-time education. In Belgium, compulsory education does not mean compulsory school attendance. It is possible to teach children at home, provided that their education complies with the legally imposed requirements.

No charge is made for education

The entitlement to education established by the Constitution means that access to education is free throughout the period of compulsory schooling. In primary education, all children, irrespective of their origin, benefit from this right. In secondary education, children from non-EU families staying in Belgium to study have to pay a statutory attendance fee.

Coeducational schooling

Pursuant to the European Commission directive of 9 February 1976 requiring member states to make provision for the equal treatment of men and women, schools have been encouraged to admit both boys and girls without discrimination. The European Directive was translated into a Royal Decree of August 1983 prior to federalization and is legally binding in all three Communities. Coeducational schools are now a standard feature in education provided by the Communities. Most single-sex schools are to be found in the denominational sector. In the Flemish Community, schools were required to become mixed in accordance with a Flemish Government decision of 26 January 1994. Today, most Community schools are coeducational, with only a small proportion of private schools still offering single-sex education. The practice of single-sex schooling is based on the principle of pedagogical autonomy, which is being challenged by a growing number of parents who are even taking the matter to court. In the French Community, following the *Decret sur la Mission de l'Enseignement* of July 1997, the number of single-sex schools is proportionately smaller. There are no single-sex schools in the *Deutschsprachige Gemeinschaft*.

Full-time attendance

Traditionally, there are three levels of education: elementary education, secondary education and higher education. Of the total school population, 20 per cent is in nursery education, 33 per cent in primary education, 35 per cent in secondary education and 12 per cent in higher education. Apart from this, there is also special education (at primary and secondary level) for children and adolescents who need special care in some way, and adult education. In the following, each sector will be dealt with separately.

Elementary education

Elementary education comprises both nursery, pre-school and primary education. Although the two levels are structurally separate, attempts are being made to achieve a smooth transition between them.

Pre-school education

Nursery education is provided for children from the age of 2.5–6 years. From this early age, all children can go to school on a full-day basis and without cost to parents. Before that, there is also a well-established network of care for children from 0 to 3 years, run either by subsidized childminders or in collective childcare centres ('*crêches*'). The position of Belgium, and of Flanders in particular, in the European context is unique in that the entire area of early childhood education is fairly well taken care of by the state. In spite of the fact that this education is not compulsory, the rate of participation is extremely high: about 90 per cent of all 2.5-year-olds start their school career at this very early age. At ages 3, 4 and 5 attendances reach levels between 95 and 100 per cent.

Nursery schools are usually organized into three age-based learning groups (except in sparsely populated areas, where different ages can be combined in one teaching group). These schools are often attached to an elementary school and supervised by the same principal, though they are regarded more or less as separate units with their own objectives, activities and upbringing ethos.

The general aims of a child's pre-school education are:

- to ensure a balanced and diversified psychomotor, cognitive and socio-emotional development;
- to develop intellectual skills;
- to encourage the growth to independence;
- to stimulate creativity;
- to learn to express oneself and communicate correctly;
- to develop social skills and moral consciousness and make the child familiar with community life.

In nursery education children's development is assessed mainly on the basis of observation, using a system for monitoring children which contains the development objectives set out.

The current practice in the Belgian nursery school has its legacy in the traditional kindergarten concept and in the leading educational philosophies of Froebel, Montessori and especially Decroly. Play and games, impression and expression, exploration and thematic work are predominant. A relatively new element has been the Experiental Pre-school Education project, which is the most important source of innovation in nursery education in Flanders. Within this approach, which grew out of discontent with current preschool practice, the child's personal experiences occupy a central place, free initiative is increased, the educational environment is enriched in a challenging way and much attention is paid to the quality of the interaction between teacher and child. The basic assumptions and the further elaboration of the project have been inspired by the emancipatory movement of the late 1960s, the theories of humanistic psychology of Rogers and Gendlin, the critical psychoanalytic movement and Piagetian theory. The conceptual framework of this innovatory model developed for the pre-school level has already proved to be fruitful in other educational contexts, such as primary school, remedial teaching, special education and teacher training.

Primary education

Primary education is intended for children between the ages of six and twelve. It comprises six consecutive school years, subdivided into three levels or grades, each of two years' duration. Primary schools are usually organized in year-classes, with one class teacher (who teaches most subjects) for every group. As with nursery education, two years are sometimes combined in a single group in isolated rural areas.

The general aims of primary education may be summarized as follows:

- to foster the balanced personal development of the whole child whilst respecting his or her personal identity;
- to facilitate the child's initiation into society;
- to help the child acquire basic knowledge and skills;
- to use the school attended and the education provided to help compensate for the child's inequalities at the start.

The primary school curriculum includes reading, writing, arithmetic, mother tongue (Dutch, French or German) education, world orientation, geography, history, natural science, drawing and arts, handicraft, singing, physical education, health and road safety. In the non-denominational Community-maintained (official) schools, ethics is taught as a curriculum subject. In denominational schools both religion and religion-based ethics are taught.

Typical of the Belgian situation is the option, widely practised, to provide lessons in a second language from the third grade (fifth year) of primary education onwards. In the Brussels area, the second language has to be offered from the second grade (third year). Belgian education pays a great deal of attention to foreign language learning. In the French Community, for example, experiments are being conducted in selected schools, trialling language education based on ideas of early language learning and using submersion methods of teaching the second language. These lessons are organized during normal school hours with the assistance of external linguistic experts, supervised by a scientific pedagogical committee.

Pupil evaluation is the responsibility of the organizing authority of the school. During the school year, pupils' progress is continuously assessed on the basis of their daily work in the classroom and their homework. At regular intervals the teacher sets formal tests, which are individually designed by the school or taken over from the umbrella organization of the network. The school report informs the pupil and his or her parents about the results that have been achieved, the actual progress made, as well as the pupil's learning behaviour and personal development. On the basis of all the information gathered during the school year, the teacher decides, usually in consultation with the headteacher, at the end of the year whether or not the child will move on to the next class.

Primary education is concluded with a certificate of elementary education, the *getuigschrift van het basisonderwijs* or *certificat d'études de base*, which confirms that the pupil has successfully completed the six-year course of primary education.

Policy outlines and innovations

From the 1970s onwards, a whole range of pedagogical innovations have been introduced in Belgian primary education.

Respectively, in 1989 and in 1990, the French and the Flemish Communities established a committee 'for the remodelling of elementary education', the aims of which are the implementation of a more differentiated approach attuned to children's individual learning progress and educational needs. A serious problem for the Belgian educational system has been the appalling number of pupils who have fallen behind because of having to repeat one or more school years in the course of their school career.

The relative organizational freedom, a system introduced in 1984, allows elementary schools to appoint a specialist teacher for religious instruction or ethics, for physical education, or for teaching arts or handicrafts. The school can also decide to set up a so-called 'adaptation class', in which a remedial teacher is responsible for organizing help for children with modest or occasional learning difficulties. For particular periods, these children are withdrawn from their normal class and taught individually or in small groups those parts of the basic subject matter which they have failed to master at a given point in time. For the rest of the school activities these children attend their regular class.

Restructuring schooling and assessment

On 1 September 1997, a new Elementary Education Decree (dated 28 February 1997) came into force in Flanders. This decree finally realized the intention to transform the complex, opaque and obsolete regulations governing elementary education into one comprehensive and simplified whole. The decree introduced a number of important innovations, the most crucial being that of giving all local schools greater autonomy and responsibility for their own organization.

The compulsory division into year classes and grades was abolished, the organizing authority of the individual school being empowered independently to define the pedagogical organization and grouping structure of the school. As a result the school can autonomously define its pedagogical organization and grouping structures.

The former list of fixed, compulsory discrete curriculum subjects was replaced by a number of 'learning areas' which includes: physical education and training, art education, language education, mathematics and 'world orientation', the latter consisting of education about nature, humankind and society.

Within each learning area, a number of 'attainment targets' (*eindtermen*) have been set up which represent the minimum objectives which must be aimed for and/or achieved in regular primary and secondary education by the majority of pupils at the end of the level and in the line of study they are in. The targets define standards of knowledge, understanding, educational attitudes and skills. In the non-compulsory nursery education sector these are called 'developmental objectives' (*ontwikkelingsdoelen*) which are to be be pursued, though they do not necessarily have to be achieved by all children. Developmental objectives have also been introduced in the first year B and in the pre-vocational second year and in special education. The learning areas for elementary education refer not so much to a subject-based classification, but are to be taken rather as a total package of objectives which must be attained as far as possible in a functional coherence. In addition, attainment targets beyond the actual learning areas are available for more general social skills and progress made with 'learning to learn'. From 1 September 1998, according to the decree of 15 July 1997, the attainment targets and developmental objectives have become an integral part of the school curriculum.

In the French Community (following the decree of 14 March 1995), an equivalent experiment is going on with a form of attainment targets (*socles de compétence*). These objectives are meant to ensure a fundamental education for everyone, which the more specialized education available in the upper forms of secondary schooling can build on.

The introduction of attainment targets has to be seen as a new phenomenon in the history of Belgian education, and can be interpreted as a clear commitment of the government to maintaining not only the educational structures but also the provision of high-quality educational contents. Many aspects which used to be determined by the organizing authorities and the schools themselves are now being defined by central government in exchange for wider local autonomy and school responsibility. Schools have to integrate the attainment targets and developmental objectives into their own self-designed curricula and subject syllabuses. However, the providing authorities, the schools and teams of teachers have been left much room for creativity and for their own objectives, emphases and decisions. Every school must present its own profile within a specific pedagogical project and a school working plan, which make up the pedagogical freedom of the school.

The pedagogical project represents the general aim and identity of the school, the sum total of its educational ideas and principles based on a range of philo-sophical, religious, ideological, social and upbringing assumptions. The working plan translates the pedagogical project into daily practice, a strategy to achieve the general goals within the conditions of each school.

There are no central or any other external forms of educational evaluation.

Compared to some other European countries, schools and their teachers have always enjoyed a large degree of autonomy with respect to assessment and examinations. In Flanders the attainment targets are primarily meant as a framework of criteria or norms which government imposes in view of its financial commitment to providing education and its guarantee of the standard of the diplomas and certificates awarded by the schools.

Regulations governing mainstream and special primary education are integrated in one and the same decree. Not only will legislation be simplified in this way, but attention will be drawn to the necessity of maximum integration and cooperation of all parts of primary education.

Recent measures concerning extending the general care taken of children and the educational priority policy are included in the decree. The school is expected to pursue an optimal care system which gives every child maximum opportunity of a full and well-balanced development of their personality. One of the aims of extending care is to develop a more differentiated approach towards weaker children, those with learning difficulties or groups of children coming from vulnerable socio-economic backgrounds on the one hand, or for extremely gifted children on the other. Besides commitment to the extending care project, educational priority is specifically targeted to cater for immigrant youngsters. It is hoped that initiatives of this kind will contribute to a reduction in the large number of repeaters of grades and the growing percentage of children who are dependent upon special education. In the future, both approaches will increasingly be integrated in the conditions attached to school project financing.

Teacher performance and employment

Teacher performance is no longer defined by the number of teaching hours but related to teachers' job descriptions. In consultation with the teacher employee, the headteacher draws up a job description, possibly with the help of government models. On the basis of these job descriptions, schools can develop a modern personnel policy. By clearly stating what is expected of the teaching staff, their evaluation is made more objective and the development of further training programmes can be geared to the needs of the individual concerned. Government has decided on a phased introduction of the new system.

All teachers are employed by the organizing authority which in legal terms is the employer. However, conditions of employment and salaries are negotiated at Community level: separately for Community provided ('official') schools and the sector of assisted public and grant-aided private schools. The difference is in respect of the responsibility of the organizing authority. All Community schools have one and the same authority, in the case of assisted and private schools the organizing authority is responsible for a few or only one particular school. The conditions of employment, for example the pension system, are similar to those of civil servants, although technically speaking teachers cannot be civil servants because some of their organizing authorities are non-state bodies.

Financing education

In the case of pre-school and primary education there are two lump sum budgets: one for teachers' salaries and one for the overall functioning of the schools, excluding investment in new buildings but including overall maintenance of facilities. The 'envelope' system introduced by the decree enables schools to organize staffing to suit their educational planning, for example to have more classrooms or specialized teachers in areas such as music, physical education or special needs.

Secondary education

Secondary education is intended for adolescents between 12 and 18 or 19 years of age and as a rule comprises six years of schooling, possibly followed by a 'specialization year' or a preparatory year to higher education.

The history of secondary education within the last three decades has been known as a turbulent period. Since about 1965, it has been undergoing thorough reforms. The evolution towards a more efficiently structured system corresponds both with the democratic call for equality of educational opportunities and with the needs of the economy for more and better-educated and skilled school leavers. The three main objectives of the remodelled secondary school (*Vernieuwdsecundaironderwijs* or VSO in Flanders, called *l'enseignement de type I* in Wallonia) were formulated mainly as a reaction to the previous traditional school system and intended to provide a broad, general and common basic education for all pupils which postpones making the decisive choice as to the precise area of study to a later age and which reduces the socio-cultural discrimination of some pupil groups.

In 1975, the VSO system, officially called 'type I', was proposed as the single type of secondary education within the state network then in existence, the result of the policy of liberalizing education and the introduction of the principle of pedagogical autonomy, The traditional type was labelled 'type II'. Private education could not be compelled to adopt the VSO structure and was able to retain the 'traditional' educational type. Relations between these diverging types became increasingly strained, and soon resulted in a competitive struggle between types I and II.

In the school year 1989–90, a new 'unified structure' was introduced in Flemish secondary education. The former 'national' legislation of 1971 (type I) and 1957 (type II) was replaced in the Flemish Community by the Decree Concerning Education II (1990) relating to a new general framework for secondary education. The compromise structure was to stop the enduring struggle between the two parallel school types, with its concomitant structural, financial, legal and psychological problems.

In the French Community, secondary education has retained the double structure. However, only a small minority of Roman Catholic schools still cling to the traditional form (affecting about 3 per cent of the secondary school population). In the German-speaking Community, secondary education now comprises education of type I only.

Secondary education in the French- and German-speaking Communities

L'Enseignement de type I: *remodelled secondary education (VSO)*

In accordance with the law of 19 July 1971, the VSO system is structurally divided into three grades of two years each, the first grade, called the 'observation stage' (*observatiegraad* or *le degré d'observation*), the second, the 'orientation stage' (*orientatiegraad* or *le degré d'orientation*) and the third which constitutes the 'determining stage' (*determinatiegraad* or *le degré de détermination*).

In the starting grade ('observation stage'), all children attend a common first year divided into types A and B. Teachers observe their pupils to discover their abilities and interests. The curriculum of the first year A consists of a broad common core (religion or ethics, French/German, a second language, mathematics, history, geography, sciences, physical education and art education) plus a range of complementary and optional activities. In the common second year, the core curriculum is the same, with various basic options added: Latin, economics and scientific, art or technical education. The first year B is intended for children who have fallen behind in primary school or who are less suited to benefit from a predominantly academic education. At the end of the first year B, some pupils are able to join the first year A, while the others go on to a second pre-vocational year.

In the second grade ('orientation stage'), the optional part is extended whilst the content of common education is reduced. This stage includes different study programmes in four educational streams:

- a general academic education stream (*Algemeen Secundair Onderwijs (ASO)* or *l'enseignement genéral*);
- a technical education stream (*Technisch Secundair Onderwijs (TSO)* or *l'enseignement technique*);
- an artistic education stream (*Kunstsecundair Onderwijs (KSO)* or *l'enseignement artistique*); and
- a vocational education preparation stream (*Beroepssecundair Onderwijs (BSO)* or *l'enseignement professionel*).

The four types of the second grade are organized in two main streams:

1 the transition stream (general academic, technical and artistic), where the first priority is preparation for higher education, whilst leaving pupils the option of choosing immediate entry into employment;
2 the qualification stream (technical, artistic and vocational), where the first priority is preparation for employment whilst allowing pupils the option of continuing their studies in higher education.

The third grade, known as the 'determining stage', is divided into three streams: the transitional and long-term qualification (TSO and KSO), on the one hand, which builds on the transition stream of the second grade; and the vocational qualification, on the other hand, which builds on the second grade of BSO. During the second and third grades the common core elements are progressively reduced, while the optional part of the curriculum is gradually increased.

Pupils who succeed in the tests of the second year of the first grade of secondary education and can submit a certificate of completion of elementary education receive a certificate of completion of the first grade of secondary education. Likewise, pupils who are successful in the second grade of secondary education receive a certificate of completion of the second grade of secondary education.

The VSO system, which is the dominant form of secondary education in the French- and German-speaking Communities, is not comprehensive in the 'integrated', entirely mixed-ability schooling sense. Only education in the first grade is common, although pupils can choose significant options already in the second year of that grade, for example by taking Latin. Some schools place all first-grade pupils in 'heterogeneous' (mixed-ability) classes while in others pupils with the same level of achievement at primary school, confirmed by the tests used at intervals, are put together in 'homogeneous' class groups. In such cases the same common subjects are taught but often at different levels of difficulty.

After the first grade the different programmes of study corresponding to the four streams can be organized either in separate schools – usually this is done only in the case of the ASO – or in one school which offers the separate programmes to different sets of pupils. The three grades can also be accommodated in combination or organized separately, usually with two grades (first and second or second and third) in one institution.

Type II: the traditional secondary education

Education of type II comprises six years which are divided into two three-year stages (a lower stage and a higher stage), and offers a choice between two types: a general academic education (ASO) and a technical and vocational education (TSO and BSO).

From the first year, pupils have to choose a line of study within one of the two types: old humanities (Latin), modern humanities (modern languages), technical education or vocational education. Technical and vocational education have been kept separate from the humanities with their own structures and statute. The two different types of education are usually provided in separate schools.

In the higher stage of the general academic type (from the fourth year on), a choice can be made from seven lines of study (depending on the chosen line of study in the lower stage): three in the old humanities – Latin–Greek, Latin–mathematics and Latin–sciences; one in the modern humanities; two in the sciences: scientific A (mathematics), scientific B (mathematics and sciences); and one in economics and human sciences.

In the technical education institutions, pupils follow a first common 'orientation' year. From the second year on they have a choice between a large number of different lines of study. At the end of the lower stage pupils obtain a first qualification. If they are considered to be capable of further study they can proceed to the higher stage. Vocational education has a similar structure. At the end of the third year ASO and TSO pupils receive *le certificat d'enseignement secondaire inférieur* (CES I); at the end of the sixth year ASO, TSO, KSO, or the seventh year BSO they qualify for *le certificat d'enseignement secondaire supérieur* (CESS).

The vertical and hierarchical structure implies that in most cases the definite choice of study will already have been made at the end of the primary school, and that a selection is made between pupils who are aimed at the lower professional echelons and executive tasks and pupils who wish to complete a secondary education which will give them access to higher education and to higher administrative and social functions. In most cases, the line of study that is chosen in the first year determines the further school career, despite the theoretical possibility of transfer from one line of study into another.

The 'unified structure' in the Flemish Community

Generally speaking, the unified structure corresponds to that of type I: it consists of six years of study divided into three grades, each of two years' duration. The compromising character of the unified, 'comprehensive' structure, though, becomes apparent from the rather weakened commonality of the first two years and the separate vertical structure from the second grade onwards.

The first grade, comparable to the observation stage of type I, consists of a first common year A and a second year. A great deal of importance is attached to a broad, general basic education which accounts for most of the teaching. The majority of pupils (90 per cent) start in the first year A. The first year B acts as a 'bridge class' between primary and secondary school, and is intended for children with learning difficulties or children who do not feel attracted by the study of academic subjects. The first year A has 32 lesson periods, 27 of which cover subjects which are the same for everybody (common core curriculum): religion or ethics; Dutch; French (and possibly English); mathematics; history; geography; arts education; science; technology; and physical education. In addition, five periods a week are left available to each school to use as the staff wish, within a legally fixed framework. This allows the school to assert its own profile, for example taking into consideration the tradition of the school or the socio-economic environment in which it is located.

In the second year, all pupils follow a core curriculum of at least 24 periods per week, 14 of which are taken by all pupils, apportioned as 10 periods for English, French and mathematics of either a highly academic or a less academic curriculum. The rest of the time is made up of the basic options (six to eight periods), which cater for pupils' personal preferences and interests, and which enable the school to project its individual character, highlighting for example Latin, Greek, modern foreign languages, additional mathematics or technology.

Besides the common second year, within the first grade there is a second pre-vocational year which is intended to cater for the small groups of pupils with learning difficulties or those unlikely to benefit from a broad general education or the more academically orientated subjects. Mostly these are pupils from the first B year who in addition to studying a common basic curriculum for 16 teaching periods choose a minimum of two vocational options consisting of a theoretical and a practical introduction to two 'vocational sectors' (16–18 weekly periods) chosen with a view to future employment. They move on to the BSO in the second grade, which is the time a vocationally orientated education can formally begin.

Attainment targets and developmental objectives for the first grade of secondary education have been in force since 1 September 1997 (decree of 24 July 1996). Concerning the subjects of the basic education, there is an A-stream (attainment targets that have to be achieved by pupils of the first year A and the second year) and a B stream (developmental objectives to be aimed at by pupils in the first year B; in the second year they will probably be in BSO). Besides these, there are attainments targets and developmental objectives relating to the syllabus content of all discrete subjects or addressing the content of a cross-curricular group of subjects. These are to show evidence of pupils' ability in 'learning to learn', their social skills, as well as the knowledge and skills of citizenship, health and environmental education. The subject-orientated objectives have to be integrated in the teaching syllabuses, whilst the cross-curricular objectives can be realized through several school subjects or educational projects.

From the second grade (that is, the third year) onwards, a distinction is made between four types of education, which are organized separately. Within each of these types, different lines of study can be chosen. These courses lay the foundation for the third grade:

- General academic secondary education (ASO) emphasizes a broad academic education, providing a sound preparation for higher education. In the second grade there are ten lines of study, which are all 'double packages' and aim at a broad basic education so as to avoid too early a specialization, for example Greek–Latin, Latin–modern foreign languages, economics–mathematics options.
- Technical secondary education (TSO) pays special attention to general and technical-theoretical subjects, although practical lessons are also included in the course of study. After a TSO education, pupils can go on to higher education or take up employment.
- Artistic secondary education (KSO) combines a broad general development with active art practice. After completing the course, young people can continue their education in a higher education institution or they may look for employment.

At the end of the third grade of general academic, technical and art education, pupils who have obtained a certificate confirming passes in the tests at the end of the second grade can be awarded the Diploma of Secondary Education. The third grade can be supplemented by a seventh year of preparation for higher education (in ASO or KSO) or a year of specialization in the TSO, KSO and BSO options.

- Vocational secondary education (BSO) emphasizes above all a practical preparation, in which pupils learn a specific occupation or trade while receiving a general education. Most leavers go on to the labour market. It is possible, however, to attend a fifth completion year at the end of the second grade of BSO or a seventh specialization year at the end of the third grade. On completion of a seventh year of vocational education and the award of the Diploma of Secondary Education, BSO pupils can also gain access to a higher education institution.

In the third grade, pupils again have to make a choice of study. Most of the study areas in the third grade build on the lines of study of the second grade. However, there are also a number of disciplines that cannot be taken up before beginning the third grade. Education can be further refined and specialized with a view to the final career choices or the future higher education study plans of the leavers.

In ASO, TSO and KSO, the following subjects are part of the basic education in the second and third grades: religion or ethics, Dutch, a second modern language (usually French), mathematics, history, geography, science, physical education, and (only in ASO) a third modern language (English or German). In vocational secondary education (BSO), basic training comprises: religion or ethics, Dutch, history and/or geography (sometimes integrated in one course of social studies), mathematics and/or applied sciences. Attainment targets for the second grade of secondary education are currently being developed.

Diplomas and certificates of secondary education (VSO) are parallel in Flanders and Wallonia.

Part-time compulsory schooling

In addition to full-time secondary education, which is compulsory up to the age of 15 or 16, there is also part-time vocational secondary education – *Deeltijds Beroepsecundair Onderwijs* (DBSO). This education comprises a combination of alternate learning and working in a sandwich structure. Pupils can attend one of the 90 Centres for Part-time Education and Training (in Flanders as well as in Wallonia), where they attend school for 15 lessons a week for specific vocational preparation and general education. For the remaining time, pupils are involved in work experience.

Another example in the context of part-time compulsory education is the retail training course. Pupils attend lessons of general education and vocational preparation for one day a week in a Centre for Entrepreneurship Training while apprenticed to an industrial employer or a small tradesman. A contractual apprenticeship is signed by the apprentice and the employer providing the training.

Policy outlines and innovations

The Flemish government holds out the prospect of a radical restructuring of secondary education. Deregulation, decentralization, autonomy and quality are the key-words. The government wants to tackle two major problems. First of all, there is the fragmentation of and overlap within current provision. There are too many small schools, free to offer too many possible lines of study, many of them (*quasi*)identical, in locations next to each other, often within the same providing network, for too small a number of pupils. The second problem is the 'third-payer system', which means that schools can off-load the consequences of their poor financial management on to the government, without assuming the responsibility for having made unreasonable decisions.

The intention is to achieve a more identifiable provision by creating cooperative ventures, a kind of school consortia, and by restricting the number of study options on offer, which will be grouped into fewer but larger study areas. By analogy with the funding of institutions of higher education, an 'envelope' or lump-sum system of financing will be introduced. Individual schools or cooperative consortia of several schools will receive a single overall sum which they can dispose of independently. This budget will be calculated in a linear way, that is directly proportional to the number of pupils on roll. Large and small schools will receive an equal amount per pupil.

However, two corrections will be built in: free choice between 'official' (Community) and private education within a particular area must be guaranteed, even if the number of pupils is too low, while those schools that recruit many underprivileged young people and make special provision for their welfare must receive extra finance for their pedagogical projects. Finally, in the light of greater local autonomy, the increased scale of projects and the system of 'envelope' financing, it is also intended to revise the legal position of tenured staff so as to enable schools to implement a responsible and flexible staffing policy, such as teachers working to job descriptions. All these reforms are to result in a new decree on secondary education restructuring the entire secondary sector along more transparent, easily manageable lines.

In the French Community, similar themes have emerged. Some years ago, fusions of schools in the Community network were achieved. Since 1996, following the growing trend towards rationalization, a more general plan of 'recomposition' of schools in all three networks has been introduced. This plan is based on four key concepts:

- the size of secondary schools, with about 450 to 900 pupils accepted as the optimum;
- equality of access to education in both rural and urban zones and free choice of either a denominational or non-denominational education;

- improvement of technical and vocational education, with more money made available for modern equipment;
- positive discrimination towards certain schools, for example those in disadvantaged areas. They can function with fewer pupils than the 'optimal' size.

Besides emphasizing rationalization of educational provision as a whole, measures have been taken to secure other priorities, such as reduction of school failure (for example, experimentation with a biannual stage of education); respecting the learning pace of individual pupils and its continuous evaluation; improving educational quality by using external evaluation; positive discrimination by taking action against school violence; and introducing intercultural education.

The internationalization of primary and secondary education

Belgium is very active in the area of international cooperation and its participation in European programmes and initiatives can be assessed as largely successful: for example, intercultural education is a firm component of the curriculum in all Belgian schools.

A start with 'European awareness' is made as early as in the primary school. Primary and secondary schools participate in the partnership and exchange activities provided by the various Socrates and Comenius programmes. In the Flemish Community, apart from European Union financial support, additional government funding is available for a variety of activities following a Flemish ministerial circular letter of 10 January 1996. Before the adoption of the Comenius programme the 'Euro classes' project had already made a start with class exchange schemes on the basis of a European Dimension cooperation agreement between Flemish secondary schools and schools from one other of the EU member states. These exchanges can be undertaken in the fourth, fifth or sixth year of secondary education. Participation in these programmes can help schools to cross the threshold before taking part in full-scale Socrates and Comenius programmes.

Primary and secondary schools also participate quite successfully in the Socrates–Lingua and Socrates–Arion mobility schemes. The Leonardo–Petra programme enables pupils in technical and vocational secondary education to participate in short- and long-term practical training periods. In Flanders between 1992 and 1994, 150 pupils in compulsory education took part in work experience programmes of three weeks' duration.

The GROS programme (1995) between Flanders and the Netherlands enables Flemish and Dutch primary and secondary school classes to exchange on the basis of long-term and intensive cooperation agreements. It also involves the payment of grants to teaching staff to prepare and follow up the exchanges.

The Three-leaved Clover programme, an intra-Belgian exchange programme, was set up as a cooperation between the three Belgian Communities. It provides exchanges of third-grade pupils in the primary and secondary schools as well as students in teacher training institutes among the three different cultural environments. The objective is to immerse the pupils in the language of the other Community and to help them discover each other's cultural backgrounds and everyday life situations through instructional, cultural, sporting and family activities. In the school year 1994–5, 27 schemes were approved; in 1995–6 this number had risen to 65 (involving 2,800 pupils). Teacher exchanges, especially teachers of Dutch, French and German, are also possible.

At the secondary education level, the Flemish Community also participates actively in the EU programmes Equilibrium, Nuori/Key, Youth Restart and Enable, as well as in the projects of the European Social Fund. A special agreement has been made with two famous Flemish institutions, the Ryckevelde (Brugge) and Alden Biesen (Hasselt) centres, aiming at the promotion of the European idea. Both centres promote the European dimension in all aspects of the school curriculum.

During recent years, the Ministry of Education of the French Community has organized a number of international projects, often with a European focus, such as: 'A secondary education for Europe', on school legislation in Central and Western Europe; a working group on the European dimension in education; and CONFEMEN, which is a Conference of Ministers of Education from French-speaking countries.

Special education

Special education is available to those children and adolescents, who cannot be taught in mainstream schools, whether on a temporary or permanent basis, because of a physical, sensorial, psychological, social or intellectual development problem or handicap and/or learning or educational difficulties. Special education is provided at three levels: special nursery education, special primary education and special secondary education for children aged approximately 2.5–6 years, 6–13 years and adolescents 13–21 years, respectively, to about 3–4 per cent of the total school population.

Special education is organized into eight types, adapted to the pupils' needs:

- type 1: children and adolescents with a slight mental handicap;
- type 2: children and adolescents with a moderate or severe mental handicap;
- type 3: children and adolescents with serious emotional and/or behavioural problems;
- type 4: children and adolescents with a physical handicap;
- type 5: children and adolescents with a long-term illness;
- type 6: children and adolescents with a visual handicap;
- type 7: children and adolescents with a hearing handicap;
- type 8: children with serious learning difficulties.

At the secondary level there is provision for four types of special education which can bring together pupils with different kinds of disability according to the precise nature and severity of their disability. Every type has its own pre-determined objectives:

- Education 1: provides a social training with a view to integration in a protected living environment (four years);
- Education 2: provides a general and social training with a view to integration in a protected living and working environment;
- Education 3: provides a social and vocational training with a view to integration in a normal living and working environment;
- Education 4: prepares adolescents (with a physical handicap but otherwise mainstrean intellectual capabilities) for studies in higher education and integration in active life.

In Flanders, the 'Integrated Education' project (*geintegreerd onderwijs (GON)*), which is also available in Wallonia (*enseignement integré*) aims at complete or partial integration of children or adolescents with a handicap or with learning/educational difficulties in mainstream schools. Certain children or adolescents are enabled to attend one or more courses in an ordinary school, in cooperation with the supporting school for special education. Recently the Minister of Education has taken the initiative to anchor in a decree the right of every child with special educational needs to an 'integrated education', provided that certain conditions are met (Decree on Education VII of 8 July 1996). Developmental objectives are currently being prepared for types 1, 2, 7 and 8.

Higher education

Higher education comprises university education and two other types of higher education, the latter organized by the *hogescholen* or the *hautes écoles* (higher education institutes), of short- and long-term duration. In the German-speaking Community there is only one type of higher education, which is of short-term duration. For long-term tertiary or university education students have to study in institutions provided by the French or Flemish Communities or go to Germany.

The Belgian open access system to higher education is almost unique in Europe. All students who are in possession of the Diploma of (upper) Secondary Education have free access to higher education. Foreign students who wish to study in Belgium must hold a diploma or certificate of secondary education recognized as equivalent. Generally, there are no entrance examinations or selective admission procedures, although a few recent exceptions have been made in the case of civil engineering and some art courses. However, the debate on new admission criteria (a *numerus clausus*) has become more lively, especially for university study, for example the introduction of an entrance examination in medicine and dentistry has been considered. Success in the current year's university examinations is a condition of students' progress to the following year of study.

University studies

Studies at a university are characterized by the integration of education and research. Fundamental research falls entirely within the universities' competencies.

The Flemish Community maintains eight universities, whilst in the French Community university education is provided in nine institutions. These can be categorized according to various criteria. At some universities, virtually all basic academic-level courses are available. As a consequence of the practice of making academic education available in the regions, several universities offer a limited number of courses or parts of some study programmes only, the others being taught elsewhere. Academic education numbers 18 study areas, with about 80 different acknowledged study programmes.

Academic education can be structured into five main types:

- *basic academic education*: the lowest academic degree is obtained after two stages of study. The first stage takes two or three years of study and in most cases leads to the *Kandidaatsdiploma*, equivalent to a bachelor's degree. This degree is not a final award but lays the foundation for the second stage of study which leads to the degree of *Licentiaat* (licentiate) or other titles such as Civil Engineer, Pharmacist, Physician and several more, according to the discipline studied, and which can be obtained after two or three (sometimes even four) additional years of study;
- *advanced academic education*: this consists of post-graduate study programmes of one or two years' duration which can be made up of complementary courses which, in the main, include subjects taken from other basic academic disciplines, or of advanced education which allows students to specialize in a specific sub-area of their original basic academic education;
- *the doctorate*: the degree of 'Doctor' is the highest degree of specialization at the level of academic research. It is based on original research that may take several years to complete, and involves the public defence of a doctoral thesis. Some institutions also require participation in an additional 'doctoral programme' covering seminars, courses, congresses and similar activities attended which relate to the specialization chosen;
- *academic teacher training*: this programme leads to the award of the qualified teacher's degree, which entitles the holder to teach one or several subjects in upper secondary education and non-academic higher education;
- *continuing education*.

Non-university-based higher education in Flanders

As a consequence of the decree pertaining to the *hogescholen* (higher education institutes) of 13 July 1994, a number of important reforms have been introduced in the *hoger onderwijs* (higher education) sector. The Flemish Education Council (*Vlaamse Onderwijsraad*) – the French equivalent is the *Conseil de l'Education et de la Formation de la Communauté Française* – has interpreted the new decree as a general framework for the introduction of a whole new policy for higher education outside the university.

It established 11 areas of study within which a wide variety of basic pro-grammes are available, ranging from architecture, health care, industrial sciences and technology, (audio)visual and fine arts, music and drama, biotechnology, teacher training, product development, adult education and social work (*sociaal-agogisch werk*), applied language studies to commercial sciences and business administration.

The distinction made earlier between short-term and long-term higher education disappeared as a result of this decree. Instead of the old structure, the *hogescholen* have been subdivided into single-stage programmes (which normally require three years of study) and two-stage programmes lasting four years, in which each stage normally takes two years depending on the general teaching objective. Single-stage higher education prepares students for various professions and occupations and focuses on practical and professional skills, such as those of social worker, physiotherapist or midwife. A graduate degree is awarded to successful candidates. Two-stage higher education is of an academic character based on scientific knowledge in the discipline chosen. A bachelor's degree is awarded, for example in civil or commercial engineering, after the first stage. The second stage leads to the licentiate (*Licentiaatsdiploma*), equivalent to a master's degree. Most higher education institutions also organize advanced studies in specific, often highly specialized areas leading to a diploma in the advanced study of a subject and/or offer the possibility of attending international master's degree programmes.

All types of higher education meet the requirements of the European Guidelines of 21 December 1988 relating to the equivalences of higher education diplomas and degrees.

As a consequence of the rapid growth of this sector of education, nearly 160 higher education institutions have been merged into 29 new *hogescholen* most of which have at least 2,000 students each.

The 1994 decree redefines the tasks and different responsibilities of govern-ment and of the higher education institutions themselves. Government is moving away from detailed centralized regulations and clearly aims at deregulation and decentralization. From 1 January 1996 every institution has received an 'envelope', covering both staffing and operational costs, which, as an autonomous entity, it can dispose of as it sees fit. This financing system involves increasing deregulation: the institutions have been given the highest possible freedom when carrying out global government policies. The institutions must learn to budget and to use government funds allocated in advance effectively to carry out their responsibility for providing high-quality tertiary-level education. Government monitors the quality of the product, though not the process of production.

There are no attainment targets determined for higher education, but professional and educational profiles (for example, basic job competences for teachers) are being worked out.

Non-university-based higher education in Wallonia

In the French Community, the decree of 5 August 1995 introduced a drastic restructuring of the higher education institutions, the *hautes écoles*, which are either short-term or long-term ones according to the following eight higher education study areas: agriculture, arts (including performing arts), economics, paramedical training, pedagogy (mainly teacher training), social sciences, technical education, and advanced training of translators and interpreters.

The French decree imposed a regrouping and a decrease of the total number of higher education institutions with a compulsory minimum of enrolled students. The 110 existing institutions have been regrouped into some 40 institutions, which are preferably multicategorical, which means that there are widely diverse study areas on offer, and multitypical, which means that short-term and long-term education is on offer in the same merged institution. As in the Flemish Community, this restructuring has been combined with an increase of institutional autonomy, coupled with quality control measures and budgetary restrictions.

Quality control

As a counterbalance to the universities' increased scope for their own policy making with respect to educational programmes and financial priorities, the managements of the universities have been made responsible for carrying out regular expert assessments of the quality of their three products: education, scientific research and scientific services. This system of quality control is based on self-assessment evaluation by fellow researchers in an inter-university cooperation exercise.

The government takes the initiative to examine quality by establishing committees of independent experts. In particular, the government plays a role in the field of quality auditing by carrying out an audit of the internal mechanisms of quality control/improvement used by the universities.

Despite their freedom to run their own affairs, universities have their output monitored more closely than was the case in the past, with special attention paid to performance. The information exchanged between the universities and government consists of an annual account and report, detailed information on individual students and staff, and quantitative and qualitative analysis of certain facets of university activities.

Universities are responsible for the teaching programmes of their courses. Education is arranged into 18 study areas, and interdisciplinary courses are also possible. Universities are free to allocate study areas or the parts of them to every university; however, government determines which academic courses can be offered in every study area as well as the name of the degree awarded. When producing programmes the laws and regulations which define the practice of the professions concerned as well as European directives are taken into consideration.

The internationalization of higher education

Involvement in actions organized to promote the European dimension or European idea are focused on two programmes: Socrates–Erasmus and Leonardo–Lingua plus a number of others. Using the figures available from the Flemish Community (those for Wallonia are not significantly different), in terms of quantity, the participation in the Erasmus and Lingua programmes has been particularly successful.

During the academic year 1995–6, 2,325 Flemish students (compared to 354 in 1988–9) were exchanged with Erasmus and 45 with the European Credit Transfer System (ECTS) grants. All Flemish universities and higher education institutes take part in 338 cooperation programmes. At present, 108 of these programmes are coordinated by a Flemish institution. For the academic year 1997–8, all institutions concerned submitted an Institutional Contract. The universities of Leuven and Ghent are counted amongst the five universities most closely involved in European exchange and cooperation activities. Since 1990, the Flemish government has been making an additional budget available to increase the number of mobility grants, which amounts to approximately one-third of the budget which Flanders receives from the European Union. During recent years the Flemish budget for the Socrates–Erasmus programme has grown from BEF12 million to BEF26 million.

Although the level of participation in Erasmus programmes can be designated as very high, it is striking that the participation of single-stage higher education courses in cooperation in Europe is considerably lower than that of universities and higher education programmes recognized as offering a full academic education. The small size of Erasmus grants (students from modest backgrounds are unable to meet the extra costs), the lack of a tradition of international contacts among some social classes, the difficulties involving the acceptance of equivalences of the educational programmes pursued in universities abroad, incompatibility of the course structures at home and abroad (such as the problem with courses organized over an entire year), the small size of some institutions which prevents them offering a wide choice of study courses, and problems with language are some of the most likely reasons for low participation. However, following the thorough restructuring of non-university higher education institutions in 1994 some of these problems are being redressed. With the establishment of the Association for the Internationalization of Higher Education (*Vereniging voor de Internationalisering van het Hoger Onderwijs* located within the Flemish Council of Higher Education Institutes, 1994), the institutions affected have united to respond more effectively to the opportunities on offer. The ready introduction of the principles of the European Credit Transfer System in the Flemish higher education regulations facilitates harmonization with programmes of study in partner institutions abroad.

The Lingua programme has also been extremely successful: the number of students and pupils participating in the different programmes has increased from 93 (in 1990–1) to 1,146 (in 1994–5). Also in this case, the Flemish Community made an effort to top up the budget made available by the European Union.

The Flemish Community and its single-stage higher education institutions also participate fully not only in the Leonardo activities (between 1992 and 1994, 250 graduates participated in work experience lasting three months in the context of Petra), but in the Tempus programme as well. The number of Flemish students who participated in student work experience in the context of Comett increased from just seven students in 1990 to 76 in 1994. There is also an active Flemish participation in other EU activities, such as the Ortelius database.

The impact of the European education programmes is expressed not only in the increased mobility of students, school teachers and higher education lecturers, but also in other forms of collaboration, for example cooperation in the development of new study programmes or teaching modules, the development of a department of international relations in most non-university higher education institutions or the establishment of large international group ventures between non-university higher education institutions. Greater attention than ever before is given to the teaching of foreign languages, and there is growing interest in creating international quality comparisons involving academic recognition of more foreign courses and qualifications.

All higher education sectors are involved in teaching for joint European qualifications under existing Socrates and other programmes. The growth of bilateral agreements to teach for foreign diplomas has grown even more rapidly, and mention should also be made of the Businet association of higher education institutions from all EU member states jointly developing European qualifications in the areas of accountancy, tourism and information technology.

Teacher training

Teacher education is provided at three levels, which prepare student teachers for teaching at a particular level or in a particular type of education. There is:

- teacher training in full-time non-university higher education institutions (single stage, short-term) preparing teachers in nursery education, primary education, the first and second grades of secondary education and vocational secondary education. These courses are of three years' duration and comprise concurrent general and pedagogical training, together with the study of one or two specific subject disciplines in the case of future lower secondary teachers;
- teacher training at universities for those intending to teach in upper secondary education or single-stage higher education. Students may obtain a supplementary certificate, parallel with or after the second stage of the basic university course, entitling them to teach specialist school subjects. Training comprises an introduction to some of the theoretical aspects of pedagogy and teaching practice;
- teacher training obtained in 'social advancement' courses: for those involved in vocational training courses and certain technical subjects at lower or upper secondary levels, for which no full-time training is available. These

part-time courses in the form of evening or weekend classes focus on both the theory and practice of teaching, and students give lessons under the supervision of an instructor. Training leads to a certificate of pedagogical aptitude.

The education provision networks are responsible for the provision and organization of in-service training for teachers.

In the Flemish Community, a 1996 decree on initial and in-service teacher training (Decree of 16 April 1996) introduced a number of reforms. This creates a distinction between general initial teacher training, completion of which leads to the award of a basic diploma, and advanced teacher training, which leads to an additional degree.

The initial teacher training programmes comprise the four levels of nursery, primary and two of secondary teacher education:

- secondary teacher education – group 1: teachers are trained in particular to teach specific subjects in the first and second grades of secondary education and in vocational secondary education;
- secondary teacher education – group 2: teachers are trained in particular to teach in the second and third grades of secondary education and in the seventh year of vocational secondary education as well as in non-university higher education institutions.

The advanced teacher training programmes enable someone who has an initial teacher training degree to obtain an additional degree which would facilitate a broader range of professional mobility and improve employment opportunities. There are advanced courses either to specialize in a particular area of expertise, for example in physical education or special education, or to extend the initial teacher training qualification to another type of education, enabling transfer from nursery teaching to primary teaching or to other subject fields applicable to secondary education – in the case of group 1 teachers.

The 1996 decree also stipulates a new system of in-service training, which will essentially be based on demand. The schools have their own means to develop an in-service training policy. In addition, there is also a limited budget available from the umbrella organizations of each network providing education and from government to spend on in-service training which is not supplied sufficiently by the free market.

Partners in the administration of education

In both Flanders and Wallonia, schools are required to have local participation structures.

Flanders

In Community education, the local school council of each school can take decisions on all matters which can be settled at local level. It is composed of an equal number of representatives elected by parents (legally not necessarily parents themselves) and of teachers (elected by teachers from among the teaching staff). Both groups coopt an equal number of representatives of the wider local community (business, social and cultural). The local school councils, chaired by the headteacher, act as a 'governing body' and jointly with the central council for all Community schools, which in turn has twelve nominated members: six by the Flemish Parliament and six representing all local school councils. Elections are held every five years. The local council ensures genuine co-management and right of decision making, which means a strong decentralization of policy and administration.

In assisted, 'non-official' schools participation councils consist, in addition to parents, teachers and members of the local community, of representatives of the authority responsible for providing the school. The headteacher can be delegated to the council. Participating councils can give advice, including more or less binding advice to the 'governing body' or 'organizing authority' responsible for providing the school. Elections are held every four years.

In secondary schools a 'delegation' of third-grade pupils (aged 17–19) may attend the meetings of local and participating councils to take part in discussions on matters of concern to pupils and to give advice. The delegates have no voting rights and no permanent membership.

The system will change, following debates in the Flemish Parliament, probably by giving more rights to the pupils. The forthcoming legislation will include councils negotiating with teacher unions and the Flemish Education Council, which is an advisory body to the government.

Former Community-organized non-university higher education institutions, no longer under Community authority and meanwhile called 'Flemish autonomous non-university higher education institutes', have their own individual administrative councils with the powers of the 'organizing authority', the *hogeschoolbestuur*; its members are elected every four years and consist of teaching and administrative staff, student representatives and members of the local and educational community. The day-to-day management of the *hogeschoolen* is in the hands of the Administrative Board, which includes the chair of the administrative council *ex officio* and three other of its members who are elected by the administrative council.

Every department has a departmental council consisting of staff and students as well as members of the local community. The departmental councils are responsible for the organization of teaching programmes, courses and research activities. Private non-university higher education institutes have councils with similar powers, but with slightly different membership elections. Every higher education institute must have a separate student council.

Wallonia

Primary and secondary school councils have structures similar to those in Flanders. All schools have compulsory *conseils de participation* (participation councils) with an advisory role (decree of 2 July 1997). Unlike the councils in Flanders, they play no part in the governing body of the organizing authority. The participation councils are not involved in the details of daily management of schools but they discuss fundamental options in specific, clearly delimited domains, stimulating the process towards more decentralization and autonomy. Councils in the assisted sector have less influence in determining curriculum details and the appointment of teaching staff. The numbers of members may vary; in addition to staff, parents and governing body representatives, the councils in Wallonia have members representing teacher unions and the pupils. They also coopt members representing the local community.

In higher education the structure is again similar: there is student representation in the administrative council, and all institutions must have a students' council. The German Community has compulsory school advisory boards with advisory powers only. There are no local community or pupil representatives.

Quality control and guidance

The autonomy enjoyed by Belgian teachers with respect to evaluation and examinations and monitoring the learning process and output has been commented upon already. Attainment targets are primarily meant as criteria imposed by the government enabling decisions regarding the financial support received and the recognition of diplomas and certificates awarded. The introduction of centrally formulated core targets or, indeed, central evaluation or examinations have never been considered and have on occasion been explicitly rejected.

Notwithstanding this fact, government does exercise control over outcomes. In the Flemish Community, a 1991 decree draws a clear distinction between inspection and pedagogical counselling. The inspectorate supervises, on behalf of the government, the quality of nursery, primary and secondary education. To that end, it has to examine the quality of the specific pedagogical projects within the curricula and syllabuses and the timetables within which these are completed. The inspectorate assesses whether the minimum goals have been properly achieved and whether the other organizational conditions have been correctly observed. It operates through team visits aimed at screening all aspects of a school's operation, instead of checking and judging individual (subject) teachers.

While the latter is merely a controlling function, the pedagogical support services, which are organized at the level of each providing network, give external support to teachers and schools in the general pedagogical and methodological fields. The 'education development service' (DVO) is a scientific staff service belonging to the inspectorate. It defines the minimum goals for all schools, and develops the instruments required to measure their proper functioning.

In the French- and German-speaking Communities, the inspection on Community level is still fulfilling a double role. With regard to Community-maintained education, its task (as the final representative of the Minister, the organizing authority of this network) still comprises all aspects of school activities: curricula, teaching methods, school organization, infrastructure and equipment. In this respect, its role is dual, in the sense of having to inspect and sanction whilst at the same time having to guide and counsel. Besides this, the Community inspectorate is also responsible for the control of assisted education, deciding on the award of financial support grants.

Psycho-medico-social guidance centres (PMS centres) deal with assistance and (non-binding) advice to individual pupils, while taking into account their social environment, parental wishes and school background. The broad task of the PMS centres requires a multidisciplinary approach, with the team including doctors, paramedical staff, psychologists, educationalists and social workers. The centres follow pupils from nursery school up to the end of secondary education. PMS centres belong to one of the three educational networks. In Flanders, plans to reorganize the tasks and the structure of the PMS system are being discussed.

Quality control and supervision of the education on offer in higher education institutes and at universities is based on self-evaluation and 'visitation committees' for peer review (decree of 13 July 1994). In the case of universities and two-stage higher education institutes the former system of *ex ante* supervision by the authorities has been replaced by an *ex post* system. It is based on the idea that these institutions are capable of independent management.

Conclusion

In some respects, the three Belgian Communities making up one nation can be seen as a microcosm of the European Community since 1993.

As in most other EU member states, the Belgian educational system has undergone considerable change over the last few years. Education has been an important area of concern of the governments of the three Communities since 1988 and has generated much policy debate and legislation. It can be said that developments in Belgium converge with current policy reforms in most other Western European countries, evidenced by:

- a trend towards more efficient, effective and accountable school management through decentralization and deregulation;
- a stricter quality control of output demonstrated by the development of attainment targets, and restructuring of the inspectorate;
- an increase in participation and input by 'society', such as growing responsiveness to the wishes and interests of the 'consumer' (parent participation, close school–business links to create a better adaptation of education to the labour market), greater influence of the principles of economic profit;

- an increase of scale resulting in mergers and cooperative ventures between schools which are actively encouraged or even imposed so that the available resources, infrastructure and manpower can be used more efficiently;
- a growth of internationalization of all sectors of education.

All these objectives should be achieved, though, under the pressure of increasing budgetary constraints. Educational expenditure has had to be cut, more has to be done with less money. Educational policy seems to be mainly orientated towards considerations of the economy: finance, efficiency, effectiveness, quality, management, and output control, which assumes and tends towards a converging and harmonizing educational process. But isn't there a danger in a unifying policy style which is subjected to this 'economism'? Is not the richness of Europe due to its very diversity?

Bibliography

Depaepe, M. and Laevers, F. (1992). Preschool education in Belgium. In G. Woodill (ed.), *International handbook of early childhood education*. New York: Garland.

Druine, N., Haak, E., Lagerweij, N., Wielemans, W. and Dewulf, L. (1995). *Verwantschap en verscheidenheid. Het secundair onderwijs in Vlaanderen – Het voortgezet onderwijs in Nederland. Een vergelijking*. Den Haag: Sdu Uitgevers.

Michielsens, P. (1996). De toekomst van het Vlaamse onderwijs in perspectief. *Tijdschrift voor Onderwijsrecht en Onderwijsbeleid*, 6(4), 219–228.

Ministère de l'Éducation, de la Recherche et de la Formation (1996). *Le Système éducatif en Communauté Française de Belgique*. Bruxelles: Secrétariat général.

Ministerie van de Vlaamse Gemeenschap, Administratie buitenlands beleid (1996). *Het onderwijs in Vlaanderen*. Brussel.

Ministerie van de Vlaamse Gemeenschap, Departement Onderwijs (1994). *Decreet betreffende de hogescholen in de Vlaamse gemeenschap, 13 juli 1994*. Brussel: Afdeling Informatie en Documentatie.

Ministerie van de Vlaamse Gemeenschap, Departement Onderwijs (1995). *Wegwijs in de ontwikkelingsdoelen en eindtermen van het basisonderwijs*. Bruxelles Afdeling Informatie en Documentatie.

Ministerie van de Vlaamse Gemeenschap, Departement Onderwijs (1997). *Wegwijs in de eindtermen en de ontwikkelingsdoelen voor de eerste graad van het secundair onderwijs*. Brussel: Afdeling Informatie en Documentatie.

Ministerie van de Vlaamse Gemeenschap, Departement Onderwijs (1997). *Sleutel. Overzicht van de mogelijkheden voor internationale samenwerking in het onderwijs*. Brussel: Afdeling Informatie en Documentatie.

Ministerie van de Vlaamse Gemeenschap, Departement Onderwijs, Administratie Basisonderwijs (1997). *Decreet Basisonderwijs, 25 februari 1997*. Brussel: Afdeling Informatie en Documentatie.

Ministry of the Flemish Community, Department for Education (1996). *Educational developments in Flanders 1994–1996*. Brussels: Information and Documentation Division.

Ministry of the Flemish Community, Department for Education, Administration of Higher Education and Scientific Research (1997). *Hogescholen in Flanders (Belgium)*.

Ministry of the Flemish Community, Department for Education, Universities Section (1997). *Universities in Flanders (Belgium)*.

Monard, G. (1995). Een ambitieus regeerakkoord. *Tijdschrift voor Onderwijsrecht en Onderwijsbeleid*, 5(4), 226–233.

OECD (1991) *Education in Belgium: The Diverging Paths* (Review of national policies for education) Brussel – Bruxelles – Eupen: Ministerie van de Vlaamse Gemeenschap, Dept. Onderwijs – Ministère de l'Education, de la Recherche et de la Formation – Verwaltung der Deutschsprachigen Gemeinschaft, Abt. Unterricht

Tielemans, J. (1996). *Onderwijs in Vlaanderen. Structuur – organisatie – wetgeving*. Leuven-Apeldoorn: Garant.

Van Craeymeersch, S. (1997). Het Decreet Basisonderwijs, geen revolutie, wel een grondige vernieuwing. *Tijdschrift voor Onderwijsrecht en Onderwijsbeleid*, 7(4), 211–222.

Van den Bossche, L. (1996). *Policy paper. Organizing education in Flanders: Creating the necessary conditions for an integrative education policy in the 21st century*. Brussels: Ministry of the Flemish Community.

Wielemans, W. (1991). Comprehensive education in Belgium: a broken lever? *European Journal of Education*, 26(2), 167–178.

Wielemans, W. (1996). *Het onderwijs in België*. Leuven-Apeldoorn: Garant.

3 Denmark

Thyge Winther-Jensen

Introduction

Three major events from the last 25 years have exercised particular influence on the formation of Danish educational policy: first, Denmark's entry into the Common Market (post-1993 the EU) in 1973; second, the advent of a liberal, right-wing government in 1982, which in many ways meant a breach with the previously pursued educational policies; third, its replacement by a government headed by the Social Democrats in 1993.

Denmark became a member of the EC in 1973 after a referendum in 1972 on accession to the Treaty of Rome of 1957. This had been preceded by a stormy public debate that to some degree influenced Denmark's relations with the EC in the following years, a characteristic feature of which was that large parts of the population found it difficult fully to accept that Danish membership was a reality.

In 1986 the government called for a non-binding referendum on the amendments to EC cooperation that the member states had negotiated in Luxembourg in 1985, the so-called EC Act (in Denmark 'the EC package'). With effect from 1 January 1993 the Act was intended to remove the last barriers to a Single Market with free mobility of goods, labour and capital. Despite the opposition of the Social Democrats the referendum resulted in a Yes vote of 56.2 per cent (with 43.8 per cent voting No). Although support had fallen by 7 per cent in relation to 1972, the Prime Minister nevertheless interpreted the result as meaning very considerable support for the actual idea of EC membership, since – unlike in 1972 – the Social Democrats had recommended a No to this extension of EC cooperation.

It is fair to say that for a while this referendum put an end to the rather hesitant Danish approach to the EC that had characterised the period between the two referendums. Up to the next referendum in 1992 none of the parties represented in parliament seriously questioned the rightness of Danish membership. Instead preparations were begun for the establishment of the Single Market from the end of 1992.

The next referendum took place on 2 June 1992. The issue this time was the so-called Maastricht Treaty, which had been adopted at an EC summit meeting in Maastricht in southern Holland on 9–11 December 1991; 17 protocols and 31 declarations were appended to the actual Treaty, a document totalling 308 pages. The Treaty can be seen as a political counterpart to the Single Market.

The Treaty contained: (a) rules for an economic-monetary union involving closer cooperation among member states on economic and currency matters; (b) a follow-up to the social charter which was adopted in Strasbourg in December 1989 by the EC heads of state and government in the form of a number of specific directives – the so-called 'social dimension' of the Treaty; (c) new powers for the European Parliament; (d) rules for the establishment of a solidarity fund to provide economic support for environmental protection and the transport infrastructure in the poorer parts of southern Europe; (e) rules for a common policy on the environment; (f) rules for a common foreign and security policy; (g) rules for asylum, immigration policy and police cooperation; (h) rules for an 'EC citizenship', which mean that EC citizens resident in another member country have the right to vote and are eligible for election in local elections in the country in which they are resident; (i) furthermore, the Treaty established the so-called subsidiarity principle, which is interpreted to mean that 'the EC acts only in areas in which cooperation at EC level is better and more effective than if each member state acts independently' (Article 3B); (j) finally, the Treaty included new areas or strengthened existing areas of cooperation in the fields of culture and education. There was a wish that in the field of education, which was barely touched on in the original Treaty of Rome, the so-called European dimension should be given more weight.

Prior to the referendum on 2 June all the political parties with the exception of the SF (the People's Socialist Party) and *Fremskridtspartiet* (the Progress Party) recommended a Yes, but the Danes nevertheless rejected the Maastricht Treaty by a narrow majority. This rejection led to the drawing up of the 'national compromise', which was adopted by seven of the parliamentary parties including the SF and approved at the EC Summit in Edinburgh in December 1992. The compromise, which exempted Denmark from participation in certain important areas of the Maastricht Treaty, was confirmed by a narrow majority at the referendum in May 1992. In 1998 a referendum was held on the so-called Amsterdam Treaty and 55.1 per cent voted Yes and 44.9 per cent voted No.

The second event was the change of government in 1982, when the then Social Democratic government gave way to a right-of-centre government, primarily because of economic problems in connection with the ever-increasing balance-of-payments deficit.

The views of the previous government on education had been formulated in *U90. Samlet uddannelsesplanlægning frem til 90'erne* (U90. A total plan for education until the 90s)[1] in 1978, while Ritt Bjerregaard was Minister of Education. The document demanded 12 years of non-selective schooling for all (though without recommending an extension of compulsory schooling from 9 to 12 years) as well as more 'socially relevant', topic-orientated and interdisciplinary teaching.

U90 will be remembered as the plan that continued the ideas from the end of the 1960s and the beginning of the 1970s concerning more socially relevant and equality-orientated schooling. It was an ambitious attempt at presenting an overall plan for education right up to the 1990s, but it was overtaken by developments, and so rapidly that within an astonishingly short space of time it acquired the status of an historical document. Some of its ideas can nevertheless still be encountered in discussions on educational policy.

The change of government in 1982 meant a radical break with the ideas behind U90. Symptomatically, the new Minister of Education, Bertel Haarder, abolished with immediate effect the Central Council for Education, which had formulated the plan.[2] In his view, there were two main expectations regarding the new government's educational policy: first, that the widespread scepticism regarding the value of even longer, uninterrupted schooling would now be manifested in practice; second, that the 'ideologisation' of and emphasis on 'social relevance' which have increasingly set their mark on education since the 1960s, and which 'have never enjoyed the support of either a majority in parliament or among the population' should cease to be favoured by the central administration.

Interdisciplinary topic-orientated teaching was also taken to task, since here 'ideologists and technocrats often meet in a shared acceptance of lower standards, which were as a rule the inevitable consequence of such practices. The projects combined a Marxist critique of the curriculum and the Social Democratic philosophy of equality with the demands of technocrats, the organisations and the business world for social utility'. U90 and the reactions to it illustrate the two educational ideologies that have characterised Danish educational planning in recent years. On the one hand, we have an ideology of equality which demanded uninterrupted, integrated schooling (a 12-year non-selective school), late specialisation and the deferment of the final choice of career, the erosion of the autonomy of the individual subjects and a focus on interdisciplinary topic-orientated teaching. On the other hand, we have a neo-liberal ideology opposed to state paternalism and therefore desirous of a decentralisation of the educational system, a reduction in the power of the institutions, shorter career-orientated courses of education, an emphasis on individual subjects rather than on interdisciplinary activities and methodological formalism. In the Danish edition of this ideology there was also a strongly Grundtvigian element, which favoured the teaching of history and literature as subjects that give pupils experiences which contribute to the development of their personalities.

It was clearly the latter of the two ideologies that set its mark on Danish educational planning in the period from 1982 up to the next change of government, even though the political process somewhat blunted its cutting edge. It was translated into plans that changed many things in the field of education. And as the government was strongly pro-European, the demand for internationalisation of the educational system also emerged as a significant element. In relation to the EC, however, it is 'not a matter of harmonising', claimed the Danish Minister of Education, 'but of recognising one another's differences, increasing the exchange of students and teachers and strengthening mutual confidence and harmony. The idea of harmonisation is dead and buried – as the fantasy it has always been. "Not harmonise, but recognise" became the motto for the government's work in the field of education.'[3]

A noteworthy element in the programme for education, as described by the Minister in *Perspektiver i uddannelse og forskningspolitikken* (Perspectives for a policy for education and research)[4] from 1986, was the focus on the historical perspective: 'As Danes,' the document stated, 'we have our common experience as a people recorded in history, literature, poetry, art, songs and hymns, scholarship and science . . . To think historically and act contemporaneously is a good recipe to follow in schools and further education in a time which in so many ways calls for change and innovation.'

A second element was the emphasis on values: 'Goals and values will be the key words in the educational debate of the future. It is not enough to "learn to learn" . . . The art will be to distinguish the important from the unimportant. That is why the debate on values will be vitally important. It will be of vital importance that we do not waste the pupils' time on trivial texts . . . The days of nihilism with regard to values are past. Concepts like value, quality of upbringing and culture are indispensable.'

A third element was the demand for comprehensive revision of objectives and teaching guides for a large number of subjects in all structures of general education. This revision was to aim at, among other things, 'the identification of central core of material . . . which should be known to all' and a 'strengthening of the cultural and artistic aspects of the subjects – as opposed to the trend in the 60s and 70s towards giving priority to the pedagogical process and to topicality.' In his demand for core material the Minister could draw on examples from abroad such as the American report *A Nation at Risk* of 1983.

A fourth element in the programme was its emphasis on the 'necessity of autonomy for schools, i.e., parental influence and free choice of school, including the freedom not to choose a state-maintained school'. Direct reference was here made to the tradition of freedom deriving from Nikolai Grundtvig and Christen Kold.

An important pre-condition for this autonomy was the demand for a transition from detailed administration to control via defined objectives and an overall framework, with respect to both educational practice and finance. With respect to educational practice there was a demand for precision in the definition of objectives together with increased freedom to decide how these objectives were to be achieved locally. In terms of finance this involved a transition to block grants. The position of the individual school management was to be strengthened, with regard to both budgeting and the formulation of the special 'profile' of the individual school within the framework of its overall objectives. The latter was considered to be especially important if the *Folkeskole* was to be able to compete with the private schools.

Increased consumer influence was also recommended, for instance through the introduction of a voucher system that placed a certain sum of money at the individual's disposal for the payment of educational and living expenses. It was maintained that such a system would ensure that pupils and students would take a keen interest in whether they were receiving value for money.

Finally, the programme recommended influence for the receiving organisations, both the vocational schools and institutes of higher education, simplification of existing agreements and the replacement of the watertight compartment system created by the organisations with an 'interconnected network in which one can move laterally and change one's place without being forced to start all over again'. This network was to be made international, as has been done through the EC programmes Erasmus and Comett.

The programme was an excellent example of the mixture of neo-liberalism – both political and economic – and Grundtvigianism that characterised the educational policy of the time with its predilection for key words like 'values', 'content', 'innovation' and 'quality'.

In particular, the concept of 'quality in the classroom' was to play an important role in the discussion. In February 1989 the Ministry of Education launched a special 'quality development programme'[5] with the aim of 'creating more precise objectives for individual courses of education, greater coherence with regard to content among them, higher quality throughout so that citizens receive more and better teaching for their money'. The real motive behind the project was, however, the idea that the quality of the educational system had to be improved if Denmark was to be able to cope with international competition on the threshold to the Single Market. 'In all Western countries', the presentation of the project stated, 'we find that increased demands are being made of the quality of teaching, education and research. This is due to, among other things, structural changes in the labour market, new technology, intensified competition and ever more comprehensive internationalisation.'

The project was initiated with a conference on evaluation and a visit by Her Majesty's Senior Chief Inspector from England. Among the sub-projects of the project were: (a) a discussion paper on quality in teaching and education (published in the same year);[6] (b) the establishment of working groups to examine objectives and content for physics[7] and English,[8] among other things to see if there was coherence between the different levels at which these subjects were taught; (c) the testing of internal and external criteria for the evaluation of selected institutions; (d) the comparison of levels in parallel forms of education; and (e) international quality and level comparisons in collaboration with IEA (the International Association for the Evaluation of Educational Achievement). This analysis of the academic levels of Danish schools in relation to those of other countries was initially to be carried out with reference to teaching of the mother tongue, and later to include English (first foreign language) and mathematics.

The third event – the accession of a new government headed by the Social Democrats in 1993 – set its mark on the new *Folkeskole* Act of the same year which, because of the Tamil Case, the outgoing government had not managed to complete before its resignation. That it was now the radical Minister of Education Ole Vig Jensen who conducted the negotiations influenced the formulation of the Act in certain important ways. Unfortunately the Act ran into the criticism of the *Folkeskole* that followed the publication of international and national studies of reading proficiency. The studies gave Denmark a weak placing in relation to other countries, especially if the results are seen in the light of expenditure per pupil. These findings occasioned the publication of two books that were highly critical of the Danish educational system.[9] The criticism did not lead to any legislative changes, but it changed the climate around the Act and strengthened demands for a revision of the latest Act on teacher training, even though it had last been amended as recently as 1993.

Reforms in the 1980s

In the following account of educational reform in the 1980s, it is not difficult to recognise the principles described in the preceding section.

The Folkeskole *(primary and lower secondary education)*

Basic education is given both in the *Folkeskole* and in the private basic schools, which are also called 'free basic schools' and have the same structure as the *Folkeskole*. The *Folkeskole* comprises a voluntary pre-school class and the first to ninth grades, possibly followed by an optional tenth year. Nearly all children attend the pre-school class while approximately 50 per cent continue to the tenth grade. After the ninth and tenth grades pupils can, if they wish, sit for the Leaving Examination or the Advanced Leaving Examination of the *Folkeskole*.

The *Folkeskole* is a municipal school free for all who are covered by the obligation to receive nine years' teaching – in Denmark there is no legal obligation actually to attend a school. Its provisions are formulated in the Act of 1993. The *Folkeskole* is a non-selective school, in which the pupils are taught in unstreamed classes at all levels. The subjects to be taught are laid down in the *Folkeskole* Act, while provisions concerning their content are formulated by the Minister as statutory orders. The Ministry issues central curricula as guidelines for the individual municipal cities. Obligatory curricula are issued by the local county councils or by the schools themselves after authorisation from the local councils.

In the 1980s the *Folkeskole* as a whole was faced by the requirement to adjust its consumption of resources to the sharp decline in the number of children of school age (from 781,000 7–16-year-olds in 1978–80 to 630,000 in 1989–90; a further fall to 571,000 in 1995–6 was forecast). This has led to school closures in many municipalities.

Side by side with the *Folkeskole* there is a private school sector – the free basic schools[10] – whose number at the beginning of the 1990s had risen to 402 schools with approximately 67,000 pupils or 10.8 per cent of the total age group. The state pays a considerable subsidy (75 per cent) to the private schools. In 1988 the subsidy scheme, in accordance with which grants of 85 per cent were given to meet certain costs (salaries, maintenance of buildings, heating, cleaning, rates and other) was replaced by a block subsidy scheme, intended to give the individual school greater freedom of disposition.

For a time, the sharp increase in the intake of the private schools at the beginning of the 1980s led to fears that the *Folkeskole* would be the loser in competition with the private sector. This fear was probably somewhat exaggerated even though the share of pupils attending private schools today (1997) has risen to above 13 per cent.

In the 1980s the *Folkeskole* was not subjected to quite as radical structural reforms as other parts of the educational system. There was, however, a mini-reform in 1985, which contained the rules for the so-called 'coordinated school start' and also expanded the framework for the voluntary tenth year. The coordinated school start derived originally from a desire for a better transition from kindergarten (pre-school class) to school. The Minister's wish, inspired by, among other things, English conditions, for an actual lowering of the school age was realised in such a way that the three youngest classes are to be regarded as a unit in which play and teaching receive equal weight. In reality this meant that the two pedagogical cultures of the kindergarten and of the school now had to try to cooperate to find a common pedagogical approach. The expanded framework for the voluntary tenth year meant that the local authorities could now formulate non-traditional educational provision at this level without a leaving examination.

For the *Folkeskole*, it was more its content than its structure that was the object of attention in the 1980s. First, this led to a revision of the curricular guidelines for Danish and history, in which older literature/the literary experience and a coherent understanding of the historical process were given greater emphasis.[11] Second, the question was raised as to what actually constitutes basic knowledge and skills. This was brought about by, among other things, surveys that indicated the presence of serious gaps in schoolchildren's general knowledge and skills.[12] An introduction to the debate titled *Om grundlæggende kundskaber* (On basic knowledge and skills) (1986)[13] was published by the Ministry and was later followed by the report *Pejling og perspektiv* (Bearings and perspectives) (1988)[14] from the so-called Perspective Committee established by the Minister to consider the question: What basic knowledge and skills and what general values shall the school system give Danes with which to meet the twenty-first century? The Committee divided its report into three sections: the first presented a number of general values (21 in all), which the committee felt that children should encounter; the second section put forward ideas as to what general knowledge and skills are; the third section discussed necessary knowledge and skills in five areas: aesthetics, man, society, science and language. In addition, the report emphasised the need for intercultural teaching. The report failed to evoke much public attention. It was written at such a non-committal, abstract level that it was difficult to disagree with its content. Its most controversial contribution would today seem to be its rejection of the concept of the 'neutral teacher'.

The report did, however, play a role in future planning. Prior to its publication – in May 1987 – Parliament had adopted a 'Development programme for the

Folkeskole and the school as a local cultural centre' (the so-called seven-point programme) as preparation for radical reform of the *Folkeskole* at the beginning of the 1990s. Over a four-year period the programme was to receive DKK100 million annually for development work in the *Folkeskole*. These funds were administered by the Development Council for the *Folkeskole*. The general development activities under this programme included – although on a small scale – projects based on the Perspective Committee's report. One such field of development is the inculcation of general values. Evaluation of these and the many other activities under the seven-point programme was concluded in the spring of 1992.[15]

Characteristic of the many development projects – about 8,000 – is the fact that they were not dictated by the Development Council for the *Folkeskole*. To a large extent the ideas for projects arose locally, from parents, pupils and teachers, which accords well with the Danish tradition of allowing reforms in the area of the *Folkeskole* to grow up 'from below'. Another tradition is that reforms of the *Folkeskole* should have broad parliamentary backing.

Among the topics for other development projects initiated under the seven-point programme are: the school as a local centre of culture; the class teacher's functions; Danish teaching in the third and fourth grades (with the aim of strengthening reading skills); foreign-language teaching (for example, starting English earlier and moving French to the senior classes); and the integration of elements of computer studies into the other subjects taught in the *Folkeskole*.

In the meantime, the revision of the existing curricular guidelines continued independently of the preparations for a reform of the *Folkeskole* Act. Thus, in addition to the already-mentioned changes in Danish and history, the demand for a clearer definition of core knowledge and skills and of general values led to a revision of objectives and content in other subjects such as Christian studies,[16] geography[17] and art.[18]

Other aspects of the *Folkeskole* – administration and teacher mobility – will be discussed below. All in all, it can be said that in the 1980s the *Folkeskole* was forced into a process of radical adaptation, partly as a result of the decrease in the number of children and partly as a result of new educational policies. Two elements of the latter have been emphasised: first, a neo-liberalism, which for market- and competition-related reasons wished to see a significant strengthening of core knowledge in foreign languages, natural sciences and social studies; and, second, a Grundtvigian conviction that attached importance to the teaching of Danish language and literature and to the nation's common historical heritage.

In the spring of 1992 – even before the evaluation work had been completed – the Minister presented his proposals in Parliament for a new *Folkeskole* Act. As a result of political pressure the Bill was not adopted until the spring of 1993. The intervening discussion was primarily concerned with the objects clause, examinations and marks, foreign-language teaching and the teaching of Danish.

Upper secondary education

To all intents and purposes general secondary education consists of the *Gymnasium* (upper secondary school) and *Højere Forberedelseseksamen* (HF) (Higher Preparatory Examination). The former takes three years, while the latter takes two years. The *Højere Forberedelseseksamen* can also be acquired through a series of courses taken in individual subjects at county adult education centres. The *Gymnasium* course is completed by the Upper Secondary School Leaving Examination, while HF is completed by the *Højere Forberedelseseksamen* itself.

Historically, the *Gymnasium* derives from the old 'Latin' schools, while HF was not established until 1966. It sprang from a desire for democratisation of the education system in the period after the Second World War. The Social Democratic government of the time wanted to break the *Gymnasium*'s monopoly of access to higher education. HF therefore became an education which, in the words of the Social Democratic Minister, was to 'be "open" not only "upwards", but also "downwards"'.

Today the *Gymnasium* and HF together constitute a general upper secondary education, which in most cases shares teachers and buildings. The *Gymnasium* is now seen as the natural preparation for higher education for 16-year-olds, while HF is intended for more mature students who have already had experience of the employment market. HF (especially as single-subject courses) has developed into a form of recurrent, continuing education. As opposed to the *Folkeskole*, which is administered by the municipality, all *Gymnasiums* and HFs are today managed by the local county council. The only remaining state-run *Gymnasium* is Sorø Academy.

In the course of the 1980s both the *Gymnasium* and HF (the latter only to a slight extent) underwent reform. The prelude to these reforms began in the period after 1978, namely in the wake of U90. This plan envisaged not only a coordination of the various forms of upper secondary education but also a new 'pedagogy'. There was resistance to the ideas in U90 regarding the *Gymnasium* from, among others, representatives of the professional associations of teachers of modern languages.[19] They criticised what they saw as the downgrading of foreign-language teaching in U90, its 'fixation on topicality' and a lack of backbone in the face of social trends that characterised both U90 and the endeavours to introduce topic-orientated, interdisciplinary teaching.

In 1982 – shortly before he became Minister of Education – Bertel Haarder co-authored a pamphlet *Kampen om gymnasiet* (The struggle for the *Gymnasium*),[20] in which the *Gymnasium* was designated as the forum for 'the most important cultural struggle of the 80s'. The pamphlet speaks of the need to combat 'democratism and its "interdisciplinary, problem-orientated group projects", of giving the individual school subjects a new identity, of strengthening Danish and history as "intellectual/spiritual subjects", of promoting the cultural aspects of foreign-language teaching and of retaining the high levels in the teaching of the natural sciences'. On the other hand, there is no mention of a structural reform of the *Gymnasium*.

During the complicated reform work from the autumn of 1985 until the reform[21] took final shape in January 1987, although changes were introduced with respect both to structure and to content, the above-mentioned severe criticism that followed the proposals of U90 did not so much result in radically new departures as in a preservation and strengthening of the tradition of individual school work as opposed to interdisciplinary and topic-orientated project work. The most important change relating to the *Gymnasium* from before the reform is a greater freedom for pupils to combine subjects according to choice.

Structurally, the three-year *Gymnasium* still consists of two 'lines': the language line and the mathematics line. Both have the same overall objective: to provide a general education as well as a preparation for higher education. This two-part objective has remained unchanged since 1850 – a thought-provoking continuity when one considers how often the objectives of other forms of schooling have been altered during the same period. The reform meant a transition from a branch structure to an options structure. Where formerly pupils chose specific branches after the first year – for example the mathematics–physics branch or the modern languages branch from the mathematics and the language line respectively – they can now choose optional subjects. Of a total of 31 or 32 weekly lessons they now have four to five optional lessons a week in the second year and fourteen to fifteen in the third year.

There were a number of reasons why in the final resort the optional system won over the branch system. On the one hand, it meets pupil needs for greater individualisation and non-traditional subject combinations, such as English and mathematics at high level; on the other hand, it has now become easier to introduce new subjects, such as business subjects, information technology and philosophy. It is no longer necessary to establish an entirely new branch in order to get such subjects into the timetable. 'In other words', as the Director of the Directorate for the *Gymnasium* and *HF* said, 'we shall be able to adapt much more quickly to the demands of society.' Perhaps this adaptability contains the seeds of the dissolution of the *Gymnasium* as an integrated and stable institution. The advantage of the branch structure was that the individual branches were composed around related subjects which supported one another.

The reform has necessitated a division of the school subjects into three groups: common core, compulsory and optional. The common core subjects are those that are the same for all pupils, irrespective of what line they have chosen. These subjects are Danish, history, biology, English, art, classical civilisation, religion. The compulsory subjects are those that are necessary for the specialist line chosen: for instance, a foreign language for the language line and physics and chemistry for the mathematics line. The optional subjects can be taken at two levels: advanced and intermediate. Pupils are required to choose at least two advanced-level subjects, one of which must belong to the group of compulsory subjects linked to the line they have chosen. The reform also meant a strengthening of written work, inasmuch as during the final year pupils now have to complete a major written assignment.

Besides these structural changes, changes have also been made in the content of individual subjects, especially with regard to Danish, history, physics, geography, biology and social studies. In Danish the linguistic and literary content, including older literature, has been considerably strengthened.

As a whole, the reform has reinforced the humanist-linguistic side of upper secondary education. Among the foreign languages taught, English now enjoys a stronger position as it can be chosen at advanced levels by pupils from both lines. Furthermore, pupils have been given greater possibilities for choice and the writing skills have been given greater emphasis.

The reform contained a number of elements that clearly pointed in the direction of the Single Market of 1992: the strengthening of foreign languages, especially English, the more flexible structure facilitating quicker adaptation to the changing needs of society, the increased degree of specialisation, the emphasis on the cultural aspect of foreign-language teaching. Finally, the importance attached to older literature in Danish teaching can also be seen as an expression of a greater attention to the nation's own cultural heritage in the forthcoming closer encounters with other European cultures. At the same time, however, the reform sought to preserve the special strength of the Danish *Gymnasium*: its balance between a broad, general education and a suitable degree of specialisation.

Technical and vocational education

This part of the educational system covers those forms of education that take place in the technical and commercial schools, that is, technical and vocational education as such, which affects two-thirds of each age group.

Both general secondary and technical and vocational education are placed under the Ministry of Education as the highest administrative authority. Nevertheless, in legal terms, administratively and in accordance with tradition there is in Denmark a relatively sharp distinction between them.

Until 1989 two parallel forms of technical and vocation education existed side by side within the various trades: the traditional apprenticeship and *EFG*, the *Erhvervsfaglig Grunduddannelse* (basic vocational education). The minimum admission requirement was the *Folkeskole* leaving certificate. To start an apprenticeship, a contract had to be drawn up between apprentice and employer. Apprenticeships lasted from two to four years depending on the trade, alternating between practice at the place of work and school attendance, and were concluded by a 'journeyman's test'. In the commercial and clerical fields, where there are no provisions for a journeyman's test, acquisition of a certificate of completed apprenticeship was conditional on passing the Commercial Assistant Examination (*handelsmedhjælpereksamen*) or the more comprehensive Commercial Examination (*handelseksamen*). EFG courses, which were introduced in 1977, were structured rather differently. They started with a basic one-year course in one of the eight main fields into which the employment market is divided: commercial and clerical trades; service trades; the construction sector; food industries; iron and metal industries; graphic industries; agriculture; and transport. The first year consisted partly of vocational, partly of general education. Its purpose was to provide pupils with an overview of the main field chosen and with a basis for their later choice of a special branch in the second part of the course. The education, including workshop training, took place entirely at school, except for visits to companies and firms. As in the apprenticeship system, the pupil alternated in the second part between school and approved trainee places of work. On completion of this education the pupil received a certificate equivalent to a journeyman's certificate.

In addition to these two forms of education, which together covered by far the major part of vocational training proper, there were other, less widespread types of technical and vocational training. The two- to four-year Technical and Commercial Diploma courses (*grundlæggende tekniske uddannelser*), which required the completion of a basic year of a relevant EFG course and trained technical designers and assistants, laboratory assistants and similar trades.

The technical and vocational system also offers courses which in reality must be described as general, upper secondary education even though they are vocationally orientated. At commercial schools it is possible to take a two-year course leading to the Higher Commercial Examination (*højere handelseksamen* – HHX), which is equivalent to the Upper Secondary Leaving Examination. Similarly, technical schools offer a two-year course leading to the Higher Technical Examination (*højere teknisk eksamen* – HTX). Such courses ensure that there is a link between technical and vocational education and further and higher education.

In the preceding years the discussion of technical and vocational education had been dominated by the existence of two types of parallel education: apprenticeship and EFG. Both types had their convinced adherents and opponents. It was therefore with considerable satisfaction that in the spring of 1989 the Minister could announce that political agreement had finally been reached in Parliament, and that 15 years of 'religious war' were now over. On 30 March of the same year – on the centenary of the first Danish Apprenticeship Act – Parliament passed the Technical and Vocational Education Act and the Technical and Vocational Schools Act, which together constituted the legislative basis for a reform of technical and vocational education.[22] This legislation was based on the work of a commission, which in the spring of 1987 published a lengthy Report on Basic Technical and Vocational Education.[23]

The Technical and Vocational Education Act laid down the structure and principles for these types of education. It aimed at combining the best elements of the apprenticeship system, EFG and of the technical and commercial diploma courses into one set of regulations in order to make the system simpler to understand both for young people and for employers. The majority of the existing types of education were to become special branches within a much reduced number of basic courses with a duration of up to four years. It was still possible to start this education in the two 'old' ways: either at school or in a firm with which one has concluded a trainee contract, but except for the first 20 weeks the teaching was to be the same for both types of pupil. The education was to be more consistently based on the principle of alternating between short periods at school and practice periods at the place of work. The latter, however, were not be solely vocational in content. The aim was for practice and school mutually to support and supplement each other.

The Technical and Vocational Schools Act gave schools new and wider powers. In future, there would be far greater possibilities for the management of a school to determine its activities in cooperation with the local community. The individual school could decide what kinds of vocational education it wished to offer. At the same time there would be free access to the various types of education. Together with their places of actual training, pupils would be able to choose freely among the schools. The individual school would receive a block grant, which would be dependent on, among other things, enrolment.

During the preparation of the reform it was stressed that basic technical and vocational education should be given a content capable of attracting and retaining young people in order to bring about the greatest possible reduction of the group (approximately 9 per cent) who receive no other education than that at the *Folkeskole*. It is mainly from this group that the young unemployed are recruited. The Chairman wrote:

> The Committee emphasised that the aim of giving as many young people as possible vocational competence also implied that this education should have considerable breadth . . . , that it should provide a basis for further education, and that it should comprise general qualifications that are not narrowly specialised, but which live up to the demands and challenges that must be made of upper secondary education.[24]

The reform of technical and vocational education in Denmark was set in motion by structural changes in the employment market, technological development and international competition. It was therefore natural that in the 1980s Denmark also became involved in Eurotecnet II, one of the EC's action programmes that aimed at raising the level of technical and vocational education through the interchange of teaching experience in the field of new information technology (NIT). In step with the realisation of the reform it must be expected that international activities will be further expanded.

Further and higher education

This sector contains many and varied types of education, provided partly at the universities in Copenhagen (founded in 1479), Aarhus (1928) and Odense (1964) and the university centres in Roskilde (1970) and Aalborg (1974), and partly at a large number of specialised institutions, among which the following have research commitments: the Technical University of Denmark (1829), the Danish Academy of Engineers (1957), the Royal Dental College of Copenhagen

(1888), the Royal Danish Veterinary and Agricultural College (1856), the Royal Danish School of Pharmacy (1892), the School of Economics, Business Administration and Foreign Languages in Copenhagen (1917) and Aarhus (1939), and the Royal Danish School of Educational Studies (1856).

Among the institutions that do not offer postgraduate research facilities can be mentioned almost 60 teacher training colleges, kindergarten and recreation-centre teacher training colleges and home economics teacher training colleges. This group also comprises the eight state-recognised engineering colleges and a number of further social and health education institutions (nursing, physiotherapy, midwifery and others).

Like other Western European countries, Denmark experienced a rapid increase in admissions to further and higher education in the 1960s and 1970s. The increased costs of this educational explosion, together with the cutbacks in resources from the mid-1970s, provide an explanation for the intensified state planning that these courses have been subjected to during the past 20 years. Another explanation is, of course, that they have increasingly become part of the production apparatus in international economic and cultural competition.

The Directorate for Further and Higher Education under the Minister of Education and Research is the supreme administrative authority for this sector. The Advisory Committees to the Ministry of Education on Engineering, Health Education, Social Sciences, Humanities and the Natural Sciences are permanent advisory bodies under the Directorate for Further and Higher Education. Under the Directorate for Research, the Research Policy Council and the six Research Councils are advisory bodies to the government and to parliament. An influential but less formal organ is the Danish Conference of Rectors, which consists of the heads of Danish universities and other research institutions.[25]

In 1977 restrictions on admissions to further and higher education were introduced. This was not simply due to capacity problems but also to the threat of unemployment among graduates – especially those with an education in the humanities or those whose education was mainly intended for employment in the public sector. (Today the percentage of unemployed humanities graduates – approximately 12 per cent, calculated as full-time posts – more or less corresponds to the national average.) Through regulation of admissions, students were guided away from 'unemployment studies' and in the direction of 'employment studies', namely studies that lead to employment in the private sector.

Another method was to remove the bias relating to narrow professional destination from the studies threatened by unemployment. Thus, in 1985 a new Executive Order for the humanities attempted to move this field of study away from its traditional field of employment, the *Gymnasium*, where it was estimated that because of the sharp decrease in the number of pupils there would be few opportunities for new posts this side of the year 2000. (That this prognosis proved not entirely correct was due to an increased interest in general secondary education – the *Gymnasium* and *HF* – at the expense of the vocational and technical schools.) The Executive Order opened the possibility for students to combine their studies with elements other than those of the two subjects traditionally taught in the *Gymnasium*. The basic education could be supplemented with a considerable variety of modules from such subjects as computer studies, the social sciences and the natural sciences, which it was presumed would enhance the usefulness of graduates to the private sector.

To some extent it was the same ideas that motivated the three-year bachelor degree courses introduced on the Anglo-Saxon model in the summer of 1990. In principle these courses consist of a two-year basic module, to which other elements corresponding to one year of study and chosen by students from outside the introductory course must be added. It is too early to say to what extent graduates with this new degree will be welcomed by the private sector, where it is still relatively unknown. In favour of this innovation it was argued that it would provide a broader basis for students and thereby improve their chances of employment. It would, furthermore, reduce the drop-out rate by giving an earlier chance of completing a degree course – in other words, shorter periods of study for the many who get stuck at a late point in their studies. It was also claimed that it would result in more places in higher education becoming available, since not all students wish to have a lengthy education, and in more researchers because the long degree courses can be made more research-orientated. Moreover, it would make it easier for Danish students to study abroad when they could refer to a completed degree course and a title that would be recognised in other countries.

With regard to research, the government adopted in 1989 a Strategic Research and Development Plan for the Period 1991–94.[26] The plan aimed at an intensification of Danish research, not only by increasing research appropriations but also by achieving qualitative improvement through better application of resources. The plan also envisaged a considerable growth in the private-sector research and development contribution. Only in this way, it was said, would trade and industry be equipped to meet the challenges and opportunities of the Single Market. The goal was to bring the total Danish research and development investment up from 1.5 per cent in 1989 to 2 per cent of GNP in the course of the next decade. To this end the programme called for greater concentration and internationalisation of state-financed research and a more stringent qualitative selection of priorities. Research environments were to be larger, the most competitive environments were to be given priority and Danish firms and researchers were encouraged to take advantage of the benefits offered by international research cooperation in the European Community as a whole, Eureka or other international bodies.

After a debate in the spring of 1990 a parliamentary majority recommended the government to take steps to ensure stable development of state-financed research through, among other things, a strengthening of the management of research institutions, less detailed administrative control and greater attention to the evaluation of results and the training of researchers. These principles were in accordance with the above-mentioned research and development programme. In the mid-1980s the Research Academy was founded with the express purpose of improving the education of researchers in cooperation with universities, other public research institutions and the research units of the private sector. Denmark has derived significant benefits from EC research. Danish firms and research institutions have participated in a range of technology programmes, making prominent contribution in such fields as wind energy, marine research, electronic language processing, tropical medicine and in various natural science programmes.

There is an increasing tendency for the European dimension to be incorporated in the curricula of the individual subjects. This can be seen, for example, at the Institute of Philosophy, Pedagogy and Rhetoric at the University of Copenhagen, where comparative and international educational theory is now a component both of the bachelor degree course and of the superstructure course.

An indication of the considerable growth of interest in the relation between education, research and the EC is the increased amount of information on this subject, among other things, Danish participation in Eurydice, the publication of a new journal *EF Forskning og Udvikling* (EC research and development), which gives information about EC programmes in research and technological development.[27] Finally, in the spring of 1990 the Ministry of Education published the first complete survey of EC initiatives in the field of education.

The education, training and mobility of teachers

In Denmark three distinct forms of teacher training prepare teachers for three different institutions: the *Folkeskole*, the *Gymnasium* and the technical and commercial schools. No formalised pedagogical training is required of teachers at universities and other forms of higher education. Teachers at the University of Copenhagen, however, have the opportunity of participating in the pedagogical courses offered by the Institute of Philosophy, Pedagogy and Rhetoric. University teachers' pedagogical qualifications are discussed in the report to the Ministry of Education *Quality in the Humanities*, published by the Advisory Committee on the Humanities in September 1989. Pedagogical departments for university teachers are presently being developed in a number of faculties and institutions.

At the other end of the scale, in the pre-school area, the term used is not, as in many other countries, 'teacher training' but 'pedagogical training', as the concern of these courses is not so much with how one teaches young children, but more with how their development is strengthened through play and other non-teaching activities. Changes in this area are, however, possible as a result of the introduction of the 'coordinated school start' mentioned above.

The training of teachers for the *Folkeskole* takes place at 18 teacher training colleges in the form of a four-year course, which gives competence for grades 1–10. The Royal Danish School of Educational Studies is responsible for the further education and in-service training of this group.

A report published in June 1990,[28] from a committee established by the Minister of Education in 1987 for the revision of the present form of teacher training for the *Folkeskole*, recommended the retention of this four-year framework. The most striking proposed change was an increase in the number of lessons devoted to the two main academic subjects, that is, the two specialist subjects chosen by the student and studied with a view to teaching them in the *Folkeskole*. The motive was to give more emphasis to the students' own choices and to raise the academic level in the subjects taught. That there was reason to do so is suggested by the fact that at the time considerable criticism was being levelled at academic standards, not least at the teaching of foreign languages (English). The working group set up under the quality development project (see above) charged with analysing English teaching throughout the educational system concluded that one-third of the teachers of English in the *Folkeskole* were not formally qualified to do so. The new Act was passed in 1991.

For the two other forms of education, teacher training is given in a special course following the completion of the relevant degree course. For Gymnasium teachers this course (called *pædagogikum*) is arranged by the Ministry of Education, while the course for teachers at technical and commercial schools is under the State Institute for the Training of Vocational Teachers.

The administration, inspection and regulation of educational provision at local-regional level and national level

Danish education is administered by the state, the counties (14 in all) and the municipalities (277 in all). The process of decentralisation that has been taking place over a number of years received further impetus during the 1980s. Under the slogans of 'de-bureaucratisation' and 'autonomy' a number of the Minister's powers were delegated to the local authorities. Greater freedom in the choice of school was introduced, so that all parents were entitled to choose a school outside their own catchment area. And, in 1989, new, simplified regulations for the *Folkeskole* were introduced based on the principle of regulation via defined local objectives and framework in place of more detailed administrative control. The new provisions meant greater financial and pedagogical autonomy, increased parental influence and a strengthening of the position of the school principal.

Each school acquired its own board,[29] consisting of five or seven representatives elected by parents, two staff representatives and two pupil representatives. The individual municipality determines whether the staff and pupil representative shall have voting rights. The board determines the principles for the school's activities, its 'profile', within the framework defined by the local authority. The introduction at the same time of free choice of school has to a certain extent forced the schools to compete in terms of deciding on a 'profile'.

Today all institutions offering upper secondary education have boards like those of the *Folkeskole*. At the beginning of the 1990s, moreover, a reform of the financial management[30] of the individual *Folkeskole* was introduced – once again in the name of decentralisation and autonomy. Instead of grants for specific functions, schools now receive block or framework grants, which they may dispose of freely. The size of these grants is determined by the so-called 'taxi meter' principle, according to which the grant paid is related partly to the number of pupils enrolled and partly to the number who complete the course of education in question. Within this framework schools are largely free to spend the money in accordance with their consumers' wishes.

Together with the administrative reform described above, the reform of financial management gave consumers relatively more influence on educational institutions, and in a period with a declining school-age population the taxi meter principle automatically resulted in cuts in the education sector. But, as the report on the financial administration system optimistically wrote: 'greater freedom for institutions to adapt to consumer wishes and new educational needs in trade and industry can contribute to a greater dynamism in the educational system and counteract a tendency towards professional stagnation that can easily be the consequence of the decline in the number of pupils'.

The issue of language

Except in a few foreign schools, teaching everywhere in Denmark takes place in Danish. At only one *Gymnasium* is an experiment in progress, with teaching in English. On the other hand, foreign-language textbooks (mainly in English, less so in German and French) are widely used in further and higher education. At the universities, actual teaching in one or more foreign languages is becoming necessary in order to attract students from abroad; for example, under the Erasmus programmes. In addition a large number of courses in English are already on offer for various subjects and topics. Conversely, a strong secondary motive for Danish students to study abroad is their wish to become more proficient in the foreign language in question.

Even though Danish is understood by more than 20 million Scandinavians, it is nevertheless a small language area seen in an international perspective. There is therefore a strong interest in foreign-language learning, which is accompanied by an on-going discussion as to its placing in primary and secondary education. At what age should we start English (the first foreign language)? Should German or French be the second foreign language? And when should the second foreign language be introduced? Is Danish foreign-language teaching good enough?

Denmark has strongly supported the establishment of the Lingua programmes for language students. There is a natural interest in becoming better at expressing oneself in foreign languages and also in strengthening the position of the Danes' own language. The closer association with Europe through the EC/EU has not so far meant that the increased interest in foreign languages has taken place at the expense of Danish. Rather it appears that the focus on foreign languages has led to a similar increase of interest in learning Danish.

Reforms in the 1990s

Two in particular of the major reforms implemented in the field of education since the accession in 1993 of a government headed by the Social Democrats merit further description. The first was the passing of a new *Folkeskole* Act in 1993 to replace the old Act from 1975. Preparations for the new law were begun under the previous liberal, right-wing government, but it was the Radical Minister of Education Ole Vig Jensen who saw it through parliament.

The new Act differs from its predecessor on the following ten points:

- an amended objects clause, which emphasises that pupils must learn about Danish culture and gain insight into other cultures and mankind's inter-action with the natural environment;
- a new compulsory project assignment in the ninth and tenth grades;
- a policy of no streaming by ability in the eighth to tenth grades;
- English introduced already in the fourth grade;
- schools encouraged to offer French as an alternative to German;
- introducing a new subject: nature/technical studies for grades 1–6;
- providing more lessons – also for the creative subjects;
- advising differentiated teaching according to pupils' needs;
- the use of interdisciplinary teaching;
- more attention paid to the needs of the weaker pupils.

The Act continued – or completed – the development towards an unstreamed school, as the streaming by ability which remained in the 1975 Act was now completely abolished. It is not yet clear how the possibilities presented by the Act for forming temporary groups of pupils from different classes and grades when there are practical and pedagogical reasons for so doing will be exploited in practice. But after the new Act the *Folkeskole* must today be characterised as a mixed ability, non-selective school for the 7–16-year-olds, even though teaching in grades 8–10 may in periods be organised in units based on the pupils' different needs and stages of development.

It is worth underlining the express intention contained in the Act that teaching in all subjects should take as its starting-point the individual pupil's qualifications and stage of development. In order to compensate for the abolition of streaming, differentiated teaching has in this way been made the basic principle for the organisation and implementation of schooling.

The compulsory project assignment in grades 9 and 10 was introduced to underline the interdisciplinary intention behind the Act. On the basis of a topic chosen by the school, the individual pupil or group of pupils formulates a task. The pupils plan, collect and process information and present the result.

As is customary in Danish school legislation, the Act was the product of broad parliamentary agreement, though not quite as 'broad' as on previous occasions, because the Conservatives chose not to support the Act, the motive for their refusal being that they did not wish to 'share responsibility for the introduction of the totally unstreamed school'.

The second noteworthy reform was a new Act in 1997 on the Training of Teachers for the *Folkeskole*. The new law was mainly motivated by the desire to strengthen the academic qualifications of teachers in the *Folkeskole*. The means to achieve this end was an increase in the number of specialist subjects studied – four instead of two, one of which must be Danish or mathematics. The goal was that teachers should only teach the subjects they have had as special subjects at teacher training college:

> Today [1997] it appears that far too many teachers teach subjects that they have not studied as specialist subjects at teacher training college. For instance, only 10 per cent of teachers of Christian studies have had the subject as a specialist subject or subsequently taken an in-service year's course in it.[31]

To make room for the new specialist subjects, cuts were made in a number of minor compulsory subjects, most of which can, however, still be chosen as specialist subjects. In addition, students must now complete a major assignment on a topic of their own choice based on one of their four specialist subjects and drawing upon the pedagogical disciplines. The general tendency of the Act is to ensure a strengthening of the academic side of teacher training through greater specialisation. Teacher training remains the province of teacher training colleges rather than of the universities.

Teacher training continues to be a four-year course of education and must comprise the following subjects (the figures in parentheses denote the proportion of the work in terms of a full year of study): Christian studies/human life (0.2), either Danish or mathematics (0.7), three specialist subjects (0.55 each = 1.65), a major assignment (0.15), pedagogical subjects (0.7), the school in society (part of the pedagogical subjects), oral communication (part of Danish), teaching practice (0.6).

Conclusion

At the beginning of this chapter three events were singled out as having exerted a major influence on the educational policies of the 1980s and 1990s: Denmark's entry into the Common Market in 1973, the advent of a liberal, right-wing government in 1982 and of a government under Social Democratic leadership in 1993. As has been shown above, a considerable number of reforms were implemented during this period, especially with respect to the various forms of secondary education for the age group between 16 and 19/20. It is difficult to determine to what extent these reforms are mainly due to the challenges expected to be met within the European Union, to the educational policies and ideologies that changing governments have sought to realise or to a general demand from a society undergoing a process of change. The three factors are inextricably mixed and have all played a part in the reform work that has been carried out.

With the completion of these major reforms there are grounds for believing that educationally Denmark is prepared to meet the challenges arising from the transition to a world that is becoming smaller and a market that is becoming bigger. Only time will show whether the reforms have been sufficiently relevant and radical. In the field of education the new challenges will manifest themselves in the areas described by the following questions. Is the general level of education sufficiently high and flexible for the individual to be able to adapt to changes in the employment market? Will Danish technical and vocational education make it possible for Danish production to benefit from technological development? Will foreign-language teaching be of a sufficiently high quality for the increased communication across cultural and linguistic borders to take place naturally and without impediment? And will research be of a quality to contribute to material and spiritual development in an international context?

Notes

The following references are with few exceptions limited to the official publications of the Ministry of Education.
1 *U90. Samlet uddannelsesplanlægning frem til 90'erne*. Ministry of Education 1978, vol. 1, ch. x.
2 'Frisind er ikke en åben ladeport', in *Politiken* 20 Nov. 1982.
3 See the preface in *Uddannelse*, 3/4–(19)90.
4 See *Uddannelse*, 1986, pp. 329–363.
5 See *Uddannelse*, 8–(19)89 and 7–(19)90, both of which discuss quality in teaching and education, and *Undervisningsministeriets nyhedsbrev* 3/3.
6 'Mål og med'. A discussion paper on quality in teaching and education. Published by the Ministry of Education (Oct. 1989).
7 *Fysik – kvalitet i undervisning og uddannelse.*
8 *Engelsk – kvalitet i undervisning og uddannelse.*
9 Henning B. Fonsmark, *Kampen mod kundskaber: et kritisk essay om en hovedstrømning i dansk skolepolitik*, Copenhagen: Gyldendal 1996; Maj C. Nielsen and Niels Chr. Nielsen, *Verdens bedste uddannelsessystem*, Copenhagen: Fremad, 1997.
10 'Frie skoler', *Uddannelse*, 5–(19)90.
11 'Historie 84'.
12 See, for example, *Uddannelse*, 7–(19)86.
13 *Om grundlæggende kundskaber*, Ministry of Education 1986. Other publications: *Praktisk-musiske fag i samordnet indskoling* (1987), *Natur og teknik* (1988), *Om mobning* (1989), *Fortællingen i skolen* (1989) and *Børn og udtryk* (1991).
14 *Pejling og perspektiv. Perspektivudvalgets rapport om almene værdier og grundlæggende kundskaber*. Ministry of Education, 1988.
15 See, *inter alia*, the so-called 'Drøvtyggerrapport'.
16 *Undervisningsministeriets nyhedsbrev*, 2/15.
17 *Undervisningsministeriets nyhedsbrev*, 1/21. Ove Biilmann: 'En ny læseplan og en ny slags undervisningsvejledning', in *Uddannelse*, 6–(19)90.
18 *Undervisningsministeriets nyhedsbrev*, 3/18.
19 *GL 100. Skole, stand, forening*, ed. Bryld, C.-J., Haue, H., Andersen, K.H. and I. Svane. Copenhagen: Gyldendal, 1990, p. 201.
20 Bertel Haarder, Jørgen Granum-Jensen and Asger Sørensen, *Kampen om gymnasiet*, Copenhagen: Gyldendal, 1982.
21 For a brief account, see *GL 100*, op. cit., pp. 131–144. See also *Undervisningsministeriets nyhedsbrev*, 1/3.
22 Mentioned in *Undervisningsministeriets nyhedsbrev*, 1/3, 1/21, 3/4. See also *Uddannelse*, 6–(19)89.
23 'Betænkning om grundlæggende erhvervsuddannelser' in *Betænkning* nr 1112. June 1987.

24 *Uddannelse*, 6–(19)89.
25 Administratively the universities are regulated by Styrelsesloven (Act on the administration of the universities of 1970 with subsequent amendments). An OECD report from 1987–8 pointed to a number of weaknesses in the present system of university management. In 1990 the criticism was followed up by a series of Danish reports from the Academy for the Technical Sciences (March), the Research Policy Council (August) and the Ministry of Finance (October).
26 *Undervisningsministeriets nyhedsbrev*, 3/3 and 4/8.
27 See *Undervisningsministeriets nyhedsbrev*, 3/16.
28 En ny læreruddannelse in *Betænkning* nr 1199. June 1990. See also Bo Jacobsen, *Fungerer læreruddannelsen?*, Ministry of Education, 1989; and *Uddannelse*, 6–(19)89.
29 See *Uddannelse*, 6–(19)90.
30 See Jens Peter Christensen, 'Aktuelle tendenser i uddannelsespolitikken', in *Uddannelse*, 6–(19)89.
31 *Undervisningsministeriets nyhedsbrev*, 2 June 1997.

4 Finland

Reijo Raivola

Historical and geographical context

Gustav Vasa (1523–60), king of Sweden-Finland was quick to assimilate the message of Martin Luther and the Reformation. The Church became an integral part of the state, that is, a state church. Luther's idea that each Christian should be able to read the holy scriptures was taken literally in the work of the Church. As early as the seventeenth and eighteenth centuries peripatetic schools, and occasions when the reading skills of the populace were put to the test, had ensured a distinctly widespread literacy. Holy matrimony was the Church's greatest weapon. No marriage could be solemnised unless those concerned could prove that they could read and had mastered the rudiments of Christian doctrine.

Finland came under Swedish domination, and for most of this period was a part of the kingdom of Sweden. Administration of the state caused a Swedish-speaking administrative staff and an intelligentsia to be brought into Finland. The schools were Swedish-speaking. Thus the children of ordinary Finns were compelled to learn Swedish on starting school. The first secondary school with Finnish as the language of instruction was established as late as 1858, although by the end of the nineteenth century the number of Finnish-speaking schools and Finnish-speaking pupils was greater than that of Swedish.

Basic education began to acquire an organisational form in the municipalities only as late as the 1860s, and the legislation on compulsory education only dates back to 1921. In the Nordic countries equality and social justice have a long tradition. When it proved problematic to establish state girls' schools (the first came in the 1840s), the American tradition of coeducation was eagerly adopted. Since the 1880s girls have been eligible to take the matriculation examination and thereafter to seek admission to university.

At the time of the Napoleonic wars Russia took Finland from Sweden and annexed it in 1809 as an autonomous grand duchy. In the following century Finland created its own political system, its own civil service and army, its own currency and organised various institutions of education into a system. The Eastern Orthodox Church increased its influence, becoming the second state church. Towards the end of the nineteenth century the Russian administration embarked upon an aggressive policy of Russification and a reduction in the degree of autonomy in Finland. This manifested itself in the compulsory study of Russian in the schools, with extremely bad results, as in many schools it became a point of honour not to do well in Russian studies.

Finland eventually began to live the life of a sovereign republic, having won its independence after a bloody war against Russia and a civil war (1917–18) – in the midst of the upheavals of the First World War and the Bolshevik Revolution. Many critics claim that independence was short-lived when, as the result of a referendum, Finland opted to join the European Union in 1995, the result of the vote being 56.9 per cent in favour and 43.1 per cent against (mostly those of the agrarian party and the left wing).

By surface area (338,000 square kilometres) Finland is one of the largest countries in Europe, but its population is a mere 5.1 million and population density 15 people per square kilometre. Finland lies between 60 and 70 degrees latitude north and is the northernmost state to carry out efficient agriculture. The arctic climate also makes its presence felt in the arrangement of school times. With one-fifth of the population concentrated in the metropolitan area of Helsinki there is a very large rural area which remains sparsely populated. The country's geopolitical position between the striving for power of both East and West has caused problems of its own. Finland has had a fate similar to that of Poland: ever since 1300 its eastern border has been subject to constant changes.

The sparse population causes expense in maintaining a dense network of schools. At the beginning of the twentieth century, when the compulsory school system was planned, it was accepted as a norm that a child's journey to school should not exceed 5 kilometres. This resulted in a preponderance of schools with one or two teachers. The major drift of the population to the urban areas as of the 1950s had the effect of thinning out the rural population still further, to the extent that it was no longer possible to maintain the existing network of schools. A difference in cost-effectiveness between the most and the least cost-effective schools might be as much as ten times expressed in terms of cost per pupil. This led to the closure of several hundred schools and the transporting of 20 per cent of pupils by bus or taxi to larger school units. Indeed, in certain municipalities school transport accounts for a large part of the costs of schools.

Despite earlier domination, less than 6 per cent of the population are Swedish-speaking now, but the influence of this minority in politics and economics is proportionately greater than this. In compulsory education Swedish is obligatory and civil servants are required to demonstrate their competence in it. The amount of time allocated to teaching foreign languages in the upper stage of compulsory schooling and at the upper secondary level renders the curriculum perhaps rather full and unbalanced. Historical reasons make Russian unpopular.

The education system

The two state churches (the larger being the Lutheran Church with 86 per cent of the population and the smaller the Eastern Orthodox Church with 1 per cent) make their presence felt in compulsory religious instruction according to which Church the pupils belong, there also being an option to take ethics instead. They are required to be a member of the Church whose doctrine they learn. The religious doctrines of the minority Churches may be taught if there are sufficient pupils in the school to form a group. Pupils receive a grade for religious instruction on their school reports and it also forms part of the matriculation examination.

In relation to the population, the number of educational institutions continues to be high. There are over 4,000 primary level schools and 800 secondary level schools. There are some 50 institutions of higher education, which means that there is a university or a non-university higher education institution (AMK) for every 6,500 of the population of university age. This may well be a world record. The overall student population in Finnish schools is 1.047 million.

In all types of institution the academic year is divided into two semesters. The summer vacation is as long as 2.5–3 months, in winter the lower and middle school stages have a one-week sport vacation, but the break between the two semesters around Christmas is a mere week or so. At the end of the 1960s the beginning of the school year was brought forward by 2–3 weeks when Finland changed to a five-day school week, but there was no desire to cut the summer vacation further. The view is that the dark autumn and long winter make a lengthy period for recuperation desirable. From time to time there arises a demand to increase academic efficiency by introducing a summer term. Students have the option of taking examinations and doing fieldwork in summer, but there is no contact teaching.

Structure of the education system

General

There is a separate network of schools for each linguistic group, Finnish and Swedish. Only a few institutions are bilingual.

Day care for children under school age is provided by municipal day care centres and in publicly supervised private homes where mothers take care of some extra children in addition to their own. There is no compulsory pre-school education in Finland. The term refers to the voluntary education of the 6-year-old, who in the following year will start school. Pre-school education is provided either by day care centres or by special classes annexed to the *peruskoulu*, compulsory comprehensive schools.

Compulsory education starts at the age of seven in the comprehensive school, which provides general education for the whole age group. It takes nine years to obtain the leaving certificate. There are very few dropouts, and the certificate entitles the school leaver to continue in any kind of secondary education. Those who have not decided on their further education or have not taken up employment or who want to improve marks in their school report may continue for a tenth year in the comprehensive school.

More than 50 per cent of graduates of the nine-year school continue their general education in the *lukio*, the upper secondary school. Studies usually take three years and end with the matriculation examination at the age of 19+. The curriculum consists of compulsory, optional and voluntary courses, and many schools are class-less, which gives the students the chance to progress at their own pace by effecting lessons of their own choice. The matriculation examination and the leaving certificate provide general eligibility for higher education.

At age 15 *ammattikoulu*, the vocational school, provides initial vocational training in most occupational fields. After compulsory schooling fewer than 40 per cent of the age group prefer the vocational track to the general (upper secondary) one. Vocational training is largely subject based. Apprenticeship training is marginal in Finland but it is increasing. Basic vocational qualifications require two to three years to complete. These qualifications confer general eligibility for post-secondary education.

Vocational colleges, or *opisto*, provide post-secondary level education (International Standard Classification of Education, ISCED 4 and 5) to those who have completed the general secondary education either in the *lukio* or in the *ammattikoulu*. It requires 2–4.5 years of full-time study to qualify, and the qualification confers general eligibility for higher education. Thus traditionally there have been two routes to higher education: a short one through the upper secondary school, *lukio*, and a long one through the vocational school and the vocational colleges (*ammattikoulu* and *opisto*). This form and level of education will be dismantled during the 1990s and for the most part redeveloped into a non-university sector of higher education, discussed below.

There are 20 university sector institutions, or *yliopisto*, in the country. Ten of these are traditional multidisciplinary full-range universities and ten are specialised institutions focusing on engineering and architecture, economics and business administration, industrial arts, and fine and performing arts. The basic degrees offered are a bachelor's degree (120 credits), a master's degree (160 credits), an optional licentiate (on the way to the PhD) and a doctor's degree (160 credits of postgraduate studies, beyond the master's degree). There is no special institution that could be called an open university, but the departments of continuing education and extension studies of the universities organise basic studies in most academic subjects, and sometimes up to the level of a full major (55 to 70 credits). However, these departments cannot award degrees.

Ammattikorkeakoulu or AMK institutions were created by legislation in 1991, first on an experimental basis, to offer non-university sector higher education. In 1998, 20 were given permanent permission to operate. The final number of institutions will be 27–30 by the end of the century. They operate parallel to the universities and award degrees equivalent to BA or BSc degrees, although the emphasis is on vocational and professional skills, applied research and product development. The study time varies between 3 and 4.5 years (120 to 160 credits).

Both supply and demand in adult education are very diversified in Finland. In 1996, 48 per cent of the population aged 18–64 years participated in some form of adult education. The main dividing line is between vocational and non-vocational adult education. The former can be categorised as self-motivated training, employment training (paid for and administered by the Ministry of Labour), apprenticeship training and in-service training. The main category in the latter is liberal education without fixed objectives which is a century old and mainly serves the need for recreation. The most important suppliers of adult education are adult education centres, folk high schools, summer universities, study circle centres, physical education centres, universities and AMK institutions. Evening classes are held in upper secondary schools and, of course, on radio and TV.

Pre-school education

In Finland pre-school education emphasises the idea of lowering the threshold to school access. Attendance is voluntary, but about 65 per cent of all six-year-olds attended in 1996. The National Board of Education and the National Research and Development Centre for Welfare and Health prepared new curriculum design guidelines for pre-school education in 1996. The aim was to create a learning environment which offers inspiring activities and an opportunity for children to develop in a holistic way. The principles in curriculum guidelines stress both the individuality of the child and its learning and socialising skills in groups. The curriculum is not divided into school subjects but into broad subject areas: language and communication, mathematical concepts, nature and environment, religion, ethics, physical education, health and arts.

The fact that the guidelines were prepared jointly by two public authorities of central government reveals the problematic nature of pre-school education in Finland. It is the responsibility of and legislated for by two different sectors: the welfare sector, which is the larger of the two, and the education sector. In 1996, 5,000 children received pre-school education in the compulsory comprehensive schools compared to 38,000 in day care centres. The original idea of the 1980s was to introduce pre-school education linked with comprehensive schools, because it would have made it also possible to offer pre-school education in the sparsely populated countryside. The major problem, however, is that day care is not free of charge, so parents of a child in pre-school education in a day care centre have to pay a fee, the amount of which depends on their income level. In comprehensive schools, pre-school education is free. The same principle applies to the cost of transportation.

In connection with preparing the new Bill for basic education, it was suggested that the child has the right to receive one year (at least 700 hours) of pre-school education, free of charge, irrespective of the provider. Municipalities were obliged to provide education, but parents could decide whether to make use of it. In the Bill of 1998 pre-school education is seen as an integrated part of lifelong learning with the aim of improving the child's readiness and willingness to learn and to help its smooth transfer from day care to education. Both lower stage compulsory school teachers and kindergarten teachers are qualified to teach in pre-school classes.

Compulsory education

The Constitution of Finland stipulates that general compulsory education must be provided free of charge. The latest legal framework for compulsory education is given in the Comprehensive School Act (1983), with Finns obliged to attend *biblio* school for a period of ten years, starting in the year in which they are seven years old. The obligation ends in the year they are 17 or when they have completed the nine-year comprehensive school curriculum, whichever occurs first. Usually it is the latter, because only 0.2 per cent of the age group leave the comprehensive school without a leaving certificate and 0.5 per cent repeat a class. Only for a tiny fraction of the age group do parents arrange private instruction. Within certain limits pupils are free to choose their school within the home municipality.

Nearly all (98.7 per cent) comprehensive schools are under municipal control and maintenance. The state supports teacher training schools for the faculties of education, a few foreign language schools in Helsinki (French–Finnish and Finnish–Russian) and schools for sensory and physically handicapped children. There are also a few privately financed schools, a Jewish school and some other schools outside the comprehensive school jurisdiction.

The comprehensive school is divided into the lower stage (years 1 to 6) taught by class teachers, and the upper stage taught by subject teachers. Pupils proceed automatically, however, from lower to upper, but usually the location of the school is different, because the proportion of the number of upper stages to lower stages is only 1:5.5. The school year begins in the middle of August and ends in the twenty-second week of the following calendar year and is divided into two terms. It consists of 190 working days. The number of lessons for an individual pupil ranges from 19–21 (1–2 class) to 30 (upper stage) on average per week.

According to the Comprehensive School Act of 1983 the aim of the school is to try to help pupils to become balanced, fit, responsible, independent, creative, cooperative and peace-loving members of society. The school is to educate pupils in morality and good manners and give them the knowledge and skills necessary for a start in life. The latest national guidelines for curriculum design were given by the National Board of Education in 1994. Local and detailed curricula are drawn up by local authorities and schools. The subjects included in the curriculum are stipulated in the Comprehensive School Act and the distribution of hours is the official government's decision. The maximum total of weekly hours over the entire six years of the lower stage is 144. The subjects are mother tongue (32 cumulative hours), arts and skills (music, art, handicrafts, physical education, 44 hours) and mathematics (22 hours). Eight hours are given over to the so-called A-languages (foreign language, usually English, or the second national language which begins in the third year). The minimum number of cumulative hours of compulsory common subjects for the three years at the upper stage is 70 and the maximum number of hours of optional subjects is 20. Most time is given to mathematics, mother tongue, A-language, biology and geography, B-language (a second foreign language in the seventh year) and physical education. An important part of the curriculum is pupil guidance in the form of two hours of individual discussions, group discussions on further studies and careers, visits to workplaces and to the upper secondary schools the pupils will attend later.

Of the 1996 age group finishing the comprehensive school, 55 per cent went to upper secondary schools and 34 per cent to vocational schools, while 4 per cent chose the extra tenth year of the comprehensive stage; 7 per cent did not continue their studies. Although more than 500 small lower stage school units have been closed since 1980 there still exist about 3,400 individual school units in the country, some of them in isolated areas. The number of upper stages is 626.

Upper secondary school

The upper secondary schooling for the age group of 16 to 19+ is provided according to the Upper Secondary School Act 1983 in 440 institutions (average size 236 pupils), maintained by municipalities. There are also some private schools. Since 1982 teaching in upper secondary schools has been organised into courses consisting of 38 lessons each. The school year is usually divided into five or six periods, each of which has a different 'menu'. The individual school can decide on the distribution of different courses into the prescribed periods. In 1994 it was made possible for all upper secondary schools to dispense with the traditional year's progression, leaving the order and placement of courses for the schools and students to decide. Some students, especially national or international athletes, take advantage of the flexible organisation to extend their own studies over four years.

The subjects and subject groups are defined in the Upper Secondary School Act and Decree of 1983. The government decides on the minimum number of courses in each subject and the National Board of Education decides on the broad guidelines for drawing up local curricula. The curriculum consists of compulsory studies, advanced studies and applied studies. The pupil has to complete 45–49 compulsory courses and the total minimum of 75 courses to be awarded a leaving certificate. Most emphasis is placed on mathematics (six basic and ten advanced courses), mother tongue, A-language and environmental and natural sciences (six courses each). Many pupils choose a C- and D-language in their programme. Because upper secondary school is no longer an elite school but the school of the majority, the workload may be too heavy for many pupils.

At the end of their study programmes, students take the matriculation examination, which comprises both optional and four compulsory subjects: mother tongue (Finnish, Swedish or Sami), the second official language, one foreign language (the A-language) and either mathematics or science and humanities. The humanities examination deals with several subjects: religion, psychology, philosophy or ethics, history, civics, physics, chemistry, biology and geography, from which the student is free to choose any combination. The different parts of the examination may be taken at the same time or spread over three different occasions. The examination is arranged twice a year. It is set and assessed at the same time nationwide by a committee appointed by the Ministry of Education. In addition to an upper school leaving certificate, a separate certificate is given for passing the matriculation examination. Each examined subject is assessed on a seven-grade scale from *laudatur* to *improbatur*. The matriculation report is extremely important for university admission, because only one-third of matriculated students are admitted to universities (a very strict *numerus clausus* is applied).

Of those who matriculated in 1996 only 17 per cent transferred to university in the same year, while 10 per cent went to the AMK institutions, 12 per cent to vocational colleges and 61 per cent interrupted their studies for a year or more. This makes it understandable that the average age of the first-year university student is higher in Finland than in most European universities: 21–22 years.

Vocational education

Radical changes and innovations have been implemented in post-compulsory schooling at age 17 in vocational education and training (VET) during the last 20 years. After reforms in the 1980s VET comprised 26 basic programmes leading to 220 school or college level diplomas or special options. The number of qualifications was further reduced to 170. In each of the basic programmes, the first-year syllabus consisted of general and vocational subjects that the three levels of VET (school level and college and higher education level) had in common. After the first year, students chose a specialist course from the different levels. Most students who studied for higher qualification levels already had a 2–3 years' school-level diploma or had passed the matriculation examination.

In 1995 the 26 basic programmes were discontinued and education in this sector was reorganised into seven extensive sectors: renewable natural resources; technology and transport; administration and commerce; hotel, catering and home economics; social and health care services; humanities and expressive education. The sectors include 77 basic vocational qualifications, which take 2–3 years to complete. The courses were originally intended for comprehensive school leavers, but in 1996 the direct route from comprehensive school to higher vocational education was blocked. The entrance to higher education level programmes was restricted to those with basic (*ammattikoulu*) vocational qualifications or the matriculation examination (a consecutive structure). There are now 53 qualifications within the above-mentioned sectors at the post-secondary or higher education level. By the turn of the century practically all the vocational colleges (*ammattikoulu*) will cease to exist, because they will be transformed into higher education type AMK institutions thus raising the level of education and qualifications of the teaching professions and merging some 200 colleges, or part of them, into 30 multidisciplinary institutions. They are the Finnish counterpart of the German *Fachhochschulen* or Dutch *HBOS*. One reason for the establishment of these institutions was the undervalued status of the vocational colleges between post-secondary and higher education (ISCED levels 5–6); another was the need to comply with the European Community directive of 1988 on the general system for the recognition of diplomas.

The aim of vocational training at the upper secondary level is to provide operational occupational skills together with a solid general education. Young people should have the competence to cope with a wide range of specific tasks in their field and to qualify for further studies. The National Board of Education prepares guidelines for curriculum design in collaboration with representatives of business and industry, labour market parties, research institutes and educational institutions. The personal learning plan of a student consists of basic studies that are common to the whole sector, orientation studies, common core studies and optional studies. Compulsory subjects are Finnish and Swedish, a foreign language, mathematics, civics and working life orientation, and physical education and health studies. Electives are taken from the following units: mathematics and sciences, arts and society, culture and philosophy, and ethics. Certain themes cut across all studies: environmental questions and sustainable development, communication and information technology skills, entrepreneurship, consumer issues, and occupational health and safety.

The Treaty of Maastricht very clearly states that questions of education are to be handled following the principle of subsidiarity. The Treaty forbids all attempts to harmonise educational legislation, structures and contents. Nevertheless, education is part and parcel of European labour and social policies, which lie at the heart of EU politics. Creating open European qualifications and education markets, demanded by Jacques Delors, makes vocational education (and training especially) a common policy issue in the entire Union. All national systems of education have to solve the same problems, which is to remove the barriers between vocational and general, scientific and practical, theoretical and instrumental curricula and their organisational solutions. The aim is to achieve parity of esteem between the two tracks of secondary and higher education. Spending too long on education in one institution, rather high drop-out rates and overlapping curricula and syllabuses were seen as a national drawback in Finland.

To answer these questions an experimental reform was initiated before Finnish entry into the European Community in 1991. The main principles guiding the work of 134 pilot institutions are freedom of choice that allows personal study programmes; cooperation between all types of educational establishments; and new learning environments and arrangements.

Organising inter-school cooperation has required modularising teaching, the joint timing of study periods, synchronising the timetables of participating schools and adapting the gradeless system of progress in student studies following interest groups. For upper secondary school students, 40 per cent is the maximum proportion of study that can be undertaken at other institutions. For vocational school students the proportion is 30–40 per cent, depending on the length of their studies. Knowledge and skills acquired outside any formal educational institution may also be recognised. The number of compulsory subjects is heavily reduced; for example, in the upper secondary school it is only four. It is possible for a vocational school student to pass the matriculation examination and for an upper secondary school student to acquire vocational orientation or even take a vocational qualification. This is expected to raise the level and prestige of the vocational sector and help Finland to compete in the EU market.

Higher education

The vocational sector

A binary system of higher education is being introduced during the 1990s in Finland. The vocational higher education reform was launched with the enactment of legislation on experimental AMK institutions, *ammattikorkeakoulu*. Under the Act, 22 institutions were established. In 1995 Parliament made the system permanent. By the year 2000 most post-secondary colleges of vocational education will be upgraded to AMK institutions, as already mentioned. A phase of experimentation must always precede the permanent foundation of an institution. Charters will be granted by the government on the basis of proven quality and achievement during the experimental period. It is thus continuous development and the gradual awarding of permanent operating permission that lie at the core of the strategy.

The main objectives of the reform were defined as follows:

- to raise the standard of higher vocational education by one ISCED degree. The diploma is equivalent to a university's bachelor degree;
- to react to changing needs for broad expertise and renewable skills;
- to make vocational education more attractive to secondary school students;
- to improve the international compatibility and to raise the status of higher vocational education;
- to rationalise and fine-tune the education system by amalgamating small colleges into larger, more efficient, multidisciplinary units;
- to decentralise the administration;
- to reinforce the regional and local impact of vocational education.

Education–workplace interaction is a key component of the reform. New institutions are expected to perform the role of innovation and service centres for local industries.

AMK studies comprise basic and vocational studies, elective studies, practical training (20 credits) to boost occupational skills, and the preparation of diploma work. Studies are organised as 120–160 credit degree programmes approved by the Ministry of Education. The fields of study are the same as the secondary stage except in the humanities and education sector, which is directed more towards sport and recreation. The institutions are owned by municipalities, federations of municipalities and private foundations. Institutions are mainly financed from the state budget and by contributions from students' home municipalities.

The universities sector

The first university in Finland was established in Turku in 1640, from which city it was transferred to Helsinki in 1828 after the great fire of Turku. With 33,000 students, the present University of Helsinki is the largest university in Finland, its constitutional autonomy also making it the most prestigious. In the 1960s and 1970s considerations of regional policy and educational equality caused an expansion of university access to the northern and eastern parts of the country. This expansion involved the upgrading of colleges of art and craft to university status and the upgrading of the education of teachers in the lower stage of the comprehensive school to that of the master's degree. In 30 years the student population has increased sevenfold in three waves: in the 1950s the growth was in the humanities and mathematical and natural sciences; in the 1960s in the fields of jurisprudence and social sciences as a project of the expansion of the welfare state; and since the 1970s in the name of economic competition in the technical and commercial disciplines. The latest reform has been to raise kindergarten teachers' education to the level of BEd in 1995.

There are altogether 20 university-level establishments in Finland, all state institutions (in which the highest category of post is that of professor), in which masters' degrees may be taken and which are entitled to award doctoral degrees. The annual intake is 17–18,000 students, the total student population numbering 135,000 (of which only 2 per cent come from outside Finland), while the teaching staff now total about 7,500. The universities themselves decide on the number of new students they take within the bounds set nationally by the Ministry of Education.

Two-thirds of the finance comes from the state budget and the remainder from chargeable services and other external sources. The cost of the universities accounts for some 0.7 per cent of GNP. Since degree students are not required to pay any tuition fees, there is little purely private financing (5 per cent). This one-sidedness in finance is problematic, since in the recent economic recession (1992–5) the allocation of finance to the universities dropped by 17 per cent, notwithstanding that the number of students increased by 15 per cent. The explanation for the marked and rapid growth in student numbers is the poor youth employment situation. Increasing the number of university places was a measure of employment policy paid for in the first year by the Ministry of Labour, but thereafter left to the universities to finance.

Each university negotiates individually with the Ministry regarding its goals for the future and the resources needed to accomplish them. The greater part of the resources allocated comprises operating costs, mostly to pay the salaries of tenured teaching posts. Some 10 per cent is to cover producing given numbers of masters' and doctors' degrees or to make up the discrepancy. Some 5–10 per cent is earmarked for the implementation of new research or teaching projects. The system is based on overall funding as opposed to the earlier precise division of resources channelled to different uses, and the universities can now themselves decide how they dispose of their funds, or as a senior ministerial official put it:

'Would you prefer to hire a professor or buy some computers?' The ruling admin-istrative ideology is management by objectives and results, which manifests itself in decentralisation and deregulation and an increase in marketisation. What was once advance planning has become retrospective monitoring of results.

Key problems facing the universities

These have been identified as: insufficient competition between universities; resulting in overlapping activities; rigid models for operations and adminis-tration; long duration of studies; and high age of graduates. The average time for the completion of a masters' degree is 6.5 years, for architects as much as 10 years. The average age of those completing masters' degrees is over 27 years, and for those completing doctoral degrees almost 38 years. In the natural sciences and in certain humanistic disciplines, dropout or change in the major subject is common. There are many reasons for dropping out or changing the major subject; it is difficult to get into university (only 35 per cent of matriculated students do so), and those entering the universities are clearly over the age of 20. The most difficult subjects to get to study are arts subjects (10 per cent or less of applicants are successful), psychology, law, medicine (15 per cent) and veterinary medicine. Places are most easily found in the universities of technology (65 per cent), where some students are admitted without an entrance examination if they have taken the long option in mathematics in the matriculation examination. Health care and natural sciences also admit over half of those who apply. Of those selected to complete the studies required of a subject specialist schoolteacher, only 27 per cent are men. The most male-dominated area is engineering, with 82 per cent men, and the most female-dominated area is veterinary medicine with 92 per cent women. Almost 70 per cent of students engage in salaried work in term time. Doctoral studies are generally undertaken alongside salaried employment. Many students take considerably more credits than the minimum required for the master's degree (160–180 credits). The poor employment situation is not conducive to qualifying quickly. Of those taking an academic degree 17 per cent already have some qualification in addition to their matriculation qualification.

At the beginning of the 1980s changes were made in subject discipline choices and free university study to encourage education programmes which respond better to the needs of economic life. These programmes include, in addition to the advanced studies in the major subject, 10 per cent of scientific and social general studies and two or three subjects taken as minors. At the same time the lower academic degree was abolished, but was restored in the mid-1990s. In 1997, the new two-cycle degree structure was adopted in most disciplines. The aim is that students complete BSc studies in three years (120 credits) and the master's degree in five. At least 75 per cent of the new entrants are expected to complete the higher degree. The purpose of the reform was to bring about a degree structure compatible with EU norms, to provide students with the opportunity to combine studies across disciplinary and institutional boundaries, and to establish closer links with the life of work (practical training is obligatory). Other essential objectives are reducing dropout numbers and speeding up studies. Students can receive financial aid for a maximum of 55 months for master's studies (plus 15 months extra for further studies).

In order to raise the quality and efficiency of doctoral studies and to lower the average age of new doctors, the Academy of Finland and the Ministry of Education created in 1995 a graduate school system for post-graduate studies. In the first year there were already about 100 schools in operation offering full-time, salaried posts for a thousand students for four years. At the end of the 1990s about 1,500 students are expected to complete their doctorates each year, and a heated debate is going on both in academic circles and in mass media about the functionality of the over-production of doctors. Doctors in medicine, engineering and natural sciences might be absorbed by huge university hospitals and the expanding hi-tech sector of industry, but what about doctors in social sciences, education and humanities? The public sector, including the universities, has stopped expanding and the private sector does not see what added value doctors could bring to the company. Critics foresee that underemployed (or unemployed) doctors will demonstrate the diploma disease and inflation of education at its worst. Certainly the rate of return on educational investment to individuals has declined very clearly since the end of the 1970s.

Adult education

Educational costs in the Finnish national budget in 1996 amounted to FIM26.5 billion, of which 13 per cent was allocated to adult education. Adult education is one of the main areas targeted by the government for further development. The reason is obvious: of Finns in the age group 25–34 the proportion of those with a qualification after the basic level is 81 per cent, but for the age group 55–64 it is only 30 per cent. This difference is the greatest in all OECD countries. Educational reforms generally reach most effectively the young age group currently involved in formal education, which has caused the disparity in education between the age groups to grow. Now, however, the population of Finland is ageing rapidly. The largest age group of all time was born in 1947, when the fertility rate was 3.6. Now it is a mere 1.8, that is, the nation will not renew itself without immigration. Within the next 20 years the average age will rise by five years to 43. The proportion of those over the age of 65 will be almost 50 per cent greater, and the proportion of those of working age will drop by over 10 per cent. At the present moment, owing to high unemployment, the maintenance ratio gives cause for concern: for every worker there are 1.7 who are outside working life. Even if unemployment could be brought down, the achievement of pension age by the large age groups (those born between 1946 and 1950) will cause the maintenance ratio to deteriorate. While in the early 1980s the maintenance ratio (children and old people per 100 people of working age) was under 50, by the year 2030 it will be almost 70. Those of working age will need to be extremely effective in order to continue to produce the level of affluence to which people are accustomed.

At the same time the change in the occupation structure will continue. By 2020 there will be 40 per cent of Finns earning their living by information work. Even those with a good basic education will need to update and expand their expertise through further education. Finns are eagerly using the services of some 1,000 institutions of adult education. Of those of working age, almost half are involved in some sort of education. In 1996, 44.3 per cent of salary earners took part on average in four days of personnel training, the most enthusiastic being those living in towns, the well-educated, women and those employed in service occupations. However, even among those aged 55–64 participation in personnel training amounted to 37.5 per cent. As the economic situation improves more personnel training will be available.

Divided by number of teaching hours, professional adult education is given for 62 per cent of the time and liberal education for 38 per cent. Of this, 25 per cent is qualification-orientated and 75 per cent is supplementary education. Fifty-one upper secondary schools provide general education leading to the matriculation examination for adults. Vocational adult education centres are mostly municipal. All 46 institutions organise mainly labour market and employment training. There are 90 folk high schools in Finland. They are privately owned, usually have an ideological mission and operate as boarding schools in the field of non-formal general studies. Adult education centres (275), owned by municipalities, aim to meet local educational needs. They provide non-vocational general education: teachers, foreign languages, arts, social studies and other; 57 private specialised vocational institutions receive state aid to meet the needs of trade and industry. Study centres are maintained by civic organisations (trade unions, political parties, Christian associations). There are 14 sport education centres and 84 music institutions categorised into three classes: music schools, music institutes and schools. Vocational training leading to certified professions is provided only by conservatoires.

Teacher education

Finnish teacher education was systematically organised in the 1860s. Uno Cygnaeus, the 'Founding Father' of compulsory education, designed a co-educative, four-year seminar with an affiliated kindergarten for the education of primary school teachers. The design and the curriculum were influenced by seminars in Wettingen and Bremen. In comparison to seminars in Europe and in the USA, the seminar was both organisationally and educationally of a very high standard. The first university summer courses for primary school teachers were offered in 1907, and in 1934 the first college of higher education for teacher training was established in Jyväskylä.

In the early 1970s both primary and secondary school teacher education was transferred to universities, and since the early 1980s all prospective teachers have to earn a master's degree. Since 1995 kindergarten teachers have to study for a bachelor's degree.

Class teachers graduate from the eight faculties of education with a major in education, and subject teachers from the departments where they study 2–3 subjects to be taught later in school. Teacher education departments organise 35–40-credit pedagogical studies with practice in normal schools which belong to the faculties of education. All teachers in vocational education must have work experience and 15–40-credit pedagogical studies in a university or in an *ammattikorkeakoulu.*

There are about 61,000 teachers in formal education, of whom 61 per cent are women. The retirement age is 63.

Internationalisation of Finnish education

The remote situation of Finland on the far side of the Baltic Sea in the north-eastern corner of Europe – it is 4,500 kilometres from Rome to Rovaniemi, the gateway to Lapland – has not tempted strangers to visit the country. For 700 years strangers meant conquerors, and the Finns have come to regard strangers with caution. Even in times of economic growth there has been no need for foreign labour. Of those living in Finland at present, only 1.3 per cent are foreign nationals, and 20 per cent of these are refugees. On the other hand, the Finns, in the hope of greater prosperity, have been keen to emigrate. Had there been no exodus after 1860 the population of the country would now be almost 40 per cent greater. The doors have been kept shut against strangers and internationalisation has taken the form of emigration. Consequently, Finland continues to be one of the world's most homogeneous countries as regards race, language and religion and so, incidentally, affords an excellent opportunity for research into hereditary diseases.

Internationalisation has been slow and has largely advanced through Nordic cooperation. In 1952 passports were abolished for citizens to travel between the Nordic countries, and the Nordic Council was established that same year. Geographical proximity, a common religion and, through Swedish, a common regional language, the common conception of the Nordic welfare state, shared values and legal tradition have held Finland to the Nordic community. The Nordic Council of Ministers has administered the exchange programme Nordplus for higher education. It was partly designed after the model of Erasmus in 1988 to gain experience for wider European cooperation. For trainee exchanges in the field of technology there is a corresponding programme Nordtek.

A more noticeable change in the internationalisation of education came about in the late 1980s. As a forerunner of full EU membership Finland joined the Comett programme in 1990 and the Erasmus programme in 1992–3. Now the target has been set that one-third of undergraduates in both universities and AMK institutions (a total of 13,000 students per year) and all postgraduate students should complete part of their studies in a foreign country. This target has not yet been reached but, in relation to population, the Finns are among the most eager participants in the Leonardo and Socrates programmes. Internationalisation is perceived to improve the quality of teaching and learning, to improve competence in languages, to afford the opportunity to study what is not available in Finland, to enhance the student's independence and ability to orientate to a foreign culture, and, with the help of visitors to Finland, to enable the Finnish educational institutions to be multicultural. The number of those participating in exchanges for vocational education between 1993 and 1995 has grown by 80 per cent for those leaving Finland and by 200 per cent for those coming to Finland.

At the present time over 90 per cent of vocational institutions are involved in one way or another in international cooperation, the most common forms being personnel and student exchange, visits, instruction given in foreign languages and participation in joint projects. In 1995 a total of 2,250 Finns left Finland to study for a total of 6,900 months in the receiving institutions. The greater part of these were from the sectors of health care and commerce. Some 1,000 exchange students came to Finland for an average stay of four months. Only in forestry and wood processing were there more incoming than outgoing students.

Practical work experience abroad continues to be more popular than student exchange. Those leaving Finland numbered 5,900 and those coming to Finland some 1,700. The main countries of destination for Finns are the EU countries, the Nordic countries and Estonia. Those participating in an exchange are likely to choose a country whose language(s) can be understood or at whose institutions of learning teaching is given in a language which is manageable. Greece and Portugal are not common choices for Finns, nor is the Finnish language known in Europe, as it is not related to the language of any other EU country. This leads to a clear imbalance in personnel exchange. In order to redress this the Finnish institutions are compelled to offer teaching generally with English as the medium of instruction. In the vocational institutions in 1995 at least 38 courses of 40 credits were offered in a foreign language, 78 courses of 10–40 credits and 673 shorter courses carrying fewer than 10 credits. Elementary courses for foreigners are likewise arranged in Finnish and Swedish and in the culture of the country.

Finland has participated in international cooperation projects, notably in the development of teaching, research and product development, the main partners being Western Europe (37 per cent), Russia (16 per cent), Estonia and the other Baltic countries (16 per cent), the Nordic countries (8 per cent) and the Far East (6 per cent). The following are typical examples of projects coordinated by Finns: multiple uses of forests; distance education multimedia; teleservices and telenetwork for farmers.

After two years of the Leonardo da Vinci programme there were 123 Finnish-led projects with 166 partners from all EU countries (plus Norway and Iceland) and 14 partners from five associated countries. The most popular pilot projects are in the sectors of information and production technologies, environmental problems, and tourism and catering. Usually most partners come from the United Kingdom, the Netherlands, Germany and Sweden. The most important themes among strand I and III projects are: open and distance learning; the content and validation of vocational qualifications; and the relationship between training and working institutions.

Finland has been involved in Erasmus cooperation since the academic year 1992–3. In four years the ICPs have increased seven- to eightfold. In 1995–6 there were 250 outgoing and 1,401 incoming participants. The main Erasmus partners are the UK, Germany, the Netherlands and France. It is only with France that the ratio of exchange is evenly balanced. Most outgoing students were from the fields of economics (25 per cent) and technology (15 per cent). It may be seen as a source of concern that of those participating only 2.9 per cent were studying humanistic subjects. High hopes rest on such students that they will act as facilitators and interpreters in the process of European integration. More participation from men would also be desirable; they account for only one-third of participants. In the universities there are some 300 courses of study covering one or two semesters. The possibility exists to take several complete degrees in English. Prognoses for the academic year 1997–8 showed that 6,300 students and 1,600 teachers were to participate in an Erasmus exchange, of which over half were from the universities and a quarter from the AMK institutions. Problems of transferability are generally taken care of by the ECTS system. In all categories Finns are generally among the most eager applicants.

Finnish schools have also been keen to participate in the Comenius programme, including schools from all over Finland with the exception of north-ernmost Lapland. The programme enables schools to achieve an international profile. More 'European ingredients' enter their curricula and can extend their foreign language teaching. Likewise pupils' language competence improves and learning outcomes are generally better. They can make first-hand acquaintance with member countries' cultures, which duly enhances their capability for inter-national cooperation later on in working life. These schools and pupils retain their international contacts long after the support for cooperation has ceased. In the first academic year the Commission supported 460 projects, 18 of which were coordinated by Finnish schools, while they were partners in 10 per cent of projects. The forms of cooperation include electronic communications, videoconferencing, materials exchange, teacher exchange and independent fund-raising for pupil exchange and outward bound schools.

The homogeneous nature of the Finnish nation is reflected in the low degree of exploitation of the Comenius 2 programme (support for migrant workers, nomadic people and education of Romany people). Of the 160 projects approved by the Commission only two were coordinated by Finns. On the other hand, Comenius 3 (supplementary education for teachers) was better utilised.

The European dimension is among the main concepts in the EU memoranda and documents on educational policy. However, it was only the Brussels Green Book of 1993 which provided a more comprehensive content for the concept, emphasising the quantitative and qualitative improvement of language compe-tence. The small languages need special support; thus there was a warm reception for the Commission's assistance for the language training programme of 1996, through which small language teaching was given intensively in small groups to students arriving from abroad. It was a comfort to hear students report that Finnish is not such a difficult language as the Finns themselves suppose.

The European dimension also includes cooperation between institutions and personnel and student exchange, teaching about Europe in the curriculum, recognition of studies and qualifications and a comprehensive information network. Although education is a mainstay in the creation of a national identity and a sustaining power and source of national legitimation, it can also serve to educate people to be Europeans. The European identity extends to the recognition of common values, mutual respect and interdependence. Citizens must comprehend the geographical, cultural and social diversity and its historical lines of development. If the subsidiarity principle in education is given a dynamic interpretation, the educational policy of the European Community can support national education in the achievement of common goals. If Europe is understood as a common culture and interest area the concept of joint qualification and education markets is a positive one, which the education programmes of the Community are intended to promote.

From the Finnish perspective the main obstacles to cooperation between institutions are not only language and geographical location, but also many administrative variations such as semesters of different lengths, different vacation periods, the different ways of organising teaching work (in Finland the system of courses and classlessness in the upper secondary school, the different integration models for academic and professional education) and the various practices for covering the costs of studies (in Finland free study in all forms of school) cause difficulties in coordination. Differences in curricula, variation in teacher education, dividing up of the educational career into different levels of education, the compatibility of teaching and students' wishes, all render choices difficult. Perceived cultural differences between countries and their educational systems may cause the newcomer something of a shock. Yet the great popularity of education and action programmes shows that there has been a considerable effort to remove obstacles. In Finland it is the Centre for International Mobility (CIMO) and the National Board of Education which serve as the coordination organs in the internationalisation of Finnish education and offer information via the Internet and elsewhere.

Developing Finland as a cultural information society

In 1995 the government decided on the principles for the development of Finland as an information society, in accordance with those of the European Council in Corfu in 1994. The starting point is that in the information society knowledge is the key resource leading to advances in information and production technology, restructuring the social and productive relationships, and becoming a common product to be sold and bought on the market. Old education cannot thrive in a new society.

Educational systems are not guided only by binding norms, that is, acts and decrees, but also by decisions of principle, memoranda and committee reports. In 1994–6 the government and the Ministry of Education were strikingly active in producing strategic documents for the development of education. The most important of these were the *Development Plan for Education and University Research* (Government Resolution, given every four years); the *National Education Strategy* (Ministry of Education); *A Finland of Knowledge and Know-How* (Science and Technology Policy Council); *Education; Training; Research in the Information Society* (Expert Committee); and *A Finland of Culture* (Expert Committee). In these documents guidelines for the coming millennium are given: goals and objectives for all levels and forms of education, criteria for curriculum work at primary and secondary levels, development plan for structural changes, and most importantly – from the practical point of view – quantitative objectives for admission to institutions and their 'end products', that is qualifications, diplomas and degrees at different levels and forms of the system.

The development of Finnish education will be focused on:

- the principle for lifelong learning;
- responding to changes in the content of work and in occupational structures;
- internationalisation;
- introducing a more varied language syllabus at all levels (especially German, French and Russian);
- implementing information strategy for research and education;
- recognising sustainable development and applying it in practice;
- improving mathematics and science skills;
- emphasising the cultural missions of schools and universities;
- providing basic educational security;
- strengthening the status of evaluation as a tool for ensuring quality of education.

All levels of education and training from comprehensive schools upwards must teach the necessary basic skills in information technology, management of information, and communication. Teachers' initial pre-service and in-service training are the key components in the adaptation to new competencies. The whole education system will be brought within the research of information network services. Open and distance learning will be promoted at all levels of education and training. Public libraries will be supported as centres in the open information network for the use of those citizens who have no equipment at their disposal at home. Finland is already fairly well advanced in the use of modern technology. One-fourth of export income comes from hi-tech. Information is readily available to people throughout Finland. The Finns have 63 per 1,000 Internet connections, more than 12 per cent of adult people over 15 years old using the net every week. Mobile telephone extensions are among the most used in the world. All scientific libraries and about 80 per cent of municipal libraries have computerised library systems. Most of them are connected to a common network.

Conclusion

In the spring of 1997 the government presented legislation to parliament in which 26 laws governing education were to be reduced to ten. Likewise the separate legislation for each individual university is to be unified. The purpose of the reform is to render the education arrangements more flexible by taking into consideration the learning needs of those of different ages and by abolishing the bureaucratic differences between the different forms of institutions. Administrative boundaries have hindered cooperation and effective operation. For example, there is now a desire to remove the structure of competence, tenured post and salaries linked to individual types of institution in order to facilitate the more flexible use of teachers in different institutions. Local decision-making power is being increased. The basic security of education, the opportunity to study according to one's own requirements is to be guaranteed to all. Places in higher education will be provided for two-thirds of the age group, of which 62 per cent will be in the non-university sector and 38 per cent will be in the universities.

Teaching and research are vital aspects of the Finnish welfare and economic development strategy, as indeed they have been ever since the 1950s. Education is being further developed with the objectives of high quality, equality of educational opportunity and the principle of lifelong learning. In EU education and research policy Finland takes initiatives but safeguards the interests of her own citizens. The view is therefore taken that there is no reason to increase the authority of the EU in the fields of education and research.

References

Council of the State 1996: *The Development Plan for Education and University Research*. Helsinki (in Finnish).

Finnish Leonardo Centre 1996: *Leonardo da Vinci Programme*. Helsinki.

Ministry of Education 1995: *Education, Training and Research in the Information Society*. Helsinki.

Ministry of Education 1996: *Higher Education Policy in Finland*. Helsinki.

National Board of Education 1996a: *International Activities of the Institutions of Vocational Education in 1995*. Helsinki (in Finnish).

National Board of Education 1996b: *The Development of Education 1994–1996*. Helsinki.

Ollikainen, A. 1997: 'Finland'. In National Agency for Higher Education, *National Policies for the Internationalisation of Higher Education*. Stockholm (in Swedish).

Raivola, R. 1994: 'Adult Education in a New Europe'. In M. Parjanen (ed.), *Outside the Golden Gate*. University of Tampere: Institute for Extension Studies.

Science and Technology Policy Council 1996: *A Finland of Knowledge and Know-How*. Helsinki (in Finnish).

5 France

Françoise Convey and Nicole Vigouroux-Frey

The education system: past – present – future

French pupils and teachers have probably lost count of the many reforms which have, since 1945, lined the pathway of the long-suffering consumer, who is always prepared for the next modification which is never long in coming once a new minister and his team take up office. This then proceeds to create turmoil at regular intervals – *démocratie oblige* – for a significant cross-section of the nation. Yet it seems that this has never really managed to endanger the pyramid-shaped edifice of the French educational system, a public service which has been built up patiently over 200 years.

The most recent measures affecting the French education system stem from the *Loi d'Orientation sur l'Education* (or *Loi Jospin*) of 10 July 1989 (Act 89–486) and look as if they may prove to be more permanent in the long term. This is so because, despite the changes that have taken place on the French political scene since then, there has been a thread of continuity in the reforms started in 1989. Indeed, the preamble to the *Loi d'Orientation* states that:

> Education is the first priority of the nation. It is a public service planned and organized around pupils and students. It contributes towards equality of opportunity.

> Education is a right guaranteed to each individual in order to allow for the development of the personality, the improvement in the level of initial and continued education, the induction into social and professional life and the exercise of citizenship.[1]

This is an education system written into the rule of law, which guarantees access to education for everyone; a system, however, which is in no way set in stone, as demonstrated by the succession of education reforms which have been implemented since 1945.

An historical overview: towards a state monopoly

In the Middle Ages, the Church in France established itself as the main source of access to education, and for a long time remained its main provider. From the sixteenth century onwards, the period of the Reformation, the Humanists struggled to transform universities into non-religious public institutions. The influence of the civil authorities increased up until the Revolution, particularly as a result of the expulsion of the Jesuits ordered by Louis XV. In the eighteenth century, the *philosophes* hoped for an education system under the sole responsibility of the state: the Revolution would draw its inspiration from their ideas. After 1791, the notion of non-fee-paying state education (*instruction publique gratuite*) became law, together with the pattern of the three successive levels of education as we know them today: primary, secondary and higher education (decree of 15 September 1793). Even though the Revolution spoke a great deal about the 'democratic school', without actually managing successfully to complete such a huge undertaking, one of its achievements was the creation of those prestigious institutions at university level such as *l'Ecole Polytechnique*, *l'Ecole Normale Supérieure*, *l'Ecole des Langues Orientales* and *le Conservatoire National des Arts et Métiers*, which still contribute so much today towards educating the nation's elite,

The Revolution did not have the time to follow its plans through to their logical end, although it had opted resolutely, by the decree of 17 Pluviôse An VI (January 1798), for tight state control over private education (including syllabuses and textbooks) and a state monopoly on all education matters. With Napoléon Bonaparte and the Empire, the principle of state pre-eminence reached its glorious zenith. The law passed on 10 May 1806 established the imperial university and the state monopoly on education. The *Grand Maître* of the university alone had the power to authorize the creation of what were then known as *établissements d'instruction*. Only seminaries, which were exclusively devoted to the training of priests, remained outside the *établissements d'instruction*. The impression that people in a number of other countries still retain of the French education system, one where all pupils open the same textbook at the same time (a conception which today is totally obsolete), originates directly from the imperial school. After the Restoration, the Bourbons retained the state monopoly, simply giving the control of religious education to the archbishop of the diocese concerned. Today, the monopoly system is slowly wasting away, with the exception of the examination system and the conferment of degrees and diplomas, which the state still retains as its educational responsibility and to which the nation as a whole remains very attached.

The foundations of the present education system were laid by the Third Republic and particularly by Jules Ferry who, as Education Minister, with the educational laws of 1881–2 established the basic principles of *l'école de la République*: an education system which is free, secular and compulsory (*l'école laïque, gratuite et obligatoire*). Under the Third Republic, education became more than ever a matter of political objective: the *nation*, the army and the school were all seen as tools for the unification of the French nation. In the long and passionate ideological debate of the time, education was seen as providing this unifying factor: the school is presented as 'the temple of the new faith' (*le temple de la foi des temps nouveaux*) and the teachers as its ministers. Indeed, the new secular moral code was based on the *morale laïque*, to be taught through compulsory lessons in *instruction morale et civique* (education for citizenship and moral education), which were to serve as a substitute for religious instruction in schools. This secular moral code was strongly associated with patriotic duty and values. The use of the French language too was seen as having a crucial function; it was a means towards national unity and unification, which would lead to the interdiction of the use of all regional languages and dialects at school and the elimination of these languages and cultures in France for a century and a half.

Since 1945, successive governments and ministers of education have shown themselves to be aware of the need to prepare young people for the next century through education, at times giving the impression of frenzy and haste which have marked the French education system throughout the second half of the twentieth century.

The organization of compulsory education: an analysis of its parts

Administrative components

Since the regional reforms of 1960, France has comprised 21 *circonscriptions d'action*. A twenty-second district (Corsica) was added in November 1970. These *circonscriptions d'action* became *régions* in 1972, before eventually being transformed into *collectivités territoriales* by the Act of 2 March 1982. The administration of these local authorities, the *collectivités territoriales*, is entrusted to a council of elected members (*conseil général*). The Act of 7 January 1983 defined the respective powers held by the *communes*, *départements*, *régions* and the state, and in addition two further Acts (those of 22 July 1983 and 25 January 1985) concentrated on the relationships between the *Ministère de l'Education Nationale* (Ministry of Education), the *collectivités territoriales* (local authorities) and the schools.

The *académies*, however, the administrative units for education, continue to correspond to the former structure of the *circonscriptions d'action régionale*, each *académie* being made up of one or more *départements* (in the case of Paris, which counts as both a town and a *département*) with a *Recteur* at its head. In total, there are 28 *académies* and, as a rule, the head office of the *rectorat* corresponds to that of the *conseil général*.

LE RECTEUR

In each *académie*, the *Recteur* is directly responsible to the Minister of Education and to senior officials of the Ministry. He or she is selected by the Minister and is responsible to the Minister for the education system within the *académie* of which he or she is in charge. The job may in fact be regarded as a kind of assignment. Normally holding a doctorate, the *Recteur* is appointed by decree by the President of the Republic and is generally chosen from amongst the body of university professors. The *Recteur* exercises authority over the three levels of education: primary, secondary and higher, and has the official title of *Chancelier* of the university or universities within his *académie*. He sees to the implementation of policies made by the Ministry and in turn informs the Minister about what is happening locally in the *académie*. The *Recteurs* also keep their local colleagues informed about developments and pass on details of directives emanating from the Ministry in order to ensure satisfactory implementation of any decisions taken at the top. However, they retain sole responsibility to the Ministry.

LES INSPECTEURS D'ACADÉMIE

The *Inspecteurs d'Académie* fulfil administrative functions. Selected according to a list of criteria based on competence and experience in the educational field (*liste d'aptitude*), they are appointed as inspectors 'in residence' in a particular *département*. This position was first created in 1808. Since 1945, however, the responsibilities of the *Inspecteurs d'Académie* have covered the organization of the entire education service within their *département*. Under the aegis of the *Recteur*, they deal with new building programmes and with the geographical organization of the services provided (or *carte scolaire*). With reponsibility for the organization of schools in their area, the task of implementing decentralization and region-alization, the transfer of powers from the central organs of government to the local education bodies initiated between 1980 and 1985, fall to the *Inspecteurs d'Académie*.

Their responsibilities are extensive: apart from being in charge of all educational services in the *département*, they also have the task of informing, advising and supporting the local *Inspecteurs Départementaux de l'Education Nationale* (IDEN), as well as individual headteachers, in matters concerning all the educational initiatives which are being taken.

The *Inspecteurs d'Académie* work in close collaboration with the *Recteur*, who delegates to them powers to inspect schools, to control their administrative management and to monitor the implementation of teaching methods. It is also the *Inspecteur d'Académie* who, on the recommendation of the headteacher, grades the individual school staff members for purposes of promotion. The powers of the *Inspecteurs d'Académie* are at their most extensive in primary education. Here, they have all the IDENs under their direct authority, they take charge of school inspections and, being responsible for the work of primary school teachers in the *département*, they effectively determine their careers. Their duties also include responsibility for technical education, extracurricular activities, sports, further and continuous education, school health services, provision of transport for pupils and the construction of school buildings. In the last two tasks they work in close contact with the *conseils régionaux et départementaux*.

Educational components

Education used to be compulsory between the ages of 6 and 14 years since 1945; however, the school leaving age was raised to 16 years by a government ordinance of 6 January 1959 which modified Article 92 of the 1958 Constitution. This has resulted in the concentration of a considerable part of the school-age population at the first level of secondary education – in the comprehensive *collège* – a tier of secondary education without any formal examinations governing the school syllabuses. With the abolition of the *certificat d'études primaires*, which used to be taken at the age of 14 years and which marked the official completion of compulsory primary education, the *collège* has become accessible to all. What remains today is the *brevet des collèges*, which now marks the end of the academic cycle of compulsory secondary education, and the *baccalauréat*, the national qualification to which the great majority of French people remain very attached and which completes the academic cycle at the upper level of secondary education. Success in this examination gives the candidate the right of access to university and other higher education.

PRIMARY EDUCATION

Nursery schooling is a fundamental stage in a child's education. Its benefits are recognized particularly in the primary school, especially where it involves children who by virtue of their immediate environment are more disadvantaged in their access to education. Children are able to start their nursery schooling at the age of 2 and those who do so have the advantage of a significant lead over other children, who would normally start nursery school at the age of 3. The aim of this lead is to restore equal opportunities as far as possible for the more disadvantaged children when they enter the primary school at the age of 6, where they stay until they are 11. An initial exposure to modern foreign languages, in the form of games and nursery rhymes, is sometimes provided. In any event, the 1989 *Loi d'Orientation* proposed that there should be a 'nationwide implementation of an experiment in modern language learning at primary school level'.

Primary school teachers, who used to be known as *instituteurs* or *maîtres d'école* and who up until 1990 were for the most part trained in the *Ecoles Normales*, have now given way to teachers who are the *professeurs des écoles*, trained in the *Instituts Universitaires de Formation des Maîtres* (IUFMs). The school syllabuses and directives, as issued by the Ministry of Education, remain just as heavily loaded and as specifically prescriptive as before. The idea in the words of the *Loi d'Orientation* is 'to give the nation a school which is strong, active, and looking towards the future'. At the heart of what has long been the pride of the education system, the permeating ethos thus seems not to have changed. However:

> In order to educate the adults of the twenty-first century, it is essential to modernize the primary school curriculum. This modernization comes with

the grouping of knowledge and skills into seven fundamental core areas of equal importance: French, mathematics, science and technology, history and geography, education for citizenship, art, and physical and sport education. Convergence does exist and interdisciplinary work is necessary among these subjects or disciplines; the essential point is to ensure the coherence of the system, as each and every one of these subjects plays a part in a child's general education.[2]

In primary education, emphasis is placed upon basic competencies, particularly the importance of learning to read. But the choice of teaching methods and the pedagogical approach adopted depends on the skills of the individual teacher: 'The teacher assumes pedagogical responsibility for the organization of school activities, within the framework defined in each *académie* for nursery and primary schools, including cases when part-time teachers are involved.[3]

Each primary school is led by a headteacher who is in charge of the school management and whose range of competence has recently been expanded to include the 'leadership of a team of teaching staff'.

Primary schools are organized into five stages, each of one year duration:

- *cours préparatoire*;
- *cours élémentaire 1*;
- *cours élémentaire 2*;
- *cours moyen 1*;
- *cours moyen 2*.

A feature of the French education system is the existence of the *redoublement*, which envisages pupils repeating a year of study considered unsuccessful. Although it is becoming less common than it used to be, it still is a *constat d'échec*, an admission of failure, since in the long term it can lead to marginalization of those pupils who have repeated a year or more in the course of their schooling. *Redoublement* takes place on the advice of teachers at primary level or the *Conseil de Classe*, where both parents and pupils are represented, at secondary level. In all cases, parents can appeal against the decision and these appeals are usually upheld, especially with younger pupils.

SECONDARY EDUCATION

The term *Collège* is used to designate the comprehensive-secondary school attended by all pupils aged 11 to 15. It includes the following classes: *sixième, cinquième, quatrième* and *troisième* (that is, years 1 to 4 of the secondary school). There is a common curriculum, both 'National and Republican'[4] which was put in place by an administrative decision issued on 14 November 1985, by Jean-Pierre Chevènement, the then Minister of Education. The allocation of teaching hours for each subject was first implemented at the beginning of the school year in 1986, starting with the *sixième*, followed by the *cinquième* in 1987 and so on.

The *collège* curriculum is a continuation of the subjects which have already been taught in the primary school. No distinction is made between major or minor subjects, the syllabus for which, as in the case of the primary school, is laid down by the Minister in consultation:

> All subjects are compulsory and aim to provide a full education. In addition to their own subject-specific objectives, they lead to the attainment of the three general objectives which are considered as having top priority: the *collège* must develop logical thinking; it must teach pupils how to master the three basic skills of reading, writing and interpreting images, as well as mathematics; and it must introduce the child to autonomous methods of working.[5]

Transforming a child who is becoming an adolescent into a socially aware human being seems to be one of the priorities in the new curriculum. From this viewpoint, the role of teachers as an educational focus is essential. As they are obliged to keep to the syllabus in force, teachers are duty bound not to go beyond what the syllabus prescribes. At the same time, they are free to choose any textbooks, according to the educational criteria and priorities to which they have subscribed in their contract of employment as teachers. Furthermore, they are free to decide on the teaching methods to be used, provided that they acknowledge pupils' right to diversity. The result is that 'it is necessary to diversify and to tailor teaching methods to suit individual needs so as to deal with the problems posed by the difficulties encountered by some pupils and the mixed ability nature of classes'.[6]

Nevertheless, the difference in the teaching time allocated to Civics and to French, for example, underlines the fact that the latter subject is regarded as the most important by parents and pupils alike. An option to introduce regional languages and cultures into the curriculum, from the *sixième* onwards, exists in some of the *académies*. This is the case of Breton, Occitan, Provençal and Corsican. In Corsica, a very successful experiment in 'Classes Med' has been conducted in a number of *collèges* where pupils are taught Latin, Italian and Corsican throughout the four years of study.

At the end of their schooling in the *collège*, between the ages of 15 and 16, pupils may take their first national examination, the *brevet des collèges*. The *brevet* is an examination which marks the end of compulsory schooling: it is not required in order to proceed beyond the *collège*, nor is it a prerequisite of the *baccalauréat*. However, the majority of pupils pursue their studies further in a traditional *lycée* (*lycée d'enseignement général* or *lycée professionnel*: LEG or LEP) or in a *centre de formation d'apprentis* (apprentice training centre).

A group of general inspectors, assisted by the *inspecteurs pédagogiques régionaux*, helps to ensure the effective implementation of the curriculum as a whole and subject by subject syllabuses of the *collège*. These inspectors also have the authority to perform a similar function in the post-compulsory *lycées*. The keystone of the organization of the *collège* is the *principal* or headteacher. He or she is assisted by a management team and a governing body (*conseil d'adminis-tration*) and is responsible for the successful running of the range of services offered within the school.

The *lycée* is structured in a similar way to the *collège*, but with a *proviseur* at the helm, assisted by a double team, administrative and academic. The principal aim of the *lycée* is the acquisition of knowledge, which is tested through a national examination, the *baccalauréat*, the passing of which opens the door to higher education.

The *lycée* is essentially a service organization and its product is education. This explains why the *proviseur* is just as much a manager as a teaching specialist. Yet, by virtue of the particularly heterogeneous nature of the school population in terms of study objectives and motivation as well as social advantages, the *proviseur* ends up by administering an education system rather than actually shaping it. During the past two decades, the range of duties of the *proviseur* has included providing in-service training within the continuous education service, alongside teachers who work on this type of activity within the framework of GRETA (*Groupement d'Etablissements pour la Formation Continue des Adultes*), continuing education forming an integrated part of the state education system. The highly successful GRETAs were created in 1974 and they now number 315.

The *proviseur* is responsible for:

- maintaining the educational and civic values adopted by the institution;
- the provision of teaching staff and material resources and presenting emergency plans;
- the organization of the teaching in classes and subjects;
- the quality of teaching;
- interpersonal relationships amongst management, teaching and maintenance staff;
- consultations and meetings.

As a result of the processes of decentralization and devolution, schools have become very much like real businesses and they require their headteachers to have a range of technical administrative skills (in law and management, for example), interpersonal skills, teaching skills and cultural and social expertise which will enable them to identify the priorities and values for which they are responsible, and which will lead them to promote, with pride, a public image of a school community with a statement of aims and principles which carries its own stamp and which can kindle the enthusiasm of everyone concerned.

The actual recruitment, appointment or dismissal of teaching staff, however, is not included within the headteacher's responsibilities. Being civil servants, teachers are recruited as *professeurs titulaires* or *maîtres auxiliaires* by the Ministry of Education and are appointed to a given school according to existing vacancies.

When she was leaving Paris at the end

Teachers cannot be dismissed: they can only be moved or suspended or they can incur a reprimand (*blâme*) from an administrative tribunal, but only in cases of gross misbehaviour. Like their counterparts in the *collège*, teachers in the *lycée* retain the right to choose their teaching methods and teaching strategies. They must, however, take into consideration the diversity of the pupils entrusted to their care in a truly comprehensive education system; that is to say that the teaching must be both diversified and tailored to suit individual needs, with the aim of stimulating pupils' inventive skills and fostering their creative activity. By insisting on the rights and duties of those being taught, the 1989 *Loi d'Orientation* emphasizes a new approach to the education system, that of a negotiated *pédagogie du contrat*, which is 'part of the process of learning about citizenship' (see note 1).

The *lycée* teacher's overall educational responsibility includes a minimum of administrative duties, but particularly that of keeping in each class a *cahier de textes* to which the teaching team, pupils, parents and inspectors can refer. This *cahier de textes* acts as a record of class activities by date and subject. As a kind of class diary, the *cahier de textes* also records the contents of the written tests, titles or brief descriptions of lessons taught, and homework given. It is also of assistance to the *inspection générale* and to the headteacher, who is responsible for evaluating the teaching and administrative work of the teacher concerned. By recording all absences from each class throughout the school day, the teacher is helping to ensure the safety of the pupils and their families. In the event of accident and/or misbehaviour, the *cahier des absences* is a record which would relieve the school staff – and consequently the state – of any liability. Asking a teacher to supervise the pupils during break time or even to undertake a certain number of extra-curricular activities (such as visits to museums, surveys, school trips) is not ruled out.

The challenge of secondary education which has been set at taking 80 per cent of a particular age group to the level of the *baccalauréat* is not an easy one to meet. In 1997, 623,000 candidates sat for the *baccalauréat*: today 61.5 per cent of an age group are successful in taking the 'Bac', compared with 30 per cent only ten years ago. After repeating the year, 90 per cent of the pupils in their last year of study (*classe terminale*) eventually succeed in the examination. There is a choice of 12 different specialist sections. The majority will opt for a 'Bac Général' (literary, scientific, economic or artistic), while a small number will take a technological or professional *baccalauréat*. These were created ten years ago to provide direct access to the employment market, but the figures of candidates for the 'Bac professionnel industriel' and the 'Bac professionnel tertiare' are too small to appear in any statistics ('Les resultats du Bac 1997' in *Le Monde*, 27 March 1998 – an analysis of the performance indicators for the top *lycées* in the country). However, in view of its symbolic role, there is no question of doing away with the *baccalauréat*. It is perceived by families as a rite of initiation and a strong social signal, and of course it is a passport allowing entry to higher education. The debate is whether quality and quantity can be reconciled and whether the system should move towards democratization or just go for mass education.

The nature of the French educational establishment has been radically transformed in the space of a few years. The elements of this change take various forms: the modernization of the *collèges*, the globalization of funds, the notion of a development plan for each school (*projet d'établissement*), and the increased role of the boards of governors (*conseils d'administration*). Linked to these changes and to the reality of school life, the role of the headteacher has also changed. The challenge of taking 80 per cent of a particular age group to the level of the *baccalauréat* does create problems.

The training of teachers

By Act 89–486 of 10 July 1989 (Article 17 – *Loi d'Orientation*), the *Instituts Universitaires de Formation des Maîtres* (IUFMs) replaced the former *Écoles Normales* training institutions. They provide both primary and secondary training. The setting up of an *IUFM* in all 28 *académies* at the start of the 1991 academic year was a key measure in the reform of the entire education system. The *IUFMs* meet two stated objectives: first, to train teachers in possession of both a good academic education and professional skills; second, to recruit a sufficient number of teachers to meet the increase in the population of children of school age and to fill the large gap which will be left by teachers about to retire.

The task of the *IUFM* is to provide initial as well in-service professional training for both primary and secondary school teachers and to contribute to educational research. Linked to one or more universities, the *IUFM* is a higher education institution and is, therefore, necessarily located in a university town. The idea was that the state could guarantee a consistent recruitment of future teachers and a transparent course of training with clear objectives. All teachers (in primary or secondary education alike) are now required to have a degree. The reason for this is the state's concern to ensure that 'professional competences are based first and foremost on a thorough knowledge and mastery of the subjects to be taught'.[7]

Entry to the *IUFM* is based on application and interview. Successful entry carries with it a financial allowance of approximately FFr75,000 per annum; this allowance frees the trainee teachers from financial worries and enables them to devote themselves fully to their training, which is both theoretical and practical. On completion of the first year at the *IUFM*, primary school teachers (now called *professeurs des écoles*) are formally recruited into an *académie* by means of a competitive examination; they will then be placed on an official *département* list as teachers for subsequent appointment. *Lycée* and *collège* teachers will be posted as before at national level, but not until they have been successful in the competitive examinations of *Agrégation* or CAPES (*Certificat d'Aptitude Pédagogique à l'Enseignement Secondaire*). Universities continue to provide preparation for the CAPES and the *Agrégation*. Once they have passed the examination, trainee teachers spend the second year of their training at the *IUFM*. The award of qualified teacher status (*certification*) does not take place until successful completion of the second year, when the newly qualified *agrégés et certifiés* obtain their *titularisation*, which confers tenure. The system ensures teacher education and professional preparation in an institution with higher university status.

Candidates from another member state of the European Union are eligible to become teachers in a *collège* or a *lycée* under the same conditions as French nationals. They need a first university qualification acquired after three years of study (equal to the *baccalauréat* or equivalent plus three years, that is, normally a degree). Since French teachers are civil servants, the state recruits teachers for the public service through open competitions (*concours*), followed by a mandatory year of professional experience (*stage en situation*). In practice, this means that nationals from another member state apply to an IUFM: after one year of study and one further year of teaching experience, they are *titularisés*, with tenure to the end of their teaching career. If they already have a teaching qualification obtained in another member state, they only have to satisfy the requirements of the *stage* in order to become fully fledged teachers.

The number of foreign applicants for the *concours* examinations rose from 661 in 1993 to 2,409 in 1997, the latter representing 1.17 per cent of the total number of applications. The largest numbers came from Germany and Spain, with the United Kingdom in fourth place. The pass rates for the Germans and British were slightly higher than those for the other foreign applicants. Even so, of the 2,409 applicants, only 279 were admitted to posts. Languages are the most frequent subject applied for. There were difficulties with the 'employment for life' status of foreign nationals.

Higher education

Two important parliamentary Acts determine the current structure of higher education in France. The *Loi d'Orientation* of 12 November 1968 (more commonly known as the *Loi Edgar Faure*),[8] amended and extended by the *Loi du 26 janvier 1984* governing higher education by the then Minister of Education Alain Savary and followed by the *Loi du 16 juillet 1984* relating to physical and sport education guarantee the autonomy of universities in France, although they do not really provide universities with the means with which to maintain such autonomy.

Anyone who has passed the *baccalauréat*, or indeed any candidate who has passed the special matriculation examination, is entitled – in theory at least – to register at a university of his or her choice. The faculties of medicine, the technological universities and the *Instituts Universitaires Professionnels* (IUPs) alone have a special status which allows them to restrict entry by limiting student numbers. The various component parts of the higher education system in France are complex. They consist of:

- the universities;
- the *Grandes Ecoles*;

- the specialized institutions, such as business schools, interpreters' or journalists' schools, to name but three;
- the institutes of further education, in which education can be provided in the *lycées*, leading to *BTS* (*brevets de techniciens supérieurs*).

Universities, including the *IUTs* (*Instituts Universitaires de Technologie*), are organized into *UFR* (*Unités de Formation et de Recherche*), the composition of the *UFR* varying from one university to another. The first two years of university education (*premier cycle*) lead to the following qualifications:

- *DUT* (*Diplôme universitaire de technologie*) issued by an *IUT*;
- *DEUG, DEUST* (*Diplômes d'études universitaires générales/scientifiques et techniques*), or *DU* (*Diplôme universitaire*), issued by a *UFR*.

All qualifications for the *premier cycle* require a pass mark in a paper in a modern foreign language, usually in a language which the student started studying in the *lycée*.

The degree (*Licence ès lettres/Licence ès sciences*) can be obtained on completion of an additional year of study. A fourth year of study after the *baccalauréat* gives access to the *maîtrise*, which is a year of initiation into research, taken by students intending to proceed to the *DEA* (*Diplôme d'études approfondies*) or *DESS* (*Diplôme d'études supérieures spécialisées*) and after three or four years of further study possibly to a *Doctorat* under the *nouveau régime* regulations.

All state universities award national qualifications; that is, qualifications which have the same status throughout the whole of France and from one university to another. Though in the scientific sector careers for young researchers seem promising, it is not the same story in the arts, where the *Centre National de la Recherche Scientifique* (CNRS) and universities offer the best prospects. The *doctorat* or an equivalent foreign qualification enables the candidate to apply for a *maîtrise de conférences* (lecturership), for which a limited number of posts become available each year. After interviewing potential candidates, the university concerned draws up a shortlist of three candidates who have the required profile for the post. The shortlist is submitted to the *Conseil National des Universités* (CNU) who makes a choice and gives its approval. The new *maître de conférences* is appointed as a 'probationer' for a fixed period lasting between one and two years. Once *titularisé*, he or she remains *maître de conférences* until they have produced a sufficient number of research articles, publications and conference papers to allow them to aspire to an *habilitation à diriger des travaux de recherches* (to become an approved research supervisor). Once the *habilitation* has been awarded by a university of their choice, the *maître de conférences* can apply for a post as *professeur des universités*, subject to the availability of posts each year. If the application is accepted by the university to which it was made, it must be approved by the *CNU* for the decision to become final.

The restructuring of the French university system is as yet incomplete. Since 1968, it has suffered from incomplete and hasty reforms. The reorganization of research in the humanities along the same lines as the sciences has had the effect of doing away with monumental doctorate theses which involved a good ten years of research. The change has not been easy, but the principle does now seem to be well established. Next in line is the overhaul of the *premier cycle* and of the *DEUG*, which should at last allow for more continuity between secondary and higher education, especially with the intake of an ever-increasing number of students who are uncertain about their future and who at present have to attend too many lectures for which they are ill-prepared. The appointment of research students as tutors has been a very positive step.

Outlook

Jospin's proposals for an education system for the future

At the request of the then President of the Republic, François Mitterrand, an extensive consultation was devised and conducted by the *Collège de France* in 1985: it was aptly called *Propositions pour l'enseignement de l'avenir* (Proposals for an education system for the future). It was the result of a long process of reflection followed by maturation, starting with the report on the *lycées* by the eminent historian of education, Antoine Prost, in the mid-1980s. In December 1988, nine commissions based on particular themes conducted a study aimed at completely rethinking the contents of the general and professional education systems from nursery school through to university. The evaluation of their findings was entrusted to a number of well-known researchers led by the sociologist Pierre Bourdieu and the biologist François Gros, both professors at the *Collège de France*. At the end of this initial phase, a set of seven principles was established. These formed the basis of the Bourdieu–Gros Report, entitled *Réflexion sur les contenus d'enseignement*, published in March 1989.[9] The report drew the main outlines of the gradual changes that were to take place in the education system. In particular it initiated a wide process of consultation and went on to offer practical proposals which were to lead to the *Loi d'Orientation*, frequently referred to above. For those involved, the consultation process, which is a relatively recent phenomenon in the history of French education, was to be a landmark. Indeed, the two periods of 'cohabitation' which intervened in 1986–8 and 1993–5 did not substantially modify the principles set out by Lionel Jospin, so that for the first time since the war there is a strong feeling of continuity in the area of education policy. Many foreign countries continue to envy France, perhaps with good reason, for its public service which provides quality education; however, the education system meanwhile has certainly become a sprawling monster and is now 'the top national priority' for attention, as stated in the 1989 *Loi d'Orientation*.

In a speech to the National Assembly on 7 June 1989, Lionel Jospin, the Minister of Education at the time, stated: 'The evolution of our education system is not decided by decree: it is the result of a building process. We must therefore unite our wills around one coherent action' (see note 1). This action has been developed in line with the principles set out in the Bourdieu–Gros Report of March 1989. The questionnaire designed by the Bourdieu–Gros Commission was used as a nation-wide consultation document. Responses came predominantly from private individuals but they were also received from trade unions, professional associations of teachers, inspectors, subject specialists and parents' representatives, as well as training and employment agencies.

Modern foreign languages

If one takes item 5 on the questionnaire which reads '*Langues vivantes, Europe, diversifier*' as an example[9] and looks at the responses obtained, it is evident that they reflect a greater preoccupation among the respondents with the improvement of modern foreign language teaching, particularly through opportunities for more oral practice, than with diversification of the languages studied, as it is the former which would enhance the value of exchanges within the European Union. Replies from the business sector were noticeably more specific: 'English must be taught as the international business language.' One of the suggestions was that certain core subjects (mathematics, history and geography) should be taught through the medium of a modern foreign language. It is worth noting that this already happens in some schools in their *sections bilingues*. A general consensus among the groups questioned highlighted the importance of learning a modern foreign language at an early age, as early as the primary school.

The Bourdieu–Gros commission had set up nine workshops; one of those workshops, which was headed by Jean Janitza, dealt with modern foreign languages. It led to the Chevalier–Janitza Report of July 1989 which highlighted the growing importance which needed to be given, with the Single Market of 1993 on the horizon, to teaching the languages of the European Community in the first instance, whilst not forgetting the other languages used in the rest of the world.

The nature and content of language teaching have changed significantly in recent years. English, for example, is no longer treated only as a literary language associated with Shakespeare, an approach which had prevailed for so long. The English now taught in the *collèges* and *lycées* is primarily aimed at exchange and communication. However, there seems to be a survival of the French Napoleonic attitudes in the way in which educationalists still expect school pupils to speak English, Spanish or German fluently, the way a native speaker would. Such an attitude shows the influence of an outdated educational approach, popular at a time when foreign languages were the privilege of an elite which had access to a secondary school education. The goal can no longer be to study languages for their own sake; languages have to resume their natural function – that of a tool. The advantage of knowing one or several languages, therefore, can only be to acquire the skill to communicate more easily, to export goods without requiring intermediaries. In France, the process is a relatively new one; it appears as a new challenge to have become aware of the necessity of trading a few English structures in order to obtain goods and ideas, intellectual or physical transactions. It provides new opportunities: to compare, to think, to reshape and eventually to re-create.

Because of such priorities, the Chevalier–Janitza Report emphasized three objectives in the teaching of languages in French secondary schools:

- communication through the artificial situation of exchange in the classroom, with the intention of mastering the language as a tool;
- culture, which, in the present context, signifies the development of the individual personality confronted with authentic aspects of a foreign culture;
- correct training in the given language so as to avoid all kinds of Babel-like misunderstandings.

The Chevalier–Janitza Report's insistence on vertical coherence from primary school level teaching, through secondary education and up to university studies is a recommendation to reconsider the mode of training tomorrow's teachers to facilitate the inclusion of the European dimension in education.

As rapid transformation seems to be a keyword in present European societies, it might be possible to envisage an approach to teach European citizens to adapt to a changing world: '*apprendre à apprendre*'. It could be achieved at a second level with language awareness and European awareness working hand in hand. Why not start on training at school level and consider right away that European awareness also signifies intercultural awareness of several meta-systems? At the moment, it is probably one of the least-considered aspects of education. School children and young adults still indulge in a collection of stereotypes about the foreign countries whose languages they try to master.

A feature of the French education system is the existence of a significant number of *lycées et collèges à sections bilingues* and of *lycées internationaux*. These *lycées à sections bilingues* prepare pupils for foreign examinations – GCSE or TOEFL for example. The *lycées à sections internationales* prepare pupils for the French *baccalauréat* as well as for the International Baccalaureate. In both, a certain amount of teaching in some subjects is conducted in the foreign language. This process is helped by the use of multiple and regular student and staff exchanges at all levels throughout the European Union.

From the 1990s onward

The Ministers of Education who followed in the footsteps of Lionel Jospin – Jack Lang, François Bayrou and Claude Allègre – have been very much aware of the need to adapt the French education system to the demands of the next century. 'Audacity, prudence and pragmatism', in the words of François Bayrou,[10] have characterized their approach. Bayrou, who did not believe that an earthquake should happen in the field of education every time a new minister takes office, advocated continuity. The general philosophy of the reform started by Lionel

Jospin has been preserved and the far-reaching reform of the French education system, which became known as the 'Jospin–Lang–Bayrou' reform, has been fully operational since 1995.

The change of government after the 1993 general election and a new period of 'cohabitation' (a conservative government, led by Edouard Balladur, 'cohabitating' with a socialist President, François Mitterrand) did not have a major impact on the French education system, because François Bayrou remained in office as Minister for Education until the spring of 1997, after the election of Jacques Chirac as President of the Republic and the return to power of the Gaullist coalition. His main stated objectives were expressed in *Le Nouveau Contrat pour l'école*, published by the Ministry of National Education in September 1994 and widely distributed throughout the country. François Bayrou described the *Nouveau Contrat* as 'a plan for change and progress, comprising 158 precise and concrete decisions'. The five principles that give the *Contrat* its coherence are:

- transparency: the crisis that affects society and the family is reflected in the school; it is therefore essential for the school clearly to state its aims and objectives that must be made accessible to all;
- priority given to the fundamental competencies: French language, reading, mathematics and work education methods to combat school failure. Introduction of education for citizenship (*l'éducation civique*) at all school levels and of the study of a foreign language as early as the *cours élémentaire* (the third year of primary school);
- individualization of educational approaches (*à chacun sa voie*): this is the end of the comprehensive *collège unique* and its uniformity. Individual methods have to be applied to individual pupils, as far as possible, particularly to those who have experienced difficulties; it is crucial to change the negative image of professional training in schools;
- more responsibility given to the base of the education system – the schools and the teachers: newly trained teachers will no longer be appointed to difficult posts; improved management of the teaching profession and cooperation of teachers and parents;
- new responses to the challenges of a new world: the introduction of new technologies, of an early start made with learning foreign languages, of twilight classes for parents or for those who have been labelled as 'failures'.

The Bayrou *Contrat* insisted on ensuring that pupils acquire mastery of the basic competencies (reading, writing and numeracy), so that the dismal figure of one child in four being unable to read or write at the end of his or her primary schooling would no longer obtain: *faire reculer l'illettrisme*. It set up a review of the structure of the comprehensive school and the *collège unique*, created by the *Loi du 11 juillet 1975*, the *'reforme* Haby', for the first four years of secondary schooling,[11] with its mixed ability classes (*classes hétérogènes*), which he considered a source of injustice and inequality (*injuste et inique*), since to attempt to provide the same training for all pupils can only lead to failure for some. He saw it as essential to create *des classes de mise à niveau* to enable pupils who had fallen behind to catch up through using the remedial classes to reintegrate into the normal stream of teaching as rapidly as possible. The *Loi Guermeur* (*Loi du 25 novembre 1977*) on the relationship between the state and private education established better financial conditions for the private sector.

A major step forward in the curricular area was Bayrou's demand to introduce the study of a foreign language at the age of 8 for all pupils in primary schools in order to compensate for the reluctance of the French to use foreign languages and to enable them to play a greater role in European economic life.

Claude Allègre, who took over from Bayrou in 1997 after the General Election which saw Lionel Jospin become Prime Minister, had in fact been fully involved in Jospin's Reform, as one of his key advisers at the Ministry of Education. He will no doubt be remembered for some of his most striking phrases: '*dégraisser le mammouth*' (slim down the dinosaur-like heavy weight of the administrative machinery of the French education system) and '*alléger le paquebot*' of the *éducation nationale* with its 1.5 million employees, in order to provide more flexibility in the rigidly structured hierarchical organization of the system. In the last resort, it is the pupils who will be the beneficiaries.

This is illustrated by the creation of 30,000 *emplois-jeunes* for the young unemployed as *médiateurs* working for the *éducation nationale* whose role consists of acting as a go-between amid pupils, parents and schools, and as a help to introduce the new technologies. A number of these young *médiateurs* themselves come from immigrant families. Allègre wanted to return to the very source and ideals of the school of the early days of the Third Republic, when Jules Ferry and Ferdinand Buisson created the 'school of the Republic'. 'I believe that it is from this proximity between the nation and its school that one must start the process of renewal of our educational system'.[12]

Allègre takes up and updates the issues left by his predecessors: the inertia of the administrative machinery, the multiethnic–multicultural problems expressed through violence in the *banlieues* and in the ZEP (*Zones d'Education Prioritaires*), by investment enabling the introduction of the basic competencies necessary to operate in the global world of today. He wants the French education system to respond to what he sees as the three main challenges of tomorrow's world:

- the recognition of the diversity of talents upon which are based the true equality of opportunities and real democratization;
- the continuous adapting of programmes and syllabus content to the needs of a changing world;
- the mastery of the new technological tools together with the deep changes that they engender, particularly in social relationships.

To achieve this, Allègre has launched a wide programme of consultation and reflection. The most significant developments of the Allègre review of the French education system, which is far reaching and wide ranging, include the fight against failure and violence in schools, particularly in the *banlieues*, the new approach to multiethnic–multicultural issues, and the reintegration of the *exclus* into the system by some very successful experiments conducted in twilight areas to salvage pupils from the so-called dustbin classes (*les classes poubelles*). His reform is aimed at adapting the French school system to the new world of the third millennium: particularly in the area of new technologies and multimedia through the *adaptation et adéquation de l'école*. A willingness to work together is needed to produce the 'European school of tomorrow', a school which makes use of language awareness, of bilingualism, of multilingual documents, of libraries, language clubs and multimedia software in foreign languages, a school which 'while educating, prepares for liberty'.

The European dimension: new future prospects

The European and international dimensions are mentioned clearly in Jospin's *Loi d'Orientation sur l'Education* in the section entitled: '*La dimension européenne et internationale dans la formation*':

> The Single European Act leads to harmonization of legislations (recognition of diplomas and free movement of people). Individuals will have to get more and more involved in exchanges and cooperation in the areas of training, research and employment.
>
> A training open to the European dimension encourages an inquiring and creative approach and adaptability. It must help to develop a knowledge of other cultures as well as the learning and command of modern foreign languages by:
>
> - the introduction of a nation-wide experiment in modern foreign-language learning in primary schools;
> - the opportunity for all *collège* pupils to study two foreign languages from the *quatrième* onwards (year three);
> - the teaching of a second modern foreign language in technological and professional sections, with better-adapted syllabuses and methods;
> - improvement in the efficiency of language teaching, particularly in higher education.[13]

Apart from the stress on the teaching of modern foreign languages from the age of 8, the integration in the syllabus of core subjects which are studied by all pupils up to the *baccalauréat* and which have a European dimension (namely history and geography), the programme of *instruction civique* (education for citizenship, which includes European citizenship) are the other obvious contributions with a European content. *Instruction civique* is a core subject to be taken for one hour per week throughout compulsory education and more particularly by all pupils in *première* (secondary year 6) who will be tested on it for the *baccalauréat*.

Some recent measures further confirm this emphasis, such as the decision to double the number of English language assistants in schools in 1998–9 in order to provide primary schools with the benefit of having a native speaker in the school, or the decision by the government to sign the European Charter of minority languages, or the stress on information technology as a key development, with all schools to be provided with computers and connected to the Internet and e-mail. School twinning is thriving more than ever, whilst links with business are developing, particularly in the context of regional cooperation at European level.

This is particularly relevant in the EUREGIOs: the EUREGIOs are border areas which have traditionally been areas of conflict, often a kind of no-man's land. In the 1970s and 1980s, a number of initiatives were developed in border areas between France, Germany, Belgium, Luxembourg and the Netherlands. A well-known initiative is the Regio Basiliensis, where many aspects of tripartite cooperation are taking place, including education between Alsace, Baden-Württemberg and the area of Basle. Transborder schemes set up by local authorities to develop joint activities and links have led to agreements being signed particularly involving languages and common cultural activities between teachers, local authorities, businesses and individuals.

In higher education, the Erasmus branch of the Socrates programme is in great demand by students who are aware of the advantages of living, studying and working in another country. Leonardo programmes, with professional work experience in business or administration, are slowly developing: *stages en entreprises* are becoming the norm in many courses as a preparation for professional life. In a society where unemployment is a tragic reality, preparation for working life in a European perspective has become another key issue.

Will higher education in France retain the means to be available free of cost to the student, whilst its European partners are implementing other systems? It is of course a political decision, but the setting up of European networks – Erasmus for example – has produced unexpected difficulties. The French host university cannot provide the social welfare or educational advantages that exchange students are guaranteed in their own universities. French students, still largely dependent upon their families, do not always have the financial means to undertake a lengthy period of residence in a foreign or distant university which in some courses (*Langues Etrangères Appliquées*) is an integral part of the course.

Even if bilateral agreements between institutions seem to operate in a smooth and satisfactory manner at both secondary and higher education levels, the notion of a European qualification or of an integrated European syllabus still seems difficult to accept. In the French way of thinking, the *diplôme* remains a national matter.

While in principle the Ministry of Education is happy to advocate a greater degree of mobility for both teaching and administrative staff, it tends to favour only short- and medium-term periods of exchange. Meanwhile on the ground, things are not so simple. The language barrier is not in itself insuperable, but the constraints of family life and the economy deter mobility and prevent time off for spouses or meeting the cost of accommodation abroad. The inflated numbers of students and the increased use of large-scale lecture classes – both phenomena practically unknown to some of France's European partners – often make exchanges between university colleagues somewhat delicate. As for the students, language students and students from the *Ecoles Supérieures de Commerce* have traditionally tended to be more in favour of exchanges, the greatest reticence coming from the students of French. In the present economic situation, where the threat of unemployment affects many families, few wish to take what they see as risks. Happily, evidence suggests that young people are becoming more enthusiastic about travelling and studying abroad and taking part in exchange programmes. As a founding member of the European Community, it is very important that France should remain active in exchange and collaboration programmes.

Conclusion

The French education system remains largely national in its outlook and a number of its concerns. It is European and international at times, mainly in exceptional situations such as in international or bilingual *lycées*, but it is at last moving in other directions. The introduction of the study of a foreign language, education for citizenship, history and geography studied as core subjects until the *baccalauréat* are essential to the process. So is the mastery of the new technological tools together with the deep changes that they bring about in the field of communication and social relationships, simplification of procedures and transparency of decisions and a school management closer to the perceived needs. The French education system is awakening to Europe in a context of social unrest and unemployment where opportunities are perceived by young people in Europe: the response must be in moving into the future where *la transmission des savoirs* is no longer the main aim of education: imparting an encyclopedic knowledge (*les savoirs*) is replaced by *savoir-faire* (knowing what and how to do) and *savoir-être* (how to conduct oneself). The new direction of thinking is education for life in Europe.

Notes

1 [Lionel Jospin] *Loi d'Orientation sur l'Education* (*loi du 10 juillet 1989*), *Bulletin Officiel du Ministère de l'Education Nationale* (special no. 4, 31 August 1989). See also A 1286, p. 22 ibid.
2 *Ecole Elémentaire: Programmes et Instructions*, Paris: Ministère de l'Education Nationale, Centre National de Documentation Pédagogique, 1990, pp. 5–6.
3 'Organisation et fonctionnement des écoles maternelles et élémentaires', *Bulletin Officiel du Ministère de l'Education Nationale*, spécial no. 9, 3 October 1991, article 12, p. 33.
4 J.P. Chevènement, *Collèges: programmes et instructions*, Paris: Ministère de l'Education Nationale, Centre National de Documentation Pédagogique, 1985, p. 8.
5 [Jospin], p. 16.
6 Ibid. p. 18.
7 *Les Instituts Universitaires de Formation des Maîtres*, Paris: Ministère de l'Education

Nationale, Direction de l'information et de la communication, document Nr. 1, September 1990, p. 7.

8 [Edgar Faure], *Loi d'Orientation de l'enseignement supérieur* (*Loi du 12 novembre 1968*).

9 *Consultation Nationale*, the Bourdieu-Gros Report, 1989 (article 5 on modern foreign languages).

Langues vivantes, Europe, diversifier

5.1 A modern foreign language is a core subject in secondary schools.

5.2 Every pupil must learn at least two modern foreign languages (*Diversification Europe*).

5.3 Every pupil must learn English.

5.4 The teaching of modern foreign languages requires certain resources (small oral groups, laboratories, trips and pupil exchanges).

5.5 Efforts must be made to increase foreign exchanges.

5.6 It is necessary to begin learning a modern foreign language at primary school.

10 F. Bayrou, *Le Nouveau Contrat pour l'école*, Paris: Ministère de l'Education Nationale, Centre National de Documentation Pédagogique, 1994, pp. 4–5.

11 [Ministry of René Haby], *Loi du 11 juillet 1975*, known as the '*réforme Haby*'; *Loi du 25 novembre 1977*, known as the '*Loi Guermeur*', on the relationship between the state and private education.

12 C. Allègre, 'Ce que je veux', *Le Monde*, 6 février 1998.

13 'La Dimension européenne', in [Jospin], p. 22.

Bibliography

Allègre, C., 'Ce que je veux', *Le Monde*, 6 février 1998 (see also various articles published in *Le Monde*, juin 1997–).

Auduc, J.L. and Bayard-Pierlot, J. *Le Système éducatif français*, CRDP de Créteil, septembre 1995.

Bayrou, F., *Le Nouveau Contrat pour l'école*, Paris: Ministère de l'éducation nationale, septembre 1994.

Bloch, D., 'Pour une stratégie convergente du système éducatif et des entreprises', in *Rapport présenté au Ministre de l'Education Nationale*, Paris: La Documentation française, 1988.

Bourdieu–Gros: *Rapport*, Consultation nationale, 1989.

Chevalier, J.C. and Janitza, J. *Rapport sur la mission de réflexion sur l'enseignement du français, de la littérature et des langues vivantes et anciennes*, Paris: Centre National de Documentation Pédagogique, 1989.

Durand-Prinborgne, C., *Le Système éducatif*, Paris: La Documentation française, 1991.

[Jospin, Lionel], *Loi d'Orientation sur l'Education* (*Loi du 10 juillet 1989*), *Bulletin officiel du Ministère de l'Education Nationale*, no. 4, 31 août 1989.

Legrand, L., 'Pour un collège démocratique', *Rapport au Ministre de l'Education Nationale*, Paris: La Documentation française, Coll. 'Rapports officiels', 1982.

Lesourne, Jacques, *Education et société, les défis de l'an 2000*, Paris: La Découverte/Le Monde de l'Education, 1988.

Prost, A., *Histoire de l'enseignement en France*, Paris: Armand Colin, 1968.

Prost, A., 'L'enseignement s'est-il démocratisé?' in *Sociologies*, Paris: PUF, 1986.

6 Germany

Friedrich W. Kron

The resolution of the European Council of February 1988[1] and the relevant clauses of the Maastricht and Amsterdam Treaties provide the new framework for the position of education and vocational training in the consolidation process of the European Union. The educational guidelines have been deduced from the economic priorities of the Union, a scenario in which the education systems of the individual member states make their own contribution to the completion of the European internal market by:

- strengthening young people's consciousness of their identity as Europeans;
- preparing the young generation for its participation in the economic and social development of the European Union;
- making the young aware of both the advantages and the challenges confronting them in Europe; and
- improving their knowledge of the Community and its member states.[2]

The guidelines sketched in show the education system as a function of the production system which leaves only limited room for a humanist approach. From the educational point of view this constitutes a central dilemma.[3]

The following exposition is based on this dilemma and attempts to search for room within which basic ideas of democracy, international understanding and European integration, inherent in the constitutions of all member states of the European Community, may be realized. In this discussion concentration will be placed on the school system, and examples will be taken from the Federal State of the Rhineland Palatinate (*Rheinland Pfalz*), which shares a long border, as well as many traditions, with France.

The chapter will proceed in three stages. The first will present the legal framework and its realization. The second will serve to demonstrate the correlation of political developments and resulting changes in the educational system of the reunited Germany. The third deals with post-school education.

The legal framework and its realization

The historical background

Responsibility for the school system in Germany does not lie with the Federal Government. The individual Federal states are virtually independent in matters concerning education and culture. The immediate historical background of this federal provision was the painful experience of the misuse of schools during the National Socialist period. For at least 12 years the school system exercised a total influence on the young generation by the centralized state by means of indoctrinating an extremist political ideology.

According to the intention of the authors of Germany's Basic Law of 1949,[4] a similar misuse would not be allowed to happen in the future of the new Federal Republic. As a result, since 1949 the Federal states have enjoyed an educational and cultural autonomy.

This independence includes responsibility for and sensibility towards social development processes as well as for the realization of guiding principles. In cultural and educational matters, therefore, federalism must not lead to a totally separate development of the educational systems within each of the constituent states (*Länder*). Indeed, the education system is meant to be coordinated. Coordination is ensured by a body called the Permanent Conference of the State Ministers of Education (*Kultusministerkonferenz*: KMK),[5] and has resulted in quite a successful coordination of educational and school policy and of legal, organizational and curricular problems ever since the conference was established. The five newly created Federal states in the former German Democratic Republic were incorporated into the coordination process on 3 October 1990. The present-day Federal Republic of Germany consists of 16 Federal states.

Fundamental ideas and values

With regard to Europe, in the writer's opinion the states' jurisdiction over education will not present a problem. Many Federal states have cultivated partnerships with regions or constituent administrative areas of neighbouring countries at all educational levels; for example, the Rhineland Palatinate with Burgundy in France. In the past, this level of relationship has proved to be stable as well as flexible in respect of local changes. The same applies to relations with Eastern European countries, or even beyond – for example, the Rhineland Palatinate maintains active relations with the African state of Rwanda, particularly in the area of vocational training. No doubt these links will grow in the future. A similar situation prevails in the provinces of the former German Democratic Republic. Over the past 40 years, these former provinces had built up relations at various educational and personal levels with Central and Eastern European countries, especially the former USSR, Poland and the former CSFR. To this effect a number of supporting associations and organizations had been founded, which were transformed into new institutions after 1990.

It remains to be seen to what extent this potential can be put to advantage for the benefit of the general mass of European peoples in the European Union. To date, the German experience shows that the federal structure of relations does not hinder but rather promotes international cooperation among schools. The individual educational sectors are able to plan and frame their European links flexibly according to their own ideas of social responsibility and educational competence. Nevertheless, central support is needed for information, innovation, evaluation and media service. Thus, experience teaches that basic concepts are best realized through local self-organization – that is 'learning by doing' – but central stimuli and support systems will also be necessary. Regrettably, government budgets are constantly being pruned, which entails curtailing promising initiatives.

The locally orientated model of European cultural cooperation could be further intensified in the future. For Germany, the Basic Law may serve as the legal framework and impulse. According to Article 24 of the Basic Law, the Federal Government may confer jurisdiction in cultural and educational matters to the Federal states. The states are all represented in the Lower House of the German Federal Parliament (*Bundesrat*[6]) and cooperate closely in educational matters via the Permanent Conference of the State Ministers of Education. Individually, in groups or together, the states can extend and deepen their cooperation with European regions and countries.

A number of legal foundations guarantee these processes with regard to contents. In this part of the chapter value guidelines for school education are considered. The following account will show that a number of these values also comprise central ideas on democracy, international understanding and European integration. A study of these value guidelines may therefore throw light upon opportunities for and obstacles to bringing to fruition in the schools the central ideas mentioned above. The following observations will focus on five documents.

The Basic Law

In a variety of articles the Basic Law of the Federal Republic (FRG) provides the political and idealistic foundation for education for democracy. In Article 2, the free development of the person is guaranteed; that is to say, the right to education. Regarding the school system, besides other provisions, equal opportunities must be established for the education of all. Article 3 guarantees the freedom of religious and political views. For schools this also means free practice of religious and political education as well as that of religious freedom and freedom of conscience, guaranteed in Article 4. Lastly, Article 5 lays down the right of free speech for every person working in the school.

The state constitutions

The constitutions of the Federal states have to be considered next. The Constitution of the Federal State of the Rhineland Palatinate[7] will be used as an exemplar of all Federal states. According to Article 33 of its Constitution, it is the fundamental task and duty of the school to educate pupils in the spirit of democracy and international reconciliation.

The Education Acts

The third document, the Rhineland Palatinate Education Act 1974, holds that the school must prepare pupils for the assumption of their rights within the state and society as well as for their acceptance of duties as citizens towards the state and society. The school must also familiarize pupils with the idea of an international community. Therefore, in concrete action and school practice, pupils are brought up to qualify not only for a profession, but also for their social commitment in their own country, in Europe and in the wider world.

The 1973 Declaration of the Permanent Conference of the State Ministers of Education

The claim of education for democracy is further reinforced and specifically related to the FRG in the 1973 Declaration which solemnly requires that the school must:

1 educate for freedom and democracy;
2 educate for tolerance, instilling respect for human dignity and man's differing convictions;
3 foster a peaceful turn of mind in the spirit of international understanding;
4 foster the readiness for social commitment and political responsibility;
5 award qualifications for the assumption of rights and duties within society.

These grand demands have not been fully realized as yet.

The school regulations

The fifth and last document, the school regulations of the Rhineland Palatinate, may be regarded as proof of the gap which exists between theory and practice in respect of an education for democracy in Germany.

According to the law, school regulations are concerned with the day-to-day running of the individual school. The school regulations of 1984, which apply to all local community and state-maintained schools, regulate relations between pupils and the school, between parents and the school, as well as the organization of lessons, the assessment of achievement, examinations and conflicts in everyday school life. They are a code of regulations, largely unknown to the pupil, which primarily serves teachers and headmasters as an instrument for orientation and justification of their own actions. Their function therefore is more that of maintaining order than of implementing guiding principles and objectives. There is only a rudimentary implementation of basic rights, such as the right of co-determination and the right of free speech in a well-ordered manner. Although Article 5 stipulates the basic right of free speech, the field of activity in which this right may be exercised is instantly limited. Pupils may express their opinion orally; however, if they wish to express their opinion in writing – for example to distribute leaflets – they must first obtain the headteacher's permission. Political meetings and the distribution of materials are not permitted. Even the freedom of speech achieved by publication in a school magazine is relative – that is to say, it is censored.

Pupils' part in co-determination regarding school life and lessons was characterized as a 'joint responsibility', thus effectively depoliticized and neutralized. The great wealth of social experience and the plurality of norms and values therefore remain outside the school gates. Only very few individual teachers take advantage of this educational opportunity, school life being reduced to particular major events authorized by headteachers. Social learning in a democratic and socially integrated form is largely a myth.

In conclusion, it may be said that the legal foundations of an education for democracy, international understanding and European integration do exist for promoting the European idea in Germany and its Federal states. However, as the basic rights are actually implemented in the organizations – illustrated by the school situation – they are replaced by the practice of organizational and bureaucratic rules.

With regard to Europe this problem requires particular attention. Centralization and bureaucratization ought to be minimized, only entering the organizational process if they are to serve self-organization at local level.

The mission of international understanding and of learning to be a European citizen must be further supported by idealistic, financial and organizational means. Besides existing European Union programmes such as Socrates, Comett and Lingua and those related to vocational training such as Leonardo, Euro-tecnet, Force and Cedefop[8] schools providing general education must be the central focus of EU programmes. Nor will the mere expansion of the educational information network Eurydice and of the YES programmes[9] suffice. The creation of entirely new European programmes will be needed. These programmes must translate the concepts of equal opportunities, freedom of religious belief and political development and education, as well as the right of free speech, into cooperative practice.

Political developments and changes in the school system

Historical development

As in other countries, in Germany too the development of the school system is bound up with socio-political change. It is only 80 years since the first move was made in Germany towards a democratization of schools providing general education. It arose from the first German democracy, the Weimar Republic. In 1920, the German Parliament decided to introduce the four-year primary school which all German children had to attend. This first phase of comprehensive schooling replaced the old, social class-orientated separate school system for the lower, middle and upper classes. The school system introduced in 1920 has been maintained structurally until today except that the then four-year primary school was followed by the four-year extended primary school (*Volksschule*), the six-year secondary school (*Realschule*) and the nine-year grammar school (*Gymnasium*). Schooling in Germany is compulsory between the ages of six and eighteen.

The school system providing a general education

Organization

After World War Two, the FRG returned to the educational system of the 'Weimar tradition'. The school system has kept its relatively firm organizational structure[10] since 1960. Following the four-year primary school (*Grundschule*) and the two-year orientation level (*Orientierungsstufe*)[11] the school system providing general education is divided into three branches: the five- or six-year extended primary school (*Hauptschule*); the six-year secondary school (*Realschule*); and the nine-year grammar school (*Gymnasium*). There are also schools for special education (*Sonderschulen*) and specialized grammar schools (*Kollegs, Aufbaugymnasien*) which may substitute for the last three years of ordinary grammar schools.

The whole system is defined as a streaming system. In some Federal states with an Anglo-Saxon tradition such as Hamburg, Bremen and Berlin or in the socialist tradition of the former GDR, the primary school is extended to six years followed by secondary I and secondary II phases. This particular system is called a setting system and it exists in some Federal states besides the general streaming system.

The goal of the four- or six-year primary school is to provide the basis for secondary education in the core areas of reading, writing and arithmetic and to foster general motivation in individual learning, achievement and competition. Little emphasis is placed on social learning, cooperation and self-reliance. Depending on the grades obtained by pupils in primary school, the recommendations of their teachers and the preferences of their parents, a school pupil is enrolled in one of the three branches mentioned. In most of the Federal states parents' preference is guaranteed by law and extensively used. The general effect is that the number of pupils attending the *Gymnasium* is constantly rising, in contrast to the *Hauptschule* which is now regarded as 'a last resort' school for marginal and immigrant groups. Pupils who have completed the *Hauptschule* must continue to attend the vocational school system until the age of 18.

In the former GDR, the socialist comprehensive school was gradually introduced after 1945.[12] Its core was the ten-year polytechnic high school (*Polytechnische Oberschule* – POS). It was followed either by the two-year extended upper school (*Erweiterte Oberschule* – EOS), or by the two- to three-year vocational training schools, in all of which practical vocational training had to be accompanied by mandatory general school education. In the FRG this twofold commitment is known as the 'dual system' (*Duales System*). In the EOS as well as in vocational training, matriculation standard could be attained. About 10–15 per cent of all pupils entered the universities. Parallel to this school system, special schools were available. A three-year nursery school preceded the primary school.

With the reunification of Germany in 1989 the school system of the former GDR was almost totally converted to the Federal Republic (FRG) system. The guidelines were developed by the Joint Education Commission (*Gemeinsame Bildungskommission*) in 1990. The key sentence of the document on conjunction of the two education systems (*Zusammenführung der beiden Bildungssysteme*) reiterates that according to the Basic Law the Federal states are exclusively responsible for education, science and culture. In this context the Reunification Act (*Wiedervereinigungsvertrag*) of 31 August 1990 gave some space for regional developments. All questions of coordination continue to remain within the competence of the Permanent Conference of the Ministers of Education (*Ständige Konferenz der Kultusminister*).

The unification process of schooling took place between 1991 and 1993 and it shows a certain flexibility. It was possible to preserve some structural ideas of the former GDR school system or to transform them into new or existing FRG models, such as the Comprehensive School (*Gesamtschule*), the merger of the *Hauptschule* and the *Realschule* into a new bilateral 'integrated school' type in which curricular ideas of the former *Einheitsschule* are partly realized. The six-year *Grundschule* and the eight-year *Gymnasium* as well as the new nine-year *Gymnasium* could also be found in the FRG. It is remarkable that there was little discussion to preserve the former GDR education system in totality in the East or to transfer or adapt structures and ideas from East to West. Nevertheless the transformation process served as a trigger to discuss the entire education system in Germany relating to more flexibility and European concerns.

School-leaving certificates

The different schools award different certificates depending on the specific professional areas covered, further or university education, for which they prepare. As a rule, the extended primary school awards a qualifying certificate after six years; the secondary school, also after six years, awards an intermediate secondary school certificate (*Mittlere Reife*), comparable to the British General Certificate of Secondary Education, while the *Gymnasium* (grammar school) certifies the matriculation standard as well as the university entrance examinations (*Abitur* or *Hochschulreife*), comparable to A levels, its only purpose being qualification for university study.

Including primary school, pupils of the extended primary school and secondary school attend a school providing general education for a total of ten years. Grammar school pupils will attend school for 13 years. In the states of the former GDR, the *Abitur* requires 12 years of schooling, which is comparable to most countries within the European Union. The latest discussion in Germany tends towards reducing school attendance at the secondary level (fifth to tenth forms) by one year. In this context, new forms, tasks and functions may be included in the final three years of grammar school, the upper level (II) phase (*Gymnasiale Oberstufe*).

At present, the final three years of grammar school are organized as a system of study courses (*Grund und Leistungskurse*) in all Federal states of Germany. At the same level, special secondary schools prepare pupils who have received a certificate from the extended primary school and the *Realschule* for university admission.

School curriculum subjects

Whereas most schools offer 12–16 subjects which are taught on a weekly basis for two to four periods throughout, in the final three years of the grammar school pupils take only about four to six compulsory and optional subjects as study courses.

Dynamic curricula operate in German schools. Teachers have 'free' classroom periods[13] when they can select the content according to the needs of their pupils. In this way, basic topics of everyday concern can be introduced into subject-related syllabuses. The same is true of European content topics, which have been integrated into most subjects, such as German, modern foreign languages, history, geography, social studies and art. However, 'European studies' is not, as yet, taught as a subject in its own right. In an important decree entitled 'European Studies' of 7 December 1990, the Permanent Conference of the Ministers of Education strongly urged a more determined consideration of European issues at school.[14] This document proposes specific measures for further development of 'European Studies' and for the preparation of specific curricula to this end. Particular attention is paid to the exchange of pupils and teachers, the study of European culture and languages, bilingual instruction and in-service training for teachers.

A Project Group Europe has started to develop further perspectives. Similar efforts have been made by the Educational Research Centre of the OECD. The topic of the year 1991 was therefore designated 'Studying for Europe – New Ways of Life and Learning'. Due to this initiative, projects and new methods are now being financed to an ever greater extent in the Rhineland Palatinate. These concentrate particularly on foreign language studies and bilingual instruction. Curriculum commissions for history, social studies and geography are working to put into effect the basic issue of European integration. Eleven experimental schools with 60 classes and about 2,000 pupils have been involved in projects experimenting with instruction in selected subjects through the medium of a foreign language, such as English and French. In 21 of 140 grammar schools, bilingual classes have been established; in 350 extended primary schools about 1,200 pupils are studying French, Spanish, Italian, Portuguese, Russian, Polish, Japanese and Chinese within the framework of study groups. Similar study groups will soon be introduced in vocational schools. At present, about DM1 million has been set aside for these projects. The state of Rhineland Palatinate meets one-half of all costs and the Federal Government meets the other half. European topics were not known to exist in curricula of the former GDR at any level.

Denominational religious education or ethics is a part of the school curriculum.

School hours

In German schools, formal instruction is confined to the morning hours. As a rule, school teaching periods run from 8 a.m. to 1 p.m. They are divided into six lessons (45 minutes per lesson) interrupted by breaks of different lengths. Special study groups are usually scheduled for the afternoon. The afternoon is otherwise free for homework, hobbies and sport activities of groups, the composition of which in most cases differs significantly from the peer group (that is the class) at school. Instruction is largely cognition and achievement-orientated. It aims at accumulation and transfer rather than at the evaluation of knowledge and skills.

Pupils who do not attain the required level of achievement in at least two subjects at the end of the school year, lasting from autumn to summer, have to repeat the entire year – not just the failed subjects. This is a heavy price to pay to compensate for low performance. In the provinces of the former GDR, the repetition of a year was not practised.

Social learning

The study of social norms, rules, values and responsibilities is restricted to the mornings. Therefore, little time remains for subject-integrated social learning. A significant factor in the democratic socialization of pupils is thus reduced. Education for democracy and other ideas such as education for Europe tend to be left to individual initiative.

Good comprehensive schools (*Gesamtschulen/Ganztagsschulen*) offering whole-day instruction are the exception. The inclusion of projects, collaborative study groups and open recreational facilities – that is, opening schools to society – has secured enriching input and ideas from outside the schools. This practice offers the opportunity to foster the readiness for social interaction and political responsibility as well as the opportunity to learn to make use of the freedom of speech and to examine and learn to respect the opinion of others. In short, values, rules and norms may be taught which are based on the central ideas of democracy, international understanding and European integration. However, learning processes of this kind which are practised daily at comprehensive schools – by no means without conflict – are left to the personal initiative of individual teachers or to small groups of teachers in other educational institutions such as those of continuing education.

The teachers: instructors or educators?

In the German school system the teacher's function is mainly that of instructor. Consequently, tasks such as teaching and assessment are emphasized, while others such as educating, advising and innovating[15] are of minor importance. The result is the formalization of socialization processes at school with teachers placed on a hierarchy regarding the prestige of the subjects taught and the required achievement levels obtained. It is not surprising that most often teachers in grammar schools (*Gymnasien*) see themselves as experts in a subject area. Teachers in secondary schools and extended primary schools share this self-assessment. On the other hand, teachers in primary schools see themselves predominantly as educators. Integrative processes of subject-orientated and social learning are most probably encountered in primary schools, for example in integrated curriculum teaching. Such teaching is usually available for two or three hours daily during which pupils actively work on topics comprising several subject areas. Projects are frequently offered to practise this approach. In this manner, basic democratic and European virtues can best be exercised functionally and practised intentionally at the same time.

Special education

The special schools are part of the school system providing general education. Pupils who suffer from severe handicaps or impairments are instructed in special schools because they need specific educational care and support which the general school system at present can provide only to a limited extent. Handicaps and impairments may be of a behavioural, linguistic, physical or intellectual nature. Pupils in special schools attend for ten years, comparable to pupils of schools providing general education. All school leavers receive a certificate, after which pupils may transfer to vocational schools offering special instruction.

Within the past decade the major increase in special schools has led to debate. Opponents of expansion of the special education sub-system advocate an integrative concept as practised in Britain and Sweden, where disabled pupils and mainstream pupils are taught jointly in schools providing general education. This concept would require external reorganization and internal transformation of the entire school system. Greater permeability of the various types of schools, or a graded system of greater individualization, a more flexible differentiation of performance as well as the cooperation of teachers, social workers and special educators, would be inevitable.

Pre-primary schooling

Nursery schools (*Kindergärten*) and pre-schools (*Vorschulen*) offer an upbringing before pupils go to any of the schools mentioned above. They are not an integrated part of the school system. Nursery schools primarily complement family education. Pre-schools prepare children for qualified transition to primary schools. Children can attend these schools from a starting age of 3 years.

The orientation phase

A further feature of the German system must be pointed out: 'the orientation phase' (*Orientierungsstufe*). It may be established in any of the schools providing general education. The orientation phase is intended to help pupils decide which type of post-primary school is most appropriate for them – the extended primary school, the secondary or the grammar school.

General education and its function in society

The diversely structured, essentially tripartite school system provides general education (*Allgemeinbildung*). According to the German educational tradition, general education comprises those mental and physical activities of every person which allow him or her to play a meaningful part in 'cultural' life. General education is accompanied by a specialized education (*Spezialbildung*), which serves to build up specific knowledge, competence and skills within one or several fields of knowledge and skills. It is virtually equivalent to vocational training (*Berufsbildung*). In the nineteenth century, the organizational implementation of the distinct concepts of general education and vocational education led to a school system which provided general education and to a separate system of vocational schools. In addition to other educational systems, these two types still make up the principal part of the German education system as a whole. The individual school systems offer diverse tracks and qualifying certificates and are of varying duration.

The requirements for these certificates are aligned with varying social needs and career areas: the extended primary school prepares mainly for skilled trades; the secondary school prepares largely for middle management; and the *Abitur*, the university entrance examinations, prepares predominantly for university study or higher management. The association of particular types of schools with corresponding career areas – that is to say, the allocating function – reproduces a functionally biased, social class-orientated, tripartite structuring of society.[16]

The social function of the tripartite school system therefore contradicts the postulate of equal opportunities as guaranteed by law. Besides, in the allocating function, contradictions are inherent in the qualifying and the integrating functions of the school system. Because qualifications required by the various types of schools differ substantially regarding content, aims, achievement level and curricula, the qualifying function reinforces the allocating function and thus contradicts the concept of equal opportunities. The integration of pupils in social and professional activities is thus largely determined by the type of school they attend, where pupils continue or acquire the corresponding values and modes of behaviour. In addition to the official value curriculum, a hidden curriculum compels pupils to adapt to specific social and professional standards.

In the writer's view, it is a matter for criticism that the general education which the school system is meant to provide should, in practice, be linked closely with particular interests in the social and professional areas because of the tripartite organization of the school system. Furthermore, German general education is no longer in line with the central principles of an education for democracy and perhaps not even with those promoting the European idea.

A general survey of the differentiated education system as a whole

In reply to the criticism made above, it may be said that the differentiated school system providing general education is paralleled by other educational organizations which supplement, support and consolidate the former. The vocational school system, adult education and further education programmes of individual businesses and youth welfare must be noted in this context. This argument makes the entire German educational system appear to be a large educational edifice in which the school system providing general education is only one of many sectors.

This differentiated educational edifice certainly increases the opportunities for advanced and individualized qualifications. However, its streaming system, as opposed to a setting system, poses a problem in relation to the postulate of equal opportunities. The decision to opt for one course of education can either not be changed at all or it can only be modified subject to certain conditions. Once the decision has been made, transfer to a different type of school, particularly to a 'higher' one, can become very difficult indeed.

The vocational school system

The school system providing general education, particularly the extended primary school and the secondary school, is complemented by the vocational school system. The vocational school system is based, first of all, on the concept of vocational preparation. This concept considers education within modern societies and in modern working conditions to be a matter of qualifying for a profession or vocation and of practising it. Therefore, interaction with socio-political and economic agencies and with a variety of cultural areas represents an integral part of vocational training. Vocational training must therefore be seen as an integrative component of modern, democratic general education. Indeed, the organizational implementation of this new concept led to the vocational school system in the first place. It comprises full-time and part-time schools which must be attended for one or two days a week. For the rest of the week, the apprentices carry on with their practical job training in what is known as *Duales System*.

The German vocational school system is highly differentiated, and accommodates the diverse interests of students and employers by offering a wide range of courses of education and qualifications. Because of this high degree of differentiation, a great number of educational professional opportunities are created, not least for disabled pupils, who are taught in separate classes.

All courses of vocational education award a specific certificate. Nevertheless, very few lead to the *Abitur* standard. Most qualifications acquired in the vocational school system rank below school-leaving, matriculation, standard.

Consequently, the vocational school system can be said to reinforce the selection structure of the tripartite school system preventing students from entering higher education.

The apprenticeship

A commendable feature of the German vocational school system is its organization. Concurrently with a two- to three-year apprenticeship in a company, the apprentice attends a vocational school, or a commercial school, for one whole day at least once a week. This procedure underpins the practical vocational qualification by theory, broadening the student's general education in the process. For example, after finishing the extended primary school, a student may serve an apprenticeship as a carpenter. At the same time he or she attends a vocational school with a department for carpentry apprentices for one day every week, theory and practice complementing each other. The *Duale System* was introduced as long ago as the 1920s and its somewhat narrow, inflexible vocationalization in modern workplaces is beginning to be questioned.

The comprehensive school

The call for a comprehensive system can be justified as follows:

1   The traditional tripartite school system emerged from the social order of the nineteenth century and is no longer suitable for the needs of modern democratic industrial societies. The separate types of schools prescribe a very rigid course offering little opportunity for transfer to another type.
2   The modern school system must be differentiated and graded: but its organization must permit easy transfer from one type of school to another.
3   School education can no longer be expected to provide the entire education for a person's lifetime: education must be directed towards lifelong learning.
4   Teaching and learning can no longer be primarily shaped by experience and tradition; both must be more firmly based on educational science and research findings.
5   Learning at school must combine theory and practice as well as subject-orientated and social learning.

The development process of the German school system was interrupted in the 1960s and 1970s when the Federal Republic was rapidly transforming itself into a modern, democratic, performance-orientated society. The most significant document of this period regarding educational policy, the Conceptual Framework for a New Educational System (*Strukturplan*), published in 1969, expressed for the first time the assumptions for further development of the German education and school systems and demanded the transformation of the tripartite (streaming) into a comprehensive (setting) system.

In the *Strukturplan* of 1969, the educational system is considered to be in a continual state of flux. Perpetual reform is to be the process as well as the task with which a modern society may exercise both its reproductive and its innovative functions. Equal opportunities in society and education will thus become reality. The educational system and the school system will differentiate as well as integrate. The replacement of the traditional schools by the comprehensive school (*Gesamtschule*) therefore appears to be a correlated reform process.

The proportion of comprehensive schools within a given Federal state varies, but it is still small in comparison to that of other types of schools. European integration may, however, tend to direct the present state of development towards a setting system.

Taking stock of the entire development of comprehensive schools from the 1960s to the present day, such schools may be said to differ from the tripartite school system in the following ways:[17]

1   Opportunities for higher education for working-class children are substantially increased; however, inequality survives within comprehensive schools to some extent.
2   Education courses are more open and more easily modified.
3   Comprehensive schools do not award a distinctive leaving and qualifying certificate of their own, but must still award the qualifying certificates of the tripartite school system. This is a major problem because the various certificates help to reproduce the traditional school divisions.
4   Repeating a year because of low performance has been abolished in comprehensive schools.
5   Self-organized learning and, above all, social learning in the sense of cooperative learning are cultivated extensively; nevertheless, weak pupils still feel this generally favourable school climate as a threat to their identity.
6   The comprehensive school has opened up life outside the school as a resource and encouraged learning through everyday life situations; specific days and weeks set aside for projects and socio-educational work are characteristic of this approach.

Despite such a radical approach to learning, traditional classes and subjects still predominate due to the academic inertia of the German educational tradition.

Summary

With respect to the idea of a 'Single Europe', the highly diverse school system described does, despite of its rigidity and lack of integrative factors, leave room for a number of developments supporting the European example:

1   All pupils start learning a foreign language in the fifth form. Usually the first foreign language is English, but in the Rhineland Palatinate, which borders on France, pupils may also start with French.

2   In the Rhineland Palatinate, pilot projects have been introduced in some primary schools regarding bilingual education and/or teaching French as the first foreign language. With this in mind, new methods and new curricula have been developed. These projects are supervised scientifically by the University of Landau-Koblenz. In cooperation with the Ecole Normale at Quimper, Brittany, new curricula have been developed for primary school teacher training. These curricula have already been tested.[18]

3   Throughout the secondary level, visits are organized to other European Union countries whose languages are studied at school. These visits are a normal component of the curriculum and financed partly by European programmes.

4   In addition, partnership programmes involving individual classes have been run. Within the framework of these exchange programmes, classes visit each other for extended periods; pupils explore the foreign country; they attend school and live with host families. The Federal state subsidizes these forms of European cooperation and covers the cost of insurance, although parents must meet the main share of expenses. Consequently, families in the lower socio-economic strata are placed at a disadvantage regarding meaningful participation in such opportunities designed for realizing the European 'ideal'. Even so, school partnerships are increasingly more common in all German school systems, which helps to share out costs.

5   A number of school curricula already provide for the theme of European integration within and across teaching subjects.

Post-school education

Teacher training

Teacher training is geared to the requirements of the different types of target schools. In some Federal states prospective teachers of grammar schools and vocational and commercial schools are trained at universities or at colleges of advanced technology (*Technische Hochschulen*), whereas prospective teachers of other schools are trained at teacher training colleges (*Pädagogische Hochschulen*). In other states, universities are responsible for the entire teacher training programme.

In Germany, teacher training encompasses two stages. The first stage covers academic studies at the university and concludes with the First State Examination (*Erstes Staatsexamen*). Usually, students study two main subjects (for example, mathematics and physics) and education as a subsidiary subject. Afterwards, graduates apply to the state ministries of education for a student teaching position. If their application is accepted, the second stage (*Referendarzeit*) follows. Student teachers complete a two-year programme which is the exclusive responsibility of the particular state ministry of education; the universities are not involved. Student teachers have to teach their subjects according to a limited timetable and must attend specialized seminars. They are supervised by experienced practising teacher mentors. The student teaching programme concludes with the Second State Examination (*Zweites Staatsexamen*). Subsequently, graduates may be fully employed as teachers, and their employing authority is the Federal state. As teachers are civil servants, they are sworn in and receive a state pension, usually at 62 years of age. Depending on the type of school, they teach between 24 and 28 hours per week. The remaining hours, making up the total work-load of 39 hours weekly, are reserved for preparation and the marking of pupils' work.

The division of teacher training into two stages is frequently criticized because it entails the separation of theory and practice as well as of education and administration in teacher training programmes. So far, an integrated teacher training programme, common in many other European countries, has not been introduced. One explanation may be the fact that teachers are employed by the Federal state and become civil servants after a trial period. The state thus assumes a dominant position with regard to training and employment. This fact, and the orientation of training and employment towards one specific type of school, contributes to a narrowing of teaching careers and attitudes focusing on one particular type of teaching experience. In consequence, flexibility and innovation in respect of the organizational, professional and attitudinal dimensions are hampered, and this includes new educational issues such as that of 'Single Europe'. Foreign nationals, including citizens of member states of the European Union, cannot be employed for life as civil servants in any subject. Those from EU countries, however, may be employed on limited contracts for up to three years, renewable, in state schools. They receive a higher salary, but no assistance with retirement pensions, and can be dismissed at short notice.

Teachers are advised to take part in in-service and other courses of further education. For this purpose, institutes and centres with full-time employed personnel have been set up in all Federal states. The state and the churches maintain most of these institutions. At this level, universities are again involved. For many years, these institutions have also offered workshops and excursions to other European Union member states. Within this framework, joint seminars of German teachers and teachers from other EU countries take place; for example, in the Rhineland Palatinate, teachers from the United Kingdom and France have been coming together. Retraining topics include the comparison of school systems, intercultural situations at school and in the classroom, and bilingual instruction in subjects such as mathematics. On the political and administrative level, this basic European cooperation enjoys strong support. Funds are made available according to the financial circumstances of the Federal states, but in order to make such initiatives really effective a substantial increase in funding will be necessary.

Further education

The area of further education consists of a diverse, wide-ranging, pluralist system which comprises and/or supplements all educational institutions. The local communities, churches, political parties, trade unions and social clubs are among those providing tuition in the further education system. Courses are adapted to all age groups and social classes. Qualifying certificates, as well as certificates which merely document acquired knowledge or skills, are awarded, and this to some extent offsets the rigid certification in the different school types. In addition to full-time lecturers, other teachers, including university professors, teach classes in further education.

The European dimension is involved in four specific areas: (a) modern foreign languages; (b) culture and travel; (c) intercultural cooperation; and (d) further vocational training or retraining. In each of these specialisms, almost all organizations maintain links with other European countries. These, however, could be further extended and strengthened. The greater flexibility of the further education sector in respect of organization, curricula and methods adopted by the individual institutions (as opposed to the school system) may be of great assistance in this context. 'Unbureaucratic' financial support will secure and preserve the necessary self-organization and purposeful initiative to face both challenge and opportunity provided by the 'Single Europe' context.

Higher education

The system of higher education is highly differentiated. Classical universities (*Universitäten/Hochschulen*) compete with colleges of advanced technology (*Technische Hochschulen*) and teacher training colleges (*Pädagogische Hochschulen*) as well as with private universities and technical colleges (*Fachhochschulen*) in many career areas. There are no tuition fees at German universities or tertiary colleges. Loans are available to cover maintenance expenses.

Due to the universal and internationally recognized quality of research in Germany, there are manifold relations with universities in all European countries. Exchanges take place mainly within the framework of partnership programmes. For example, the University of Mainz has entered into partnership with the universities of Dijon, Glasgow, Valencia, Parma, Warsaw and Baku as well as with the Erfurt Medical College. Not much teaching is included in this rather traditional transfer and exchange of academic expertise. Language studies require a stay abroad and practical training. The same does not apply to the social sciences, including education. The Erasmus programme has been the first to provide for cooperative European studies in the field of education. Positive results are already making themselves felt. It would be desirable for Erasmus programmes to be extended, and indeed supplemented by new programmes, especially for teachers. So far, higher education has been most closely involved with European collaboration programmes.

German attitudes towards a Single Europe

Germans view the prospect of European integration on the whole positively; this goes especially for the younger generation. Ironically, the recent disturbances in the provinces of the former GDR have not affected EU citizens. The education system, particularly its provision of modern language skills (at least one language is available in all post-primary schools after the fourth year, and from year 7, except in the *Hauptschule*, a second foreign language must be chosen), seems well prepared to cope with the challenges of the European labour market. The prospect of integration does not affect Germans' self-concept of their identity as Germans. Indeed, some educationists believe that a European curriculum is more likely to promote the formation of a national identity that is flexible and adaptable than a narrowly national one in cultural and linguistic terms. A European perspective is well developed among those Germans who have completed a vocational education, including the unique dual system. On the other hand, the existence of the thirteenth year of schooling runs contrary to the trend elsewhere in Europe. Also, widespread participation in school of parents and experts from the world of business and industry is discouraged by teachers and their professional associations. Recently, however, a more *méthode directe* approach to teaching has been taking over in classrooms, especially with the European dimension parts of the curriculum: exchanges and language work. In response to enquiries school authorities confirm that European concerns 'are realized in all schools in a great variety of informal ways'.

Because of the spending limits, grants are not generous in the case of education, there are few teaching vacancies, and thus there are few chances for regular teaching posts in German schools for European Community nationals, except as language assistants and in language schools. The civil servant (*Beamten*) status of teachers, which is still the rule, as suggested earlier does not make things any easier.

As a function of changing processes all over Europe, the German education system will change to more European ideas and standards. There is great expectation on the part of teachers, parents and educators that this process will be given a stronger push ahead in the near future, resulting in Internet projects and the introduction of innovatory curriculum components such as Awareness of Language and Intercultural Education, both helpful in the changing European scene.

Notes

1 *Bulletin der Europäischen Gemeinschaften Kommission*, EGKS-EWG-EHG 5–1988, no. 2, pp. 10–15.
2 Ibid., pp. 10–11.
3 See Kron (1996, pp. 279–327).
4 The FRG was founded in 1949. The Basic Law was introduced on 23 May 1949.
5 This conference has existed since 1948.
6 In the *Bundesrat* the ministers and presidents of all Federal states are represented.
7 The State Constitution was passed on 18 May 1947.
8 See Müller-Solger (1990, pp. 816–18).
9 See *Bulletin der Europäischen Gemeinschaften Kommission*, EHG 5–1988, p. 1.
10 See Arbeitsgruppe am Max-Planck-Institut (1984).
11 The two-year orientation phase may be integrated in a separate educational establishment.

12 See Bundesminister für Bildung und Wissenschaft (1990, pp. 354–79). Dr Manfred Wandersleb, of the Teacher Training College Erfurt, was so kind as to supply the information on the current situation in the former GDR.
13 See Kron (1989). Mr Gerd Schmitz, Coordinator of European Education, Ministry of Education of the State of Rhineland Palatinate, Mainz, kindly supplied this information on the latest developments.
14 This decree applies the Basic Guidelines of Brussels (cf. *Bulletin der Europäischen Gemeinschaften Kommission*, EHG 5–1988) to the FRG. The statements on 'European Awareness' and the 'Guidelines for Implementation' as well as the 'Recommendations for Further Development' are particularly significant.
15 See Deutscher Bildungsrat (1971, pp. 217–20).
16 See Fend (1977).
17 See Tillmann (1986).
18 See Hegele and Rück (1990, pp. 22–5).

References

Arbeitsgruppe am Max-Planck-Institut für Bildungsforschung (1984) *Das Bildungswesen in der Bundesrepublik Deutschland: Ein Überlick für Eltern, Lehrer und Schüler*, Hamburg: Rowohlt.

Berggreen, I. (1990) 'Europa 92: Konsequenzen der Europäischen Einigung für den Kulturföderalismus in der Bundesrepublik Deutschland', *Zeitschrift für Pädagogik*, 36(6): 827–47.

Bund-Länder-Kommission für Bildungsplanung und Forschungsforderung (1989) 'Wie öffnet sich die Schule neuen Entwicklungen und Aufgaben?', paper presented at OECD/CERI-seminar, Bonn.

Bundesminister für Bildung und Wissenschaft (ed.) (1990) *Grund- und Strukturdaten 1990/91*, Bonn: Eigenverlag.

Committee of the European Communities (1988) 'Der Beitrag des Bildungswesens zur Vollendung des Binnenmarktes', *Bulletin der Europäischen Gemeinschaften*, 21(5): 10–15.

Deutsche Gesellschaft für Erziehungswissenschaft (1988) *Pädagogen-Handbuch 1988/89: Verzeichnis der Institutionen und des Personals erziehungswissenschaftlicher Forschung und Lehre*, Weinheim and Basel: Beltz.

Deutscher Bildungsrat (1971) *Strukturplan für das Bildungswesen: Empfehlungen der Bildungskommission*, Stuttgart: Klett.

Fend, H. (1977) 'Gesellschaftliche Bedingungen schulischer Sozialisation', *Soziologie der Schule I*, Weinheim and Basel: Beltz.

Grundgesetz für die Bundesrepublik Deutschland und Verfassung für Rheinland-Pfalz (1971) Mainz: Institut für Staatsbürgerliche Bildung.

Hegele, I. and Rück, H. (1990) 'Lehrerausbildung auf dem Weg nach Europa', *Uniprisma: Zeitschrift der Universität Koblenz/Landau*, 12: 22–5.

Kron, F.W. (1989) 'The nature and limitations of teachers' professional autonomy', in W. Tulasiewicz and A. Adams (eds), *Teachers' Expectations and Teaching Reality*, London and New York: Routledge, pp. 261–81.

Kron, F.W. (1996) *Grundwissen Pädagogik*, 5th edn, Munich and Basel: Reinhardt.

Kultusministerium Rheinland-Pfalz (ed.) (1983) *Bildungswege in Rheinland-Pfalz*, Speyer: Kultusministerium Rheinland-Pfalz.

—— (ed.) (1982a) *Die Berufsbildende Schule in Rheinland-Pfalz*, Speyer: Kultusministerium Rheinland-Pfalz.

—— (ed.) (1982b) *Mainzer Studienstufe: Informationen für Schüler Eltern und Lehrer*, Mainz: Kultusministerium Rheinland-Pfalz.

Ludwig, H. (ed.) (1981) *Gesamtschule in der Diskussion*, Bad Heilbrunn: Klinkhardt.

Müller-Solger, H. (1990) 'Bildungspolitische Zusammenarbeit der Europäischen Gemeinschaft in Europa', *Zeitschrift für Pädagogik*, 36(6): 805–25.

Sekretariat der Ständigen Konferenz der Kultusminister der Länder in der Bundesrepublik Deutschland (ed.) (1990) *Europa im Unterricht*: Beschluß der Kultusministerkonferenz vom 8.6.1978 i.d.F. vom 7.12.1990 (Anlage IV z. NS 251. KMK 06/07.12.1990), Bonn und Berlin.

Tillmann, K.-J. (1986) 'Zwanzig Jahre Gesamtschulentwicklung', *Westermanns Pädagogische Beiträge*, 1: 12–19.

—— (1990) 'Welche Schule? Zur deutsch-deutschen Bildungsdiskussion', *Dialoge*, 1: 14–15.

Tulasiewicz, W. and Adams, A. (eds) (1989) *Teachers' Expectations and Teaching Reality*, London and New York: Routledge.

7　Greece

Michael Kassotakis

The present study seeks to assess the impact which the participation of Greece in the European Union (EU) has on Greek education. To this end, the most important reforms which have taken place in Greek education after the 1980s which aim to adapt Greece to the European reality and enable it to respond successfully to the challenges emanating from the changes in the European space, are briefly described. Finally, the main problems associated with the Greek educational system are also addressed in the study.[1]

Greek education in the context of the European Union

The creation of the EU, the free circulation of capital, goods and workers in the single European market, the perspectives created by economic and monetary European integration and the institutional changes provided in the recent Treaty of Amsterdam have established a new economic, social and political reality in Western Europe. New perspectives for further development are open to all members of the EU. The recent changes will potentially cause remarkable rearrangements in the labour market and will produce new conditions for the employment of young people. They will also bring the European nations closer and mark the beginning of deeper social, political and cultural changes in Europe, which, together with the socio-political 'transformations' occurring in the Eastern European countries after the dissolution of the Soviet bloc, have led to the creation of a 'New Europe'.

The globalisation of the economy is continually increasing economic and commercial competition in the world and exposes Europe to new challenges. Such competition is expected to have an impact not only on Europe as a whole, but also on each of the EU member states. This impact will be more significant on the smaller and less-developed countries, like Greece, the economy of which is still characterised by several weaknesses and which will probably have more difficulties in responding efficiently to the emerging challenges and in coping with the competition successfully. Most of the small and technologically antiquated Greek enterprises will be forced either to close down or be absorbed by bigger European units. Such an eventuality will have far-reaching repercussions on the Greek economy and society, especially on the labour market in which the existing rate of unemployment is approximately 10 per cent. The support given, therefore, to Greece by the EU in order to enable it to restructure its economy, improve the effectiveness of its educational system and converge on the standards of the other European countries is of great importance.

In the new European market, Greek employees must show that they have the same qualifications and professional skills as other European workers, so as to be able to demand occupational placement on equal terms. On the other hand, the expected increase in contacts amongst Europeans, the free mobility of workers and the inevitable gradual adoption of similar ways of living will progressively lead to a general 'Europeanisation' of the cultural and social life of all European nations. This 'Europeanisation', being a necessary condition for the integration of Europe, will very likely cause the erosion of some ethnic, cultural and social characteristics of the European nations, especially the smallest ones. The less frequently used languages, like Modern Greek, will probably face the threat of a greater 'shrinkage' in the future, which will have undesirable effects on the national identity of those who have them as mother-tongues.

In view of such an eventuality, Greek education will have to provide the labour market with a properly equipped workforce, contribute to the modernisation and reconstruction of the economy, and also satisfy many other needs which will be generated in the above perspective. It will undertake, for example, responsibility for upgrading the functioning of state mechanisms by improving the initial and in-service training of civil servants. The increase in the efficiency of state mechanisms is an indispensable precondition for Greece to take the maximum advantage of the opportunities offered by the European Union.

Education will be called upon to contribute to the dissemination of the European idea and help the Greeks to acquire the necessary knowledge and language skills to enable them to understand, communicate and cooperate efficiently with other Europeans. On the other hand, the preservation of Greek history, tradition, culture, Orthodox religion and Modern Greek language, which are considered essential components of the Greek national identity, will also have to be accomplished through education.

Greek education has another additional responsibility in the New Europe: to stress that the Greek origins of European civilisation have been the formative link between all European nations. Therefore Greece must play one of the leading roles in the study of the roots of European culture.[2]

In view of the above, the following questions can be raised: Can Greek education satisfy the increasing needs generated by the integration of Europe? Is Greek education able to compete with education in other EU countries, especially the most developed ones, as far as the training of scientists and workers is concerned?

Views and attitudes of the Greek people

The views of the Greek people on the above questions differ. Some fear that Greek education is not well prepared to respond successfully to the aforementioned demands or to take full advantage of the opportunities offered by the European Union.[3] This is one of the reasons why some Greeks believe that intensive attempts are required to improve the educational system. The following quotation from an article by the Prime Minister K. Simitis, written some years ago (1992), reflects this point of view:

> the problem of the Greek educational system becomes more intense as 1992 approaches. In competition among the educational systems, Greece lags behind. Tomorrow, in the united Europe, all the opportunities, all the possibilities and all the benefits will belong to the others, because they will be better qualified and better prepared to cope with the emerging problems. If we do not stop going backwards, we will be providing the European market with low-level personnel in jobs requiring merely mechanical skills and not creative work.[4]

Similar views are being expressed nowadays despite the remarkable progress made in Greek education.

A small minority of Greek people, affiliated with the Communist Party, express more negative attitudes towards the integration of Greece in the EU and the changes which were brought about in education and the labour market in the context of the EU directives. These attitudes derive from the position that Greece will become subjugated to the interests of the metropolitan centres and also the view that the compliance of education, the economy and the labour market with European directives will aggravate the dependence of Greece upon the centres of capitalism.[5] Progressively, these reactions have ceased. It seems that the majority of Greek people support the position that the integration of Greece into the EU will exert a positive influence upon Greek education, society and economy. They argue that competition will urge Greek people to systematise their education, and work towards its improvement more consistently and effectively. In addition, the economic support offered to Greece from the structural funds of the EU and/or any other scientific and technological assistance will positively contribute to that.[6]

In brief, the idea of an integrated Europe has been gaining acceptance in Greece. At the same time, Greeks are becoming aware of the weaknesses and the problems that the economy, the labour market, public administration, the educational system and some other sectors of Greek society are faced with. They have realised, moreover, that the adjustment of Greece to most developed European countries will be achieved only if these problems are solved. The improvement of education will contribute positively to overcoming the present difficulties. It will also help to secure the opportunities required for the active participation of Greece in the construction of the 'New Europe'. The growing awareness of the role that education can play strengthens the demand for educational renewal.

Several changes enabling the educational system to respond to the new necessities have been observed since the 1980s, leading to a number of significant steps taken in all sectors.

Recent changes in Greek primary and secondary education

The educational reforms during the period 1980–96

In the 1980s, Greek education underwent a number of reforms introduced by the PASOK socialist government. These reforms aimed at the democratisation and modernisation of the educational system. Such changes encompassed the structure and the administration of education as well as the school curriculum. The main structural changes at the level of primary and secondary education can be detailed as follows: (a) the establishment of the comprehensive Multilateral Lyceum (*Polykladiko Lykeio*), the aim of which was to combine general with technical and vocational education. In the educational reform which took place in 1997, the *Polykladiko Lykeio* was the basis on which a new type of Comprehensive Lyceum was formed; (b) the abolition of entrance examinations to the Lyceum (upper secondary school); and (c) modification of the selection system for entrance to higher education. The system established at the beginning of the 1980s was based on national examinations (*Genikes Exetaseis*) in four subjects in each of four branches of studies (*desmes*). However, this system will be abolished in 2000 as provided by the education law 2525 of 1997, the main features of which will be presented below.[7]

The nursery and primary school curriculum was entirely revised after 1981. New subjects such as environmental studies, health education and civil education, the teaching of foreign languages and supplementary teaching for slow learners have been introduced into primary schools. In addition, primary school textbooks as well as the methodology of teaching and evaluation of pupils have been updated.

In secondary school curricula the major innovations are as follows: (a) the introduction into the curriculum of new subjects like information technology, political economy, technology and production, requiring the writing of new school textbooks; (b) supplementary teaching for low achievers; (c) the introduction of optional courses and educational activities into the curriculum of the Multilateral Lyceum; and (d) the organisation of creative afternoon activities in some schools.

It should be noted that in its administration the Greek educational system has always been centralised and bureaucratically organised. All decisions pertaining to curricula, textbooks, school timetables, the appointment, salaries and promotion of teaching staff, the establishment, equipment and operation of schools, are made by the Ministry of Education and uniformly introduced into all schools. With law 1566 of 1985 for primary and secondary education, some steps towards the decentralisation of education, mainly relating to the allocation and administration of school grants, were taken. The same law provides for the participation of the local authorities and representatives of social bodies in educational committees functioning at school level as well as at regional and national levels. However, the measures taken towards this end have not brought about very satisfactory results. Greek education still maintains its traditional hierarchical, centralised and bureaucratic structure, which makes difficult the realisation of a substantial change.

The school unit remains the core of the system. It is governed by the school headteacher, supported by a deputy headteacher and the teachers' council. Their autonomy is, however, limited due to their strong dependency on the local and, mainly, on the central educational services. The educational institutions operating in every region are administered by educational directorates which are different for each level of education (primary and secondary). There are 108 Directorates of Primary and Secondary Education in the 54 prefectures of the country. In some prefectures there are also Education Officers. The basic responsibility of the Directors and Officers is the coordination and supervision of the functioning of schools. The Minister of Education, supported by one or two Deputy Ministers, is the top educational authority overseeing education in the country. The Pedagogical Institute, a service of the Ministry of Education, is responsible for curriculum development, the school syllabuses and the supervision of in-service teacher training activities. It is also one of the main advisory bodies of the Minister of Education.

Teachers are given advice and information concerning educational matters by school counsellors who are selected from among teachers with 15 years' teaching experience and adequate academic credentials. Their service lasts for four years and is subject to renewal.

Further, law 1566 of 1985 provides for the participation of secondary school pupils in the administration of the school and their involvement in extra-curricular activities. Two types of school organisation have been developed: (a) school communities and (b) school cooperatives. The former seek to promote collaboration among pupils, to emphasise freedom of expression, encourage the free flow of ideas as well as activities aiming at the self-development of pupils. They also aim at pupil–parent cooperation in a variety of school and community activities. School cooperatives are responsible for the organisation of fund-raising activities in schools. In reality, the role of pupil organisations in the relation between school, society and the world of work is marginal.[8]

New changes in the Greek educational system were put forward by the right-wing New Democracy government which was in power between 1990 and 1993. The emphasis on student and teacher assessment, the increase in school control, the introduction of the teaching of older forms of the Greek language in lower secondary schools (*Gymnasium*), the establishment of a National System for Professional Training have been some of the main characteristics of the changes occurring in Greek education in this period.

In October 1993 the PASOK socialist government came to power again. The educational policy of the period 1990–3 was revised at some points. Although the new government brought back the educational policy of the 1980s, a number of the previous measures, like the teaching of older forms of the Greek language and the National System for Professional Training, were maintained. The effort to adjust education to new socio-economic conditions and to reinforce Greek education in order to comply with the European reality has been stronger during recent years. To this end, it has been used more often as a context of reference by educational reformists now than in the 1980s. The emphasis shifted from the democratisation of education, which was the prevailing goal during the 1980s, to the qualitative upgrading of education, the effectiveness of which has been the subject of continuous criticism in recent years.

The situation in primary and secondary education

According to the existing statistical data, the enrolment ratios in primary and secondary education compare favourably with those of the most developed countries of the EU.[9] However, enrolments in the pre-primary schools are lower. An increase in the number of pre-primary pupils, therefore, must be one of the priorities of educational reform. Such an increase is necessary in view of the continued increase in female employment.

Compulsory attendance in Greek schools is of shorter duration (nine years) than that reported for the most developed European countries. Furthermore, there is no provision for further compulsory vocational training for those who complete their education at the age of 15. This lack of provision, together with the underdevelopment of adult education, deprives the educational system of the necessary flexibility and the possibility of satisfying the need for continual retraining of the workforce, imposed by the changing labour market.

Despite the educational reforms which have taken place during the period 1981–96 general education curricula still maintain, to a large extent, their academic orientation. Indeed, the whole school system is marked by its authoritarian and formalistic character. Many Greeks complain about the quality of education offered to pupils and especially about young people's inability to use the Greek language correctly. On the other hand, limited practical and technological knowledge is offered to pupils who attend the *Gymnasium* and to those who had selected a General Lyceum until 1997 (about 60 per cent of post-compulsory education pupils). The use of new information technology in schools is limited despite its usefulness in the world of work. Career education and guidance is not well developed; it mainly focuses on the provision of general information about jobs and studies.

Further, technical and vocational education has not been well developed. The quality of studies is considered low and the practical experience of the students has been inadequate. It is difficult, therefore, for technical and vocational school graduates to find a job commensurate with their studies.[10] It is likely that this problem will be greater in the future due to the expected increase of competition in the labour market on the one hand and the probable modernisation of Greek industry and economy on the other, unless technical and vocational education is improved. The creation of the National System for Vocational Education and Training implemented with the financial support of the EU has been a significant step towards the improvement of professional training, but it is not sufficiently well developed yet fully to satisfy existing demands.

Until recently (1996–7), the majority of Greek students attended general secondary schools, leaving technical and vocational schools to atrophy. The reasons for this one-sided orientation are: (a) the low prestige and the under-development of technical and vocational schools; (b) the difficulties vocational school graduates have with finding jobs; (c) the availability of better opportunities of access to the universities from the General Lyceum,[11] one of the recently abolished types of Lyceum. The attempts made to increase the number of pupils who attend technical and vocational schools have not achieved the expected results.

The proportion of secondary school graduates who succeed in entering universities is approximately one-third of the candidates. This imbalance between supply and demand for higher education is the cause of several educational and social problems in Greece. The great majority of Lyceum students attend *frontisteria* (private schools) in order to pass the highly competitive entrance examinations to the universities. Many of those who fail to enter tertiary institutions go abroad in order to receive higher education. In 1992, for example, the number of Greek students abroad represented 12.1 per cent of the total student population in Greece despite the remarkable decrease noticed in the mid-1980s. According to other estimates, however, this number is higher. In 1993 Greek families spent more than US$231 million on the education of their children abroad on the basis of official evidence. According to the data reported in recent studies, this cost is greater than the total of current expenses for higher education in Greece.[12]

Some Lyceum graduates who fail to enter tertiary institutions attend vocational courses in non-accredited private educational centres called *Ergastiria Eleftheron Spoudon* (centres for further studies). The degrees awarded by these centres are not recognised by the state, a fact which minimises the opportunities of graduates to find a job. Further, a number of secondary school graduates enter the labour market without having received any specific training apart from the general education required for unskilled white-collar workers. The shortage of jobs in the public and private sectors increases their difficulties in finding suitable employment.

These weaknesses in the educational system negatively affect its socio-economic efficiency, and will not facilitate the role which Greek education must play in the European space.

The recent educational reform

The Greek government passed a Bill in Parliament which became law in September 1997 in order to face the above-mentioned problems and to prepare education to cope successfully with the present challenges. The main changes brought about in Greek education with this new educational Bill are:

- the establishment of the *Eniaio Lykeio* (Comprehensive Lyceum) as the only type of Lyceum;

- the creation of the 'daylong' school at the level of primary education (kindergartens and primary schools);
- the reformation of the evaluation system of pupils: the new system aims at a more reliable and multilateral assessment not only of pupils' knowledge – which was emphasised by the previous system as well – but also of skills and critical thinking;
- the enlargement of accessibility options to tertiary education, and the new way of entrance to universities and higher education institutes which will take place in 2000;
- the abolition of the 'waiting list', on the basis of which teachers had been appointed, and the upgrading of their initial and in-service training;
- the re-establishment of the evaluation of schools, teachers and educational cadres which had been inactive for about 20 years;
- the creation of the so-called schools of 'second opportunity' for those who have not finished compulsory education; and
- the reformation of careers and vocational guidance activities.[13]

The creation of the *Eniaio Lykeio* (Comprehensive Lyceum), which replaces all previous types of Lyceum (General Lyceum, Technical and Vocational Lyceum, Multilateral Lyceum) and the abolition of the entrance examinations to higher education are considered the most important characteristics of recent educational reform. The *Eniaio Lykeio*, the first class of which is attended by all students, comprises the following three directions of studies, which start in the second class: (a) theoretical; (b) scientific (pure sciences); and (c) technological. The last direction has two separate cycles in the third class.

The above reform emphasises the provision of general education combined with technological knowledge and the development of a wide range of skills. Thus it is expected that *Eniaio Lykeio* graduates who do not follow higher education will be able to get professional training offered by a flexible and easily adjustable reaction to the changes occurring in the labour market system. This system will be based on the present National System for Vocational Education and Training which is composed of a network of public and private institutes for professional training (*Institouta Epagelmatikis Katartisis, IEK*). IEKs operate in cooperation with local productive agencies under the supervision of an Organisation for Vocational Education and Training, called OEEK (*Organismos Epagelmatikis Ekpedefsis kai Katartisis*) in several cities throughout the country. OEEK is a self-governing body, the administration of which comprises representatives of various Ministries and social partners (employers–employees). Although IEKs are the responsibility of the Ministry of Education, they function outside the formal educational system and offer various flexible programmes of educational training which are of different duration.

The previous secondary technical and vocational schools attended by those who had not followed Lyceum after finishing their compulsory education have also been replaced by the newly established technical and vocational institutions, called TEE (*Technika Epagelmatika Ekpedeftiria*) which are a part of the formal educational system. Those schools comprise two cycles of studies lasting 2 and 1.5 years respectively. The graduates of the first cycle are entitled to three choices: (a) to have a profession; (b) to complete the second cycle of the *TEEs*; and (c) to get registered for the second class of *Eniaio Lykeio*. The graduates of the second cycle of studies are awarded a certificate which allows them either to follow a career or to get registered, upon certain conditions, at tertiary non-university level technological institutions. The graduates of *TEEs* can upgrade their education by attending *IEKs*. In addition to the structural changes taking place in the *TEEs*, the educational reform provides for new programmes of studies and flexible schemes of professional training. The creation of the *TEEs* and the upgrading of the *IEKs* are expected to enhance the possibility for the Greek education and economy to respond to the challenges of the 'New Europe'. It is worth mentioning that Apprenticeship Institutions (*Scholes Mathiteias*) operate out of the formal educational system under the supervision of the Manpower Employment Organisation (OAED) which belongs to the Ministry of Labour.

The following issues are also under consideration in the context of the educational reform: (a) the upgrading of the education offered to Greeks living abroad and those returning home as well as to people coming from other countries; (b) the implementation of multicultural education in Greece and the systematisation of the education of minorities and special social groups (such as Gypsies); and (c) the development of a new national curriculum and school textbooks, which are among the highest priorities of the recent educational reform.

The new National Curriculum aims to:

- secure coherence in subject matter among the different school grades thus abolishing overlapping information and knowledge discontinuities;
- renew and update the content of education;
- allow regional educational authorities to adjust a part of the national curriculum to local needs;
- reinforce the interdisciplinary character of various subjects; and
- integrate related separate subjects into wider thematic areas.

In addition, attempts are to be made to replace the single textbook for each subject with one book chosen by the teacher from among three books written under the supervision of the Pedagogical Institute. The implementation of this innovation started in the school year 1999–2000.

The expected qualitative improvement of the education offered in the Lyceum along with the progressive abolition of the *numerus clausus* of those entering universities and technological institutions will potentially decrease the demand for *parapedia* (education offered in private preparatory schools called *frontistiria*) and the high demand for studies abroad.

The recent reform is supported financially by national resources and a pro-gramme for educational development called *EPEAEK* (*Epixeirisiako Programma*

Ekpedefsis kai Arxikis Epagelmatikis Katartisis) funded by the second European Community Support Framework 1995–9 (Second CSF). *EPEAEK* amounts to about Dr600 billion, 75 per cent of which is covered by the European Structural Funds. This programme aims to innovate education, boost human capital by enhancing education and skill levels, increase competitiveness and enhance employment prospects.

Although the recent educational reform has been accepted positively by the majority of Greek people, the reactions of teachers' unions, the negative attitudes of political parties from the Opposition and some problems related to school infrastructure create difficulties for its successful implementation. None the less, the changes introduced by the recent educational reform have been necessary, and the existing difficulties will be eliminated soon. In order, however, for this reform fully to achieve its goals emphasis should be given to the following issues:

- realisation of a political consensus as to the way educational matters should be addressed;
- reinforcement of the dialogue between the state and the social partners and especially those involved with education;
- development of more links between school and the world of work;
- decentralisation of the educational system and increase of the role that regional educational authorities and committees should play;
- clarification of the professional rights of school graduates;
- provision of compulsory supplementary training (part-time courses) for those who terminate their schooling after age 15;
- systematisation of lifelong education and provision of supplementary training or basic training at any age;
- the increase of the share of the gross domestic product (GDP) invested in education must gradually reach the corresponding levels of the rest of the European countries, since Greece has the lowest share of GNP allocated to education.[14]

European educational cooperation and Greek primary and secondary education

Greece has made efforts to foster participation in EU educational programmes despite difficulties related to language and lack of appropriate infrastructure existing mainly at regional levels. A separate directorate, which functions in the Ministry of Education, is responsible for the promotion of cooperation between Greece and the rest of the member states and also for the dissemination of educational information among teachers and pupils. The national unit of the Eurydice network has been incorporated into this directorate. The Greek Scholarships Foundation plays an important role in the promotion of European educational cooperation and the implementation of the Socrates programme. Similar bodies (such as the Pedagogical Institute, the National Foundation for

Youth and the Centre for Educational Research) are also responsible for the coordination of some European educational programmes.

The General Secretary for Youth, who is supervised by the Minister of Education, plays an essential role in the development of youth exchange programmes. The National Labour Institute is the national agent for the Leonardo programme, supervised by the Ministry of Labour which has the responsibility for the implementation of programmes concerning the professional training of workers and unemployed people. Furthermore, the General Secretariat for Research and Technology is responsible for cooperation in research programmes, while other ministries, organisations (private and public), banks and local authorities participate in European projects and/or organise seminars supported by the European Commission.

The participation of Greece in the European programmes of educational cooperation and teachers' exchange schemes has been increasing continually in recent years. As an indication, in 1995, 43 Greek schools participated in the Comenius programme, while in 1997 this number increased to 220. In 1994, 244 teachers participated in the Lingua programme (action 3). This number doubled in the next year. In the context of the Arion programme, 85 Greek teachers visited other European countries during 1995–7.[15] Greek participation in the actions of the Socrates programme referring to school education is also considered satisfactory. Participation in the rest of the European initiatives which concern vocational training, employment, exchange of young workers and other related activities is satisfactory as well. For example, in the transnational projects of placement and exchange in the Leonardo programme (action 1I.1.2.a,b,c), 259 trainees, 73 young workers and 68 trainers participated during 1995–7 (data 31 May 1997).[16] The experience obtained by these activities has been assessed by the Greek National Labour Institute as very useful and constructive.[17] It is also worth mentioning that the participation of teachers and pupils in the mobility programmes funded by *EPEAEK* (Second CSF) which complement the corresponding Socrates and Leonardo actions is of great importance: 1,509 secondary school teachers took part in these programmes (individually and collectively) after they were first advertised (March 1997). This number increased to 2,212 after the next advertisement (June 1997).[18] The participation of teachers and pupils in the mobility programmes as well as in those of the multi-partner schemes funded by the *EPEAEK* has also been significant.

All the above activities have contributed positively to the development of the European dimension in Greek education and the feeling of belonging to Europe, and reinforce the convergence of Greek education with that of the most developed member states.

Despite the progress made in the field of educational cooperation between Greece and the other EU countries, some problems still exist. A rapid increase in the number of pupil and teacher exchanges is difficult to achieve due to difficulties related to the lack of appropriate administrative infrastructure, language problems and insufficient economic support, especially for primary school teachers who are not allowed to participate in exchange actions funded by the *EPEAEK* programme. In addition, there are difficulties related to the distribution of information about the educational activities carried out in the EU and the opportunities for educational cooperation. The following can also be added to the difficulties concerning the expansion of Greek participation in educational cooperation programmes: (a) the lack of motivation on behalf of teachers; (b) the dependency of the school units upon the central administrative services of education, which restricts the possibility for the development of initiatives in schools; and (c) the absence of previous experience as far as international cooperation is concerned. Further, the inflexibility of the school curricula, the detailed definition of school activity by the central educational services do not facilitate the integration into the school reality of the experiences teachers acquire from their participation in European programmes. What is also lacking is the effective coordination and continuity of the innovating educational attempts supported by the European Union and a systematic evaluation of the results obtained.

Despite the existing difficulties, the willingness and zeal characterising those involved with education guarantees the further development of educational cooperation. It is considered that if more emphasis is placed on the teaching of foreign languages in Greek schools and in teacher training institutions, if the national and community funds for pupil and teacher exchanges are increased, and if the programmes for educational cooperation are improved and more systematically evaluated, the above cooperation will be strengthened.

Greek higher education and the European challenge

The present situation in higher education

According to the Greek Constitution, higher education is to be provided free of charge and only by the state. The creation, however, of private higher education institutions has been widely discussed in recent years, since a number of non-recognised higher level institutions, known as *Ergastiria Eleftheron Spoudon* (Centres for Further Studies), operate in cooperation with various foreign universities.

Higher educational institutions are of two kinds: university and non-university level. Both underwent radical structural changes in the 1980s (Bills 1268/82 for the university level and 1404/83 for the non-university level institutions). The main changes in the universities are of a structural and administrative nature (for example, division of the faculties into departments; increase in student and teaching staff participation in decision making bodies; replacement of the chair system by academic domains (*tomeis*) including teaching personnel of related speciality; ranking of the teaching staff into four grades – lecturers, assistant professors, associated professors, professors; and the establishment of a National Council for the Higher Education). All courses have been reorganised into semester courses with modernised curricula, including optional courses and interdepartmental programmes of study.

The organisation of the non-university level institutes, *Technologika Ekpedeftika Idrymata (TEI)*, is similar to that of the university level institutes, *Anotata Ekpedeftika Idrymata (AEI)*. They are divided into schools, departments and sectors. They differ from the *AEI*s in their aims, administrative operational details, qualifications and promotion of their staff, duration of courses (three to three and a half years) and the absence of postgraduate courses. The new Bill for the *TEI*s also provides for the establishment of two advisory services operating within the Ministry of Education: the Council for Technological Education (*Symboulio Technologikis Ekpedefsis, STE*) and the Institute for Technological Education (*Instituto Technologikis Ekpedefsis, ITE*). Regional Technological Councils operate as well.[19]

The recent educational reform provides for the creation of a wide network of inter-university and interdepartmental programmes (*Programmata Spoudon Epilogis, PSE*). These programmes aim at increasing the provision of tertiary level education and the creation of flexible educational schemes in the universities and higher technological institutions, thus enabling them to adjust to recent changes and perspectives, among which the participation of Greece in the European Union has a pre-eminent position. The establishment and recent functioning of the Open University is considered a remarkable change in tertiary education, the promotion of which has been accelerated in view of the European perspective of Greece.[20]

Problems and necessary changes in higher education

Greek higher education has gone through a crisis which has lasted for many years. The main characteristics of this crisis are:

- the inability of the higher institutions to satisfy the social demand for post-secondary education;
- the lack of systematically organised postgraduate studies;
- limited research activities;
- unilateral orientation towards the production of civil servants mainly for the state central government services;
- little involvement in productive activities and few links with the world of enterprise;
- outdated organisation of studies such as the use of one textbook which is usually the only source of knowledge for the students, traditional examining methods, teacher-centred (*ex cathedra*) teaching, and so on;
- low student attendance;
- inadequate funding, which causes insufficiencies in the infrastructure (buildings, libraries, laboratories, and so on).[21]

These drawbacks have had a negative impact on the quality of studies, which has led to reservations as to how well prepared Greek higher education is to face the European challenge and to make the maximum use of the opportunities which will be offered. The socio-economic efficiency of higher education still remains low and the involvement of its institutions in the productive processes is not satisfactory. In addition, the upgrading of the quality of higher studies, especially of postgraduate studies, has not been as expected. Further, some new problems have emerged, such as difficulties pertaining to the employment of university graduates, the increasing lack of balance between needs and resources, the inflexibility of decision-making processes due to the multiplicity of the bodies involved in them.

The recent reforms which have taken place in Greek higher education aim towards the elimination of the above weaknesses. Remarkable progress in the democratisation of the administrative structures has been noticed. New universities and new technical institutes as well as new departments have been established while the creation of 70 new departments has been announced for the next five years. The number of teaching and research staff has increased and the ratio of available university and non-university places to applicants has improved. The creation of the Programmes of Choices (*Programmata Spoudon Epilogis*, PSE), the operation of the Open University and the announced changes concerning the reinforcement of the autonomy of the universities have been mentioned. The reorganisation of undergraduate and postgraduate studies and the promotion of research will enhance the quality of higher studies and enable tertiary education to respond successfully to social and economic demands. They will also link it with the needs of the country and allow it to function as a lifelong education thus increasing its socio-economic efficiency. The funds of the Second Community Support Framework play an important role in the upgrading of Greek tertiary education, enabling the development of new programmes of studies, the improvement of teaching equipment, postgraduate studies, research and practical exercises for students, the modernisation of libraries, the evaluation of institutions, and the streamlining of their administration.

Greek higher education is not lacking in dynamism or the potential for further development. The necessary infrastructure exists, and is continually improving. Many prominent Greek scientists who work abroad, especially in the United States and Western Europe, are returning home now that better work conditions have been created. It is hoped that the challenge of the integrated Europe will accelerate the efforts for the creation of the conditions required for further advances.

Greek higher education and European educational cooperation

Cooperation between institutions of higher education in Greece and those in other European countries has been better developed than cooperation involving primary and secondary level institutions. The bilateral contracts for cultural and scientific cooperation signed by Greece and various other countries, including some EU members, provide for academic staff exchanges and research grants awarded by the governments of the participating countries. A significant increase has also been noticed in the tertiary educational institutions participating in the European programmes of educational cooperation in recent years. After the reservations and doubts expressed by a number of students affiliated to the radical left political parties at the beginning of the implementation of the Erasmus and Comett programmes, the expansion of Greek participation into all EU educational activities has been steadily continuing. In 1995 and 1996, for example, the tertiary educational institutions participated in 763 programmes of inter-university cooperation and in 81 thematic networks, despite the fact that they started functioning in 1996 for the first time. The number of Greek students who had been approved to participate in the Erasmus and Lingua programmes increased from 467 in 1988–9 to 4,800 in 1995–6, while the number of those participating in programmes which had been concluded was 195 in 1988–9 and 2,000 in 1994–5.[22] A similar increase has been observed in other programmes which refer to employment and training, the formation of links between educational institutions and enterprises, participation of educational institutions in regional development and social policies, education of women and special social groups. The expansion of Greek participation in such programmes contributed to the support of the mobility of students and teaching staff, the development of cooperation between universities and higher technological institutions and institutions abroad, and the promotion of the European dimension in Greek education.

Despite the recent remarkable progress in the field of educational cooperation, problems still exist, mainly related to the limited use of the Greek language by foreign students who want to come to Greece. Greek students who wish to participate in European programmes of educational exchanges also face similar problems, but not to the same extent.

The increase in the living cost and expenses of studies abroad, which cannot be fully covered by scholarships offered in the context of the Erasmus programmes, the insufficiency of the administrative infrastructure for the promotion of the above activities and the inadequate dissemination of the related information can be added to the above problems.

Inter-university research cooperation

European funds for the development of research are of great importance due to the fact that expenditure on research in Greece is lower than in other EU member states. In Greece, 0.46 per cent of GNP was allocated to research activities in 1991, as compared to 0.61 per cent in Portugal, 0.87 per cent (1990) in Spain, 0.90 per cent in Ireland, 1.38 per cent in Italy, 2.42 per cent in France and 2.58 per cent in Germany.[23] The number of people who are employed in the research sector must also increase. In Greece 2.7 of every 1,000 persons are employed in the research sector as compared to 2.5 in Portugal, 4.7 in Spain, 6.1 in Ireland, 5.8 in Italy, 11.9 in France and 12.9 in Germany (1991 data except for Portugal, which are for 1990).[24]

In 1996, the total research funding given to Greece by the European Community was Dr21.5 billion. This amount of money represents 23.4 per cent of the total research funds in Greece. Much of this amount was allocated to higher institutions and the remainder was absorbed by the research centres, some of which cooperate with universities.

The advanced technology introduced into Greece from the EU countries and also the modernisation of the infrastructure might not have reached the present level of development without international research cooperation and EU support. The most important cooperation concerns projects to do with computing, energy, protection of the environment and agricultural development. Quite often, experts or representatives from institutions from EU countries get involved in these projects. Institutions often organise seminars on computing, social affairs, marketing, livestock production, teaching methods, gender equality, or they develop various educational projects or conferences which are supported financially by the Community.

In sum, participation in educational programmes seems to have had a positive influence on Greek higher education. The progressive replacement of previous curricula by new curricula based on the credit system in order to facilitate student exchanges are some effects of this influence. Greek higher education has not, however, taken the maximum advantage of the opportunities offered.

Initial and in-service teacher training in Greece

Greek primary and secondary school teachers receive initial and in-service training in different institutions. In the past, all courses organised for the initial training of primary and pre-primary school teachers lasted two years and were offered in teachers' colleges and nursery teachers' colleges, called Pedagogical Academies and *Scholes Nipiagogon* respectively. The training of secondary school teachers lasted four years and focused mainly on subject discipline study in the universities. In 1984–5, the Pedagogical Academies and *Scholes Nipiagogon* were abolished and were replaced by university-level departments of education for primary and nursery school teachers. Students of these departments attend undergraduate courses in several subject areas (such as language and literature, history, mathematics, sciences) and receive professional training concurrently.[25] On the other hand, the preparation of secondary school teachers still focuses on subject specialisation. Their professional training is not considered satisfactory.[26]

Currently, a number of changes to eliminate these weaknesses and to harmonise teacher education with that existing in most advanced EU countries have been introduced. The most important of these changes are as follows. The previous system of teachers' appointment based on a waiting list (*epetirida*)[27] has been replaced by a system requiring examinations at a national level. During the 1998–2002 transition period of its application, a gradually increasing number will be appointed through examinations while the rest of the positions will be covered by teachers from the waiting list. When the transition period ends, the examination system will be the only way for appointment in schools. The organisation of examinations on subjects of speciality (for example, mathematics, physics, literature, history) and also pedagogy and teaching methodology is the responsibility of the National Council for Appointments, called *Anotato Symboulio Epilogis*. After the transition period, participation in the examinations will require a Certificate of Educational Competence awarded after one year's studies at university in addition to a bachelor's degree (*ptychio*).

Teachers are civil servants. Their appointment is made permanent after a two-year probationary period. Their salaries as compared with those of the rest of Greek civil servants are considered satisfactory, but they are not comparable with those of other countries. According, for example, to data from the OECD,[28] salary per statutory teaching hour in equivalent US dollars is 29 in Greece while the corresponding mean salary in the rest of OECD countries is 36.

Teacher education in Greece aims at preparing teachers for Greek schools only. There is no provision for training that will enable Greek teachers to find employment in another EU country, despite the fact that there is a surplus of teachers in Greece and a shortage in other EU countries. The foreign-language skills which students acquire in the universities do not enable them to teach in a school abroad, although the learning of at least one foreign European language is compulsory in most higher education institutions.

The expansion of the European dimension in teacher training curricula is likely to assist in the reorientation of teacher education. It is encouraging that one of the aims of the Greek authorities is the promotion of the European idea through teacher training curricula. The participation of Greek teachers in joint programmes, short-study visit programmes, and inter-university cooperation programmes enables them to become familiar with European lifestyles and with the idea of seeking a job in another country.

Thus far there are no teachers from other European countries in Greek public schools. There is, however, a great number of them working in private schools for the teaching of foreign languages (*frontistiria*).

In-service teacher training in Greece consists mainly of the following:

- a two-year post-initial training course (*Metekpedefsi*) given in a separate institution. Attendance is conditional upon examinations. This type of training, which affects a very small proportion of the teacher population, is now available only for primary school teachers. That for secondary school teachers was abolished a few years ago;
- seminars of short or long duration organised by educational institutes specialised in the in-service training of teachers.

Until the beginning of the 1990s, a one-year in-service training course was given in the above educational institutes, which were called SELME for the teachers of secondary education and SELDE for primary education teachers. They operated in eight different cities in the country. Enrolment was based on a draw; however, the number of those who had the opportunity to attend these courses was limited and the cost of the offered in-service training system was high.[29] Furthermore, they could not satisfy the need for the improvement of teachers' competencies, which is considered one of the indispensable pre-requisites for Greek education if it is to respond to the challenge of the new European reality. For this reason the system was replaced by a more flexible and shorter one in 1992, based on the establishment of regional centres for in-service training of teachers called *Periferiaka Epimorfotika Kentra* (PEK). These centres offered compulsory training lasting three months and compulsory introductory training for the beginning teachers during 1993–5. This training system, however, changed again in 1995. Seminars of short duration (40 hours) on specialised subjects replaced compulsory courses of three months. These seminars are offered to teachers during non-teaching hours while in service. In parallel, PEKs, which were restructured as far as their administrative autonomy is concerned, developed training activities of short duration in a number of different districts within their responsibility in order to offer in-service training to teachers who find it difficult to travel to cities where PEKs operate. A number of changes aiming at the introduction of a multiformed in-service training system involving universities, scientific societies, teachers' associations, and school units authorised to organise in-service training courses, and the formation of links between teachers' training and the upgrading of Greek education have been under consideration recently. The whole attempt to reform the in-service training system has been supported, to a large extent, by European Structural Funds.

In addition, intensive short in-service training seminars have been organised by counsellors and experts or agents of the Ministry of Education in order to inform teachers about changes in the curricula, textbooks and teaching methods or other potential educational innovations. Special emphasis has been placed on the in-service training of *Lykeio* teachers in order to help them implement the recent educational reform pertaining to this level of education.

The Greek language in the European context

The Modern Greek language is not widely used in the EU. It is the language of a small number of European citizens and in the new European context it will inevitably be at a disadvantage. The marginal use of the Greek language makes the development of cooperative schemes between Greeks and other Europeans difficult. It restricts the opportunities for work, which will be opened in the framework of the integrated European market. The use of the Greek language is likely to shrink owing to the expansion of the languages which are more widely used in the European Union. Such an eventuality will provide support for those who are not enthusiastic about European integration.

Therefore, the spread of Modern Greek should have been one of the highest priorities of Greek governments, which, for various reasons have not paid proper attention to such an important national issue. It is fortunate that recently an increasing interest is being shown by the Greek government in the dissemination of Greek. The development of programmes and the production of materials for the teaching of Greek to foreigners, the establishment of centres for the teaching of Modern Greek in EU countries, and the offer of support to and coordination of the activities of those centres which already teach the Greek language and civilisation abroad must be among the priorities which Greek governments should address.

It is likewise imperative that EU policy-makers should place greater importance on the issues related to the maintenance of its less-used languages. Special funds must be given for the development of programmes for the expansion of these languages. The idea expressed in Greece that a centre for the teaching of the less commonly used European languages should be established in Athens with the support of the European Commission deserves further consideration.

The teaching of foreign languages in Greece

Two European languages, English and French or German, are taught in the lower level of secondary education (*Gymnasium*). At the upper level of secondary education (*Lykeio*), English is compulsory and there is a choice of a second European language. English is also taught in primary schools.

However, the teaching hours for foreign languages in state schools are not enough for the pupils to acquire a sound command of these languages. For this reason the majority of pupils take additional lessons in private schools which function all over the country. But not all pupils have the same opportunities: some families, for example, cannot afford to send their children to private schools while others have no access to such schools because they live in remote rural districts. To solve these problems the Greek government has decreed the establishment of 30 Centres of European Languages throughout the country and three Multi-centres of European Languages in three cities (Athens, Thessaloniki, Volos) which can be attended free of charge by secondary school pupils during non-school hours. These centres will award the National Certificate of Language Proficiency.

The increase of contacts between Greek youth and youth from other EU countries, the expansion of youth exchange programmes and the systematic offering of information to Greek people about employment opportunities in the European market will increase the motivation to learn foreign languages.

Conclusions

Many changes have taken place in the Greek educational system recently. These have aimed at reorganising the system in order to cope successfully with the European challenge. The educational cooperation between Greece and other EU countries, the exchange of experience and the financial support from European funds have also had a positive impact on the reform of Greek education. Despite recent remarkable progress, weaknesses still exist. The socio-economic efficiency of education is still considered low. The preparation of young people for transition to working life does not seem to be very satisfactory. In addition, not every opportunity offered by the EU through its various educational programmes has been taken up.

It is hoped that the existing difficulties and problems will be eliminated with the recent educational reform and that the changes already discussed will take place. The implementation of these changes will enable Greek education to play a livelier role in the expansion of the ideals of Greek civilisation in the New Europe and the maintenance of the national identity of Greeks within the 'cosmopolitan' context in Europe as well as to take maximum advantage of the opportunities offered by the European Union for the further socio-economic development of Greece. Western Europe has been regarded by modern Greeks as the main source of scientific and technological knowledge and a place for renewal of educational ideas and practices. This situation, in combination with the slower socio-economic development of Greece compared with that of most EU countries, has made Greeks see Europe more as a source of assistance than as a field for creative competition. This position has been changing gradually. Its complete rejection is one of the indispensable prerequisites for the challenge of New Europe.

Ancient Greek civilisation has been the fountainhead of European civilisation. Modern Greece must face the European challenge and prove that it is a worthy successor to Ancient Greece.

Notes and references

1 The study is based on data available to the writer until the summer of 1998. Information about educational cooperation between Greece and the rest of the EU countries is not exhaustive.

2 See Kazamias, A. and Kassotakis, M. (1990). Η Ελληνική Εκπαίδευση και η Νέα Ευρώπη. Εκπαίδευση και Επάγγελμα, 3,199–216 [Greek Education in the Context of New Europe. Education and Vocation, 3, 199–216]; and Kazamias, A. and Kassotakis, M. (eds) (1995). *Η Ελληνική Εκπαίδευση. Προοπτικές ανασυγ–κρότησης και εκσυγχρονισμού* [Greek Education: Perspectives of Upgrading and Modernisation]. Athens: Seirios.

3 For more information, see Institute of Educational Research of the School 'Vaska' (1990). *Η Ελληνική Εκπαίδευση στο κοινοτικό πλαίσιο* [Greek Education in the Context of the European Community]. Athens; Tsaousis, D. (ed.) (1990). *Η Ευρωπαϊκή πρόκληση στην Τριτοβάθμια Εκπαίδευση* [The European Challenge for Higher Education]. Athens: Gutenberg; OLME (National Union of Secondary School Teachers) (1991). *Εκπαίδευση και 1992. Προοπτικές και επιπτώσεις* [Education and 1992: Impact and Perspectives]. Athens. See also various articles published in *Εκπαίδευση και Επάγγελμα* [Education and Vocation], 1990, 3.

4 Simitis, K. (1989). Τα σχολεία μας παράγουν μικροκαπιταλισμό και κρατισμό [Our Schools Produce Microcapitalism and Etatism], in the newspaper ΤΟ ΒΗΜΑ (TO VIMA), 10 December.

5 See Η νέα παρέμβαση της Ε.Ο.Κ. στην Ελληνική Εκπαίδευση [The New Intervention of the EEC in Greek Education]. *Πανεκπαιδευτική* [Panekpedeftiki], May 1985, 6–7.

6 See Institute of Educational Research of the School 'Vaska'.

7 Another structural change which took place while the socialist government of

PASOK was in power was the establishment of post-*lycea* preparatory centres for higher education (*metalykeiaka proparaskevastika kentra*), whose purpose was to help those who failed to enter higher institutions and wanted to try again. These centres were abolished in 1990 by the right-wing government of New Democracy.

8 For more information about the educational system of Greece, see Commission of the European Community, Eurydice Unit (1988). *The Greek Educational System*. Brussels and Athens; and European Commission (1995). *Structures of the Education and Initial Training Systems in the European Union*. Brussels.

9 European Commission (1996). *Key Data on Education in the European Union 95*. Brussels.

10 For this problem, see Demetropoulos, V. (1983). Η απασχόληση των αποφοίτων των Τεχνικών και Επαγγελματικών Λυκείων [The Employment of Technical and Vocational Lycea Graduates]. *Εκπαίδευση και Επάγγελμα* [Education and Vocation], 1, 3, 147–155; and Markopoulos, K. and Stavropoulos, P. (1989). Οι προοπτικές των αποφοίτων του Γεωργικού Τομέα των Τεχνικών και Επαγγελματικών Λυκείων [The Perspectives of Technical and Vocational Lycea Graduates: Section of Agriculture]. *Εκπαίδευση και Επάγγελμα* [Education and Vocation], 2, 135–144; Kassotakis, M. (1997). *Από το Πολυκλαδικό στο Ενιαίο Λύκειο* [From the Multilateral to the Comprehensive Lyceum]. Athens: Grigoris.

11 For more information about the problems of technical and vocational education in Greece, see Fragoudaki, A. (1979). Η Τεχνική Επαγγελματική Εκπαίδευση και η Ιδεολογία της [Technical and Vocational Education and its Ideology], *Σύγχρονα Θέματα* [Current Issues], A, 9–22; Kassotakis, M. (1981) 'Technical and vocational education in Greece and the attitudes of Greek youngsters towards it'. *Journal of the Hellenic Diaspora*, 2–3, 81–93; and Kazamias, A. and Kassotakis, M. (eds) (1986). *Οι εκπαιδευτικές μεταρρυθμίσεις στην Ελλάδα: Προσπάθειες, αδιέξοδα, προοπτικές* [The Educational Reforms in Greece: Attempts, Impasses and Perspectives], Athens: Grigoris; Psacharopoulos, G. and Palaiokrassas, S.T. (1990). Η Τεχνική Επαγγελματική Εκπαίδευση. Προβλήματα και προοπτικές μπροστά στο 2.000 [Technical-vocational and Technological Education: Problems and Perspectives in View of 2000]. *Εκπαίδευση και Επάγγελμα* [Education and Vocation], 1990, 3, 217–230.

12 Kassotakis, M. and Papageli-Voulioyri, D. (1996). *Η πρόσβαση στην Ελληνική Τριτοβάθμια Εκπαίδευση* [Access to Greek Higher Education], Athens: Grigoris.

13 Ministry of Education (1997). *Εκπαίδευση 2.000. Μια Παιδεία ανοικτών οριζόντων* [Education 2000: For an Education of Wide Horizons], Athens; and Kassotakis, M. (1997). Η αναβάθμιση της Ελληνικής Δημόσιας Εκπαίδευσης και η πρόσφατη εκπαιδευτική μεταρρύθμιση [The upgrading of Greek public education and the recent educational reform], O.E.L.M.E.K. *Αναβάθμιση της Δημόσιας Μέσης Εκπαίδευσης. Εκπαιδευτικό Συνέδριο* [The Upgrading of Greek Public Education. Educational Symposium], Nicosia (pp. 168–199).

14 See: OECD (1997). *Education at a Glance. OECD Indicators*, Paris: OECD, p. 52.

15 Data given by Greek Foundation of Scholarships.

16 Data given by National Institute of Labour.

17 Greek National Labour Institute (1997). *Synopsis: Mobility Programmes*, Athens.

18 Data given by the Direction of Community Support Framework/Ministry of Education.

19 See also Kassotakis, M. (1991). 'Greece'. In Wickremasinghe, W. (ed.), *Handbook of World Education*. Houston: American Collegiate Service; Kassotakis, M. and Labraki-Paganoy, A. (1994). 'Greek education and its legislative framework'. In Tulasiewicz, W. and Strowbridge, G. (eds), *Education and the Law. International Perspectives*. London: Routledge.

20 Ministry of Education (1997). Op. cit.

21 Psacharopoulos, G. and Kazamias, A. (1985). *Εκπαίδευση και ανάπτυξη στην Ελλάδα. Μια κοινωνική και οικονομική μελέτη για την τριτοβάθμια εκπαίδευση* [Education and Development in Greece. A Social and Economic Study for Higher Education], Athens: National Centre for Social Research. Tsaousis, D. (ed.) (1990), op. cit.; Initiative Group: Science and Society (1983). *Το Νέο Πανεπιστήμιο και ο κοινωνικός ρόλος* [The New Universities and their Social Role], Athens.

22 European Commission, Socrates, Community action programme in the field of education: Report of results during 1995–96. Additional information obtained from the Greek Foundation of Scholarships.

23 Ministry of Industry, Energy and Technology/General Secretariat for Research (1995). *Δείκτες Επιστημονικής και Τεχνολογικής Έρευνας* [Indices of Scientific and Technological Research]. Athens.

24 Ibid.

25 Kazamias, A. (1988). 'Education of teachers in Greece'. In Kazamias, A. and Kassotakis, M. (eds), *Teacher Training in the European Community*, Iraklion: University of Crete Press. In the same volume there are also interesting contributions by a number of Greek scholars concerning the initial training of teachers in Greece. See also Flouris, G. (1987). 'Maestri all' Universita in Grecia'. *Scuola Italiana Moderna*, 2, 16–17; National Union of Secondary School Teachers (1985). *Η αρχική εκπαίδευση και η επιμόρφωση των εκπαιδευτικών της δευτεροβάθμιας εκπαίδευσης* [Initial and In-service Training of Secondary School Teachers], Athens; Kakavoulis, A. (1990). *Προοπτικές και προγράμματα για τη μόρφωση του ευρωπαίου εκπαιδευτικού* [Perspectives and Programmes for European Teacher Education]. In Institute of Educational Research of the School 'Vaska', *Η Ελληνική Εκπαίδευση στο κοινοτικό πλαίσιο* [Greek Education in the Context of the European Community] (pp. 115–123).

26 Only students from the Faculties of Philosophy and Theology are obliged to take courses in pedagogy and psychology. They also get limited teaching practice at schools. Some science departments also offer optional courses in pedagogy. Higher education graduates wishing to teach in technical and vocational schools are obliged to attend six months' professional training at a pedagogical school called PATES, a division of the school of SELETE.

27 It was a list of higher education graduates based on the date of application for appointment and kept at the Ministry of Education.

28 OECD (1997). *Education at a Glance. OECD Indicators 1997*, Paris: OECD, p. 10.

29 Kassotakis, M. *In-service Teacher Training in Greece*. A case study carried out in the context of the programme: World Perspectives in Adult Education, University of Wisconsin (Reference No. A17); and Pedagogical Society of Greece (1983). *Αρχική Εκπαίδευση και επιμόρφωση των εκπαιδευτικών. Πρακτικά 1ου διεθνούς συνεδρίου* [Initial and In-service Teacher Training, Proceedings of the First International Conference], Athens.

8 Ireland

Kieran Byrne, Peadar Cremin and Rosarii Griffin

The European dimension: general

Ireland, being geographically peripheral to mainland Europe, was both positive and enthusiastic towards European entry. This confidence about the enterprise was remarkable given that much of what was to happen could not be fully anticipated. The fall-out benefits in economic terms, both directly by subsidy and by subvention, was obviously a major causal factor. This is particularly true in relation to Ireland's agricultural base, which was to benefit enormously from the immediate impact of direct subsidies and a wider market for export produce. These were factors which straightway heightened Irish awareness to the European dimension as far as the economy and society in general were concerned. There were others; for example, the operation of the European Regional (and Structural) Development Fund was the subject of much debate and anxiety, serving yet again to raise the profile and consciousness of Irish participation within the European Union.

By way of contrast, the obvious implications for the educational system were not fully understood. A process whereby education would contribute to a greater transnational understanding with levels of cross-cultural appreciation were not at first held in view. Indeed, within the overall context of the opening years of Irish membership the emphasis was clearly in accordance with the economic and fiscal lexicon. Nor is this difficult to understand when it is considered that there was no reference to education in the Treaty of Rome; it did however state that the European Commission was charged with a responsibility for the governing of general principles towards the establishment of a common training policy. It may also be added that there seemed little prospect that the Common Agricultural Policy would be matched by a common education policy. The importance of education in the evolution of a growing and integrating community was yet to be acknowledged.

The recent treaty on political unity (Maastricht, December 1991) stands in sharp relief to this omission. However, the confidence in educational cooperation implied in it has only been made possible by the initiation of the Commission's action plan of 1976, which resolutely included education. Since then a growing suite of educational programmes has been introduced with the aim of transnational and cross-cultural understanding. This, in turn, brought into view the prospect of a more tightly integrated Europe. Irish support for this integrative approach has been strongly evident in respect of programmes such as Socrates/Erasmus, Eurydice, Arion, Leonardo da Vinci which incorporates other programmes such as Force, Petra, Comett and Eurotecnet, as well as the Iris network and the Lingua programme.

From the Irish perspective, a critically important vehicle towards the activation of these programmes and other initiatives is the Association for Teacher Education in Europe (ATEE). This association was founded in 1976 and its principal objective is to bring together professionals involved in the area of teacher education towards the promotion of better understanding and awareness of the teacher-education programmes on a comparative basis. The promotion of research and the dissemination of information is considered central to the accomplishment of the aspiration. Irish participation in the work of ATEE has been very pronounced since its inception. Individual and institutional membership has increased over the years, which has heightened awareness both of the European dimension in education and the concept of a European educational community. Further to this, links have been formed between the Irish Educational Students and the European Teaching Association for the purpose of exchanging views and promoting a stronger sense of collectivism and collegiality on matters of mutual interest.

The Irish educational system: historical background

In many of its principal features, the current structure of the Irish educational system owes its origins to developments which took place during the nineteenth century. The seven decades between 1831 and 1900 were marked by a series of initiatives. A national system of elementary education was established in 1831. With this fundamental basis secured, educational policy-making became more fertile and assured. This new enthusiasm led to the expansion of educational institutions with the introduction of the Queen's University, with three constituent colleges at Belfast, Galway and Cork, in addition to those already in existence such as Trinity College Dublin. These colleges celebrated their one hundred and fiftieth year in existence in 1995–6. Additional changes in the late 1800s included the passing of the Intermediate Education Act in 1878 and the establishment of a Department of Agriculture and Technical Instruction in 1899.

Except for the latter legislative instalment, Irish education in its process and systems may be seen as having evolved from the centre towards the periphery. Attempts to pattern from the local authority thrust, evident in the evolving educational system in England at the turn of the century, were not to prove successful. An exception is to be found, however, in the case of technical and agricultural education. Largely because this was an attempt to link educational policy to the needs of local industrial and economic demands, a decentralised approach was cultivated.

After the establishment of the Irish Free State in 1922, little change in the fundamental structure of the system was entertained. In the general casting of government constructs, a new Department of Education was established to oversee the structure already in place. Again an exception here was the passing in 1930 of the Vocational Education Act. With policy concerns which were markedly close to those evident in the earlier 1899 legislation, vocational education embraced a wider definition of its terms of reference and was calculated to evolve within a decentralised local authority framework. It would be inaccurate to portray this departure as the making of a dual system which might suggest parity. For in most, if not all, instances, vocational education was to accommodate what were considered the less able pupils and correspondingly the socially disadvantaged.

However, one fundamental educative change occurred. With political freedom of a sort secured, the fledgling Free State embarked on a policy for the revival of the Irish language. Political freedom, it was argued, must be matched with the triumph of cultural freedom, and the Irish language was identified as the central component in that aspiration. Education was identified as the vehicle which would transport the nation to an all-Irish speaking destination. In the event, the heavy burden of this responsibility was not evenly shared. The primary school, since it was compulsory for all the children of the nation to attend, was singled out to provide a special and emphatic emphasis. In the haste to realise the objective, the ideal policy changed with varying degrees of intensity from a situation where all subjects were to be taught through Irish to one where a select number were to meet this requirement. Not to be overlooked either are the implications which this had for teacher-training programmes and their entry requirements.

Within the new Free State, at post-primary, secondary and vocational level, policy on the Irish language (Gaelic) occupied a central position. Irish was made a compulsory subject for teaching and examination. Failure in Irish meant a failure overall in the examinations at Intermediate, Vocational and Leaving Certificate levels. Not satisfied with pressures already exerted at primary level, a terminal examination was introduced which marked the completion of compulsory schooling – the Primary Certificate – with similar Irish requirements. At third level, Irish was also a matriculation requirement for entry. It was felt, however, that this language policy, which dominated curricular concerns and approaches, turned the focus of educational thought inwards rather than outwards and that it removed Irish educational policy-making in part from the mainstream of developments as the educational system became artificially self-conscious. Although it is not the purpose of this chapter to offer an appraisal of these decisions as they evolved, one implication is of relevance.

Today, the issue is still hotly debated. Some claim that '*tíre gan teanga*' is '*tíre gan teo*' (a country without its language is a country without culture). The value of the language is considered intrinsic to the cultural identity of its people. Recently, there has been a revival of interest in the Irish language; this is particularly evident with the increasing demand by parents for *gaelscoilenna*

(Irish-language primary schools) for their children. This resurgence in interest in the Irish language, the first official language in Ireland (though few claim to use it on a regular basis), is often associated with ethnic identification in the face of being culturally integrated into Europe. In any case, although it is still debated, Irish is a compulsory subject in primary and post-primary education. It is also an obligatory component in order to gain entry into one of the constituent colleges of the National University of Ireland although newer colleges have relaxed this rule.

An overview of the current structure and provision of the Irish school system

Overall responsibility for the Irish educational system resides with the Minister for Education, who is a member of the government. The minister is responsible to the Irish parliament. The structure of the department's interior accommodates in various sections the categories of the overall educational provision – primary, post-primary, university and other institutions of higher education. The jurisdiction of the department also includes responsibility for the state examinations at post-primary level, junior and senior.

In 1995, the Minister for Education published the *White Paper in Education* which was the result of a unique consultative process in the history of Irish education, the National Education Convention of 1993, where all the partners in education had an opportunity to contribute to the practice and development of Irish education into the next century. The Convention, and its *Report* of 1994, was critical of the *Green Paper* (1992) which had introduced a market-driven notion in support of a quantitatively informed parental choice. The *Report* (Coolahan 1994) was followed by the *White Paper* of 1995 which describes a 'comprehensive agenda for change and development'.[1] An Education Act was envisaged for 1997 amending the Intermediate Education (Ireland) Act of 1878. However, before it could be enacted, there was a change of government and consequently the Bill of Minister Niamh Breathnach, Education Bill 1997, was replaced by current Minister Micheál Martin's Bill, Education (No. 2) Bill, 1997. Entitled the Education Act, 1998, it was enacted in 1998.[2] It includes among its provisions sections on:

- the recognition of schools for the purposes of funding from public funds;
- the establishment of the inspectorate on a statutory basis;
- the establishment of the National Council for Curriculum and Assessment;
- the establishment of boards of management of schools;
- the establishment and role of parents' associations;
- the establishment of student associations and councils;
- the functions of principals and teachers;
- appeals by students or their parents;
- teaching in Irish and educational disadvantage;
- regulation of the state examination system.

These provisions aim to strengthen existing practice rather than to effect radical reform. However, it is also envisaged through all aspects of this legislation to address the issue of special educational needs.[3] Furthermore, a discussion paper on early childhood education and a Green Paper on adult education were published in 1998. Meanwhile, the Youth Work Act of 1997 was enacted, strengthening the services promoting young people's opportunities for employment.

Under the Irish constitution it is the duty of the state to provide free primary education and to subsidise other educational agencies and endeavours which are deemed worthy of support. School attendance is compulsorily required of children between the ages of 6 and 15 years. An Education Welfare Bill provides for raising this to age 16 over the coming year.

The universities are traditionally autonomous bodies, although they are funded by the Department of Education through the Higher Education Authority which was established in 1971. This authority also advises the Minister on the needs of this sector. A recent development by the government was the abolition of undergraduate tuition fees within the publicly funded third-level institutes. It is now necessary to look at the current school system in more detail.

Pre-school provision

In Ireland there is no state system of pre-school, play-group or nursery education. Flanking the early childhood provision of the primary school are many voluntary and privately run nurseries and playgroups. These have recently been regulated by the implementation of the relevant sections in the 1991 Child Care Act in 1996 in order to monitor and standardise their work.[4]

Primary school provision

Children normally begin primary school at the age of 4 years and continue to the age of 12 years. Inclusively this amounts to eight years in total. In the initial years, 4–6, there is a marked emphasis on informal learning which corresponds to the learning-through-play strategies of early childhood education evident in many pre-school and nursery approaches.

The 'new' curricular approach, implemented in the primary school since 1971, is child-centred and allows for a considerable amount of flexibility and integration of subjects. Team teaching, theme teaching and project work are encouraged. However, the National Council for Curriculum and Assessment (NCCA) is currently revising this curriculum to facilitate the early identification of pupils who are falling behind in the areas of numeracy and literacy.[5] Other changes include a revision of the Irish language curriculum, the expansion of the arts education curriculum, a more specific science programme, a greater emphasis on oral skills in English and the introduction of a programme in social, personal and health education.

No summative assessment of pupils takes place at primary level but teachers are formally encouraged to maintain records of progress. Profiles of pupil performance and development are assembled, and these, in some instances, are made available to the post-primary school on the transfer of pupils. This arrangement is not uniformly observed, and there is much debate on the merit of introducing regulations designed to ease the process of transition from a child-centred primary curriculum to the more academically orientated, subject-centred post-primary curriculum.

The primary schools are not state schools, but they are state-aided. They are mostly denominational schools owned and controlled by the Church. With the increased recognition that Ireland is not a homogeneous society, there has been a movement towards interdenominationalism. The importance of pluralism is formally recognised in the White Paper on education. However, the government's aspiration to pluralism and the Church's desire to maintain the current position may cause tension in the future.[6]

Post-primary school provision

In Ireland, children normally begin secondary school at 12 years of age. There are four types of post-primary school: secondary, vocational, comprehensive and community. In all of these schools education is free, although there is a convention of donation or subscription to cover ancillary running costs. There are approximately 775 post-primary schools catering for approximately 370,000 students.

Secondary schools

This is the traditional intermediate school. Two-thirds of all post-primary schools (452 schools) are in this category. Over the last two decades these schools have broadened their curriculum from a base that was quite academic and humanistic to include a wider range of subjects from the areas of technology, business and craft design.

Vocational schools

In the founding years these schools were devoted with singular vision to a programme of practical and manual skills. This narrowly conceived curriculum has changed radically, and at present most subjects are available to students. There are approximately 247 vocational schools.

Comprehensive schools

These schools were established in the mid-1960s in an attempt to make adequate provision for school facilities in an expanding educational system. The nomenclature was borrowed from the counterpart movement in England but was not an ideological match.

Community schools

These schools are the same as comprehensive schools except for a slight difference in management structure. The changed title of the schools was an attempt to point the educational system in a more democratic direction and to encourage more community participation in policy-making, planning and structure. Sometimes these schools represented an amalgamation of institutions which sought greater security and viability in collaboration. There are approximately 76 schools classed as community or comprehensive.

Examinations

Intermediate (Junior) Certificate

This examination, currently referred to as the 'Junior Certificate', is taken by nearly every pupil after three years of post-primary schooling (usually at the age of 15–16 years). It is generally conceived of as a middle marker of scholastic attainment prior to advancing to one of the Leaving Certificate courses. At this point, the latter of either passing of this examination or the student's fifteenth birthday, compulsory schooling is completed.

Leaving Certificate(s)

This is the terminal examination at post-primary level. Students have a choice to follow one of three Leaving Certificates: the Leaving Certificate Applied, the Leaving Certificate Vocational Programme or the traditional Leaving Certificate Programme. These examinations are important in terms of career prospects and for entry to third-level education. Students taking these examinations are usually aged 17–18 years old. Those following the Leaving Certificate Programme must take at least five subjects, including Irish. This programme is currently being revised to give a greater vocational orientation (Ireland 1998, p. 18). The Leaving Certificate Vocational Programme (LCVP) concentrates more on technical subjects and also has a high vocational orientation. It entails five Leaving Certificate subjects including two vocational subjects, a modern European language and three mandatory Link Modules, while the Leaving Certificate Applied is a 'self-contained' two-year programme which takes a vocationally orientated cross-curricular approach and consists of a number of modules under the following headings: General Education, Vocational Education and Vocational Preparation. While this does not entitle direct entry into third-level courses, those who complete it successfully may proceed to Post-Leaving Certificate courses (ibid., p. 19).

Two decades of reform: general

In view of the fact that the influences of the reforming decades, 1960 to 1980, broke hard with the past and still inform current practice, it is necessary to consider them in some detail. While it must be admitted that a growing degree of disenchantment was evident among educationists by the 1950s, the changes that were to ensue stemmed from a wider domain. Consequently, to establish perspectives here, consideration must be given to a wider suite of concerns which were evident at that time.

Towards the end of the 1950s it was being increasingly recognised that Irish social and economic policy lagged behind that of many other European countries. That under-development was attributed in part to a lack of imagination in policy and planning and also to the conservatism which is so often the mark of a post-revolutionary state. By this time also, many of the founding fathers had retired and thus left the path clear for younger, innovative and more energetic minds.

Ironically, it was Sean Lemass, himself an activist during the revolutionary period and a patient *Tánaiste* (assistant leader) to Eamonn de Valera as *Taoiseach* (premier), 1958–64, who set new sights and standards for Ireland with two programmes for economic expansion. For the first time politicians were identifying education as a major infrastructural component which recognised how central it was to any prospect for social and economic reform.

Flanking this fresh approach in thinking were the recommendations of the OECD report on Irish education, suitably and challengingly entitled *Investment in Education* and published in 1966. This was in fact the first full-scale in-depth analysis of Irish educational provision since the founding of the Free State. Its findings were bleak and its recommendations daring. A complete realigning of the system was required, and theoretical aspiration would have to be matched by a robust fiscal commitment, it was stated. So the motivation for reform was springing from all quarters, old and new. The slide needed to be reversed; genuine reform was very urgently required. Investment in education would make valuable returns and was seen as an act of faith in the future. More than these motivating factors there was, however, the emergence of the 'European dimension'. Ireland was beginning to build on the approach work towards assembling a successful application for entry to the European Community. Consequently the country's major 'industrial plant' item would be scrutinised with rigour. Preparations were to be made to withstand the test.

It will serve the purpose here to brush in broad strokes the individual measures which were taken. The newly found commitment was to increase schooling provision and participation; through an injection of much-needed funding, to erect new schools, revamp curricula, introduce new teacher-education programmes, and expand third-level education with new institutions alternative to the traditional universities. It will be convenient in the next section to deal more specifically with the details and the implications of these changes as they affected educational provision at individual levels.

As part of the Second Programme for Economic Expansion in 1963, expenditure on education was taken by the government to be an investment in the nation's future. One statistic which will encapsulate the new drive forward for reform and progress is to be found in the Annual Report from the Department of Education for the year 1965. It revealed that 154 new schools had been sanctioned at a cost of over £4 million; there was no precedent, only a future. Since the 1960s, investment in education has risen from an estimated 4.1 per cent of GNP to 8 per cent of GNP in the 1990s (Hyland 1997). Such investment in education appears to have been an important contributing factor to the high economic growth rates in Ireland. This current buoyant economic climate has commonly been referred to as the 'Celtic Tiger'.[7]

Primary schools

In relation to pupil participation much improvement has been secured. A policy whereby pupils were promoted from class to class and not held back gathered a healthy momentum of progression, and it was aided considerably by the introduction of free post-primary education in 1967, which sharpened the ambition to transfer and stay on. A far better pupil–teacher ratio was allowed (in 1965 it was 34:1, in 1995 it was estimated at 22:1) and this in turn was of assistance to the quality of learning and the quality of teaching.

The environment in which this newly acquired commitment was to be found was enhanced considerably by a building programme which sought to offset the deterioration in plant, which had been allowed to fall into disrepair over decades of neglect. Capital grants were advanced for building and maintenance. Smaller schools were also amalgamated to facilitate, to some degree, the fiscal demands of the building programme.

There were two other major changes in Irish primary schooling which were to impact in a positive and enduring manner. In 1971 a new primary-school curriculum was introduced, which was to effect a major change and accomplish a radical reform in the curricular arena of education. The vision of the new aspiration was creative, inclusive and expansionist. When compared with what had gone before, it was quite radical. Child-centred in thrust and dominated in much of its thinking by beliefs espoused by John Dewey, the new prospect made for an exciting time for pupils and teachers at school. New subjects and new approaches were introduced, and the traditional concentration on the core 3R subjects, branded rigid and time-warped, was left behind by the new tide.

The 1970s' primary curriculum is currently being revised in preparation for the new millennium. While its child-centred approach was endorsed by two review bodies' reports published in 1990, the reports highlighted the concern that the child-centred approach may result in lower literacy and numeracy standards. As a result, guided discovery teaching and learning methods were recommended. Other changes that will be introduced to all schools include greater emphasis on the oral aspects of English, the expansion of the arts, particularly the visual arts, a practical approach to mathematics and a more specific science programme. Other issues of concern include the early identification of pupils with learning difficulties. A European Awareness Programme is also to be included so that students will learn to appreciate the different aspects of the European Union.

A European dimension in the primary school curriculum

The 1971 curriculum was subjected to a review during the period 1989–90, and the Report of the Review Body on the Primary Curriculum was published in 1990. In its report the Review Body reappraised all aspects of the 1971 curriculum and made specific suggestions with regard to the overhaul and updating of the various curricular areas. One area of particular concern relates to the area of language, and the debate which took place on this item was clearly and predictably divisive.

In Irish primary schools, two languages (Irish and English) are taught from infant to senior levels (4–12 years of age). A number of suggestions were made to the Review Body recommending the inclusion of a modern European language as an area of study for the senior class levels. The Review Body considered the various arguments, particularly those involving educational, cultural, social and economic factors. It also considered precedents in other European countries, but concluded that it could not recommend the inclusion of an additional language area. Pressures relating to time and curriculum overload, as well as the demands of the two languages currently included in the present programme, influenced the Review Body in arriving at this decision. Strong opposition to the decision was voiced by the National Parents Council for primary level, which had its reservations on this matter appended to the report. This Council produced figures indicating that, in the absence of official support, as many as 21 per cent of schools were already providing foreign language tuition as an extra-curricular activity, and they called for the recognition of parents' wishes in regard to the inclusion of a modern European language as part of the work of primary schools.

Since then, the 1995 *White Paper* on education has incorporated this desire into the plan for primary education. Within the newly proposed European Awareness Programme other European languages will be included as part of the effort to instil in the students an appreciation of European life, languages and culture. A pilot project to this effect was commenced in 1997 involving the teaching of French, German, Italian and Spanish in 200 primary schools for fifth and sixth level classes (Ireland 1998, p. 14). This programme also aspires to foster links between Irish and European schools in such programmes as Socrates, which aims to promote cooperation between educational institutes at all levels and to encourage students to make contacts with their European counterparts. The *White Paper* specifies that Irish schools will be actively encouraged to participate in such programmes, which it hopes will 'contribute to greater awareness of our common [the European] heritage and in particular human rights'.[8]

Post-primary schools

The advent of the new enlightenment which characterised educational thought in Ireland in the 1960s was also to impact on the post-primary sector. Change here took the curricular route, for the most part. New subjects were introduced;

old syllabuses were revised with a more forward-looking approach. This was particularly marked in the area of languages, with new approaches to teaching being adopted and an emphasis placed on oracy and auracy. The possibility of travel and residence abroad for short periods was explored and promoted. For many Irish teachers, the European Teaching Association provided a welcome outlet towards professional development and the acquisition of progressive ideas.

In keeping with the child-centred approach in primary school, although here the intensity was less, project work and fieldwork were advanced as important contributors to processes of learning and self-instruction. Across the various school types a common curriculum was emerging as the liberal ideology of equality of educational opportunity began to assume the central focus of the ideational base.

The tightly centralised nature of the Irish educational system has been the subject of much debate over the decades. The argument has centred on two principal themes: administration structure and curricular/assessment policy. It is the second of these which is more pertinent to considerations here. The traditional Intermediate and Leaving Certificate Examinations are centrally set and assessed on the content of a tightly prescribed course. This has led to a lack of variety in pedagogical approaches and an adherence to directive-type teaching. In an attempt to shift thinking and commitment further away from this hemisphere a major breakthrough was made in 1990 when a new Junior Cycle syllabus and examination were ushered in. Here the density of prescription is diluted and a much wider and more open approach is entertained. Gone are the days of the set courses and the learning by rote and the reading of surrogate notes in place of the original text. The first cycle of this period came on stream in June 1992. The Junior Certificate Elementary Programme is an alternative programme which, unlike the Junior Certificate Programme, includes innovative approaches to assessment such as Profiles of Assessment which are recorded over a period of time (Hyland 1997).

Following the Junior Certificate year, students have the option of taking a 'Transitional Year' which has been introduced as a bridging year between the Junior Cycle and the Senior Cycle to provide students with enriched opportunities for personal development (Ireland 1998, p. 16). This year is student-centred and interdisciplinary. It encourages students to take responsibility for their own learning while teachers have greater flexibility in designing the curricula and course work, which are usually tailored to the needs of the students. It is also used as a time to examine Irish culture and its place in Europe.

The majority of students still follow the traditional Leaving Certificate Programme (LCP) which allows for direct entry into higher education, particularly the universities. Although this programme is currently being revised, it is still very academically orientated. While certain percentages are allocated for orals, aurals and some project work, the majority of subjects are still assessed through the medium of a pen and paper, external, summative, terminal-type examination (which, too, is currently under review). As it has been universally recognised that this type of programme is not suitable for a considerable number of students, two other programmes have been devised: the Leaving Certificate Vocational Programme (LCVP) and the Leaving Certificate Applied (LCA). The Leaving Certificate Applied will link to further vocational training. The main aim of this programme is to 'prepare students for the transition from school to adult and working life, including further education' (ibid., p. 52). Oral competence in European languages is also an important feature of this programme which will also have strong links with the local community. Students following this course will not have direct entry to third-level courses (as mentioned above) but rather to Post-Leaving-Certificate courses whose educational and training courses are certified by TEASTAS – the Irish National Certification Authority. The Leaving Certificate Vocational Programme's aim is to expand the vocational dimension through the link modules which it offers. These are Enterprise Education, Work Experience and Preparation for Work. Portfolio assessment is an important part of the assessment procedure of this programme. Students following this course have full opportunity for direct access to third-level courses. Again, European languages are an integral part of this programme.[9]

The European dimension in the post-primary school: foreign language teaching and exchanges

If not actually part of a deliberate design that laid emphasis on the European dimension, the post-primary school did traditionally include a European content in a number of its courses; for example, history, geography, languages, music and art. There are, moreover, as will be readily agreed, quite strong links between Ireland and the European mainland which go deep into the recesses of time. This connection was perhaps most manifest in the area of education, scholarship, learning and religious studies. Many Irish colleges had been established in European cities from early medieval times. The values of this part of Irish culture were always cherished, and through teaching texts in language and literature, music and art, they were transmitted in acknowledgement of that heritage and its safeguarding.

In more recent times, because of the current context of European integration, these aspects enjoy a greater emphasis and are taught with a greater degree of currency and relevance. At junior and senior cycles there is a strong European component in several of the subjects studied. Where relevant, the Irish connection or influence is always highlighted, as also is the manner in which mainland European developments impacted on Ireland and influenced the course of events there. European Community institutions and the history of the EU are also studied. A recent development highlighting the importance of the European dimension to Irish education was the introduction in 1996 of civic, social and political education as a compulsory examination subject in the Junior Cycle. This course devotes special attention to Europe and to Ireland's role in a new and integrated Europe.

Again, as part of the overall educational reform of the last 20 years or so, language provision in Irish post-primary schools has improved with the introduction of more progressive language teaching approaches. The largely literacy syllabus which predominated has been displaced to allow for one which recognises the oral and the aural. The principal concern is for communication, and the communicative method is now the most commonly used pedagogical instrument in post-primary schools. In relation to language, the approach is for as wide a provision as possible. The *White Paper* emphasises the fact that all students should have access to the study of a modern European language (Ireland 1995, p. 49). A European language is a compulsory requisite, and certainly an added advantage, to gaining entry to a large number of third-level courses.

At second level, a European visit of about ten to twelve days' duration is now a common feature in many Irish post-primary schools. The purpose of this kind of travel fieldwork is to provide students with a first-hand encounter with the multifaceted historical and cultural heritage of the various European mainland countries. The programme does not have an explicit language objective, although that is part of it, since language exchange is catered for through other means. Museums, galleries, schools, the Parliament in Brussels and other EU institutions are the most popular locations to visit.

In 1988 the European Commission issued its paper, *On the Teaching of Foreign Languages*, where it was argued that language was a key factor in mobility. This communication was to cause much heart-searching in Ireland, since the number of citizens with the kind of language competency required for mobility was found to be very low indeed. Of the Irish population as a whole, 80 per cent cannot speak a foreign language, 17 per cent can speak two foreign languages, and only 3 per cent can speak three foreign languages.

On studying the statistics concerning the take-up of languages at post-primary level, a grave disparity is to be found from language to language. The pattern is set at Junior Cycle level. Here, 70 per cent of pupils take French, less than 6 per cent take German and less than 3 per cent take Spanish; a remaining few take Italian. Alert to this disparity – all the more paradoxical because Germany is a major market for Irish exports – the National Council for Curriculum and Assessment has identified a number of strategies which are designed to establish a degree of balance. It has suggested the introduction of shorter courses, the design of courses to meet special needs and the introduction of more entry points which would facilitate access to language courses at various levels from Junior to Senior Cycle. More pertinently, the Minister for Education has been presented with proposals to allow pupils beginning the Senior Cycle to take up a language other than that taken at Junior Cycle. In addition, senior language foundation courses are being promoted. The purpose of this departure is obviously calculated to reduce the near monopoly enjoyed by the French language in Irish schools.

The debate at present has brought other vistas to the language policy. A more common approach to language teaching is advanced from the quarter which is committed to the holistic approach to learning. This view concludes that a suite of languages can be learned in an integrated way. A further feature of this debate is the emergence of a concern for the study of the cultural underpinnings of language. Here runs the argument that language without a cultural appreciation of the civilisation from which it emerges is too narrowly conceived and, therefore, inert.

A further source of potential for the development of language within the EU is the Lingua programme announced by the Commission in 1988. This programme operates at five levels: teacher in-service; the universities; the workplace; youth exchange; and supplementary measures. The budget estimated for the first five years was ECU250 million.

In Ireland there is a national advisory committee for Lingua. Represented here are associations of teachers of French, German, Spanish, Italian and Irish. Included too are the Irish Linguistic Institute, Higher Education Authority and the Youth Education Bureau. It is the function of the advisory body to decide on overall priorities for the programme.

Prior to the advent of the Lingua programme a scheme for exchange of experienced teachers with France had been in place, with some support from the cultural services at the French Embassy in Dublin. This scheme continues to operate and is taken up by approximately 20 teachers on a reciprocal basis. A similar scheme operates for Germany, Spain and Austria. The aspirations for the scheme are set out in Circular Letter no. TEX 1/92 which states:

> The exchanges will take place in the second term of the school year. The duration of the exchange will be that portion of the second term during which both schools are open. Subject to regular and satisfactory full-time service, the Irish teacher, while on exchange, will continue to receive salary in the usual way and the French authorities will continue the salary of the teacher from France. The Irish teacher will, in addition, be paid an extra tax-free allowance each week while resident abroad under this scheme.

The scheme provides Irish teachers with a unique opportunity to perfect their knowledge of French and the experience of working in an educational system different to the Irish system. The Irish pupils benefit from the presence in the school of a native speaker of French.

Teachers wishing to participate in this scheme should be graduates in French who have at least two years' experience of teaching the language. They should be competent and prepared to teach English language and literature at all levels in the French school and may also be expected to take an interest in out-of-school activities, particularly those connected with the teaching of English. Teachers who have applied to participate in this scheme, and who are selected to do so, may not normally withdraw from participation. Applicants may be required to attend for interview and the applicant will be responsible for any expenses incurred.

As the teacher from France will usually be in a position to take French classes only, heads of schools should be prepared to make appropriate adjustments to time-tables so as to make the best use of the exchange teacher.

European Studies Project

For pupils taking the Junior Cycle course, one of the more exciting and targeted programmes towards the integrating of the European dimension in education is the European Studies Project. Currently nearing completion, this is a curriculum development programme consisting of three schemes for the following age groups: 11–14/12–15; 14–16 and 16–18. At the time of writing over 11,000 students are involved and 90 schools from England, the Republic of Ireland, Northern Ireland, Scotland, Belgium, Germany, France and Denmark. The undertaking has been funded by the departments of education in these countries and from the EU. Below are examples from each of the three phases:

- *The 11–14/12–15 programme* This is an agreed programme of study in history and geography between schools in Northern Ireland, England and Ireland (six in each). Common language links are built upon, with the intention of getting pupils to work together as European neighbours.
- *The 14–16 programme* Involved in this programme are 18 schools in total: three in England, three in Northern Ireland, three in the Republic of Ireland, three in Belgium and six in France. The schools are brought together by computer link to establish a target audience for communication skills in English and French.
- *The 16–18 programme* Involved here are 47 schools in Northern Ireland, England, the Republic of Ireland, France, Germany and Belgium. The schools are clustered into five groups for logistical purposes. The emphasis is on research, with students being required to engage in research projects which examine current European issues.
- *The 16–18 programme – language, industry, trade* This was the latest scheme to be introduced in 1991–2. Involved are schools in Northern Ireland, Scotland, England, the Republic of Ireland, France, Denmark, Belgium, Holland and Germany. Language for business and enterprise is the dominant element in the course.

Five strategies for achieving the aims of the European Studies Project have been identified: specially designed curricula; school links; information technology; active learning approaches; and residential courses. An outline of one unit of study from the 11–14/12–15 programme will serve to provide an example of approaches adopted.

The European dimension in teacher education

At a meeting of the Council of Ministers for Education on 9 February 1976 a resolution was passed which endorsed commitment to an action programme in the field of education. The purpose of this programme was to introduce in a more formal way a European dimension to the experience of teachers and students in the primary and secondary schools in the European Community. This resolution was followed by similar supportive statements from the Council of Europe in a

Solemn Declaration adopted on 19 June 1983 and followed by similar sentiments expressed at Fontainebleau on 25 and 26 June 1984.

The action to be taken was:

- the promotion of the teaching of foreign languages as an important factor in strengthening the European Community;
- promoting measures designed to encourage contacts between students from different countries;
- highlighting the European dimension in curricula in teacher training courses and in teaching materials;
- the designation of a European Awareness Day.

Teacher education

Courses in education and in eight other subject areas – Irish, English, French, history, geography, mathematics, music and philosophy – are offered leading to a Bachelor of Education (BEd) degree. There is no subject on Europe *per se* on the curriculum, nor is there a period marked on the timetable for European affairs or European studies. However, that is not to say that the European dimension is neglected or ignored, or that attention to it is negligible. On the contrary, there is an increasing awareness of the European connection, and policy is to highlight and underscore the European dimension in the existing curriculum in areas where this is most appropriate; that is to say, through the process of permeation:

- with the undergraduates at their own level;
- with the undergraduates at the level of the primary school;
- with mature students taking evening classes;
- in activities undertaken specifically with the undergraduates.

The European dimension in the existing curriculum of teacher education is therefore evident in a number of ways.

Academic subjects

Most of the subjects on offer afford an opportunity to increase 'Euroawareness', and lecturers capitalise on this opportunity to form attitudes to 'integration' or 'European studies' as a subject to be taught, say on the same scale as environmental studies. Yet there is every scope for Europeanising and internationalising the Irish primary school curriculum within the existing system, and of leading Irish children to a greater appreciation and understanding of their European partners. Every subject area has a contribution to make in this regard because of the degree of flexibility and scope allowed to the individual teacher to select a programme and approach appropriate to the students being taught. The contents of these subject areas was considered in the section dealing with primary education.

Activities undertaken by staff and students: experiential learning

Students visit the EU institutions in Strasbourg, Luxembourg and Brussels annually with the assistance of the EU office in Dublin. While visiting they have a chance to speak with MEPs. In recent years philosophy students have gone to Greece to visit the classical archaeological sites in Delphi, Mycenae and Athens.

Geography students

Geography students have done fieldwork in Italy, Austria, Germany and Switzerland.

History students

History students have made educational tours to European countries and have visited EU institutions and the European parliament.

Students of French

Students taking French visit France for some weeks before their final oral examination.

Exchange programme

Mary Immaculate College, Limerick, has special facilities provided under the Erasmus programme to participate in an exchange project with Trinity College, Carmarthen. The principal purpose of this linking is to enhance the Gaelic/Welsh connection in the context of a common Celtic heritage.

Irish participation in the Reseau d'Institutions de Formation (RIF) initiative

By the mid-1980s it was becoming increasingly evident that a more broadly based and intensive approach was required if the European dimension was to occupy a more central focus of attention within the formal teacher education programmes of the member countries. A resolution on the European dimension in education which concentrated on this concern was passed by the Council and the Ministers for Education meeting within the Council on 24 May 1988. The RIF teacher education network was established in the same year.

Higher education: recent developments

The expansion evident at the other levels of the Irish system found a correspondence at the higher level also. Two new universities were designated over their former titles of National Institutes of Higher Education at Limerick and Dublin. These new institutions, untrammelled by the baggage of tradition and convention, have pioneered paths to substantial progress. By introducing modular degree systems, greater versatility was facilitated. At Limerick, which is the larger of the two institutions, new degree courses were fashioned with periods of off-campus study and experiential learning a central requirement; for example, travel. At the National University of Ireland (NUI), with colleges at Dublin, Cork and Galway, similar changes were initiated, although the change here is less visible and more difficult to gauge. None the less, it may be said that, in general, higher education has undergone significant expansion in terms of degree courses and student participation.

Patterning from the regular model fashioned in England and Wales, new institutions of higher education designed for technological and industrial development were introduced in the form of regional technical colleges in the mid-1970s which have since been redesignated as institutes of technology. These institutes respond to the call of the market place with alacrity and provide for a qualified workforce to encourage economic development and industrial progress. Here again new courses and new qualifications attuned to current and near-future trends are now a firmly established feature of the Irish educational landscape, including a heightened awareness of the European dimension.

Participation in international cooperation programmes

At the level of higher education, considerable progress has been accomplished through the various EU programmes, particularly Socrates/Erasmus and Leonardo da Vinci. Chief among the objectives of this programme is the concept of mobility at undergraduate level leading towards mobility of graduates to attain both higher qualifications and employment. The official record of member state participation in Inter-University Cooperation Programmes (ICPs) over the period 1987–91 shows that Ireland has increased its relative involvement over that period, and has a very healthy record proportional to its population size. For example, Irish higher education institutions were involved in 73 per cent of ICPs in 1987–8, and 10.4 per cent in 1990–1.

It is probably more instructive, however, to cite particular examples of institutional interest in the European dimension. For the year 1991–2 the participation of University College, Cork, may be given as one example of the many possibilities. The University College participated in 31 inter-university cooperation programmes. It also acted as coordinator for four of these programmes: English language, linguistics, international relations and European studies.

Case study of a European studies degree course

One of the most prominent European Studies courses is presented at the University of Limerick. The course objectives here are quite unequivocal in regard to the concept of European participation and integration. Similar courses, though with some structural differences and syllabuses which are cast in a different mould, are offered at other university institutions. An integral feature of the European studies course at the University of Limerick is that students take three terms off-campus over the four-year course on a work-experience basis. All European Studies students now complete at least one placement abroad.

The objective of the University of Limerick's European Studies programme is to develop a 'European' – an internationalist who can transcend national boundaries and socio-cultural differences to help realise the aspirations of a developing Ireland in an increasingly interdependent world. By producing graduates who speak continental European languages and have been educated to understand how to relate to modern European society, the European Studies programme at the University of Limerick is training the executives and technologists of tomorrow. These young people will be ready to seize the opportunities created by the transnational cooperation and expanded market already emerging as a result of the EU and other European organisations.

The major proportion of the programme is devoted to the origins of the EU and the part played in its evolution by its major member states. Unlike many other European studies programmes elsewhere, the University of Limerick's programme is utilitarian, reflecting the career orientation of the university. While sufficiently broad to provide students with the knowledge and skills necessary for pursuing satisfying and rewarding careers in a wide range of employment opportunities, the programme is specifically geared towards meeting national and local needs in such fields as the public services, semi-state bodies, the tourist industry, mass media, export-orientated industry and commerce, the insurance industry and law.

The bachelor's degree programme in European Studies is structured around a common group of core modules designed to lay the basis of the student's knowledge of contemporary Europe. During the first four terms, for example, the student is introduced to courses in economics, history, law, politics, sociology and one modern European language (French, German or Spanish). During the third year, following cooperative education, while continuing to take core modules in each area, students also take specialist modules from their chosen option area. During the fourth year, students concentrate on specialist options and related modules.

The objectives of language study are to develop written and oral abilities equally. Teaching is conducted in small groups, and from the earliest possible stage the majority of teaching is conducted in the foreign language. Once the fundamentals have been mastered, the emphasis shifts during the third and fourth years to studying the history, culture and society of each language area from original sources. Students read widely not only in literature, but also in the press, history and the social sciences. In addition to scheduled classes, students are required to do private study in the language laboratory to improve comprehension and fluency. There are three option areas from which students, at the end of a first common year, may choose one.

Case study of the use of the Comett programme

Furthermore, at the University of Limerick the EU Comett programme has been used to support some 33 engineering and science placements in France, Germany and the Netherlands. This has also included a language and acclimatisation course in Germany for grant recipients. The programme has helped to overcome some of the constraints in marketing the international programme in Europe by:

- subsidising the placements, with each student receiving a travel grant and accommodation allowance to defray cost of living differentials;
- providing Comett contacts and University of Limerick recognition to overcome the traditional reluctance of continental employers who had hitherto employed their own nationals;
- compensating for lower employment contribution.

The growing interaction with European companies has resulted in an increase in the number of University of Limerick graduates receiving offers from continental employers located primarily in Italy, Germany and the Netherlands.

European interaction initiatives

European liaison centre

The European Liaison Centre has continued to promote the development and expansion of EU initiatives in education, research and development and training. The centre was established in 1987 under the auspices of the EU Comett programme as a partnership between the University of Limerick, Shannon Development and the National Technological Park, Passey, Limerick, with transnational partners in the University of Sussex in the United Kingdom and Twente University in the Netherlands. The Centre has maintained and developed its on-going direct contact with the European Commission. This interaction, together with links to universities and Comett centres throughout Europe and access to EU-sponsored electronic information databases, has supported the centre's role in coordinating an institutional response to relevant EU initiatives.

The European Liaison Centre has continued to develop its participation in the Comett 11 programme, having received renewed recognition as a University Enterprise Training Partnership (UETP) and Commission support. The Centre has built on this renewed UETP status to expand on-going links with partners throughout the EU and EEA network of Comett centres. These initiatives have included the further enhancement of tripartite linkages with Sussex and Twente as well as collaborative programmes with other Comett partners in Portugal, France, Germany and the United Kingdom. In addition, links with EEA partners have been developed in accordance with the expansion of the Comett programme to allow full participation by the EEA countries. Current joint initiatives include the extension of the International Cooperative

Education Programme to Sweden and Austria and the involvement of Chalmers University of Technology, Göteborg, in the design of advanced high-technology programmes as a basis for collaborative R&D activities under EU programmes in the future.

European Community student exchange programmes

Student exchanges took place under four University of Limerick coordinated and eight University of Limerick endorsed Socrates/Erasmus Inter-University Cooperation Programmes. Several hundred students have participated to date. The university is also involved in a Lingua programme (now under the auspices of the Leonardo programme). Participation figures increase each year, with strongest growth recorded in the College of Humanities.

Incoming students came from 38 different universities spread over each of the continental EU states, while Limerick students went to France, Germany, Spain, Belgium, the United Kingdom, the Netherlands, Italy and Portugal. Among the universities involved are Universität Konstanz, Université de Grenoble, Universidad de Valladolid, Universidade de Coimbra, Université Catholique de Louvain, Erasmus Universiteit Rotterdam and LUISS Roma. In addition to EU students, the university welcomed six 'free-movers' from Poland. Their stay was funded by the EU Tempus programme (also under the auspices of the Leonardo programme). Student exchanges are expected to increase by at least 25 per cent per year. Other Irish universities, of course, have also been involved in EU initiatives.

Summary

It is clear from the above account of the European dimension in Irish education that reaction in Ireland to the European ideal and the practical possibilities it offers has been very positive indeed. This account is by no means exhaustive, especially as the authors have chosen to exemplify some of the key initiatives in some detail rather than present a comprehensive coverage.

Furthermore, the spirit of European involvement and cooperation is operating at all levels of Irish education so that there is not likely to be any significant time lag before the curricular initiatives have some effect. Of course, until recently, the Irish people have been accustomed to migration, including emigration on a large scale, to Anglophone destinations, especially the United States and the United Kingdom. The European opportunity, once the Single Market is fully operative, will open up the possibilities for which the Irish government, through its educational system and other agencies, is actively preparing the population at large. The attitude of young Irish people is particularly positive and this augurs well not only for their participation in the societies and economies of mainland Europe but also for the welcoming of other Europeans who may increasingly avail themselves of opportunities to visit, work and perhaps even settle in Ireland.

Notes

1 Government of Ireland: Council of Education, *White Paper: Charting our Education Future*, Dublin: Stationery Office, 1995, p. i.
2 Personal communication from Professor Áine Hyland, University College, Cork.
3 Ireland, *Education (No. 2) Bill* (Explanatory and Financial Memorandum), Dublin: Stationery Office 1997.
4 Denis O'Sullivan, 'From theocentric to market paradigms in Irish educational policy: equality, difference, virtue and control', in K. Mazurek, M.A. Winzer and C. Majorek (eds), *Schooling and Society in Today's World: Comparative Studies*, New York: Allyn & Bacon, 1998.
5 A report from the Educational Research Centre has not yet been published.
6 Government of Ireland: Council of Education, *Report of the Constitution Review Group*, Dublin: Stationery Office, 1996.
7 O'Sullivan, op. cit.
8 *White Paper*, op. cit., p. 206.
9 Ibid., p. 53.

References

Coolahan, J. (ed.) (1994) *Report on the National Education Convention*. Dublin: Stationery Office.

Gleeson, J. (1998) 'A Consensus Approach to Policy-Making: the Case of the Republic of Ireland' in Finlay I., Niven, S., and Young, S. (eds) *Chancing Vocational Education and Training: An International Comparative Perspective*, London, Routledge.

Hogan, P. and Williams, K. (eds) (1997) *The Future of Religion in Irish Education*, Dublin, Veritas Publications.

Hyland, Áine (1997) 'Primary and second-level education in the early twenty-first century', in F. Ó Muircheartaigh (ed.), *Ireland in the Coming Times. Essays to Celebrate T.K. Whitaker's 80 Years*. Dublin: Institute of Public Administration.

Ireland, Government of (1992) *Green Paper: Education for a Changing World*. Dublin: Stationery Office.

Ireland, Communications Unit of the Department of Education and Science (1998) *Brief Description of the Irish Education System*. Dublin: Stationery Office.

Mulcathy, Donal G. and O'Sullivan, Denis (eds) (1989) *Irish Educational Policy: Process and Substance*. Dublin: Institute of Public Administration.

O'Flaherty, L. (1992) *Management and Control in Irish Education: the Post-Primary Experience*, Elo Press Ltd., Dublin.

O'Sullivan, D. (1996) 'Cultural exclusion and educational change: education, Church and religion in the Irish Republic', *Compare: A Journal of Comparative Education*, 26(1): 35–50.

9   Italy

Attilio Monasta

The rapid development of the European integration process has had a decisive influence on the transformation of the Italian education system, which was relatively static until recently.

Until the early 1990s education in modern Italy could have been defined as a 'sleeping beauty', dreaming of her glorious past, when Latin was spoken all over the (known) world, the first University in Europe was created in Bologna 400 years before the discovery of America and Renaissance artists and philosophers influenced all other European schools.

From the death of Lorenzo il Magnifico (1492) to the new Italian kingdom in 1861, Italy was not an independent state, and modern Italy, during the past 130 years, while developing economically and financially, did not awaken as far as the educational system is concerned.

Despite their common origins, education systems within Europe differ in many respects from each other, and very few people in Italy had a clear opinion as to the effect European integration could have upon the Italian educational system. However, after the growing debate on the various influences of the Maastricht Treaty of 1993 on people's day-to-day lives, a greater number of people began to question why the Italian education and training system differed from all other European systems, what effect this could have on Italian participation within a single Europe and whether it would be possible and even useful to change and adapt it for the coming events. The process of unification in Europe is seen by many, therefore, as an opportunity to cancel negative aspects and to share with other European countries the positive aspects of the system.

The main differences found in the Italian education system, in comparison to most other European countries, are: the short duration of compulsory education (eight years: from 6 to 14), the integration of all disabled pupils into mainstream education, the lack of adequate teacher education and training, the absence of an efficient advisory and guidance system for pupils, the centralised school management and administration and, finally, a rigid higher education system exclusively based in universities.

Italian public opinion, which is rather sceptical about any possible radical change in the solid old traditions of education and culture, does not seem to believe in a panacea for all educational problems. However, among the specialists, teachers, educators and an increasing number of decision makers, the unification of Europe is perceived as the only real opportunity to raise the age of compulsory education to at least 16; to create an adequate system of teacher education and training at university level; to take all the measures for facilitating the transition of pupils from school to adult and working life; to reorganise and improve the regional training system and to up-date and diversify the higher education system, according to the needs of the new European citizen for cultural, scientific and professional preparation.

The Italian government created after the April 1996 elections and based on a rather different alliance from previous governments aimed at these reforms but not without difficulties and contradictions.

The Italian education system

General information

Centralisation, inherited from the Napoleonic French school reforms, was the main characteristic of the Italian school system, similar in this respect to that of France,[1] until March 1997, when a relevant process for decentralisation of public administration started with a new Law (*Legge* 59, of 15.3.1997) which gave autonomy to schools. The central government, that is, the Ministry of Education (*Ministero della Pubblica Istruzione*) is the head of the school administration (whose local authority is the *Provveditore agli studi*, the head of school administration in each province, appointed by the government), as well as the employer of all school teachers. Centralisation affects also the content of school programmes: we cannot, therefore speak of a proper curriculum, since national laws and governmental regulations define the content of the teaching 'programme', rather than learning objectives and standards to be achieved. However, in 1997, the European Centre for Education (CEDE), the Ministerial Institute for research on school and education, was given the task of setting up a national agency for the evaluation of the education system, and a study on possible national standards began. The central government is still the only validating body for any certification, and this appears to be the approach deeply rooted in the Italian judiciary system and not likely to change: external examiners are appointed as government officers (*commissari*) for the final state exams (*esami di stato*) at the completion of primary and secondary school.

While the general structure remains intact, formal declarations within the governmental programme and preparatory work and rumours on the reform of school administration seem to verge toward the reduction of the power of bureaucracy, both central (reform of the Ministerial General Directorates) and peripheral (*Provveditori agli studi*) while new ministerial coordinators, appointed at regional level, have the task of supervising the autonomy of individual schools.

If so, the point of reference for this relative decentralisation of ministerial power (a full federalisation of school education was rejected by the government), will be the regional administrations, included in the 1948 Republican and

Democratic Constitution, and implemented from 1972 onward.[2] From this date Italian regions have dealt with vocational training, industrial training and further education, the *formazione professionale* (including all types of vocational training for young people and training for adults). The ongoing process of decentralisation of public administration is already seen as the way toward a closer cooperation between school education and vocational training, and between school institutions and the local environment. Below progress made and the problems of the Italian regional training system are discussed. Education in terms of primary, secondary and higher education is managed centrally, and training in terms of vocational and initial training, training for adults and further education, is managed regionally. Some regions have already approved regional laws for closer cooperation with schools, and agreements at local level are being signed between the peripheral organisations of the Ministry of Education and local administrations.

One of the most disputed areas of the Italian education system is religious education. From 1929, and the international agreement between the Roman Catholic Church and the Italian State (the *Concordato*), until 1989, religious education 'in the form inherited by the Roman Catholic Church' was a compulsory subject in all primary and secondary schools, except for children from families of different denominations, who could be exempt. But from 1989, all families could choose whether or not to include this aspect of education. However, religious education is still intended 'in the form inherited by the Roman Catholic Church', and teachers of it, while paid by the central government, are appointed by the local bishop and are never given permanent posts.

Parliament has considered a law concerning the funding of private schools, which are mainly Catholic, thus providing an opportunity to discuss and review the 'religious education question', one of the most difficult issues in Italian politics.

The most relevant changes in the Italian educational system during the last 20 years have occurred at the bottom and the top of the system: that is to say compulsory education and, partially, higher education. No relevant changes have been introduced into the upper secondary school (the *scuola secondaria superiore*). In May 1997, a proposal for a full reform of the education system was submitted by the government to the Parliament (details of which will be examined further in this chapter).

Compulsory education in Italy is of eight years' duration. This includes primary and secondary lower school, from 6 to 14 years of age, and it is within this area that some relevant innovations have been introduced. From 1977 (*Legge* (L) 517/1977), the assessment of pupils is no longer based on numerical marking, but rather on a detailed description of their learning achievements; a personal profile in each subject and overall. From this same year all disabled pupils have been mainstreamed into ordinary classes. In these cases, the number of pupils per class cannot exceed 20 and another 'support' teacher is appointed for special education, within the normal curriculum. In 1979 (*Decreto Ministeriale* (DM)

9.2.1979) the curriculum of the lower secondary school (the *scuola media*) was reformed to give greater freedom to the teacher in curriculum planning. In 1985 (*Decreto del Presidente della Repubblica* (DPR) 104/1985), the primary education curriculum was reformed. From 1990 (L 148/1990), the whole structure of primary schools was changed: each primary school now has three teachers for every two classes, attendance at school has been increased from 27 to 30 hours per week, and it is also possible to plan the weekly timetable on a five- rather than six-day cycle. Furthermore, one foreign language has become part of the primary curriculum.

As far as higher education is concerned, the changes refer to the status of researchers, lecturers and professors (L 382/1980), to the administration and management of higher education institutions; and, more recently (L 341/1990), university grades and curricula. Until 1988, the system was centralised under the Ministry of Education. After that date, the creation of a new Ministry, within the central government, dealing with universities and scientific and technological research (*Ministero dell'Università e della Ricerca Scientifica e Tecnologica*), and the 'creeping' and rather controversial 'autonomy' of tertiary institutions have been the most recent changes which can be related to the imminent European integration process. The most important change concerning autonomy of higher education institutions is the approval of the Law 217, in May 1997. It concerns decentralisation of public administration in general, but it allows effective autonomy for universities, including the organisation of curricula, which previously had to follow strict central regulations.

Pre-primary and primary education

Primary school for Italian children starts at 6 years of age and lasts for five years. It is normally of four hours' duration per day, for 6 days a week, from mid-September to mid-June. It must be noted that during their primary career pupils are assessed by the teacher at the end of each year and may 'pass' or 'fail'; pupils who fail may be asked to repeat the full year of study. In recent years the rate of primary school children having to repeat has become minimal. This could be related to the fact that most Italian children aged from 3 to 5 attend nursery schools (*scuola materna*).[3] Therefore many children receive initial education before entering primary school, and the level of some experience of nursery education in Italy (such as the well known 'Reggio Emilia' model) is recognised world-wide as being very high. Some local administrations, particularly in the centre and north of Italy, are experimenting with the introduction of foreign language learning within nursery education and the experiment seems, to date, to have been very successful.

The main changes in the organisation of teaching and in the content of curricula within Italian education are those which have occurred in primary schools, from September 1987 (implementation of the DPR 104/1985) to September 1990 (implementation of the L 148/1990, *Nuovi ordinamenti didattici per la scuola elementare*).

As a result, for the first time in the history of Italian education, the new programmes for primary school adapt the old philosophy of a centralised curriculum to the need for curricular change according to the aptitudes and personal learning needs of the pupils. While a long list of subject content is still suggested to the teacher in old and new disciplines such as sciences, social studies, one foreign language, musical education and psychomotor education, in subjects which are introduced for the first time the learning issues are presented in the form of learning objectives to be achieved by pupils. Also the implementation of the new curriculum is given strong support by the new regulations for primary teaching: from 1990–1 three teachers teach in two classes, and the teaching time is becoming rather similar to that of many other European countries, including school meals and afternoon classes. Primary teachers, however, are now being asked to plan their teaching in teams, of which they have little experience.

School exchanges with other European countries, which were quite the exception until 1994, within the ordinary provision of state primary schools, have become increasingly frequent within the new Socrates (Comenius) programme of the European Union. Local administrations, particularly in the larger towns of northern and central Italy (such as Bologna, Florence, Genoa, Milan and Turin) are supporting extra-curricular initiatives, including school exchanges with other schools of both west and east European countries.

Secondary education and technical/vocational education

From September 1962, secondary education in Italy was divided into two very different parts: an initial cycle of compulsory and comprehensive school, lasting three years (from ages 11 to 14), named *scuola media inferiore* (or *scuola secondaria di primo grado*, that is, lower secondary school), followed by a variety of different streams of non-compulsory upper secondary schools (*scuola secondaria superiore* or *scuola secondaria di secondo grado*). Most of these streams, for example, the classic and scientific lyceums, the technical institutes and the new experimental professional institutes, last for five years (ages 14 to 19). However, other streams provide a shorter curriculum, such as the traditional professional institutes (three years) and *istituto magistrale* (a type of early primary teacher education, lasting four years).

The relationship between the compulsory, lower secondary school (*scuola media*), reformed in 1962, and the upper secondary school (*secondaria superiore*), still structured as in 1923 and non-compulsory, is one of the most difficult problems facing the present Italian education system, and it is at the core of the reform proposal being discussed in the Italian Parliament.

The scuola media

The *scuola media* is a comprehensive school. However, compared with the British secondary school, the main difference is that there are no options among the subjects taught. In all of Italy, each *scuola media* includes religious education as explained above, Italian, history, geography, mathematics and science, one foreign language and technical, art, music and physical education.

The present curriculum of the *scuola media* comes from the governmental regulation of 1979 (DM of 9.2.1979: *Programmi, orari di insegnamento e prove di esame per la scuola media statale*). The long 'Foreword' (*Premessa generale*) to this regulation is considered the most progressive educational document relating to the Italian school system. It implies that compulsory education has to implement the constitutional aim of removing 'the social and economic obstacles which limit the freedom and equality of citizens and prevent the full development of human beings and their full participation in the political, economic and social management of the country'; it describes the general aims of basic education in terms of human and social development, links with the family, society and the world, orientation rather than selection for adult life, adaptation of school to child development, including the individual needs of disabled children; it gives indications to the teachers for curriculum planning and their professional development. Most of the descriptions for individual subject teaching are based on learning objectives, rather than on a list of contents.

The implementation of the good intentions of this *Premessa*, however, has met strong obstacles during the last ten years. The centralised bureaucratic machine does not help in taking the infrastructural measures (buildings, equipment, personnel) needed for such an open educational perspective. The basic preparation of teachers is still strongly related to the academic structure (both in terms of methods and of knowledge acquired) of university learning. Finally, lack of pedagogic theory and practice prevents teachers from carrying out the new educational measures suggested by the few advisers of the central administration.

Two main factors from the new regulation for the *scuola media* will decide whether the good intentions will result in good practice. First, the short school day, with classes finishing at 12.30 or 13.30, restricts the school to the role of a mere 'teaching place', while the learning process is confined to home work. Each school can apply for full day education (*tempo prolungato*), but financial constraints (mostly related to the greater number of teachers required) and prejudices on the part of some parents have resulted in only a minority of schools introducing full day education. Second, the assessment procedures, which were reformed in 1977 by abolishing numerical marking and introducing a large and diversified system of continuous assessment, still remain old fashioned. This is due to a lack of professional preparation of teachers: oral assessment is still predominant, written class work for summative assessment is still considered 'more important', or even the only 'real' assessment. Individualisation of teaching is almost impossible without practising formative assessment.

Most of the obstacles to the implementation of new pedagogics probably result from the importance given by the entire educational system to summative assessment. Teachers must, every fourth month (*quadrimestre*) devise individual assessment papers (*scheda di valutazione*) for each pupil. In 1996 this summative assessment was put back to an alphabetical scale (from A to E), overturning the reform of 1977 and the analytical statements which had replaced the 0 to 10 numerical scale. At the end of any school year pupils are assessed and they may pass or fail. If they fail they have to repeat the full year.

The rate of *scuola media* pupils who have to repeat is much higher than in primary school. In all of Italy, in 1990–1, 11.1 per cent of lower secondary school pupils were kept back by one year or more. In the more deprived areas of the country these rates tend to be even higher. At the end of the *scuola media*, Italian children sit their first state examination in front of their own teachers, but under the supervision of an external *commissario*.

The secondaria superiore

The Italian upper secondary school is not compulsory. However, a high percentage of pupils who obtain the 'diploma' from the *scuola media* (86.3 per cent in 1990–1)[4] enrol in the first year of upper secondary school. This school is the most selective within the Italian education system: only half of the pupils who enrol survive to the end of the five-year curriculum. The great majority of pupils who have to repeat a full year of study are found within the first two years of it; and many of them, after one or two years of failure, abandon school altogether.

The main structure of the *secondaria superiore* is the same as that which was created in 1923 by the first Ministry of Education of the Fascist dictatorship. The classic and the scientific lyceums do not give professional preparation; they traditionally prepare students for a university career. The pupils must study Italian literature, Latin, Greek (in the classical lyceum) or one foreign language (in the scientific lyceum), mathematics, physics, natural science, philosophy, history, art and physical education. The *istituto magistrale*, which was meant to prepare primary teachers in four years, is now in fact transformed into a type of five-year-long experimental secondary school, since a recent Ministerial Decree abolished the possibility of obtaining a teacher qualification at the end of it, in accordance with the new curriculum for university teacher education prepared to start in 1998–9. Upper-level technical and professional schools (*istituti tecnici* and *istituti professionali*) offer vocational training and professional preparation for hundreds of different jobs (from the more usual mechanical engineering or secretarial studies to the more unusual in the wine industry, building musical instruments, and arts and crafts). The present development of technical and professional schools, as a stream of vocational education, has continued despite the creation of a parallel regional system of vocational training to which reference is made below.

The only relevant changes to have occurred within the Italian upper secondary school do not refer to the structure or to the curriculum, but rather to the final examinations and the entry requirements for access to university. At the end of any upper secondary school, Italian students sit their second state examination before external examiners. This is very similar to the French *baccalauréat* and is called the *esame di maturità*. Until the late 1960s the examination included all the subjects learnt during the final three years. There were several written papers (from three to five, according to the type of school) and two sessions of oral examination (one for each subject area: humanities and science). However, access to the university was strictly limited according to the type of secondary school attended. Following the medieval hierarchy of disciplines, only students from the classic lyceum (that is to say, those gaining the *maturità classica*) were allowed to enter all university faculties; the scientific lyceum pupils were restricted to the faculties of science and law; from all other streams pupils were allowed to enter the university only after passing an entry examination.

In 1969 a new state examination was introduced, whereby all pupils who successfully completed their school curriculum sit the *esame di maturità* in the form of two written examinations (an Italian composition, with a choice of themes given by the Ministry of Education, and an examination in a specific subject depending on the type of school attended) and an oral interview on two of the final year subjects.

The new formula of the *esame di maturità* seems to be less selective, as the present pass rate for this examination is very high. However, as previously stated, selection within the Italian education system occurs during the school career rather than at the end. In the first two years of the upper secondary school, repetitions (*ripetenze*) affect a high proportion of pupils. It is still likely that almost one-third of pupils attending the final year of upper secondary school were delayed by one year or more.

The other important change in 1969 concerning access to university has opened all faculties to all upper secondary pupils who have achieved a five-year upper secondary school certificate, regardless of the type of school which they attended. This 'free access' to university is particular to the Italian education system and could have the greatest impact with the unification of Europe.

In 1997, the reform of the *esame di maturità* was approved by Parliament, reintroducing oral examinations for all the subjects studied in the final year and a third written examination in the form of a 'general culture' multiple-choice test. Schools and experts have already criticised this reform, as it is not related to the general reform of the school system.

Although the basic structure of the curriculum of the upper secondary school in Italy has not been reformed during the last 20 years, the Ministry of Education has allowed a large number of 'experimental' streams (*sperimentazioni* or *indirizzi sperimentali*), which do not replace the previous streams, but rather have been added to the existing school structure. These schools submit a new curriculum to the Ministry of Education, and this usually entails the modification of the type and number of subjects to be taught and, therefore, the qualification to be delivered. Most of the 'experimental' upper secondary schools aim at improving the relationship between school and working life, and frequently the process of European unification is mentioned in the basic documents. The new streams are concerned with computer education, foreign language learning, business studies, secretarial studies, health and social care, and other instrumental areas. After authorisation from the Ministry, the schools implement their renewed curriculum. However, no relevant decision has been taken concerning the assessment of the results of these experiments to date.

Technical, vocational and further education

At the upper secondary school level, the highest number of 'experimental streams' is found within the technical and professional institutes. Vocational education can be considered the weakest link of the Italian school system. The functions of central state-maintained technical and vocational schools (*istituti tecnici* and *istituti professionali di stato*), on the one hand, and of the regional system of vocational training, on the other, are still under discussion, and the relationship between the two systems is not clear.

Most of the resources for vocational training and technical education still go to central government upper secondary schools, while regional vocational training is mostly funded by European Social Fund resources. There is a conflict, however, within the basic structure of this type of upper secondary school. It tends to privilege general cultural preparation, through a 'core curriculum' based on Italian, history, geography and mathematics, which are allocated greater space within the weekly time schedule and which are highly selective in terms of 'cultural content'. Technical and professional preparation is based on specific vocational subjects.

As previously pointed out, the greatest impact for pupils is within the first two years of upper secondary school (the *biennio*). At the end of compulsory education, because of lack of guidance and career advice, many pupils who are not considered able enough to attend the classic or scientific lyceums, are advised by secondary school teachers to attend technical or professional schools, which eventually may not be easier than any other upper secondary school. Teachers of the *biennio* usually emphasise general and cultural preparation, teaching methods are rather academic and many pupils find it difficult to continue.

In many regions of Italy, pupils who fail, both at the end of the *scuola media* and during the first few years of upper secondary school, enter the vocational education system of local authorities. This, in fact, is considered to offer the least prestigious qualification. In reality, however, the 'Regional Training System', mainly in central and northern regions of Italy, has been greatly reformed and improved during the last twenty years. The training centres of regional administrations such as Lombardia, Piemonte, Emilia Romagna, Toscana and Umbria have become very flexible structures, able to change and to plan new curricula, according to the needs of the job market, much faster and more easily than the technical and vocational schools of the central government. The training centres, from a first phase during the 1970s, when they focused their attention mostly on the young deprived workforce, are now centres of services for technical and professional advice to the companies and enterprises of the area they serve. Indeed, they run most of the training initiatives for both the adult employed workforce and for the young and adult unemployed people, mainly within European Union training schemes related to its so-called Structural Funds.

It would be difficult to describe the large variety of regulations of the different regional governments within Italy, as vocational training and industrial training are the main domains in which Italian regions have exercised their autonomous decision-making powers. The influence of central government, however, is still evident. Regional legislation must follow the framework Bill on vocational training (*formazione professionale*: L 845/1978), the principal aim of which is to harmonise the school system (which is centralised) and the training system (which is regionalised), and the preparation of the workforce in all fields and at all levels to meet the changing requirements of the job market. The national Bill on *formazione professionale* was approved by the Italian Parliament at the end of a long period of conflict between unions and employers' associations. Therefore, it is already considered out of date.

Funding of the regional plans for training is provided by the central government, within the Ministry of Employment (*Ministero del Lavoro*), which also has an important role in the process of regional applications for European Union funding.

Finally, a central *istituto* attached to the Ministry of Employment (ISFOL, *Istituto per lo Sviluppo della Formazione Professionale dei Lavoratori*) was created in 1973, to assist both the central government and the regions in their training policy. ISFOL produces interesting research on training needs and the development of the jobs and professions, and it publishes a yearly report on training in Italy.[5]

The Ministry of Employment and ISFOL are at present the main links with similar institutions in other European countries, with the European Commission and with its main agent in the field, Cedefop. Under the Italian Constitution, regions were not allowed to develop their own foreign policy, which central government considers its own jealously guarded prerogative. After Law 217 was approved in May 1997, more autonomy has been given to regions which may now open European offices in Brussels, as a consequence of the Maastricht Treaty. However, only the full political unification of Europe could in reality give Italian regional governments a larger opportunity for direct contact with other European institutions and organisations.

As far as further education is concerned, it would be difficult to find an equivalent reality, or even an equivalent concept, within the Italian education system, whose nature rather encourages the development of 'adult education' and 'continuous education' (*educazione permanente*) instead. Until recently, adult education in Italy was intended to help illiterate adults or young people who had not completed compulsory education, by providing an additional learning resource. However, after the Second World War, a number of opportunities for 'informal education' developed beside the formal adult education system: many initiatives for social and cultural development have been taken within the largest social organisations, such as Catholic associations, on the one hand, and Socialist and Communist parties and workers' unions, on the other. A relevant transformation of the Italian political parties of the left which occurred in the 1990s does not seem to have affected their large social organisations for culture and leisure, such as the ARCI clubs, which are widely spread throughout the centre and north of Italy.

In the early 1970s, some relevant changes could be found concerning adult education and continuous education. Within the strong social struggle which developed in Italy between 1968 and 1974, union negotiations and agreements included a number of 'paid study leaves', the so-called '150 hours', from which a new deal on mass adult education was introduced both within and outside the school system.[6] Thousands of mature workers attended intensive courses for basic education, which in 1976 was still not completed by 72 per cent of the Italian workforce.[7] New methods of teaching and learning affected even higher education, in so far as some of the university courses and seminars were opened to mature workers and union leaders. Nowadays very little survives of this experience. The '150 hours' courses still remain at basic education level, but they are attended mostly by young dropouts, the unemployed workforce, illiterate elderly people and lower-class unemployed women.

Perhaps the best heritage of the early 1970s is the policy of local administrations to provide continuous education. The *educazione permanente*, like vocational and industrial training, is administered from within the regions and it covers a very wide range of educational and cultural initiatives funded by local authorities, from music and drama to leisure studies, from art and literature to cookery or parapsychology. A national framework regulation on this matter is still under discussion.

Higher education

'Further education' as it is understood in the English-speaking world, is probably one of the implicit functions of Italian higher education, which awards an academic qualification to less than 30 per cent of the students who register in universities, but which allows everybody to attend a large variety of courses, no matter what their objectives. During the last 30 years, the number of students registered in universities increased by 500 per cent, but the number of graduates increased by only 388 per cent.[8] The number of students entering the university is still increasing (+26.7 per cent from 1986 to 1990).

The Italian model of higher education remains at present quite unique, being the only model incorporating all different functions in one type of institution: 'the university',[9] and allowing some of them to grow to more than 200,000 students (University of Rome 'La Sapienza'). The data from the UNESCO *Statistical Year-book*[10] confirm the relatively atypical position of Italian higher education. If we look at the proportion of students attending all the higher education institutions of an individual country, we find that Italy is the only country where the concept of university is virtually identical with the concept of 'higher education' (99.3 per cent). In recent years, a few private initiatives for specific professional preparation at post-secondary level in some fields (such as fashion or photography) have grown up outside the university sector.

Each university is divided into faculties, and some of the faculties include more than one 'curricular stream' (*corso di laurea*). Faculties and 'streams' are responsible for teaching and curricula. Scientific research is organised and managed by departments (*dipartimenti*), which may concern cross-faculty research areas, and therefore bring together professors and researchers from different disciplines. As far as the real output of this type of institution is concerned, it must be said that, even if there is no clear distinction between the several functions the institution should develop, the traditional *educational function* (that is lectures and examinations) is the largest one, frequently separate from the *scientific research* university staff are involved in. Professional *training* as such is not explicit in most fields of study, other than through the acquisition of knowledge, and therefore 'work experience' is almost non-existent within the curricula of the various universities.

Italian higher education, however, is probably the part of the Italian education system which has been most affected by the wider European influence. The most important trends, which can be related to the development of a European awareness, concern the creation of a new Ministry for University and Scientific and Technological Research, separate from the Ministry of Education, which until 1987 dealt with all educational matters, and the approval, from 1990 onward, of a number of measures which could make the Italian higher education system more like that of other European countries. Until now, the main curriculum available for university studies, and frequently the only one, is the *corso di laurea*, leading to a first and, very frequently, only grade: the *laurea*. The official length of a *corso di laurea* is four years, in most cases, and five or six years in those such as engineering or medicine. Postgraduate studies do not exist in the majority of faculties, but graduate schools of specialisation are found mainly within medical studies. Since 1982, doctoral studies (*dottorato di ricerca*) have been created in most faculties, but the university must apply every year to the Ministry for University and Scientific and Technological Research for a very limited number of posts of *dottorato*, which must attract a state grant incompatible with income from any other job. The Law 341/1990 allows the institutions to create three levels of university diplomas: a 'university diploma', which has already been defined by journalists as the 'short laurea' (*laurea breve*); the usual four-year diploma of *laurea*; and a postgraduate specialisation (*diploma di specializzazione*), which is different from the *dottorato di ricerca*. This regulation is gradually being implemented through a growing involvement of external 'sponsors', since severe financial constraints (as a consequence of the march toward European monetary union) have obliged universities to introduce only no-cost innovations. First degree diploma courses are almost always created with external financial support from private and regional funds.

In so far as we can consider the Italian education system to be the 'sleeping beauty' of the tale, the steps of the 'prince' can be heard in Italian universities. European Community programmes for mobility of students and professors throughout Europe are creating the most significant changes in the mentality and structure of the Italian university. Italian participation in EU programmes such as

Erasmus, Comett, Lingua and Tempus, and now within Socrates and Leonardo, is growing and approaching the standard European average. The geographical distribution of the programmes among Italian regions, however, is still very unequal, accentuating the traditional disparity between the north and the south of the country. However, the involvement of many Italian universities in European programmes, both for research and for mobility of students, has started to be very relevant. In 1994–5 Italian universities were coordinating 226 Erasmus programmes and were involved in 58.6 per cent of all the Erasmus programmes.[11] Under the Socrates–Erasmus regulations, the 'institutional contract' of some Italian universities such as Florence and Bologna includes partnerships with more than 400 higher education institutions from all EU member states, and in 1997–8 the University of Florence received the highest financial support of all the EU for Erasmus institutional contracts. After a few years of difficulties caused by the impact upon a very rigid and bureaucratic structure within Italian public administration and university management, EU cooperation programmes are now beginning to affect, in several key Italian institutions, the style of work and the method of dealing not only with research and education, but also with finance and administration.

Selected issues and areas of reform

The education, training and mobility of teachers

Initial teacher education, too, is very particular to the Italian education system. However, it will soon be one of the fields most strongly affected by the process of European unification. Until the late 1990s, nursery and primary teachers were prepared at secondary school. A three-year upper secondary school stream (*scuola magistrale*) prepared nursery teachers and a four-year upper secondary school stream (*istituto magistrale*) prepared primary teachers. This preparation has been mostly theoretical, including Italian, Latin, history, geography, philosophy, psychology, theory of education, mathematics, science, fine arts, music and physical education. Some school experience (*tirocinio*) was required in the final years.

Secondary school teachers do not receive initial teacher education. They must have a relevant university degree in the subject area they are going to teach, and must pass a competitive national examination if they want to have a permanent post.

Personal experience and in-service training, therefore, are the most relevant factors of Italian teacher preparation. Within the last decade, in-service training has increased in quantity and importance, and it is now compulsory for about 40 hours per year for all teachers. Most of the in-service training is still run in terms of refresher courses (*corsi di aggiornamento*), which are frequently related to the need to up-date teachers on new information in their individual subjects. However, within primary and lower secondary school (that is, compulsory education) there is a growing demand for in-service training in pedagogy and methodology, curriculum planning and evaluation – the focal areas for Italian teachers. In-service training is mostly organised by IRRSAE (the Regional Institutes for Research, Experimentation and In-service Training in Education), created by the Ministry of Education in 1977. However, the *Provveditorati agli studi* and the individual schools also organise courses for this purpose.

Initial teacher preparation is being introduced within Italian universities. L 341/1990 obliged the universities to create, by the end of 1992, university curricula for teacher training: four-year concurrent courses for nursery and primary trainees, and one or two years' postgraduate specialisation for secondary trainees. A vigorous debate is presently going on as to the structure and content that this teacher education will have. In July 1996 the curricula for these university courses were approved by the government (DPR 470 and 471), and the courses should have started from November 1997. However, the 217/97 Law on teaching autonomy of universities and the proposals for school reform delayed the start of teacher education at university level until November 1998. This reform seems to be paradigmatic of some radical change within Italian university history and, accordingly, of the resistance which innovation finds within the academic world.

University staff seem to be supporting a broad academic preparation, involving many examinations to be passed to achieve the teaching qualification. Given the habitually low attendance and highly theoretical nature of Italian university curricula, very little space would be left for teaching practice, methodology, simulations and active learning methods. However, other proposals are trying to focus rather on the structure of the curriculum, asking for compulsory and assisted teaching practice, exercises in pedagogy in individual subjects and active involvement of students in the acquisition of both theory and practice.

Apart from the existing provision of explicit in-service training and the planned provision for initial teacher education, many primary teachers and fewer secondary teachers attend university courses on a voluntary basis, both for their personal cultural interest and for learning theory of education, methodology and pedagogics. Educational studies are provided mostly within the faculties of 'magistero', which were renamed in 1995 the Faculty of Educational Sciences (*Facoltà di Scienze della Formazione*).[12] It can be said that about 40 per cent of the students of this faculty are mature students of whom teachers are the largest number.

Here we can find a little, but none the less highly meaningful, experience of the European dimension within Italian teacher education. As university students, some of the teachers gain Erasmus grants to spend a study period abroad in one of the other countries of the European Union. Permanent teachers are allowed by the Ministry of Education to have from three to nine months' paid leave for this purpose, and the effect of studying abroad on their experience and qualification is exceptionally important. A European Diploma in Education and Training is being experimented with in one of the Erasmus programmes in education, and it could become an example of a joint qualification of European teachers from different countries, even if the number of student teachers who can achieve it is at present very small.[13]

The opening of Comenius action within the Socrates programme has increased the participation of Italian teachers within European programmes, both in partnership with the universities and independently from them.

The possibility of teachers qualified in other EU countries to take up regular teaching posts in Italian schools is still subject to the procedure for recognition of the 'equivalence' of their qualification to the Italian entry requirements, and therefore is not yet automatic. The equivalence is determined by the universities for secondary school teachers, who have to hold a university degree to get access to the national competitions for permanent posts (or for temporary appointments at local level).

The reform of education and school administration

Relevant changes have been introduced within the strong centralised administration of education and schools in Italy. The most visible innovations introduced to date are the following. A growing autonomy is being given to schools, as far as the organisation of teaching hours and time schedules are concerned, as well as curriculum planning and staff management, within guidelines given by the central government. From 1994, a new type of basic school organisation has been experimented with, within the so-called 'comprehensive' schools (*scuole comprensive*), which include under the same organisation and with one headteacher, both nursery, primary and lower secondary pupils. Initially established for reasons of economy in rural and mountain areas, due to pupil numbers this model is now spreading all over Italy, and a group of schools is presently being monitored by the Ministry of Education as a possible laboratory for the school reform which is being discussed in Parliament. The first aim of this reform is to extend compulsory education from eight to ten years of schooling (that is, from 5 to 15 years of age) and, the second, to create continuity between nursery, primary and lower secondary education. In a preparatory document,[14] inspired by advisers who have a wide experience of the school systems of the EU member states,[15] the relationship between the proposal and the school reforms recently implemented in Europe was explicitly mentioned.

Other relevant aspects of the proposal are the reform of upper secondary schools (still centrally controlled, but with increasing autonomy), whose alternative streams should be reduced, and which must create links with the regional system for vocational education. The proposed law also envisages the possible creation of a second channel for non-university higher education, aiming at higher professional preparation. The problem of school management still remains. The new regulations on school autonomy have found school personnel unprepared and uncertain as to how this autonomy can be practically implemented.

A significant movement for democratisation of school management grew up during the early 1970s, and in 1974 new regulations were adopted (the so-called *Decreti Delegati*), both for the legal status of school personnel and for the 'democratic' management of schools. The first of them (DPR 416/1974) resulted in elected boards of management which have been created at school, district, provincial and national levels. They include representatives of headteachers, teachers, parents and, from upper secondary schools, even pupils. At district and provincial levels, some members of the school boards are appointed by the local administration, the largest workers' unions and employers' associations. However, their power is limited and the funds they really manage are very small. Therefore, the initial enthusiasm of parents and teachers, which resulted in high participation in voting for their representatives in the first few years, fell away sharply. The present reality of the Italian democratic management of schools seems to be in contradiction to the almost unexpected autonomy given to schools at the very moment of a crisis of democratic representation within the school boards.

Problems and policies in respect of languages

The Italian language is the medium of instruction in general education almost all over Italy. In some parts of northern Italy, abutting with France, Switzerland, Austria and Slovenia, the medium of general education in some schools is respectively French, Ladin, German or Slovene. Very recently the Parliament accepted a regional law of Sardinia, which introduces for the first time Sardinian language in the schools and universities of the region.

As far as the Italian language is concerned, it must be said that Italy, as a unified nation, has a very short tradition of teaching Italian as a common language. Up to 1861 most of the people of different regions spoke different dialects or even different languages (as in Sardinia) and the only common Italian was the sophisticated language used by dramatists, novelists and poets from the time of Dante Alighieri (thirteenth to fourteenth century) until an 1876 governmental committee, chaired by Alessandro Manzoni, declared that the Italian official language was the one spoken by the 'educated Florentine person'.

The gap between the language of literate people and the common language has affected (and perhaps still affects) the school curriculum, as the teachers knew and taught a language which most of the pupils had never really heard. This is why the Italian school has remained intrinsically selective until recent years, and the dropout rate within compulsory education is still quite high. A real change seems to have happened (and is continuing) because of the influence and diffusion of television, which is the first common cultural medium of the Italian spoken language. This positive role played by television, however, is counterbalanced by a negative effect on foreign language learning: all the foreign films Italian people see are dubbed, even if in very recent years some more foreign languages are offered by television channels and cinemas.

As a result of the incoming unification of Europe, foreign languages are beginning to be taught from primary school upwards. An increasing number of university students now take the opportunity to spend a study period abroad, mainly under EU inter-university cooperation programmes, and the number of university language centres providing both Italian teaching for foreign students and foreign language teaching for Italian students is rapidly increasing.

Foreign language teaching in secondary schools is probably the only subject area which adopted, by governmental decision, a modern pedagogical approach. Policies for in-service training of language teachers have been implemented using special EU funds from the late 1970s onwards. At basic education level, the highest demand for foreign language teaching is now for the English language; the second foreign language taught is French. However, in some schools it is now difficult to find a sufficient number of pupils to build up a French language course. Some local administrations, following the initiative of foreign countries and cultural associations, are now trying to encourage the introduction of other languages such as Spanish, German, Russian and even Chinese.

Immigration processes have created within the last few years a growing interest in intercultural education within Italian schools and it seems that one of the major changes in the school environment in the coming years will be a change in the student population and the experience of cultural diversity, which has never previously been considered.

Conclusion: Italian education in a state of flux

The history of Italian culture and education has been viewed as providing an international and world dimension rather than as the development of a national civilisation. The overpowering heritage of Rome, both in terms of classic culture and Catholicism, has prevented the growth of an independent and modern civilisation on the basis of national identity, as developed from the end of the Middle Ages in most other European countries. Therefore Italian language, culture, education and society have flourished at a national level only during recent decades, coinciding with the crisis of the national state all over Europe and the creation of the European Union. Many opinion polls, and the official policy of Italian governments, show that Italians seem to be among the most enthusiastic toward European unification, even if Italy is one of the countries which has most difficulty in implementing the decisions and regulations of the European Union.

This can be explained by using the metaphor of Italy as a microcosm of Europe, reproducing, from the Alps to the 'African sea', all the differences, imbalances, contradictions and strengths and weaknesses of the whole continent. On the one hand, the expectation of a modern, peaceful, democratic Europe is a type of projection of national expectations still unsatisfied: the European ideal could be the elusive image of what our individual societies are unable to achieve. On the other hand, the differences between all the European regions and countries encourage people to hope that the strong points of one could replace the weak points of others. The implementation of the free circulation of peoples and resources within the European Union is considered the nearest approach to this perspective. Education is one of the concerns which still shows the greatest diversity within member states. This is a contradiction in itself, since, of all the factors which are considered at present, the most unifying elements of the European Union (industrial development and international competition, new technology, trade, communications) seem to be built upon the most heterogeneous and to rely upon the most diversified elements of education and training.

In order to join the European single currency, the new Italian government has had to impose on the Italian people the largest financial sacrifice that has ever been made. Unfortunately the education system is also being affected by this policy, at the same moment when Italy should be investing much more than before in education: Italy has a GDP per capita which is higher than the European average, but has always invested less than the European average in education. This is something which must radically change with Italy joining the European single currency.

If we assume, as a realistic hypothesis, that, whereas the educational systems are very different, the real problems facing pupils and teachers are fairly similar, the following list of weak and strong points of Italian education could represent the perspective toward the best convergence of the Italian school system in Europe.

Nursery school seems to be the best aspect of Italian education. The very high percentage of children from 3 to 5 attending both public and private nurseries, and the good quality of school life, could probably be taken as a good example in Europe. The role of the family is not at all diminished in Italy, but rather transferred to the level of education which is the nearest to family education.

Here we come to one of the first weak points of Italian education. The competence of teachers is not based on proper teacher education and training, but rather on personal commitment, practical experience and human relations with pupils. It seems that for the early stages of education this could be a positive quality rather than a defect. However, the further one goes into the educational process, the weaker the system becomes. This should however change quite soon.

The same ambivalence can be seen within one of the most emphasised characteristics of Italian education, the integration of the disabled within mainstream schools. In Italy many speak of simple 'insertion', rather than a real integration, since little attention is given to the particular needs of all the different types of disabilities and the professional preparation of teachers is not specialised enough to meet the aims of such a policy. However, some positive results seem to make this action irreversible: on the one hand, the presence of disabled people has encouraged positive attitudes within the whole society; on the other, the competence of teachers and other professionals dealing with this problem tends to focus rather on human relations and personal commitment than on specialised training and technical solutions. From the many contacts already established with other European countries concerning special education, it seems that in this matter Italy could learn much as far as specialised knowledge and practice are concerned, but could also offer some interesting experiences relating to human commitment.

In general, the weakest point of Italian education seems to be related to the process of training for jobs. From the most simple manual work to the highest level of professional life, most occupations are learnt by practice, on the job and by the job. Learning by experience has been one of the strongest features of industrial development in a country where most of the economy was based on hundreds of thousands of very small companies and workshops, and during a period in which the nature of work, and therefore the kind of experience needed, did not change very rapidly. Some large and modern training structures for various levels of the workforce have existed in Italy mostly within the industrial areas of the north. Large companies such as Fiat, Olivetti and Pirelli have both created their own training centres and facilitated the development of training centres managed by local authorities. Therefore, in the few areas of Italy where a tradition of industrial training was developed, some adaptation to the present phase of industrial development and the important changes related to the opening up of the European Single Market can be seen. Many initiatives are taken by large private companies or foundations for training young managers in preparation of this. However, the Italian system of training (that is, the lack of a real preparation for jobs, in a flexible and changeable work situation) is still affecting the whole of public administration, including teachers and trainers themselves. Therefore Italian public administration, at any level, can be considered one of the most problematic points of European unification. Goodwill and personal commitment by some of the personnel will not be sufficient for successful adaptation to the incoming changes.

This pre-industrial type of education and training is being transformed and possibly overtaken within Italian higher education. While universities are still seen as the only type of higher education institutions, greater attention is given to the specialisation of the different functions, mostly in relation to international cooperation programmes both of scientific research and teaching. The two opposite models of higher education – one based only on large universities, as in Italy, and the other based on a variety of different kinds of institutions, meeting the different needs of the industrial society and frequently small and well-equipped, as in Britain, France and Germany – seem today to converge.

While Italy is considering splitting the mega-university into smaller units and facilitating the development of specialised higher education institutions for some new professions, a process of clustering several functions in one institution is going on in some other European countries. This is particularly accelerated today in Britain for economic and financial reasons. Many institutions are asked, if not forced, to 'merge', to reduce their number, possibly awarding to all of them the formal status of the university. The planned smaller number of larger institutions should apparently combine several, if not all, functions, but in fact is emphasising professional preparation to meet the demands of the Single European Market.

It seems that the Italian education system is being awakened by the 'kiss' from a prince named Europe. A prime concern of Italians has to be whether the driving force will be the realisation by millions of Italians that the new Europe presents opportunities worth striving and even moving for, or whether it will be the power of externally generated innovations of a systematic and centrifugal nature. Italian education in recent decades has been informed by both these forces, and the capacity for innovation has been developed. Whether the bureaucratic traditions will enable this capacity to be realised remains to be seen.

Notes

1 For concise information on the history of the Italian school system, see D. Ragazzini, *Storia della scuola italiana*, Florence: Le Monnier, 1983.
2 Article 117 of the Italian Constitution specifies among the matters over which the regional administration has jurisdiction, *istruzione professionale e artigiana* (vocational training for art and craft jobs).
3 Until 1968, nursery schools were provided in Italy by local authorities (*Comuni*) and by private organisations, namely religious orders of nuns; in 1968 the state nursery school, *Scuola materna statale*, was created. In 1990–1 about 1,550,000 children were attending nursery schools, i.e. 91.6 per cent of the age group; about one-third of them within the private sector. See ISTAT, 'La popolazione scolastica italiana nell'anno 1990–91', in *Notiziario*, XI, 2 (ser. 4, vol. 41).
4 Pupils passed at the *licenza media* in 1989–90 = 764,239; students registered in the first year of secondary upper school in 1990–91 = 659.572 (86.30 per cent). See ibid.
5 ISFOL, *Rapporto ISFOL 1996 sulla formazione professionale in Italia*, Milan: F. Angeli, 1997.
6 See A. Monasta, M. Mostardini, P. Pecile, *Le 150 ore*, Bari: De Donato, 1975.
7 In five years, from 1976 to 1981, the number of adults without basic education decreased from 71.9 per cent to 62 per cent, also because of the larger diffusion of this new kind of adult education (the '*150 ore*'): from 1976 to 1981 the number of participants in the intensive courses for adult workers grew from 70,157 to 92,327 (see ISTAT, *Annuario Statistico dell'Istruzione*).
8 University students and graduates: Rome, 1989. 1933–4 (st. 57,294, gr. 9,349 = ratio 16.39); 1953–4 (st. 218,917, gr. 20,058 = ratio 9.16); 1973–4 (st. 840,497, gr. 62,944 = ratio 7.49); 1983–4 (st. 1,054,768, gr. 74,096 = ratio 7.02); 1987–8 (st. 1,153,774, gr. 77.869 = ratio 6.75) (ibid.).
9 See A. Monasta, 'Memorandum sull'Istruzione Superiore e l'Università', in *Scuola Democratica*, XIII, 2/3, 1990, pp. 210–232.
10 UNESCO, *Statistical Yearbook 1988*, tab. 3.7 (the datum refers to 1984).
11 See *Erasmus Directory of Programmes*, Luxembourg: Commission of the EC, 1995.
12 See A. Monasta (ed.), *La ricerca in scienze della formazione*, Rome: La Nuova Italia Scientifica, 1996.
13 See A. Monasta (ed.), *The children of Japhet: A European programme for the new professionality of teachers and trainers*, Florence: McColl, 1989.
14 MPI (Ministero della Pubblica Istruzione), *Riordino dei cicli scolastici (documento di lavoro)*, gennaio, Rome, 1997.
15 A. Monasta, *Proposte europee per il sistema formativo italiano*, Florence, 1996 (unpublished document).

10 Luxembourg

Germain Dondelinger

The central significance of language

Any survey of the Luxembourgish school system and its place in Europe must begin with a consideration of the language situation in the country.

A Luxembourgeois is often said to be bi- or even trilingual, and although this survey will not indulge in an academic discussion of what bilingualism entails, the claim nevertheless needs clarifying. The first language with which the toddler comes into contact is Letzeburgesch, a Moselle-Frankish dialect with a French influence spoken mostly within the Luxembourgish borders which in 1984 was given the status of a national language by Act of Parliament. It was also recognized for official status as a teaching subject by the 1989 decision of the European Union Lingua programme.

Letzeburgesch is mainly based on oral tradition, although there is fiction written in the language and a few years ago a dictionary was compiled and published. However, the main importance of the language lies in the fact that it is the medium used when people try to convey their innermost thoughts and feelings. It thus contributes significantly to establishing a personal and national identity. Even so, when the child enters primary school the three basic Rs are taught in German. This would undoubtedly not be possible if Letzeburgesch were not closely related to High German. True, it does take extra effort to master High German, but so it does, for example, for the users of Schwyzerdütsch. At the age of seven – that is, in their second year of primary education – pupils start to learn French. It is these three languages that are the official languages of Luxembourg.

Letzeburgesch is the medium of everyday life. German is most widely used in newspapers and magazines, and German television has the highest viewing rates. French is the language of Parliament, of the courts, of commerce and of cultured usage in general. It is also the most widely used language in administration, although a citizen writing to the government can choose to write in any of the three languages. French is not acquired spontaneously; it needs to be taught. However, the everyday environment lends its support: indeed, apart from the different domains mentioned above, French is also spoken in shops and restaurants, there are newspaper articles written in it and French and Belgian television channels have a fair share of the Luxembourgish audience.

English is taught at secondary school from the age of 13 onwards. It goes without saying that the rise of Luxembourg as a centre of international banking has strengthened the position of English in the school curriculum.

Thus generally speaking the linguistic climate is one of everyday multi-lingualism. In schools the situation is one of functional bilingualism in the sense that French and German are the languages of instruction, English is added as a third language, compulsory in all streams of compulsory education. Language acquisition has always been viewed with favour in Luxembourg; indeed, its people's proficiency in a number of languages is one of the most important reasons given why foreign companies choose to establish themselves in the country. Educational policy is intent on maintaining the relatively good record in this respect achieved so far. A multilingual facility is believed to be one of the major assets held by Luxembourg since the Single European Act came into force on 1 January 1993.

In recent years the language issue has become even more urgent and complex, since Luxembourg boasts the highest rate of immigrants in any member state of the European Union. The total population of Luxembourg is 450,000 inhabitants, a third of whom are immigrants or other foreigners living in their midst. Besides, the workforce is highly international and 55 per cent of the people working in Luxembourg are non-native. Although a number of people commute into Luxembourg from the neighbouring regions of France, Belgium and Germany, a considerable number choose to settle in Luxembourg. They are to be found in all walks of life, which means that everyday communication tends to be conducted in a foreign language. As noted above, French prevails in bars and restaurants, and it is the language most commonly used among tradesmen or craftsmen. Also users of another Romance language – especially first-generation immigrants – will opt for French in their everyday discourse. The high ratio of immigrant workers poses one of the great challenges to the country, as efforts are made to integrate young people into the school system and into society in general.

Obviously the emphasis put on the acquisition of a second and of a foreign language requires that the standards expected of the students are extremely high, and the ensuing failure rate is one of the most serious worries the education system now has to face. There is the feeling that more pupils ought to access higher education or should at least leave school fully qualified. This is confirmed by developments in the world of work, where there is virtually no more need for unskilled workers. In the case of Luxembourg, pressure on the local labour market from the neighbouring regions calls for an educational system that can equip its students with all the required skills if they are to compete successfully with their 'foreign' colleagues. This applies also to those natives who may wish to seek employment outside of Luxembourg.

Seen from this perspective, the 1993 Single Europe deadline has not presented Luxembourg with a totally new situation, inasmuch as the country has had to accommodate to the pressure of competition for a considerable period of time. On the other hand, this does not lull either the government or the general population into a false sense of security. On the contrary. But while the opportunities are great – the school system still manages to qualify its students at a high level of performance – so are the perils. There is always the danger that a small country may be engulfed – even if not in a military sense – by more powerful neighbours. A sound educational system is the most effective weapon both to preserve a sense of identity and to cope with the demands of an increasingly multinational society.

An introduction to the system of education

The Luxembourg school system is a centralized one similar to the French *éducation nationale*; headteachers are appointed by the Minister of Education (*Ministre de l'Education Nationale*). They are chosen from among the teachers of the school and in most cases have themselves taught in the school of which they become head. They are supported by a deputy head, whose tasks are to guarantee the smooth day-to-day running of the school and to maintain a general atmosphere of discipline. In each school there is a *conseil d'éducation*, which is an advisory board whose members come from the teaching staff, the parents' association and the pupils' union. The headteacher and the deputy head also sit on that board. It generally meets once a term to discuss the general situation in the school and to formulate the necessary recommendations.

The schools do not manage their own budgets; a department in the Ministry of Education is in charge of those matters. However, the overall policy now is to hand over the management of their budgets to individual *lycées* in order to increase their autonomy.

As far as the curriculum is concerned, it is the Ministry that establishes the overall framework and fixes the guidelines. However, the *commissions nationales pour les programmes*, which are bodies grouping teachers from each subject taught at school and from each *lycée* of the country, enjoy a high degree of autonomy and work out the different syllabuses of each subject.

Education is free and compulsory for children between the ages of 4 and 15. Although the vast majority of schools are publicly maintained, there are a few private schools, most of which are under Roman Catholic auspices, such as the coeducational convent school, where fees are charged. One private school is run by the Luxembourg steelmakers, and provides relevant vocational training in the skills required by the company. The state offers subsidies to all private schools and exercises some curriculum control over their operation.

The system as a whole consists of the following sectors:

- ages 4–5: pre-school education (*Spillschoul*);
- ages 6–12: primary school education;

- ages 12–19: secondary school education: adolescents go to either the *lycée* or to the *lycée technique*;
- age 19+: either university education (there is only a first-year preparatory course taught in Luxembourg) or higher professional education.

The system also includes special schools for the disabled.

Pre-secondary education

General structure of primary education

Primary education is anchored in the Constitution of the Grand Duchy (Article 23); in 1912 compulsory education between the ages of 6 and 15 was introduced by Act of Parliament. Full-time education now starts at the age of 4 when children begin to attend kindergarten. At the age of 6 they enter primary school, which takes them up to the age of 12. In other words, there are six years of primary education.

There are 30 lessons taught throughout the week, 26 at kindergarten level, spread over six mornings (Monday to Saturday, with free Saturdays in the kindergarten) and three afternoons (Monday, Wednesday, Friday). School hours are from 08.00 till 12.00 and from 14.00 until 16.00.

The organization of the primary school sector is largely decentralized. The local municipalities, *les autorités communales* (*die Kommunalbehörden*) provide the necessary infrastructure and hire the teachers. Teachers are, however, quasi-civil servants and to a large degree are paid by the state. School inspectors have the task of advising teachers and providing the Minister with information on the curriculum and the textbooks that are to be used. They share the responsibility with the local politicians: the *maire et le collège échevinal* (the burgomaster and the aldermen) when it comes to supervising the day-to-day running of the school. In their function as advisers to the Minister, inspectors do not act alone; there is also a *commission d'instruction*: that is to say, a panel comprising the chief inspector, parent delegates, teachers and a representative of the Church.

L'éducation préscolaire

The kindergarten has long ceased to be a mere playground where children could while away their time. Nowadays it is conceived of as the earliest pattern of their schooling proper. Children's spatial and temporal awareness is fostered, and they are made conscious of their own environment. The curriculum is varied, including drawing, manual work, physical exercises, singing and observational skills. Some emphasis is also put on the development of moral habits, and there is a first introduction to reading and even arithmetic.

The *éducation préscolaire* is thus very much part of a child's schooling, and this is also the reason why the two-year attendance is compulsory. It is now a major instrument of social integration and it significantly contributes to the acquisition of Letzeburgesch. A mastery of this language is vital if language acquisition at primary school level is to work effectively. This is also the reason why, from September 1999, early schooling (*éducation précoce*) will be established on a voluntary basis for any three-year-old child.

Primary education, with special reference to language

Primary education is fully comprehensive. The programme is the same for all children. Reading and writing, German, French, arithmetic and the metric system, history and geography, first notions of natural science, drawing, singing, manual work and physical training are taught. But by far the most significant dimension, as mentioned above, is that of language.

When education in literacy begins at the age of 6, German is used as the medium for that programme. The fact that Letzeburgesch is so closely related to German makes this possible. However, this may also pose serious problems for immigrant children, many of whose parents speak a Romance language. Thus for the last few years there has been a nationwide debate as to whether the first steps towards literacy should be based on French instead. This was thought to be fair towards those pupils who are of Italian or Portuguese origin and reasonable for the average Luxembourgish pupil, who will have to become fluent in French anyway.

The suggestion has been dismissed for a number of reasons. First, such a literacy programme would not do justice to the indigenous pupils, whose mother tongue is much closer to German than to any other language. Second, it would not foster the integration of the immigrant pupils into the multilingual Luxembourgish context. Even so, Letzeburgesch and German prove to be barriers which prevent the immigrant pupils from being easily integrated into school. As a result, special measures, such as extra tuition in German, have had to be adopted. However, the concept of intercultural exchange has had to be given more serious consideration, since it is felt that it would be wrong to deprive immigrant pupils of their original cultural background. In some municipalities, therefore, these pupils are offered courses in their own mother tongue at a rate of two periods per week.

The need to pay special attention to the problems posed by the integration of so-called 'foreign' children can be exemplified by the following information supplied by the local administration of Kehlen, a *commune* situated to the west of Luxembourg. This former village has now developed into a middle-class area and is situated outside the modest urban sprawl of Luxembourg City. In the school year 1994–5, 371 children attended primary school in Kehlen, 72 of whom were of foreign nationality. Quite significantly the Portuguese, the Belgian and the Italian communities were by far the most important elements among them. The proportion of immigrant children is, of course, considerably higher in more predominantly working-class areas, although the phenomenon is not confined to these areas. In 1997–8, 51.37 per cent of the children attending primary school in Luxembourg were non-native; indeed, in Echternach, a small market town situated in a rural area, the figure rose to 52.59 per cent for the same period. Generally speaking, 67.41 per cent of the children attending primary school in 1997–8 are of Luxembourgish origin, while 18.33 per cent have a Portuguese background.

French is the second language to be introduced in all primary schools. It is started in the course of the second year, and at that stage the syllabus focuses on oral skills. The acquisition of the written language is taught from the third year of primary school education. This French course has been redesigned; in its new version it attempts to strike a balance between grammatical accuracy and fluency via communicative practice, with genuine lively exchange of information and opinions. It is thus set within the relatively recent tradition of a multisyllabus, cross-curricular course design.

Secondary education

There are two main types of secondary school: (a) the *lycée*, which provides a liberal and scientific education up to the age of 19, preparing pupils for the *examen de fin d'études secondaires* and for university entrance; and (b) the *lycée technique*, which also provides a general education, but it emphasizes practical instruction as well as vocational subjects related to commerce and industry.

Luxembourgish school education aims at the cultivation of reason and the intellect, the objectives being, in terms of content, to impart a general education (*culture générale*) stressing literary, historical, scientific and technological dimensions. Moreover, admission to either type of *lycée* is based on a system of guidance (*avis d'orientation*) which stresses parental involvement in the choices to be made.

Education is a national enterprise at both primary and secondary level. State laws provide the framework within which the schools operate, and the Ministry for Education and Vocational Training establishes the standards to which the schools ought to conform: it decides what is to be taught and to a large extent how the teaching is to be carried out.

The secondary system is highly centralized. At its head is the Minister of National Education, who is assisted by a number of administrators and by a body representing the various headteachers. The *Commissions Nationales pour les programmes* report to the Minister on matters to do with the courses of studies taught and textbooks used. They are representative bodies, to which each school sends its delegate according to the subject that is to be discussed. All the schools in this sector are also funded by the national budget.

The lycée

The present structure of the *lycée* is the result of two successive Parliamentary Acts. The first of these is the *Loi Organique du 10 mai 1968*, which made all schools coeducational. It also introduced a number of specializing streams at upper secondary level, and established the *conseil d'éducation* composed of the headteacher and deputy head, plus teachers, parents and students, but whose function is solely an advisory one. The *Centre de Psychologie et d'Orientation Scolaires* (CPOS) was also set up by that law.

In this context the role of the head is an administrative one whose tasks pertain to the running of a school. Besides these, however, he or she also has the right of 'inspection' of their own school. In recent months two *lycées* have participated in an evaluation project run within the Comenius programme and one is about to have an external audit carried out by a firm of consultants. These developments are all the more important since there is no national inspectorate. The head is directly accountable to the Minister of Education. This also goes for the technical schools.

The second milestone for the *lycée classique* is the *Loi du 22 juin 1989* which reorganized the upper forms of the *lycée*, so that the overall structure now looks as follows. The first year is a year of transition (*7-e d'orientation*) and is in many respects not very different from primary school. This is underlined by the fact that no new subjects are introduced at this stage. In the second year pupils opt for either the modern or the classical stream. If the former is chosen, the students have to study English; if the latter, they have to take up Latin as a new subject. In the classical stream, English is introduced in the third year of secondary education. Together, the first three years of the *lycée* form the *division inférieure* and the last four the *division supérieure*. The latter is in turn subdivided into two phases, *le cycle polyvalent de la division supérieure* (*4-e, 3-e*), and *le cycle de spécialisation* (*2-e, 1-re*). Successful completion of secondary education is marked by a baccalaureate-like examination, the *diplôme de fin d'études secondaires*, often called *baccalauréat*, taken after the *1-re*, the *classe première*.

The *cycle polyvalent* was introduced by the 1989 Act of Parliament, and its main aim is to defer over-specialization for another two years as well as to emphasize general knowledge. At the same time, the first phase provides for more differentiation: on the one hand, there are two basic streams within the *cycle polyvalent: l'orientation littéraire* and *l'orientation scientifique*, the only difference being the more detailed mathematics syllabus in the scientific stream. On the other hand, optional courses are organized within the two phases (*cycles*) which cater for the students' specific interests and talents and which are available independently of the two streams chosen. These courses should enable the students to choose the stream best suited to their individual needs in the second phase, *le cycle de spécialisation*. At this point there are various specialisms on offer, languages and literature (section A1) , social sciences (section A2), mathematics (section B), natural sciences (section C), economics (section D), fine arts (section E) and music (section F).

In spite of these special interests, the notion of general education is not abandoned altogether. Modern languages, history and philosophy are compulsory for all streams. As can be seen from the above survey, the *lycée* provides a mainly academic education for students who want to go on to university, and once again languages loom large in the curriculum. In the *cycle inférieur* and in the language streams of the upper forms they take up 50 per cent of the weekly periods; in the other streams their time allocation varies from between one-third and one-fifth.

The Parliamentary Act of 1989 was meant to be a framework within which fundamental reforms would ease the burden put on the students, while at the same time safeguarding the achievements and standards of which the system could rightly be proud. Changes of teaching method or approaches go beyond the purely mechanistic fashion of instruction being set within the wider perspective of educational aims and provision. For example, computer studies have now been firmly established in the curriculum. Moreover, the newly introduced optional courses rely on a multidisciplinary approach.

The greatest effort now goes into the practice of teaching by objectives. A new department within the Ministry of Education, the *Service de Coordination et d'Innovation Pédagogiques et Technologiques* (SCRIPT), was created in 1992, and its main function is the management and implementation of innovation.

A second major innovative project is the *projet d'établissement*. As its name suggests, each school is encouraged to draw up its own work project. In order to realize new objectives it may initiate proposals for change and eventually install new components. One school, for example, may envisage a multimedia course, another may encourage exchange programmes with countries abroad. The purpose of the *projet d'établissement* is a twofold one. Individual schools should be granted greater freedom to develop their own ideas and should be allowed to experiment in an attempt to give the students the greatest possible scope for developing the talents they possess. What it ultimately amounts to is that it encourages the schools to assume their own responsibility in the area of curricular development. In this way the traditional ethos of the system is turned into one in which individual autonomy survives within an overall hierarchy of objectives. Furthermore, the *projet d'établissement* has to be set into an economic environment, and the links between the school and industry are fundamental to it. These acts of negotiation contribute to the profiling of the school, and ultimately influence what kinds of knowledge are created and exchanged.

It goes without saying that both SCRIPT and the *projet d'établissement* do not see their roles confined to the *lycée* but are also relevant to the *lycée technique*.

L'enseignement secondaire technique

As suggested above, the *technique* caters for the needs of the vast majority of the school intake and provides the *enseignement secondaire technique*, which comprises three phases: *le cycle inférieur* (the lower school: age groups 12–15); *le cycle moyen* (the middle school: age groups 15–17); *le cycle supérieur* (the upper school: age groups 17–19).

The overall purpose of the lower school phase is two-fold. On the one hand, it still focuses on language acquisition, mathematics and sciences (that is, on a liberal education); on the other hand it gradually differentiates between the students' various talents. Thus in the course of the first three years students begin opting for various stream lines, which range from the general to those concentrating on vocational skills. At first these streams do not so much differ from the general objectives and orientation of the subjects taught, but rather from the emphasis given to them. Indeed, all three school phases include the teaching of manual skills, and the more practical orientation of this part of the course is to acquaint the students with different crafts and trades. Students are to be put in a position which enables them to opt for a later stream line best suited to their individual needs. It has to be noted that at the end of the lower school phase the student will also have reached the end of compulsory education.

In fact, hardly any student leaves school at that age, over 90 per cent staying on and opting for one of the more specialized streams of the second phase, *le cycle moyen*, whose objectives are defined much more precisely in the form of three streams: *le régime technique, le régime de la formation de technicien, le régime professionnel.*

The *régime technique* leads to a *diplôme de fin d'études (baccalauréat) technique* to be taken at the age of 19. Its main aim is to equip students to enter professional life at the age of 19 without, however, precluding access to university. Students who have obtained the *secondaires*, the school-leaving certificate taken at the age of 19, can aim at positions in the middle management of banking institutes if they have been attending the commercial stream of the *régime technique*. There are also streams catering for the needs of hotel management, of farming and agriculture in general, and of nursing and other jobs in the health service. One stream prepares pupils to pursue higher professional studies in the field of engineering. In all cases, however, the student has to opt for a specializing stream, the curriculum of which combines specialization and general subjects. Languages continue to be taught with varying intensity right into the last year.

The diploma is organized centrally, each paper is marked by three independent examiners, the questions are the same for every *lycée* according to specialism in which the examination is taken in the presence of a presiding *commissaire de gouvernement*. In its range of subjects examined the diploma resembles the *baccalauréat*, and, like it, gives access to the European sector of higher education.

The *régime de la formation de technicien* also focuses on channelling students towards a particular type of career in industry, mostly revolving around the concept of engineering. The student is meant to become a highly skilled technician capable not only of carrying out projects but also of taking part in their conception. This occupational training is much more specialized, more orientated towards a particular vocation; at the end of the course, aged 19, the student sits for the *diplôme de technicien*, the diploma of technical studies which also gives entitlement to study in a technical college of higher or further education.

The *régime professionnel* is to a large extent a traditional apprentice system. It combines theoretical subjects taught at school with a practical training taking place in a firm. This duality may be consecutive or simultaneous; in the former case the student spends the first two years at school acquiring the theoretical background needed before being confronted with the reality of working life. If the latter is the case, the student spends, say, three days a week working in a firm and receives theoretical training in the classroom on the other two. At the end of their course students sit for the CATP, the *certificat d'aptitudes techniques et professionelles*, the certificate being a qualification giving access to the skilled labour market and the traditional crafts and trades of the *vie active*.

The third possibility is that the student may sign a contract of apprenticeship with an employer and follow a more loosely structured syllabus at school. This is intended to give more practically minded students the opportunity to pursue a theoretical training at their own pace. The syllabus is based on a modular system, leading to an employer's certification which in turn enables the students to move on to the CATP. The diplomas of professional studies are important, since tradesmen are required to pass government-regulated licensing examinations before they are allowed to set up their business.

It is possible to conclude from the above general survey of the two types of *lycées* that Luxembourg finds itself at the crossroads of French and German influence. The Luxembourgish support of a traditional apprentice system is in many ways similar to German policy in the same area. Similarly, the *lycée* is to some extent modelled on both the German *Gymnasium* and the French *lycée*.

Continuing vocational education

The vocational strand of education in Luxembourg has been the focus of some innovation, especially with the creation of the *Institut National de Formation Professionnelle Continue*. The thrust for this development came from the findings of a survey which showed that small and medium-sized firms are reluctant to be responsible for the continuing (in-service) education of their own staff. This newly created institute is not only intended to raise awareness in those firms which may have been oblivious of modern needs but also to give extra vocational education support to other firms. Moreover, it is meant to do so in a European perspective.

Obviously such a readjustment of criteria is not dictated to Luxembourg by Brussels. It is, rather, motivated by the intrinsic wish to streamline the system in such a way that its assets are maximized and its weaknesses overcome. In other words, there is the general feeling that in view of the Maastricht agreements and the Amsterdam Treaty the school system must be made more innovative and more flexible. This is not only to ensure sound knowledge of school subjects, but also to lay foundations for general competences on which additional learning in later professional life can be built.

Another initiative in this field is a large project piloted in a joint venture by decision makers from the Ministry of Education and managers from industry and the banking sector, and implemented by teachers helped by German and Dutch institutions. It is intended to define job profiles that could serve as objectives in the area of vocational training. In the context of this initiative it is essential to bear in mind that the law, besides strengthening the links between general education and vocational training, also reinforces those existing between school and industry.

Higher education

Higher education was reformed in 1996 by the *Loi du 11 août portant réforme de l'enseignement supérieur*. As a result of this Act of Parliament, higher education, which is offered in the *Centre Universitaire* (CU) and in institutes of higher education, is organized on a decentralized basis which reinforces the autonomy of the various institutes and institutions. At the same time a system of quality assessment is envisaged.

Le Centre Universitaire de Luxembourg

The *Centre Universitaire* was created by the law of 18 June 1969 regulating higher education and the recognition of foreign qualifications and degrees. The law of 11 February 1974 legislated on the statutes of the University Centre. The *Loi du 11 août 1996 portant réforme de l'enseignement supérieur* defines the current framework within which all higher education institutions may operate. It also enumerates the institutions of higher education and specifies the overall objectives these institutions are to pursue.

The term 'university' may be misleading in the sense that the centre only offers first-year courses. However, as a result of the 1996 law, the development of the *Centre Universitaire* (CU) has achieved a momentum of its own, and the provision of two-year courses in a number of areas is being considered. It currently comprises three main departments: law and economics; languages and humanities; sciences (medicine/pharmacology/biochemistry/mathematics/physics). The *Centre* may not run a full undergraduate course since the need to pursue one's studies abroad has always been felt to be being extremely beneficial for the intellectual life of the country as a whole.

Indeed, mobility has always been one of the cornerstones of Luxembourgish higher education, and the fact that students have to pass their examinations abroad has been seen as a source of cultural enrichment as well as of open-mindedness. On the other hand, this exerts enormous pressure on the *lycée*, since after their '*bac*' students must be in a position to cope with the demands of the various university systems in the neighbouring countries.

Those students who pass their examination at the end of the year in Luxembourg may register for a second-year course at one of the universities with which a special agreement has been reached, the *l'octroi d'équivalences*, and which are in fact to be found in several European countries (France, Belgium, the United Kingdom, Germany, Austria). The *Centre Universitaire* is thus embedded within the overall framework of European higher education, and this is also reflected in the composition of its teaching staff. In addition to local professors, it calls upon the services of lecturers and professors from neighbouring universities such as Nancy, Trier and Liège. Such links are vital to the functioning system of a small state, and various attempts are currently being made to strengthen them.

At the same time the new legal framework allows the setting up of various research units at postgraduate level. This new structure safeguards the advantages of the old system (the need for students to spend a considerable time of their university career abroad and to obtain their diplomas there), while at the same time providing a firmer base for research to be carried out in Luxembourg itself. In addition to the obvious advantages this would bring to students, it is felt that it would attract highly qualified researchers to Luxembourg. Furthermore, this extension of the *Centre Universitaire* would be accompanied by greater financial autonomy, the *autonomie de gestion*.

Such a widening of provision could in fact be based on the *Institut Universitaire International*, created by the *reglèment grand-ducal* of 22 April 1974, which organizes a regular series of courses and seminars on international and comparative law, economics and international studies and European research, and which is located in the *Centre Universitaire*. The postgraduate students must have a reference from an academic authority in addition to a degree.

A generously funded *Centre de Recherche Publique* (CRP) has been set up within the structure of the *Centre Universitaire*. This so-called CRP-CU (*Centre de Recherche Professionelle: Centre de Recherche Public – Centre Universitaire*), *Etablissement d'utilité publique*, though located within the *Centre Universitaire* and profiting from some of its facilities, has financial, administrative and scientific autonomy. Its main objective consists of carrying out research related to the areas of interest represented in the *Centre Universitaire*. Most of its research projects are carried out in partnership with private firms as well as with other European universities. Thus the institute does not only engage in research carried out for its own sake but, as a public body, it is also intended to strengthen the economic structure of the Grand Duchy. Technology transfer training in the new technologies figures high on its list of priorities. Among the research projects are information technology (*Cellule de Recherche, d'Etude et de Développement en Informatique*), environmental technology, and history and sociology, the last consisting of *histoire contemporaine* and *recherches pédagogiques*.

The Institut Supérieur de Technologie

The Higher Institute of Technology (IST) created by the *Loi du 21 mai 1979* offers three-year courses in civil engineering, general engineering, electronics and applied computer studies. The *Institut* has much the same links with foreign universities as the *Centre Universitaire*, but it also awards its own diploma.

The curriculum avoids over-specialization, although, needless to say, the studies concentrate on mathematics, science and advanced technology. The most striking feature, though, is the close links the *Institut* has with local industry and with another *Centre de Recherche Publique* called 'Henri Tudor'. Its title of *établissement d'utilité publique* means that the teaching is set within the perspective of practical application. However, the courses offered are full-time courses of study, although students are required to obtain some practical working experience in a firm. Generally speaking, this lasts up to a month and takes place at the end of the second year of study. The idea behind this option takes up the French concept of *stage pratique* or *faire son stage en entreprise*.

The IST is now firmly embedded within the legal framework provided by the *Loi du 11 août 1996 portant réforme de l'enseignement supérieur* and, like the *Centre Universitaire* (CU), has its own board of directors and is run in a spirit of autonomy. It also hosts a public research centre. This, too, focuses on the concept of transfer of technologies, and one of its aims is to improve its capacity for industrial innovation. Thus a multisectoral resource centre, concentrating on applied information technologies, has been established around the laboratory for applied microelectronics. The centre is also embedded in the SITec, a joint organization of Luxinnovation (Luxembourg), Institut Industriel de l'Etat (Arlon, Belgium), Institut Universitaire de Technologie (Longwy, France) and the CRP Henri Tudor in Luxembourg, which is a product of a European Union Comett project. Within the SITec organization centre are offered high-level training workshops in the field of information and industrial technologies.

Institut Supérieur d'Etudes et de Recherches Pédagogiques

The Teacher Training Institute (*Institut Supérieur d'Etudes et de Recherches Pédagogiques: ISERP*), created by the *Loi du 6 septembre 1983*, trains prospective primary school teachers and thus has been mainly an exclusively Luxembourg institution. Indeed, until recently it was the only institution entitled to train primary school teachers and it operated in a seller's market. Admission has always been restricted, and acceptance would *de facto* mean a job and security of tenure after the three-year course.

The education, training and mobility of teachers

Teacher education forms an important sector. In detail, as in all countries, the teaching force of Luxembourg has the task of mediating between the providers and the consumers of education, and the school curriculum in particular.

Until recently, the system was closed to foreigners, since Luxembourg teachers, like other civil servants, had to be citizens of the Grand Duchy. Now, of course, there is mutual recognition of teacher qualifications as between all European Union member states. Consequently, the ISERP is faced with stiffer competition from abroad, since it no longer is the only channel through which prospective teachers have to pass. The result is a large increase in applicants for teaching posts. The applicants are of two kinds: they are either Luxembourg students who, because they did not meet the entry requirements to the ISERP, turned to similar institutions abroad, or they may be other European citizens who feel attracted by the greatly advantageous working conditions in Luxembourg. Indeed, primary school teachers are quasi-civil servants enjoying security of tenure and earning a salary above the European average.

As a result the conditions regulating access to the profession have also changed. An *examen d'accès à la profession*, which is the consequence of the changing European educational environment, now regulates entry to the teaching profession at primary school level. Indeed, the ISERP may have to adapt its own overall function. It may have to concentrate more on the development of materials as well as on research. This has been one of its preoccupations in any case, and it is in this area that it has well-established links with departments of pedagogical studies in the neighbouring universities, as well as with the two CRPs referred to above.

Educating and training secondary-level teachers

Under existing arrangements in Luxembourg, generally speaking the teacher is, as mentioned above, a civil servant who as a teacher is given the task to teach a certain number of lessons, with the added responsibility of preparation and evaluation to be carried out off school premises. Thus, at secondary level, the main focus is on the cognitive development that the teacher is required to impart to his or her students, which, of course, distinguishes him or her from colleagues at primary level, where a balance is struck between the cognitive domain and socialization, with its inculcation of social attitudes, norms and behaviour. Whereas primary school teachers have so far been trained at a non-university higher education institution, those for secondary level must have a university degree. There is the added proviso that modern language teachers must have a degree from a university situated in the country where the target language is actually spoken. Thus a teacher of English has to have a BA in English literature and/or language. Languages also play a role in the teaching of other school subjects since they are taught through the medium of either German or French –

the higher the age range, the greater the share of French. The teacher's fluency in both languages is therefore a condition *sine qua non*.

Entry into the profession is via an entrance examination, similar to the French *examen concours*, followed by three years of training, the *stage pédagogique*. Training comprises professional preparation, lesson planning and delivery, classroom management, assessment of the trainee's practical experience of teaching, and educational studies grounded in psychology and sociology. During these three years the candidates are also asked to write a scientific dissertation and at the end they have to take an examination. Teacher trainees start teaching in their own classes straightaway after passing the *concours de recrutement*. At the same time, though, a more experienced teacher assists them by giving them practical advice on how to manage a class, on how to prepare lessons and on how to set up and mark tests.

This system of initial training is now being redesigned. On the one hand, the course design will see a shift from a content-based approach to one that is skill-based so that the new course requirements replace those sections of the current criteria which do not cover competences. On the other hand, initial teacher training will be more securely anchored in the newly reformed higher education sector and qualified teacher status given after the award of a certificate. Generally speaking, the new course requirements lay down criteria in relation to course type, partnership arrangements and quality assurance.

The issue which emerges most clearly is that of the teacher's professional task. As in the other EU member states, there is the general view that the new responsibilities society is placing on the teacher call not only for revised initial teacher training courses but above all for regular professional upgrading by the provision of INSET.

The idea of mobility is certainly part of this overall reassessment of the role of the teacher. In the Luxembourg context the issue of mobility has been linked with exchanges which are subject to the severe constraints of time. Under the Arion programme initiated by the European Commission, headteachers have in recent years increasingly seized the opportunity of acquainting themselves with other school systems throughout Europe. For the teachers who take part in a similar scheme set up between Denmark and Luxembourg, this exchange has always been based on reciprocity. It is still early days to say whether this involves a real flow of experience from one system to the other.

In the view of the writer there is an urgent need for Luxembourg's teachers and educationists to widen their perspectives through greater interaction with colleagues from other countries. Up to now, commitment to new methods and the enthusiasm generated by collaborating research groups has been conspicuously absent from the Luxembourg scene, which has tended to adopt a rather detached attitude towards innovative trends. This tendency is exacerbated by teachers' work conditions and teachers' attitudes. As far as working hours are concerned, they are amongst the most advantageous anywhere in Europe. On the other hand, the teacher's self-perception is that of an educational scientist and not that of a pedagogue: the 'what' of teaching being of greater importance than the 'how'. This brings about great thoroughness as far as teaching content is concerned, but is offset by an extreme conservatism in matters of methodology and pedagogical innovation.

Innovation and the challenge of Europe

Despite the somewhat 'traditional' nature of the teaching profession in Luxembourg, there has been a great deal of educational reform going on, and the role of the country in the European Union has become increasingly influential in this respect.

Some recent reforms in secondary education

The first to be mentioned is the *réforme du cycle supérieur de l'enseignement secondaire en un cycle polyvalent et un cycle de spécialisation*, which aims to extend general education while delaying specialization until the last two years of secondary schooling.

At a European level there seems to be a growing consensus among decision makers that, in the wake of an ever-increasing body of knowledge in all fields of specialization, school pupils ought, above all, to be equipped with basic knowledge in core subjects as well as with certain methodological tools enabling them to transfer their knowledge to other areas and to solve problems in an imaginative, creative way. This particular reform is set within this perspective; but it also reinforces the emphasis commonly put on language teaching, the assumption being that linguistic competence is one of Luxembourg's assets.

The second reform, the *réforme du cycle supérieur de l'enseignement secondaire*, aims to match new qualifications with new patterns of work organization, especially since the labour market is affected by skills shortages. The third one seeks to make courses more accessible to school pupils through revised *critères de promotion*.

The Luxembourg system of general secondary education is generally considered very demanding, and the result is a high rate of failures every year. Five years after first entering secondary school only 36 per cent of the pupils will have passed to the next year every year; that is, rather less than two-thirds require more than the five years foreseen for the course. Fortunately, this does not mean that there is a high drop-out rate, since the majority of students and their parents are persistent. In any case, there are alternatives: students may retake the year, they may opt for the *secondaire technique*, or they may pursue their studies at one of the *lycées* in Belgium or in France.

The European dimension

Although there is no specific place allocated on timetables for the European dimension in education as such, it implicitly permeates various subjects in the curriculum at all levels. In any case, with the size of Luxembourg being what it is – a microstate, in fact – 'Europe' is a daily felt reality rather than a vaguely threatening concept. Moreover, hardly any textbooks for secondary schools or tertiary studies are actually written and produced in Luxembourg. This reliance on foreign publishing houses actually encourages pupils and students to have a wider European perspective; this is most keenly felt in subjects like history and geography.

The European dimension is also enhanced by involvement in European programmes such as Socrates and Leonardo da Vinci, which are thought of as good opportunities to establish partnerships with other institutions in foreign countries. Participation in these schemes is usually very high.

The issue of national identity

It is fair to say that a sense of national identity, such as is known today, has only developed in the last hundred years or so, and it is the events of World War Two that have really cemented this feeling of belonging to a nation. But what is equally important for the people of Luxembourg is that their language, their economic pursuits as well as their way of life reflect their multiplicity of interests and relations with neighbouring countries. The future of Luxembourg has always lain within greater alliances, and giving up part of its sovereignty has invariably proved to be the most successful way of defending its own interests and of fostering its national identity.

Thus it is hardly surprising that Luxembourg is now very much an international place, with one-third of its population being 'foreign'; besides, on the labour market two out of three newly created jobs tend to be filled by foreigners. This is the case at all echelons in the various organizations. The opening up of frontiers does not pose a threat; on the contrary, it has been a reality for a number of years already. Acceptance of what the European Community stands for in Luxembourg has always ranked high in the opinion polls conducted in the country, while belonging to this Community is deemed a *sine qua non* for the existence of the Luxembourgish state. Indeed, Luxembourgers feel that being a full member of the EU in itself guarantees the survival of their independent state.

None the less, there is a feeling that efforts ought to be made to protect Luxembourg's national identity, and the means to achieve this is by protecting the language. So although Letzeburgesch is mainly a spoken language, a dictionary has been laid down. An ever greater number of courses are being offered for foreigners to learn it, and they are encouraged to mix more socially with the native population. For the last year CLT/ RTL, the local/international broadcasting company, has been televising a half-hourly news magazine in

Letzeburgesch on a daily basis. A convention between the government and the company has led to the creation of this TV service, which symbolizes the commitment of the government to preserve both the language and the national identity. At the time this caused alarm, but the election results showed that this was unwarranted. Indeed, there is a consensus among the major political parties not to use such 'language policy' topics for election campaigns.

The fact that the Luxembourg system has always had to measure up to the educational standards set by the neighbouring countries, perhaps to better them even, has been a double-edged sword. On the one hand, Luxembourg cannot turn a blind eye to the reform movements influencing the educational systems of Germany, France and Belgium; on the other hand, there is a refusal to rush headlong into change which might ultimately prove to be a 'blind alley'. Two factors account for this cautious, not to say ambivalent, attitude. By any standard the Luxembourg approach to politics is a conservative one; the Luxembourgers are an earthbound people or, as Edmond Heiderscheid, the managing director of the Luxembourg daily with the largest circulation, the *Luxemburger Wort*, once described them: *'un peuple épris de sécurité'*.

The second factor pertains to the education system itself. Luxembourg is on the receiving end as far as research is concerned. Except for ISERP, where research is carried out into the didactics of course materials, no institute or university department engages in pedagogical research.

Despite the high degree of dependency, this very experience has provided Luxembourg with the skills of intelligent selection from outside while safeguarding the internal culture with its distinctive national language. As far as education is concerned, beginning with a relatively traditional situation may be no bad thing. For the policy-makers, alternative, but not mutually exclusive, options are clear. On the one hand, the option that has been taken is to put an even greater emphasis on a liberal education and to avoid the trap of over-specialization. On the other, compensatory measures in the marking system are intended to 'reward' particular talents and gloss over certain weaknesses. This strategy is one way of attuning the Luxembourg system to the European mainstream.

The balance of popular and political feeling is that if Luxembourg's education system does not accommodate to change it may well lose its competitive edge, notably in language teaching and in vocational training. In that sense, the reforms are being forced upon the system by an awareness among the social partners that immobility will amount to a 'loss of terrain' in view of the challenges induced by the 1993 Single European deadline. Even so, the account given above of significant aspects of education in Luxembourg illustrates a healthy accommodation to change and a capacity for innovation. This bodes well for the successful fusion of the best from inside with the best from outside. It also preserves the situation whereby foreigners would, and do, find it easy to live, work and study in Luxembourg.

Bibliography

'Babel. Les parlers au Luxembourg en 1997', *Forum* 177, July 1997. Luxembourg.

Enseignement secondaire 1939–1989 (Ré-création 5). Luxembourg: Editions APESS, 1989.

'Instruction et education', in *Mémorial 1989. La société luxembourgeoise de 1839 à 1989.* Luxembourg, 1989.

Luxembourg: Langue, culture et communication. Madrid: Fundación Actilibre, 1996.

Magère, Ph., Esmein, B., Poty, M. *et al.*, *La Situation de la langue française parmi les autres langues en usage au Grand Duché de Luxembourg.* Luxembourg, 1998.

Ministère de l'Education Nationale, *Courrier de l'éducation nationale.* Luxembourg: Ministère de l'Education Nationale (specialized issues).

Ministère de l'Education Nationale, *Education in the Grand Duchy of Luxembourg.* Luxembourg: Ministère de l'Education Nationale (published annually).

11 The Netherlands

Luusi A.H.M. Hendriks and
Sylvia G.M. van de Bunt-Kokhuis

Policy, plans and climate of opinion

When in 1985 the European Commission published its White Paper, *Completing of the Internal Market*,[1] a general discussion in the Netherlands began to develop on the economic effects of the completion. By then education was not really a topic in the discussion, because the White Paper did not pay much attention to this aspect. Nevertheless, the European Commission created a taskforce, Human Resources, Education, Training and Youth, in which European educational programmes such as Force, Eurotecnet, Lingua, Petra and Comett were brought together. After the signing of the Treaty of Maastricht in 1992, in which articles were introduced on general education and vocational training (Articles 126 and 127), education became an explicit concern of the European Union.

A similar development can be seen at the Dutch national level, where in the Dutch policy-making on internationalisation, facts, figures and advice of the Organisation for Economic Cooperation and Development (OECD), the Dutch National Advisory Council (NAR) and the Higher Educational Advisory Council (ARHO) are taken into account.

From 1987 to 1997 the Ministry of Education, Culture and Science published a series of documents in which the policy towards internationalisation of education was stated.[2] In this chapter particular attention will be paid to the recent documents and the implementation of the European educational programmes. It started with the memorandum on the internationalisation of education and research (*Internationalisering van Onderwijs en Onderzoek*, 1987), a collective document of the Ministry of Education, Culture and Science, the Ministry of Agriculture, Nature Management and Fisheries, and the Ministry of Economic Affairs. This deals with the opportunities for international cooperation in the field of education and science, including policy plans on technology. Participation of foreign partners in Dutch research programmes was encouraged. The policy stated in this document has been supported by the major advisory bodies in the Netherlands such as the Advisory Council on Government Policy (WRR), the Science Policy Advisory Council (RAWB) and the Higher Education Advisory Council (ARHO).

Another, more general, policy document of the Ministry of Education, Culture and Science is entitled *Hoger Onderwijs en Onderzoek Plan* (HOOP) (Dutch Higher Education and Research Plan). This document sets out the main trends and issues on higher education and has to be updated every two years. The first *HOOP* was published in 1988, and the most recent one in 1998. Until 1988 internationalisation of education focused mainly on higher education. In 1988, another policy document was published: *Onderwijs en Wetenschappen in de Europese Interne Markt* (Education and Science and the European Internal Market), in which special attention was given to secondary general education and vocational education in the Netherlands. Through this policy document internationalisation became a widespread issue in Dutch education, with emphasis on Europe. In order to support education and science in preparing for the consequences of the internal market, the Minister set up an action plan of which the main issue was 'orientation on the European labour market'. It was clearly indicated that the relation between education and the labour market would grow significantly. In anticipation of this development in the Netherlands, the Dutch National Bureau for Labour Provision (*Landelijk Bureau Arbeidsvoorzieningen: LBA*), in which social partners and government work together, was asked for assistance. Vocational education and training programmes were to be developed to anticipate the European labour market and to prepare students to work in a European context.

In 1990 the Ministry of Agriculture, Nature Management and Fisheries published a memorandum on internationalisation of the Dutch agricultural education *Internationalisering Landbouwonderwijs*.[3] In this memorandum the Ministry presented the outlines for internationalisation of this sector. As in higher education, internationalisation goes far beyond the borders of the EU. Africa, Indonesia, Central and Eastern Europe are of great importance for this sector and networks and cooperation with institutions in these countries are being established.

Internationalisation of the curriculum is one of the logical steps that have to be taken to prepare students for the European labour market. In higher education there is a longer tradition of internationalisation of education. In the so-called *Ontwikkelingsplannen* (development plans) prepared by each institute of higher education, much attention is paid to internationalisation. In secondary and vocational education a big impulse was given by the national policy plan *Grenzen Verleggen* (Widening Horizons), published by the Ministry of Education, Culture and Science in 1991. In this document the national policy on the internationalisation of education in the Netherlands from 1991 to 1997 is set out. Besides the internationalisation of the curriculum and investment in extra technical equipment, the number of apprenticeships and training places should be increased, both on the national and on the European labour markets, to raise the quality of education and to keep up with European standards of education. From 1991 on, the Netherlands has also participated in such European programmes as Petra, Force, Lingua and Comett.

Increasing the mobility of students would depend on the mutual recognition of courses, diplomas and qualifications in the European Union. In the Netherlands, Nuffic (Netherlands Universities Foundation for International Cooperation), Colo (Central Office of the National Apprenticeship Training Bodies) and the IB-groep (Information Management Group) are responsible for the comparison and recognition of diplomas, both Dutch and foreign, in close cooperation with Cedefop (Centre for the Development of Vocational Education), the European centre working on this subject in order to replace the hierarchical European Community classification system of occupations and introduce a multidimensional approach.

To improve the quality of education, knowledge of foreign languages is encouraged. Although there are still good language learning facilities in the Netherlands, quality seems to have deteriorated. In this context the Lingua programme was of great importance for the Dutch educational system, as was the National Action programme 'Foreign Languages'. In the latter programme the Dutch government set up a departmental workgroup and a 'resonance' group of language experts under auspices of the 'National Platform' (see next section). Within this programme, policy measures were formulated, such as:

- defining a national action plan;
- mastering preferably two member states' languages by students in secondary education (one has to take into account that with the increasing number of immigrant children in Dutch education, Dutch is a foreign language to many of the school population);
- introducing native speakers as teachers;
- increasing the motivation of students through European inter-school projects;
- paying attention to specific language skills in labour market-orientated training;
- providing extra training for language teachers.

By then the main conclusions of the departmental workgroup were that it was necessary to stimulate better interaction between the suppliers of foreign language knowledge and the demand for it, and to enhance the quality of foreign language teaching. In the new national policy document *Onbegrensd Talent* (1997) much attention is paid to this subject again, maintaining the same starting-points.

Dutch national policy documents

Grenzen Verleggen

In 1991 the government adopted the policy document *Grenzen Verleggen* (Widening Horizons) with reference to the initiatives mentioned above. In this document the initial impetus was given to set up a coherent system of internationalisation for all types and levels of Dutch education. The main impulses for the internationalisation were four national programmes on mobility, especially focused on primary and secondary education, vocational education and training, adult education and higher education. In these programmes a great number of students, adults (teachers) and institutions took advantage of the possibilities offered. A second important theme was the so-called *Grenslandenbeleid* (policy on stimulating cooperation between institutions within the border regions). A special programme gave support to cooperation projects between educational institutions in these regions.

The Ministry of Education, Culture and Science appointed three intermediary institutions to manage the programmes (see below). The programmes under *Grenzen Verleggen* are in the completion phase: projects ran until 1997. The total budget for *Grenzen Verleggen* over five years was about 19.5 million Dutch guilders.

HOOP 1996

In this plan, it is emphasised that the main reasons for the internationalisation of higher education and research must be found in a European context; in other words, in the fact that globalisation affects Dutch education and policy.

HOOP 1996 emphasised the *Kennis export* (export of knowledge) and *Grenslandenbeleid. HOOP* 1996 also stressed the importance of foreign language education. In higher education the starting point, set by law, is that Dutch has to be the language for teaching and examinations. But, because of the increasing number of foreign students from inside and outside the EU and the orientation of a European labour market, instruction in another language or in a mix of Dutch and a foreign language might be justified. *HOOP* 1996 also pointed to the importance of mobility, and the necessity to solve the problems of financing mobility and the accreditation of studies in another country. The Ministry recognised these problems, referring to them in the new memorandum *Onbegrensd Talent* (1997).[4]

In 1998 the Dutch government adopted a new *HOOP* in which new policies for the internationalisation of higher education will be presented.

STIR (Stimuleringsgelden Internationalisering)

To realise the goals set for the internationalisation of higher education, the Dutch Ministry of Education, Culture and Science made funds available for the *STIR-HBO* (stimulating internationalisation in higher professional education). This programme ran from 1991 to 1997 with a budget of about 11.5 million Dutch guilders each year. Because of the Dutch policy on education and science, the *STIR-HBO* funds were only accessible to institutions for higher professional education. Activities stimulated under *STIR-HBO* were mobility of students and teachers, visiting lecturers and projects to enhance the international market position of higher professional education. A first evaluation of this programme indicates that about 60 per cent of the funds are for mobility.

Parallel to the policy of the Ministry of Education, Culture and Science, the Ministry of Agriculture, Nature Management and Fisheries, responsible for agricultural education, made funds available for projects in that field, *STIR-LO* (stimulating internationalisation of agriculture education). From this programme projects in secondary and higher agricultural education could be subsidised. The programme aimed to enhance cooperation with other countries in research and education on a common interest basis. Activities stimulated under *STIR-LO* were mobility of students and teachers, increasing foreign language training, internationalisation of curricula, and cooperation between educational and research institutions. The *STIR-LO* arrangement was intended to run until 1997. During this time, the funding for mobility decreased in favour of funding for actual collaborative projects. The *STIR-LO* budget was about 2.1 million Dutch guilders per year.

Onbegrensd Talent

In this policy document the Dutch government emphasises the importance of the internationalisation of all sectors of education for the Netherlands. It is meant as the follow-up to *Grenzen Verleggen* and is still the subject of debate between policy-makers and educational experts. After finishing the debating rounds, the programmes could start at the end of 1997. Spearheads of Dutch policy pointed out in this memorandum are:

- to maintain programmes for mobility and exchange in primary, secondary and vocational education with a stronger focus on quality and embedding into the qualification structure of regular educational activities. This means that mobility structurally has to be part of education, contribute to the educational objectives, be complementary to the European programmes for mobility and be accessible to all pupils, students and teachers;
- to stress cooperation between educational institutions in the border regions. Policy intentions are, for example, to set up common curricula, to bring about transnational universities or schools for higher vocational education, to increase student mobility in the border regions and to enter into bilateral agreements between the Netherlands and Belgium (Flanders) and between the Netherlands and Germany. The ambition is to extend these bilateral agreements to the United Kingdom, France and the Scandinavian countries;
- to build up synergy between the national programmes and the European programmes on education and to promote the development of the European Union into a Knowledge Union. Furthermore, the Netherlands strives for an active role in the evaluation of the Leonardo da Vinci and Socrates programmes;
- to extend cooperation beyond the European Union, emphasising higher (scientific) education, to set up a programme for the export of Dutch education and knowledge, which focuses on Japan, Indonesia and South Africa.

The total budget in this programme for five years is about 198 million Dutch guilders.

European educational programmes

Not only Dutch programmes of internationalisation of education run in the Netherlands. As a member of the European Union, the Dutch participate in all European initiatives. Most important for Dutch education and training are Leonardo da Vinci, Socrates and Adapt/Employment. General information about these programmes is easily accessible. Below, Dutch implementation of the programmes is explained.

Leonardo da Vinci

Leonardo da Vinci is a European programme for vocational and professional education. The scheme is aimed at improving the quality of education and at increasing the capacity for innovation of the various institutions and organisations that offer training. In the Netherlands social partners and ministries established the National Leonardo Committee which sets out national policy towards Leonardo da Vinci. So, for instance, added to the European priorities, the following Dutch priorities were formulated by the National Leonardo Committee:

- encouragement of transparency of qualifications and training;
- description of key qualifications, that is, international comparative professions;
- improvement of flexible learning by improving the transfer from school to work;
- improvement of foreign language learning in vocational training;
- development of information and communication technology.

The National Coordination Unit (Cinop and Nuffic, NCU) handles the management of the programme. In 1995 information materials and a special newsletter were developed, general information meetings organised and a help desk established. In 1997 new material was developed. Instead of general information meetings, more tailor-made regional information meetings were arranged. Besides the information meetings, the NCU organised several contact seminars for partner-search. Here we see the same development: from huge general seminars in the first year to more demand-driven ones in the following years. In cooperation with the NCUs of Belgium and Luxembourg, a Benelux conference was organised on the role and position of small and medium enterprises (SMEs) in the programme and on dissemination and impact. What is the impact of the Leonardo da Vinci programme in the Netherlands? In spite of the relatively small number of projects awarded in the Netherlands, the number of Dutch organisations participating as partners in the programme is large. For instance, in the 26 Dutch projects of 1996, 80 Dutch organisations were participating. When we look at the European figures, 375 Dutch organisations are in one way or another active in Leonardo da Vinci projects, working on innovation in vocational education and training. Recently some criticisms have been heard about the Leonardo da Vinci programme: complex and non-transparent procedures and application forms, reduction of budget and high expenditure on (interim) reports.

Socrates

Socrates encourages transnational collaboration at all levels of education and gives a European dimension to the education in the home country and abroad. In the Netherlands, it is the general secondary schools, universities and institutions for higher professional education who benefit the most from this programme. Activities in general secondary education are exchanges between groups of students and teachers.

At higher education level, financial support is given through the Erasmus programme. Activities include student mobility, language preparation in the sending and receiving country, short intensive programmes and the joint development of study programmes. Individual universities formulate an institutional contract with the European Commission. Finally, thematic networks are set up in a European forum of experts in a given subject area. In the Netherlands, Socrates at higher educational level is coordinated by Nuffic, in the International Academic Relations European Programmes Sector. The other programme elements of Socrates (Comenius, Lingua, Adult Education and so on) are coordinated by the European Platform for Dutch Education.

Adapt/Employment

The Bureau Uitvoering Europese Subsidies (BUESI) is the national coordinator of the Adapt programme and the Employment and ESF-4 programmes. These encourage the training of unemployed people and employees with a high risk of becoming unemployed. The programmes are financed by the European Social Fund. BUESI organised a conference in 1998 to encourage networking within the current ESF-4 programmes. To support project promoters, BUESI organises information meetings and training sessions in which themes such as financial administration of projects and general project management are taught.

Intermediaries in the management of programmes

The Dutch Ministry of Education, Culture and Science has appointed three institutions to manage the programmes on internationalisation of education. Each institute has its own expertise on one of the types of education that make up the Dutch educational system. These three organisations, described below, collaborate in a number of fields, including communication and the provision of information. Their umbrella organisation is known as Bison: Beraad Internationale Samenwerking Onderwijs Nederland (Dutch Education Council for International Cooperation).

The European Platform

The European Platform Foundation was set up in 1993 by the then Ministry of Education and Science to contribute to existing and new activities in the area of Europe and education. The board of the European Platform consists of representatives of educational umbrella organisations and councils, such as the Dutch Non-denominational Private Schools Council (NABS), the Dutch Catholic Schools Council (NKSR) and the Association for the Advancement of Public Education (CBOO/VNG). The activities of the European Platform focus on primary and secondary general education. The major tasks of the Platform are:

- to inform educational institutions in primary and general secondary education of relevant developments and programmes within Europe;
- to arrange institutional agreements and mobility schemes for those institutions;
- to coordinate activities focused on the European dimension of Dutch education;
- to advise the Ministry and other policy bodies on internationalisation of primary and general secondary education;
- to promote the European and national programmes, give advice to potential project promoters and publish relevant material on implementation of the programmes in the Dutch educational system.

The Platform makes use of a broad scale of networks: the European Centre Foundation (SEC), European Secondary Heads Organisation (ESHA), European Parents Organisation (EPA), the National Bureau for Labour Provision (LBA), the European Movement in the Netherlands (EBN) and the Workgroup of Modern Foreign Languages (Werkgroep Moderne Vreemde Talen).

The European Platform executes the programme management of several European and national programmes. In the European programmes the organisation is responsible for the management of Arion, Lingua, TES, TBS, ESD, the Multilateral School Partnerships and the European School Exchange Databank. The European Platform is also responsible for the management of the Socrates programme for primary and general secondary education. At national level it took responsibility for the bilateral programmes with Germany, the United Kingdom, Belgium and Canada and for the programmes in the framework of *Grenzen Verleggen*: IKU, Plato and Gros.

IKU is the programme for intercultural exchange of school-classes in primary and general secondary education. In 1995 about 7,600 pupils and 1,200 teachers were involved in it. Plato is the programme for teacher exchange. Its aim is to give teachers experience in teaching in another country or to follow courses in one of the countries of the European Union. In 1995 about 1,750 teachers in primary and general secondary education took advantage of this programme. Gros is for common projects between educational institutions in a border region. The aim is to intensify and set up structural cooperation between institutions in Flanders, Wallonia, North-Rhine-Westphalia and Lower Saxony. In 1995, 38 projects started in this programme.

As stated before, all these programmes ran under *Grenzen Verleggen*, the policy programme that came to an end in 1996. When the new memorandum *Onbegrensd Talent* becomes fully operational, the European Platform will most probably continue the management of programmes for the primary and general secondary education.

The European Platform developed a policy plan 'Platform-2003'. Policy towards 2003 aims at the stimulation of internationalisation. At the same time research on the effects of the programmes through statistical analysis and evaluation reports must show the results that have been achieved. Some qualitative models of internationalisation have been created which will be disseminated.

Cinop

Cinop (Centre for the Innovation of Education and Training) was founded in 1997 through merging CIBB (Centre for Innovation of Vocational Training and Industry) and SVE (Foundation for Adult Education). Both institutions have a long tradition in education and training and have built up considerable expertise. Cinop is an organisation which is involved in the innovation of (adult) education and vocational training. It works at national and international levels to modernise training courses in the light of developments within the labour market. It has an extensive range of innovative products with which to achieve this aim:

- research and studies relating to educational issues (occupational practice, effects of training);
- design of training courses (qualification structures and attainment targets, organisation of training courses, curriculum and methods, tests and examination);
- development of training course materials, both written and multimedia;
- advice on setting up training organisations and supervising changes;
- schooling and training of staff and teachers.

The main activities in Cinop are focused on the field of vocational education and training, with an emphasis on secondary vocational training and adult education. The tasks of Cinop include programme management for national and European projects. It also makes available a variety of products on the international market. Cinop carried out the management of *Grenzen Verleggen*. Programmes included Sesam, Plato and Gros.

Sesam focuses on student mobility and cooperation between Dutch institutions and institutions in the EU for vocational education and training. Cooperation is aimed at building up common exchange programmes that contribute to vocational qualifications. In 1995 about 1,700 students were involved in an exchange programme subsidised by Sesam. With Plato, the mobility programme for teachers in vocational education and training, teachers can spend some time in another country to teach, to gain work experience in industry or to follow courses. In 1995 about 1,360 teachers in vocational education and training participated in this programme. With Gros, intensive cooperation between Dutch institutions for vocational education and training and similar institutions in the border regions could be realised. In 1994, 24 projects started in the Gros-programme.

Cinop (the former CIBB) also has coordinated Dutch participation in former European programmes: Petra, Force, Eurotecnet II, Lingua and Iris, which proved very successful. Currently Cinop carries out programme management of Leonardo da Vinci in close cooperation with Nuffic, although Cinop is responsible for the overall coordination. To implement it in Dutch education, information meetings are organised, a periodical has been developed (*Leonardo Nieuwsbrief*), information materials are distributed among target groups and a help desk has been established. Cinop advises potential project promoters in the field of vocational education and training; when a project is approved, Cinop in close cooperation with Nuffic and the European Commission carries out the monitoring of the project.

The European Study Visit programme, initiated by Cedefop, formerly a separate programme, is now part of Leonardo da Vinci although carried out by Cinop. Cinop provides Cedefop every year with updated information on the Dutch educational system. Besides the capacity Cinop has in coordination, research, developing educational materials (including software) and open and distance learning on regular vocational (adult) education and training, it has built up expertise in the field of internationalisation of this sector.

Nuffic

Nuffic coordinates and administers Dutch and European programmes that help the higher education institutions to become more international, for example by encouraging staff and student mobility and by providing information about these programmes. Nuffic issues recommendations regarding the comparative value of degrees, diplomas and education systems in different countries. Nuffic also conducts studies of education in developing countries and evaluates forms of cooperation as well as the quality and impact of internationalisation. The organisation's last main area of activity involves support for international networks of researchers and consultants which aims to help developing countries to improve their teaching and research infrastructure. Nuffic administered Dutch programmes such as STIR, whose grants were meant as 'seed money' to encourage the institutions' own efforts to become more international. STIR grants could also be used to help cover the extra costs of studying or doing an internship abroad. STIR ended in 1996.

The PASSAGE programme offers people from Central and Eastern Europe opportunities for obtaining management training in the Netherlands. Dutch enterprises and other organisations are granted funds to invite managers to come for a course or for in-house training. PASSAGE is funded by the Ministry of Economic Affairs.

Finally, the Japan Prize Winners' Programme can be mentioned. This Dutch scheme offers each year 20 Dutch graduates the opportunity to spend a year learning the Japanese language and culture and become acquainted with Japanese business. After several months taking courses at Leiden University, the graduates go to Japan for a period of study and work placement. The programme, set up in cooperation with industry, is funded by the Dutch Ministry of Education, Culture and Science.

The management of internationalisation programmes, training, consultancy and surveys on the internationalisation of higher education is a main task of Nuffic.

Primary education

Developments in structure and provision

Primary education, given at elementary schools, lasts eight years. It is for pupils between 4 and 12 years of age and is administered by the WBO (New Primary Education Act). The education is set up to allow pupils to progress through an uninterrupted development process in line with the rate of development of each individual child. Special programmes strive to make primary education accessible to all children in this age group. Primary education is available from 4 years of age, but compulsory from 5 years up. Teaching aims to promote the development of the emotions, of the intellect and of creativity. Furthermore, the acquisition of essential knowledge and social and physical skills is encouraged. The underlying assumption is that the pupils are growing up in a multicultural society.

The *schoolwerkplan* (schoolwork scheme) and annual reports are the key instruments in planning, teaching and quality control. They give an insight into the organisation and content of teaching.

The curriculum and the European dimension

As regards the content of education, subjects must appear if possible in an integrated form. Some major subjects are sensory and motor coordination, physical exercise, Dutch, arithmetic and mathematics, national history, geography, expressive activities, self-reliance and healthy living. In 1985, together with the introduction of the WBO, English was introduced as a compulsory subject in the last two years of primary education. The educational design is part of the main interest, and by development of the content and methodology, the training of teachers and improving the link with secondary education, progress is made in raising standards. Since the boards of schools have much freedom in the arrangement of the curriculum, except of the major subjects, there might be found many differences in the way schools practise their teaching. By giving schools such freedom to arrange their curriculum, they can distinguish themselves either in religious, moral-ethical or pedagogical courses.

Knowledge concerning the European Community is no part of the compulsory subjects. They stress that young children have to become familiar first with basic knowledge and skills, which enables them to understand their fellows. In the opinion of the policy-makers, knowledge about other countries, cultures and languages should be incorporated into existing subjects. As stated in the memorandum *Onbegrensd Talent*, internationalisation of the curriculum in primary education has low priority at policy level, although language training is an exception. Some primary schools in the border regions started an experiment in teaching the 'neighbour language' as the second foreign language. The principle is to teach the so-called 'encounter language' (*ontmoetingstaal*), *Begegnungssprache* or *langue de rencontre*. Research should reveal if these experiments in primary education can be embedded into the regular curriculum.

Case study[5]

One of the activities undertaken with a grant from the Plato programme was a visit of 20 teachers to Reggio Emilia in Italy.[6] The *Hogeschool Gelderland* supervised this study trip which was aimed at the education of young children. In the Netherlands as well as in Flanders there is considerable interest in this issue at policy level.

In Reggio Emilia the Italian women's movement (the UDI) was involved with the development of childcare. After some experiments a public 'pre-school' for children of 3–6 years was established. In 1972 the first 'Infant Toddlercentre' for children from 3 months of age up to 3 years followed. At this moment there are 19 public pre-schools and 13 'Infant Toddlercentres' established in Reggio Emilia. In these centres a unique pedagogical concept is based on the theory of Piaget, of which interaction between child and adult is the most important pillar. The Dutch teachers were so impressed and inspired that they started a working group in the Netherlands on the 'Reggio concept'. This concept is also successful in other countries, and European Platform plans to organise and subsidise a study visit to Berlin, one of the places outside Italy in which schools have worked for some years with this concept. If teachers can experience new and successful pedagogical concepts and have the chance to integrate this experience in their way of working, the quality of basic education will increase.

Secondary education

Developments in structure and provision

Secondary education comprises four educational types. In the Netherlands, it is divided into a first phase (*basisvorming*) and a second phase (*tweede fase*), which run straight through the educational types. This two-phase distinction stems from a recent substantive educational innovation. Since 1993, a 15-subject collective educational programme has been offered during the first three years of secondary education. This takes up 80 per cent of the instruction time and is devoted to teaching 'the basics'. Instead of organisational integration of training into a single type of education, this substantive integration was preferred which left the original types of education intact. Included in the first phase are different parts of the four educational types in which teaching 'the basics', including technology, information science and health and care, is predominant:

- Preparatory vocational education (VBO, ages 12–16). This lasts four years and offers general and vocationally orientated and vocationally preparatory courses. It aims to equip students with a first practical orientation for a vocational education.
- Junior general secondary education (MAVO, ages 12–16) also lasts four years and is primarily intended as a preparation for senior secondary vocational education (MBO). However, some students advance to senior general education (HAVO) or pre-university education (VWO). In 1994, 17 per cent of the students went from MAVO to HAVO and VWO.
- General secondary education (HAVO, ages 12–17) lasts five years, of which the first three years count towards the first phase of secondary education. HAVO is primarily a preparation for higher professional education (HBO), but in practice graduated HAVO students also go to MBO and VWO. In 1994 approximately 25 per cent of HAVO graduates continued on to MBO and 18 per cent to VWO.
- Pre-university education (VWO, ages 12–18) lasts six years, the first four of which count towards the first phase of secondary education. Although originally intended as a preparation for university, in practice many graduates choose higher professional education (HBO), which is more attuned to the labour market. In 1994, about 30 per cent of VWO graduates went to HBO.

The second phase of secondary education includes the last two or three years respectively of HAVO and VWO. Policy development aims to start in 1999 with a new educational concept for those two or three years when the student can choose out of three (VWO) or four (HAVO) 'streams' or 'profiles': 'Culture and Society', 'Economics and Society', 'Natural Science and Health Care' and 'Natural Science and Technics'. Adapting the study to those 'profiles', the student is supposed to be better prepared for the higher education of his or her preference. Until 1999, students had the freedom to choose an examination in seven subjects of their choice, although not every package gave entry to all studies in higher education. A new subject introduced with the implementation of the two-phase-structure is the *Studiehuis* (study-home). In this concept, students work largely on their own and regular classical teaching is reduced to the minimum. Schools offer places to the student to work independently on assigned tasks.

In the Netherlands all the forms of schooling that comprise secondary education (VBO, MAVO, HAVO and VWO) are organisationally merged into large combined schools, called 'colleges' or 'combined schools' (*scholengemeenschappen*).

The curriculum and the European dimension

Although the Dutch authorities have no direct influence on the content of education (freedom of education is specified in the law) and nowadays policy is aimed at more self-regulation and autonomy of schools, they can, *inter alia* through inspection provide incentives and influence the European dimension in the curricula. Up to now, there has been no uniform definition of the European dimension in terms of pedagogic aims and objectives. In general one agrees that the European dimension is teaching about Europe in the sense of informing, reducing ignorance and making students aware of their common objectives. It is also teaching for Europe in the sense of preparing young people for greater mobility and teaching them the skills of living and working together with people from different countries and cultures.

The most important tool to reach these goals is to have command of a foreign language. Language training is one of the main issues nowadays and policy-makers in the Netherlands stress that in secondary education more attention can be paid to foreign languages, especially German, French and English. The curriculum also offers possibilities to integrate an international orientation into history and economics. Within the examination profiles in HAVO and VWO, one of the demands is to acquire knowledge of foreign languages, other countries and cultures and to apply it in the examination on the history of European integration from 1945 to 1997. In this way the European dimension comes into the curriculum and young people are prepared for European citizenship. European and national exchange programmes for students and teachers in secondary education also contribute to this phenomenon. As mentioned before, the European Platform has been working on these programmes since 1992 to encourage school exchange schemes.

Consideration can also be given to the project approach in close cooperation with curriculum development, further training, test development, material development and research. The law provides a framework for development of curricula in which areas such as European integration are covered as far as the examination demands, but it also gives space to go into more depth in studying European integration. Educational support is given by the Foundation for

Curriculum Development (SLO), the Central Institute for Test Development (CITO) and the Foundation for Educational Research (SVO).

Difficulties are encountered in attempting to promote the European dimension. Since the Treaty of Maastricht, the Dutch have become more aware of European integration and its consequences for education. Nevertheless, there is a general lack of a systematic approach to the topic in terms of curriculum development. A first impulse is given through European and national programmes. The other side of the coin shows that integration in the curriculum depends too much on the character of the programmes and on funding. The fact that Europeanisation often comes on top of the curriculum, which is already far too full with all the educational reforms and retrenchments, may lead to internationalisation often being considered unimportant.

An overview of programmes and results in secondary education[7]

In the Socrates programme strand II, Comenius is intended for secondary education. In 1995 approximately 90 schools were involved in setting up school partnerships. Through a substantial increase in the budget in 1996 the opportunity occurred to involve 300 schools. Since in Comenius the use of new technologies is encouraged, teachers exchange materials by e-mail or Internet, and they visit their partners in the project. Pupils communicate with each other in the partnership in the same way, although telephone and fax are also used.

Lingua, now part of Socrates, offered between 1991 and 1995 over 7,000 students in secondary education and some 900 teachers the possibility of participating in an educational exchange programme or a refresher course. Italy, Spain and the United Kingdom were the most popular destinations in student exchange. For the refresher courses for teachers, the United Kingdom, France and Germany were especially favoured. This is because of the fact that only language teachers could participate in Lingua, and English, French and German are the most common foreign languages taught in the Netherlands. Now under Socrates non-language teachers can also participate, but participation figures are not yet available.

Study visits under Socrates (the former Arion) is one of the actions that contribute to the European dimension, under which school-leaders are enabled to visit another EU member state to set up partnerships. Each year the European Commission sets themes for those study visits. In 1995 the themes for the Netherlands were:

- the role of the parents in (secondary) education;
- education for migrant children;
- teaching as a profession;
- education in foreign languages.

Another action programme is 'Europe in the School', an initiative of the Council of Europe and funded by Socrates. This is a competition in which students have to write an essay on a European subject. Prize-winners aged 15 years and up are enabled to visit one of the participating countries, when meeting with contemporaries is the central theme. The Netherlands also organises a one-week meeting for foreign prize-winners.

Besides the European programmes, secondary education schools could participate in the national programmes mentioned in *Grenzen Verleggen* and to be continued under the new policy *Onbegrenst Talent* with Plato and IKU. As mentioned, policy demands that internationalisation has to be integrated in the school policy document (*schoolwerkplan*).

The Dutch government signed bilateral educational agreements with several countries in Europe, to stress cooperation. In 1996 bilateral agreements ran with Germany, Flanders and Austria. Within the bilateral agreement with Germany two programmes were added to the existing 'Youth Programme' and 'Prämien Programme': 'Germany Plus' (1994–5) and 'Language Assistance' (1995–). Cooperation with Germany is important because it is one of the Netherlands' border countries and considered one of its most important trading partners. Other reasons are the fact that Germany is subdivided into 16 *Länder*, each with full autonomy in educational design and legislation, so cooperation offers the possibility to choose one of these regions, of which several are more or less similar to those of the Netherlands in area and number of inhabitants. Furthermore it is important to reduce prejudices against Germans.[8] Last but not least, the German language is of importance to the Netherlands. Over the last 20 years interest in German language training had diminished to a minimum, but nowadays, in the growing awareness of European integration, it is clear that the German language is important. Regions in Germany to set up joint projects are North Rhine Westphalia; Lower Saxony; Euregio Rhine-Maas; and Ems-Dollar.

Within the bilateral agreement with Germany activities such as information exchange, advice, acquisition and development of curricula, financial aid and student and staff exchange are encouraged. Activity within the agreement with Flanders was limited in 1995–6 to study visits to set up networks. With Austria some projects started in 1995 involving student and staff exchanges.

Internationaal georienteerd onderwijs (IGO)

Besides the regular primary and secondary schools, eight so-called Internationally Orientated Education (IGO) primary and eight secondary schools exist in the Netherlands. This education is intended for specific international target groups such as:

- children of foreign parents who live and work in the Netherlands;
- children of Dutch parents, if they have been working in a foreign country and if their children have been educated in that country;
- children of Dutch parents who stay in the Netherlands between two jobs in a foreign country.

Internationally Orientated Education meets the wishes of the Dutch and international industry to adapt education to the needs of children who are temporarily in the Netherlands. The curriculum aims to prepare children for follow-on education in the English language in a foreign county. Internationally Orientated Education is taught in two languages: Dutch (one-quarter of the curriculum) and English (three-quarters of the curriculum).

IGO schools are part of the regular Dutch educational system and are integrated into regular schools for primary and secondary education. Teachers in IGO need an extra qualification to teach which is recognised by the Dutch government. Most of those who teach the basics are native speakers. Dutch teachers teach subjects such as Dutch language, physics, art and music. Internationalisation of the curriculum in IGO schools is standard. Several aspects illustrate the 'ideal international school':

- there is a natural awareness of international alliance;
- student population is a mix of different nationalities and cultures;
- staff are also a mix of nationalities and cultures;
- social intercourse between students of different cultures is common;
- there is a broad know-how about teaching in different languages;
- schools often have good connections with international schools and industry.

The curriculum and the European dimension

Dutch law regulates IGO schools: primary education under the Primary Education Act and secondary education under the Secondary Education Act. Curricula of IGO are based on the British curricula for primary education and on the international curriculum of the International Schools Curriculum Project (ISCP) called 'Curriculum Framework for English Streams in Dutch Primary Schools'. In that framework, areas of education are formulated in line with those of regular primary education in the Netherlands. Specific areas for IGO are English language, English as a second language and Dutch as a foreign language. The curricula for secondary education are attuned to international standards. In the Dutch IGO school system three levels of qualification can be obtained:

- the International General Certificate of Secondary Education (IGCSE), similar to the English GCSE and to the standards of the Dutch General Secondary Education (MAVO/HAVO);
- the International Baccalaureate Middle Years Programme (IBMYP) similar to the standards of Dutch MAVO/HAVO;
- the International Baccalaureate (IB) to the standards of the Dutch pre-university education (VWO).

IGO schools have their own national network. Furthermore they participate in national working groups and organisations. The European Platform is one of the contacts for IGO to discuss and extend internationalisation of the curriculum, through the development of two-language education and language education in general.

IGO schools in the Netherlands participate in the International Schools Association (ISA), a world-wide cooperation agreement between international schools.

Case study

In Enschede, near the German border, the Kottenparkcollege cooperates with partners in Germany. In the vocational guidance sector, much information about the German labour market and vocational education is made available to students. All students in the first years of college are expected to 'cross the border' in order to get in touch with German students. Students of 13–15 are more open to new experiences, dare to speak German and are not afraid to make mistakes. In the next years, students join German students in their practical period. The Dutch student stays about three days with the German student at his or her work experience place. Through this, Dutch students become familiar with the German language, the informal as well as the formal and technical aspects of the language; meanwhile they get a good view of the German labour market.

Secondary vocational education and adult education

Developments in structure and provision[9]

In the Netherlands a distinction between initial and continuing vocational education and training is hard to make. The Dutch policy toward vocational education and training is not set up in such a way as to create two separate systems, but is based on the belief that all residents of the Netherlands, of both native and foreign origin (recent immigrants), have a right to obtain a qualification that provides a solid starting point for entrance into the Dutch labour market. So most of what is said here about vocational education is valid for initial as well as continuing training.

One of the characteristics of the Dutch 'consultation' economy is the mix of legislation and self-regulation. In initial vocational education the primary responsibility lies with the Ministry of Education, Culture and Science and the Ministry of Agriculture, Nature Management and Fisheries. This responsibility is manifested in legal arrangements. The foremost responsibility for continuing vocational training lies with the social partners. A legal framework is absent here because self-regulation is given priority. A legal framework only exists where social partners share responsibility with the Ministry of Social Affairs and Employment, as is the case with training programmes for those seeking employment.

In the Netherlands, the field of vocational secondary education has a structure that corresponds to the various business sectors. It comprises courses for types of work within four sectors: the technical sector, the economic-administrative sector, the service and health sector, and the agricultural sector. There is one law of paramount importance for secondary vocational training and education: the Education and Vocational Training Act (WEB). The advent of the WEB, which also includes regulation of adult education, is an important development for secondary vocational education and training. Although the law took effect on 1 January 1996, it was actually implemented in phases. The last measure prompted by this law will be implemented no later than 1 January 2000. The WEB aims to bring more cohesion between secondary vocational education and adult education, establish a better link with developments in the (regional) labour market and increase the autonomy of educational institutions. An example of the possibility to act more autonomously is the opportunity to develop educational tracks tailored to individual needs and abilities, or a further elaboration of the national exit qualifications in consultation with the regional business community. Social partners are more involved in the development of vocational training, laws and regulations are developed in close cooperation between social partners and the Ministries of Social Affairs and of Economic Affairs. Arrangements for job-seekers are made, and schooling regulations are foreseen for workers in collective labour agreements.

To reach more cohesion between secondary vocational training and adult education, training programmes have been brought together in Regional Training Centres (ROC). In practice it means that ROCs offer a broad range of initial and post-initial degree programmes in vocational and adult education, except for agricultural education.[10]

The WEB brings together all levels of secondary vocational and adult education into one educational structure. Levels of education correspond with European SEDOC achievement levels. In the BVE sector (which involves secondary vocational training and adult education), the following levels have been established:

- assistant vocational education courses, which prepare participants for simple operational work in an occupation. The course lasts no more than one year (approximately level 1 SEDOC);
- basic vocational education courses, which prepare participants for operational work. The course lasts two or three years (approximately level 2 SEDOC);
- advanced vocational education courses, which prepare participants to work fully independently. The course lasts three or four years (approximately level 3 SEDOC);
- middle management courses, designed to train participants to be able to function fully independently and give them a basic qualification in management. The course usually lasts four years (approximately level 4 SEDOC). Graduates can move on to higher vocational education;
- specialist training courses, which are open to graduates from the advanced

vocational education course. The course lasts one or two years (approximately level 4 SEDOC).

There are several active parties in the field of vocational education and training that jointly determine, monitor and guarantee quality of education and training under the WEB. Amongst these are educational institutions, the national vocational education bodies, local authorities, trade and industry, social partners and two ministries (Education, Culture and Science, and Agriculture, Nature Management and Fisheries).

The curriculum and the European dimension

Dutch policy on internationalisation of education aims to adapt programmes and curricula to the demands of an international society and an internationally orientated labour market and to stimulate contacts and cooperation between vocational education institutions, students, staff and teachers in EU member states. To educate students for the international labour market and to enable them to work in another member state, the most important goal for Dutch vocational education is the mutual recognition of qualifications in the European Union. Tools to reach this goal are to offer students a work placement in one of the member states, to work with other member states on the mutual recognition of qualifications and to implement the European dimension in the curriculum. Activities on student exchanges and placements are undertaken in almost every centre for vocational training. Experience from this activity brings the European dimension into the curriculum. Students have to be prepared to work or stay in another country. In that way the students are taught *about* Europe as well as *for* Europe. Giving students the opportunity to spend some of their study time abroad gives them a broader view on labour market possibilities and makes them more flexible. Nevertheless, there are many obstacles to mobility which prevent students from going abroad. One example is that for organisational and financial reasons only a selected number of students actually go to a placement or exchange. Those who can experience a foreign placement or exchange run across other obstacles. Most of these obstacles are pointed out in the European Commission Green Paper on Mobility[11] and also apply in the Dutch situation.

The work on mutual recognition of qualifications in secondary vocational education and training is done by Colo (Central Office of the National Apprenticeship Training Bodies) in the Netref project, a Leonardo project in which about 12 member states work together on a national reference structure geared to each other's national structures. In that way there will be more coherence between member states and recognition of qualifications.

To support vocational institutions in bringing a European dimension into the curriculum, Cinop developed the 'International Curriculum Comparison', a tool to make a first comparison between their own curriculum and the curriculum of the partner school.[12] In that way people learn from each other and obtain a solid base for working together. In the Netherlands nearly all schools for vocational education and training started their cooperation after they had made this curriculum comparison.

An overview of programmes and results in secondary vocational education

In vocational education and training much experience is gained from European and national programmes. In Petra I, intended for secondary vocational education and training, only very few activities were undertaken, but in Petra II activities increased. Petra II comprised three major strands: pilot projects, placements and exchanges, and vocational guidance/career counselling. The programme started in January 1992 and ended in December 1994. In Petra II, 52 pilot projects were involved, an internationally orientated career guidance centre was established and about 2,000 young people had the opportunity to go on work experience, placement or exchange. Petra II is considered a very successful programme in the Netherlands.[13]

Through this programme (and the Dutch national programme) secondary vocational educational institutions were able to broaden their horizons and to experience the European dimension. In the pilot projects materials were developed and disseminated, with modules implemented in the regular curriculum. As important or even more important were the personal experiences and 'European awareness' brought to the European dimension in the curriculum.

Together with Petra II, the Dutch national programmes Plato, Sesam and Gros started as part of the earlier mentioned *Grenzen Verleggen*. Figures from the final report for 1995–6 show that in that year 1,619 staff and teachers (Plato) and 2,517 students (Sesam) were involved in an exchange.[14] Most-favoured countries in these programmes were the United Kingdom, Germany, Belgium and Denmark. This coincides with Dutch internationalisation policy, the *Grenslandenbeleid*, which focused on cooperation between institutions in the border regions.

Other European programmes in which Dutch vocational centres participated were Iris, Eurotecnet, Lingua and Force. In Iris only very few projects were executed because of the limited means available. In Eurotecnet, Dutch research centres participated in an active way. In the Lingua programme enterprises participated and developed materials such as language courses tailored to poorly educated employees. Iris as well as Eurotecnet and Lingua were relatively small programmes. On the other hand, Force offered possibilities to many projects. All of these projects focused on the cooperation between education and enterprises, especially SMEs.

In the Netherlands, these programmes are considered very successful; there is much interest in the new Leonardo da Vinci programme, the successor of the former European programmes, especially in secondary vocational education and training, as shown in pilot projects. In the first call (1995) the national coordination unit received 167 applications for pilot projects, of which only

21 were honoured. Out of this 21, only two projects were assigned to secondary vocational education. That caused disappointment in that sector. In the 1996 call, the number of applications decreased to 99, of which 26 were approved. In the 1997 call the number again decreased (to 54) which made them more likely to be accepted. Apart from the fact that only a few projects can be approved, another reason for the declining number of applications is the non-transparent and time-consuming European procedure. High interest not only affects the pilot projects: in Leonardo da Vinci placements and exchange projects are also popular. Placements and exchanges in secondary vocational education and training are handled in a national selection procedure, in more direct contact with the applicant. In the 1995 call the coordination unit received 74 project proposals on mobility projects, of which 57 were approved. In the next two calls (1996 and 1997) the figures were respectively 92 proposals of which 71 were approved and 109 proposals of which about 60 were. Figures from the 1995 evaluation of the placements and exchange programme show that not all approved projects are carried out. Out of the 57 projects, only 50 were completed, which means that from the original figure of 815 students in the project, only 677 participated in a placement or exchange.[15] Inquiry of the project leaders showed that their project plan was forced by the application deadlines, but was hard to realise for organisational reasons.

Case studies

The next examples are chosen from the Leonardo da Vinci projects in secondary vocational education and training.

A project of STOAS (Agriculture Research and Training Institute) focuses on the education of employees in craft bakeries. The aim is to improve efficiency and strengthen the economic position of craft bakers in SMEs by increasing quality. Craft bakeries in Europe meet with competition from industrial bakeries. The craft bakery sector, however, is important for employment. In this branch about 3,500 enterprises exist in the Netherlands in which about 10,000 people find employment. In Europe the figure is estimated to be one million. To compete with industrial competition a solution can be found in the upgrading of product quality. In this project, in which four member states and the European umbrella organisation of craft bakers work together, a handbook has been developed in which a description is given of the whole process from raw material to final product. Everything is amply illustrated with cartoons, so the material is useful for low-skilled employees as well as employees skilled to the level of secondary vocational training. Instruction material is also developed to support employers in passing on knowledge to their employees. The developed material will be available in Dutch, English, French and Italian. Employees as well as employers who participated in the project were very motivated to learn to raise standards. This project is an illustration of the way in which SMEs can keep up with economic developments and formulate their own answer to the competition they experience from industry. It is also a good illustration of cooperation between education and enterprises in an economic development that affects all EU member states.

The Alexis project affects primarily the Dutch vocational education system as it is aligned closely with a huge national project in vocational education and training, the ATB project (increasing attractiveness of technical education and training) initiated by the Dutch Ministry of Education, Culture and Science, together with the social partners in the technical branches. In the Alexis project the Dutch partner works together with partners in three EU member states on the accessibility of educational applications of multimedia in the field of secondary vocational education and training. The heart of the project is the database on the Internet. From this database one can download all kinds of educational simulation games: for example, using the 'Chernobyl' simulator one must prevent meltdown by the correct operation of machines. Alexis aims to bring together all simulation games of high pedagogical and technical quality used in the member states in technical education and training. To select the simulations quality standards are developed. Furthermore, Alexis has built a library on the Internet site filled with articles, magazines, on-line examples, names of organisations, technological subjects and design tools. In the cyber café one can take a virtual break and chat with other users.

An example of good practice in placement and exchange projects is the 'Up and Down' project of Clusius College, an agricultural educational centre. In this project partners of three member states work together. They create a multinational setting, and students of two countries come together in the third country. In this way five Dutch students went to Spain, three to Portugal, while Clusius College received students from Spain and Portugal. The project was structured into a course on elementary knowledge of the country to be visited, a language course, a course on technical aspects of agriculture in the other countries, followed by a seven-week placement.

During their stay abroad Dutch students were offered jobs in SMEs, but all chose to go back to the Netherlands to study to obtain a higher qualification. This project shows that students with a qualification in secondary agricultural education and international experience are in demand in the labour market.

Higher education

Recent developments in structure and content

Higher education in the Netherlands can be divided into two branches, university education and higher professional education (HBO). In 1985 the Open University system came into being. In contrast to other western European countries like Germany and the United Kingdom, the Open University in the Netherlands was established quite late. Many people have shown interest in this type of second-chance education, since no formal qualifications are needed to enter. Universities and HBO institutions, on the contrary, require an appropriate type of secondary school-leaving certificate. The government may impose a limit (a *numerus clausus*) on the number of students for a particular programme.

The 14 universities (including the Open University) and the HBO institutions were traditionally two separate worlds. They work more closely together nowadays, although status differences still exist. An important example of a closer collaboration between HBO and universities is that students who have completed the first year at an HBO institution can be admitted to university, as long as they take courses in the same sector as they did in HBO. In financial terms, the institutions for higher education are heavily dependent on the government. These and other aspects of the relationship between the Dutch government and the institutions of higher education are primarily laid down in the following Acts of Parliament: the Open University Act (1985), the University Education Act (1986) and the HBO Education Act (1986). These ensure that individuals have access to higher education, on the basis of academic aptitude as expressed in formal qualifications, regardless of social background or financial resources.

The Higher Professional Education Act came into effect in 1986. For a period of seven years it regulated all aspects of higher professional education (*Hoger Beroepsonderwijs*, HBO). The most important changes brought about by this Act were:

- HBO became for the first time officially a form of higher education, alongside university education;
- the length of all HBO programmes was standardised at four years;
- regardless of their discipline, all HBO graduates can use the title bachelor.

Since August 1993, HBO has been regulated by the new Higher Education and Research Act. In the summer of 1993, an entirely new higher education Act came into effect. The Higher Education and Research Act (*Wet op het Hoger Onderwijs en Wetenschappelijk Onderzoek*, WHW) broke away from years of tradition by combining legislation governing HBO, university education and the Open University into one Act. Some of the most important changes are:

- study programmes are for the first time referred to in Dutch as *opleidingen*, whereby the institution and not the national government determines the content and educational objectives;
- the length of study programmes is no longer expressed in years, but in credits. The workload for full-time students is 40 hours a week, 42 weeks per year;
- student evaluations of study programmes are included in the institutional evaluations, which are part of the quality control system.

The WHW provides a statutory basis for the planning system. The Ministry of Education, Culture and Science every two years draws up a Higher Education and Research Plan (*Hoger Onderwijs en Onderzoek Plan*, HOOP), outlining plans for the following two years. The HOOP serves as a basis for the ongoing dialogue between the Ministry and the higher education institutions. The programmes of international education, designed mainly for students from developing countries, are generally conducted in English.

International features of international collaboration

Higher education institutions are involved in numerous international co-operation programmes, for example, EU programmes such as Socrates, Central and Eastern Europe (Tempus), America (STIR). As a result, staff and student mobility have increased dramatically; nowadays nearly 10 per cent of Dutch students participate in a foreign study programme. There is a relatively small number of foreign students taking a complete study programme at a Dutch higher education institution: they account for about 2.2 per cent of the total number of enrolled students. Dutch government policy is geared towards increasing the number of foreign students in regular education.

Among funding sources such as NWO and VSB Bank and (formerly) STIR, the KNAW plays an important role. The KNAW (Koninklijke Nederlandse Akademie van Wetenschappen), is a Dutch funding agency for research and one of the leading organisations in the Netherlands for the promotion of internationalisation. In a recent policy document,[16] KNAW suggests a more explicit choice for bilateral collaboration with countries or sister organisations (academies), envisaging more differentiation in the type and intensity of collaboration. Current agreements will be continued at a low level. With a selected group of countries, new or reshaped agreements will be made. The duration of these agreements will be limited to, say, five years. In these countries, specific incentives, regions and instrumentation will be selected, one of the new instruments being the exchange of guest researchers. Formerly, exchanges usually lasted one or two weeks in the host country, which is only sufficient for orientation in the new working environment. In the future policy setting, a 3–6-month stay abroad will make it possible to develop real research activities at the host institution.

The agreements with sister academies will be based on an analysis of the collaboration pattern between the two countries involved. The incentives and instruments will be introduced to those areas of academic collaboration which can be identified as being underdeveloped but high in potential.

A new reason for collaboration will be solidarity among faculty members. Some academics are limited in their academic work due to the political climate in their countries. Until recently, the KNAW exchange programmes with Central or Eastern European academies formed one of the few opportunities to meet colleagues. These agreements will be continued in order to re-establish the free academic tradition in these countries. The Dutch Minister of Education, Culture and Sciences decided to concentrate on two Central and Eastern European countries, namely, Hungary and Russia. The KNAW, in contrast, prefers a broader pattern of collaborative Central and Eastern countries and, at the same time, is compensating for the Minister's policy of concentration on two.

In the government memorandum *Internationalisation of Education and Research*, the Netherlands Universities Foundation for International Cooperation (Nuffic) is mentioned as the intermediary for the internationalisation of higher education. Nuffic was founded in 1952 to stimulate cooperation with universities in developing countries. It now coordinates and administers Dutch and European programmes that help higher education institutions to become more international. One of these is the European Leonardo da Vinci programme. Most institutions of higher education in the Netherlands collaborate in Leonardo through the UETPs (University Enterprise Training Partnerships), founded in the earlier Comett days. The UETPs enable the institutions to become part of a regional consortium which takes care of the acquisition and dissemination of the Leonardo grants. In particular the UETP consortium has advantages for the staff and student exchange programmes, because most higher education institutions do not have enough skilled staff members to run them. An application procedure coordinated by Nuffic is the so-called 'cultural treaties', which are agreed on a bilateral basis. There are limited numbers of grants for the exchange of students and staff.

The infrastructure within the higher education institutions has improved, although within higher vocational institutions it is still in a starting phase. Within universities, besides the central office for international relations, small offices have been established at departmental levels. Nuffic has an information centre connected with national information on European matters and a strong history in the comparison of certificates and diplomas. It is evident that Dutch certificates have been underestimated abroad.

The Netherlands as a country of destination

Until recently the Netherlands was underrepresented in comparison with other European destinations. On the one hand, it was seen as 'provincial', and on the other, the quality of its higher education was not appreciated. The Dutch language complicated the negative image; foreign students were not familiar with the Dutch higher education system and its degrees. Finally, there was no financial aid system in most institutions of higher education for visiting students and rather poor facilities at postgraduate level. To create a more attractive environment for visiting students and staff, Nuffic suggested the following measures:

- an international recruitment and information campaign;
- postgraduate research and training courses;
- strengthening of adult education;
- encouragement of double degree courses within EU programmes.

Double degrees

Institutions of higher education have become more interested in awarding double degrees jointly with a sister institution abroad. For example, the Hogeschool Holland started a course in European business administration run in partnership with the Business School in Wolverhampton Polytechnic. After successfully completing the four-year course, students receive a Dutch HEAO diploma and a Bachelor of Arts degree.

Some scepticism about the double degree system can be noted in the Netherlands. For British and French institutions it is a matter of survival; this is also the case for quite a few Dutch ones, filling vacancies with EU-financed students. The aim is to attract more students by offering two diplomas. In the end this may lead to diploma inflation in Europe. Overall the opinion on double degrees in the Netherlands is positive; they are seen as means to gain recognition of qualified Dutch students in the European market.

Education, training and staff mobility

Reform in teacher training

Teacher education in the Netherlands is structured on four levels. Teachers in primary education have to complete the programme of the Teacher Training College for Primary Education (PABO). The PABO, which came into effect in 1984, offers a four-year programme with a propaedeutic first year. Methodology and practical training are integrated in the current programme.

To become a teacher in secondary education there are three possibilities. The New Teacher Training College for Secondary Education (NLO) awards second and third degrees in teaching. Students have to choose a principal subject and a subsidiary subject. Methodology and practical education are integrated into the programme here as well. In 1988, the Basic Education Advisory Council (ARBO) published a paper on the 'professionalisation' of the teacher's job. In the opinion of ARBO, more attention should be paid to teachers' career structure and reviews of their function.

In addition, there is the post-doctoral university teacher training programme known as *universitaire lerarenopleiding* (ULO). ULO trains teachers for the highest teaching qualification (*leraar, eerste graad*). The ULO requires an additional one year (42 credits) beyond the 'doctoral'. Most of the programme consists of studies in the theory of education, subject-related teaching methods and research, but at least 250 hours are also spent in the classroom.

The European dimension

During the past few years more attention has been paid to the European dimension in teacher education. The most recent report is the government memorandum *Europa in het Onderwijs* (The European Dimension in Education).

One of the measures mentioned in this report is the development of a strategy to stimulate attention to Europe in the curriculum, both in initial and refresher courses for teachers. Concrete results in this field have been achieved already, for example at the University of Groningen where the University Social Studies Teacher Training Institution initiated a course for social studies, economics, history and geography teachers.

PABO's regulations for final examination syllabuses do not specifically mention the European Union as a subject. In NLOs the topic does arise, though only a few training courses expressly cover this theme, which fares best in geography and economics, and less well in history and social studies.

Staff mobility

An aspect which until now has been under-developed is mobility among teachers in training. In the Socrates programme to date only a few institutions for teacher education were represented.

Attempts are being made to extend the limited time available for training periods. Under the Joint Study Programmes there are links with teacher training colleges in other member states. Assisted by Nuffic and the Council for Higher Vocational Education (HBO-Raad), links between establishments are encouraged. With the participation of ATEE (Association of Teacher Education in Europe) other forms of cooperation with associations and centres for European education are being set up. There is no government initiative for this in the Netherlands. In forming links between training institutions across Europe, difficulties are encountered mainly through lack of funds for exchange schemes. Differences in working methods between the teachers of member states also give rise to problems.

Despite these problems, international travel has become an integral part of the work of most Dutch faculty members in universities. In institutions for higher professional education staff mobility rates vary enormously, with high numbers in, for example, agricultural studies. Some staff members, however, are hampered in their international mobility by professional and personal circumstances, and the actual number of staff taking part in international mobility is lower than expected. In the earlier mentioned KNAW plan,[17] the relationship between the academic work of faculty members and growing internationalisation was analysed. First, according to KNAW, academic work is intrinsically international in character, and this becomes evident in the communication among academics. International orientation and collaboration can create a stimulating and competitive environment, which is essential to the production of highly qualified research results. Second, scientific work is more complex nowadays as a result of increased specialisation, increased capital intensity and an exceptional growth in the number of scientific publications. Third, hand in hand with the increased international character of academic work, the shift from national to international financing and science technology needs to be mentioned.

The European Union and its Framework programmes are an example of this phenomenon. Worldwide, the importance of international research organisations and multilateral collaboration is growing, even outside those disciplines with an established international tradition such as astronomy and physics. The consequences of this trend are many. Dutch researchers and policy-makers at universities and governmental organisations need to have sufficient influence on the decision-making process in various international fora, otherwise they will miss out on an equal share of international financial resources. The crucial question is whether the Dutch academic infrastructure is solid enough to survive in this international arena. To achieve this, not only protection of national expenditure for research and development is needed, but continuing concentration and collaboration in Dutch research as well.

Obstacles to mobility in Dutch higher education institutions

The obstacles to international staff mobility in Dutch higher education institutions have been analysed in a study conducted by van de Bunt-Kokhuis which examines the incentives and barriers which play a role in the decision of Dutch faculty members to go abroad.[18] The extent to which the determinants 'academic position', 'discipline', 'age' and 'gender' influence the frequency and durationof travel was investigated in a national survey of Dutch university faculty members in the period 1994–5. The data indicate that faculty members with higher rank or those with a technical background, senior members and males travel more frequently. Dutch faculty members with a technical background are internationally more active. This appears to depend largely on the involvement of these faculty members on boards of international scientific and professional organisations, on editorial boards of international scientific journals, and so on. Moreover, travel frequency is also related to productivity in publishing in international (co)publications.

Males travel significantly more than their female colleagues and this holds true in particular for older males. It is most likely that married females anticipate potential (double career) conflicts by making shorter trips. In particular senior lecturers mentioned 'too much work pressure' as a reason for the reduced number of trips. There is an upward spiral of increased work pressure and higher academic positions. Professors are an exception: possibly they have more facilities to reduce work pressure and eliminate barriers to travel. Practical recommendations are presented to provide organisations with guidelines for implementing international mobility in their human resources policy.

Institutional policy should be focused not only on faculty members going abroad, but also on visiting faculty members and their home institutions. The curriculum itself should become more internationalised. An intensive use of international networks is recommended for conducting mobility programmes, for pooling resources, for offering foreign language instruction in less commonly taught languages, for research cooperation and/or dissemination of materials.

The Human Resources department should develop a financial 'bonus' system and should facilitate return visits if longer stays are required. Training could be offered to non-travellers to enhance their teaching skills for international activities. Special chairs for visiting professors and a system of lending experts could be implemented.

Sabbatical leave

Dutch regulations (a general law which is also applicable to other civil servants) provide sabbatical leave of one year under certain conditions and may be granted with or without salary, depending on the situation. Special conditions are that the faculty member has to write a report after completion of this period; if he or she leaves the job within two years after completion of the sabbatical, the salary paid during the sabbatical has to be reimbursed. An exception is made for faculty members moving to another public or university institution.[19] Various funding schemes are available to faculty members, for example, STIR and NWO research grants (Ministry of Education, Culture and Sciences), cultural agreements and smaller funds from private foundations. There are only *ad hoc* facilities for staff replacement.

The administration, inspection and regulation of educational provision at local, regional and national levels

The government pursues education policy at three administrative levels:

1   *at central level*, through in particular the Ministry of Education, Culture and Science. The Ministry ensures adequate facilities and their distribution; it lays down the minimum numbers of pupils/students needed to legitimise a school's existence; it determines which subjects must be taught and it sets the standards of competence to be met by teaching staff;
2   *at provincial level*, through the provincial authorities, that is, the Provincial Council and the Provincial Executive. It takes the form of statutory supervisory and judicial duties, such as ensuring that there is an adequate number of public authority schools in the region. Finally, their concern is adult education and the structuring of regional consultation;
3   *at local level*, through the municipal authorities, that is, the Municipal Council and the Municipal Executive. This level is in effect the school board for public authority schools. They also act as the local authority for all schools (publicly and privately run) in the area. Their duties include ensuring that the Compulsory Education Act is observed and allocating funds.

The distinctive feature of the Dutch education system is that it combines a centralised education and funding policy with the decentralised administration and management of schools.

The issue of language

Medium of instruction

In the European Union about 20 million people speak Dutch. In comparison with languages such as English, French, German and Spanish, this is a small number. It is therefore justifiable to suggest that the internationalisation of Dutch education has been handicapped by language. Foreign students are reluctant to visit a country with a language which is difficult for them to understand. Also, owing to the principle of reciprocity in European programmes, Dutch students have more difficulties in finding placements abroad. One solution of this problem could be the introduction of education through the medium of English. This has been partially realised in some institutions of higher education and in a number of vocational secondary schools.

Opportunities and problems

There are various opinions on what language should be used as a medium of instruction in higher education. It is possible to distinguish two trends. On the one hand, there is already a strong drive to use English; the Dutch feel that this is a way to open up education to larger groups of foreign students. As a consequence of this trend, several Dutch universities have introduced English-medium courses (integrated or separate) in their curricula. A leading example is the University of Amsterdam, where extra efforts were made to have about 25 per cent of the courses available in English. Clearly, theirs is an influential view that successful internationalisation can only be achieved when there is a sufficient knowledge of English and/or other foreign languages at higher educational level. Most Dutch people are, of course, reasonably fluent in two or more foreign languages for everyday purposes.

On the other hand, other influences strongly support the use of Dutch as a language of instruction. As an example of those influences one can mention the strong link that exists between the Dutch lowlands, Germany and Flanders. In these regions Dutch is the major language and influential groups in society cherish this cultural heritage. Also on the academic level strong links exist; for example between the universities of Gent, Antwerp, Tilburg and Eindhoven. There is also the issue of so-called 'small country languages' such as Danish, Dutch and Portuguese, to which the European Commission gives priority. In the opinion of the Commission it should be compulsory for students visiting one of the small countries to learn the local language. It is a way to get to know the people better and therefore become better Europeans. The Commission launched the Lingua programme (now part of Socrates) to improve foreign language teaching and learning. The programme is aimed at language teachers and students in universities, institutions for vocational training and firms.

Dutch is quite popular amongst visiting students. Even if students enter an English-medium course at a Dutch university, they often choose to attend a

Dutch course as well. Last but not least, there is the fact that Dutch is taught to first degree and postgraduate levels at foreign universities (Canada, United Kingdom, Germany). For example, in Germany there are more students studying Dutch (more than 100,000) than there are Dutch students studying German.

The attitude of young Dutch people towards the European Community

There has been no systematic research on this in the Netherlands. From personal interviews with young people in the final grade of pre-university education (VWO), it appears that the concept of a 'Single Europe' is understood as an economic union with consequences for everyday life such as taxes, wages and trade, or as a cultural union: having no boundaries will mean that you feel more like a European and your nationality will disappear. One of the respondents made a comparison with the United States of America: 'We shall live in the United States of Europe.'

A research study at Clingendael on the relationship between Germany and the Netherlands (mentioned earlier) showed that the young Dutch generation has a hostile view of Germans. Possibly this negative opinion is caused by the Second World War, which is surprising, because the young respondents were born since that time.

Conclusion

Due to technological developments the process of globalisation is an ongoing process in which the European Union follows its own course, turning Europe into a global village. Initiated by economic and technical trends, education followed these developments and had achieved a base by the Maastricht Treaty. The educational aim of European globalisation is that with the completion of the internal market, Europeans will be able to choose any place in Europe to live, to work or to study. In terms of education, people will move to those places where the best education is offered for their particular needs. Due to the language barrier, the Netherlands might be less popular to European students in comparison with other EU member states. On the other hand, OECD reports show that the quality of the Dutch educational system can compete with other systems in the EU. The Dutch Ministry of Education, Culture and Science is aware of the fact that the teaching language is an obstacle for foreign students entering Dutch education. To make the Dutch educational system more accessible to foreign students (including students from outside the EU), some projects have started in which Dutch schools and universities offer, still on an experimental basis, (a part of) the education in the English language. Within the border regions experiments are undertaken to set up bilingual courses in projects (the so-called 'encounter language', 'Begegnungssprache' or 'langue de rencontre') with educational institutions across the border. Recently the Dutch Ministry of Education, Culture and Science signed the GENT IV agreement with the

Ministry of Education of Flanders (Belgium).[20] Activities undertaken in this scheme include exchange of students who can carry over loans of their country of origin (money follows student), exchange of information and exchange of civil servants.

Language is also a barrier for outgoing students. Although within the Dutch educational system foreign languages are offered to all students at all levels of education, some loss of active knowledge of foreign languages occurs, especially of French. In secondary and vocational education language training will be emphasised. The Dutch government considers it an educational task to support students sufficiently to continue their studies in another country or to work in another EU member state. In the new policy document *Onbegrensd Talent* priority is given to language training.

According to all plans and policy towards the internationalisation of education, one can say that it must become a part of people's general attitude. To prepare people for the European labour market internationalisation (and multicultural education) is part of the initial training. In higher education international cooperation is sought in scientific networks, student mobility and staff exchange, not only within the EU but also beyond. Still, for initial education as well as higher education emphasis is placed on cooperation between institutions in the border regions.

Although in the past internationalisation was a domain of higher education, through the Dutch policy in *Grenzen Verleggen* and European policy in Petra, Force, Lingua, Socrates and Leonardo da Vinci, it now meets all levels of education, the aim being to implement internationalisation in the regular curriculum. Sharing experiences in national networks can provide a more efficient organisation of internationalisation. Setting up national networks will be stimulated.

Despite all positive reactions and experiences, there are still obstacles to overcome. Dutch researchers and policy-makers at universities and governmental organisations need to have sufficient influence on the decision-making process in various international fora, otherwise they will miss getting an equal share of international financial resources. Only the strongest areas, research groups and institutions will survive the international selection processes. The crucial question is whether the Dutch academic infrastructure is solid enough to survive in this international arena. To achieve this, national expenditure for research and development must be secured as well as continuing concentration and collaboration in Dutch research projects encouraged.

Students suffer from the fact that they do not get automatically a residence permit to study abroad, young workers are confronted with a very difficult and non-transparent system of tax and national insurance contributions. Then there is the fact that students cannot take study grants with them, in spite of the fact that mobility is an expensive activity in itself. Practical problems can also become an obstacle, such as accommodation, lack of information and preparation for a stay abroad. A major problem to be solved is the mutual recognition of qualifications. The internal market with free movement of labour depends very much on the fact that there is an international system of recognition, such as the national reference structure. As far as it concerns staff and teacher exchange, there are the extra costs of replacement teaching time. Last but not least there is the fact that European application and project management procedures are very time consuming. In the new Dutch policy document *Onbegrensd Talent* these problems are recognised and actions are announced to minimise the difficulties.

The Dutch Ministry adopted the 1996 theme of Lifelong Learning and gave special attention to subjects such as 'Open and Distance Learning' and 'Information Technology Developments'.

During the first half of 1997, the Dutch government chaired the European Community. In this context the Ministry of Education, Culture and Science organised three major international conferences, respectively focused on internationalisation of the three levels of education: general education, initial and continuing vocational education, and higher education.

Three major issues are set out in the line of policy: to stimulate mobility; to increase the possibilities of distance education; and to improve the efficiency of cooperation in education through reduction of policy committees and obstacles to mobility. In that way the impact on the Dutch educational system will increase and the Netherlands can compete with educational systems in other EU member states.

Notes

1 Commission to the European Council, White Paper, *Completing the Internal Market*, Milan, 28–29 June 1985, Luxembourg: Office for Official Publications of the European Communities.
2 Published documents and memoranda of the Ministry of Education, Culture and Science include those published by the former Ministry of Education and Science.
3 In the Netherlands, agricultural education is the responsibility of the Ministry of Agriculture, Nature Management and Fisheries.
4 Free translation: 'Talent Unlimited'.
5 The case studies presented in this chapter are just an illustration, taken out of a list of good projects.
6 See 'Jaarverslag 1995 Europees Platform', Alkmaar.
7 See ibid.
8 Results of research executed by Clingendael Research Centre in 1996 showed that, among Dutch students in secondary education aged 12–18 years, (negative) prejudices against Germans are common.
9 A complete overview of developments in initial and continuing vocational education is given in A. Westerhuis and L. Hendriks, *Vocational Education in the Netherlands*, 'sHertogenbosch: Cinop, 1997.
10 Agricultural education is offered by AOCs (Agricultural Education Centres). AOCs are run under the authority of the Ministry of Agriculture, Nature Management and Fisheries and provide senior secondary cycle vocational training, apprenticeship training and pre-vocational education in agriculture and natural environment or in food technology and management.
11 European Commission, *Education, Training, Research: The Obstacles to Transnational*

Mobility, Green Paper, Luxembourg: Office for Official Publications of the European Communities, 1996.

12 Cinop, *European Curriculum Comparison*, 'sHertogenbosch: Cinop, 1995 (available in Dutch, English, German and French).

13 Evaluations of this programme can be found in: L. Hendriks and C. van der Stege, '*Over de grens van . . .*' *Europese stages en uitwisselingen in Petra 1a*, 'sHertogenbosch: Cinop, 1995; F. Meijers and M. Cox, *Petra-stages, betere kansen op de arbeidsmarkt?*, Bergen: Stichting Uitwisseling, 1994; L. Hendriks, *Petra in Holland: Effecten van een Europees actieprogramma voor het Middelbaar Beroepsonderwijs*, Amsterdam: Max Goote Instituut, 1997.

14 W.J. de Jong, R. van Seters, A. van Dongen, *Eindrapportage 1995/1996. Stimulerings-programma's Internationalisering BE: GROS, SESAM, PLATO*, 'sHertogenbosch: Cinop, 1996.

15 *Jaarrapportage 1 mei 1996 – 1 mei 1997*, NCU Leonardo da Vinci Nederland.

16 Koninklijke Nederlandse Akademie van wetenschappen, *De Academie en de wereld*, KNAW, 1995, pp. 13–14.

17 ibid., pp. 8–9.

18 Sylvia G.M. van de Bunt Kokhuis, *Academic Pilgrims*, Tilburg: Tilburg University Press, 1996.

19 See *Rechtspositiereglement wetenschappelijk Onderwijs*, The Hague, 1987, pp. 94–5.

20 GENT-IV stands for the fourth agreement on cooperation of *Gehele Europese Nederlandse Taalgebied* (Complete European Dutch Speaking Language Region).

12 Portugal

Margarida Belard

The Comprehensive Law on the Education System

The Comprehensive Law on the Education System (*Lei de Bares do Sistema Educativo* – Law 46/86, 14 October 1986) was drawn up so as

> to contribute to preserving the national identity and strengthening loyalty to the historical background of Portugal by raising awareness of the Portuguese nation's cultural heritage within the framework of the universal European tradition and the increasing interdependence and essential solidarity between all nations of the world.
>
> (Article 3, paragraph a)

Article 3 goes on to emphasize (in paragraph d) 'ensuring the right to be different through respect for individual personalities and ambitions and consideration and appreciation for different learning and cultures'. In the terms of Article 7, paragraph f, regarding the objectives of basic education, it is necessary 'to develop national awareness in the context of universalist humanism and international solidarity and cooperation'. Article 9, paragraph d, highlights the imperative of educating young people interested in solving their country's problems while aware of those of the international community, 'on the basis of the realities of regional and national life and respect for the permanent values of society in general and Portuguese culture in particular'.

In accordance with the principles laid down in this law, the preservation of national identity and 'loyalty to the historic background of Portugal . . . the solidarity between all nations of the world' is commended, and the 'European universalist tradition' evoked along with the 'enhancement of international cooperation'.

The Comprehensive Law, passed in 1986 after a large-scale public debate, provides the framework for the reform of the educational system and the curricula of basic and secondary education. In its preamble it sets out that:

> The curricular structure now adopted endeavours to fulfil the complex requirements that our education system must satisfy both at national and

international levels. This is in order to draw up the project of a society which, while preserving national identity, assumes the responsibility of meeting the challenge of modernization raised by our joining the European Community.

The two four-year PRODEP programmes of educational development for Portugal (*Programa de Desenvolvimento da Educação em Portugal*) of 1989–93 and 1994–9 designed to achieve a more effective integration of Portugal into the European Community recommend a systematic and recurrent investment of substantial sums of money in the education sector with a view to catching up with the achievements of other European countries. The analysis of the situation as presented in PRODEP reveals that 'Portugal is a country where the regional asymmetries are striking', especially in comparison with the situation in other European Community member states.

Following the analysis of the current situation, the PRODEP document further states that the essential target to be pursued is building an educational system to meet the challenge of European integration at the end of the second millennium:

- access to education made widely available in order to bring Portugal's school attendance rates closer to those in the European Community, balancing regional asymmetries and correcting the non-functional discrepancies between technical, vocational and academic education;
- educational substructures to be modernized to ensure reaching an educational standard suitable for the needs of the human, democratic and technological development of the country;
- the quality of educational provision to be improved in order to create an efficient school system to deliver success.

This programme will require massive investment in education for building a solid foundation of values, knowledge and attitudes.

Organization of the education system

The entire system is organized in three different subsystems:

- pre-school education, which is complementary and supplementary to education in the family and in close cooperation with it;
- school education, which includes basic, secondary and higher education, encompassing special education and including structured leisure time activities;
- education off regular school premises, which takes place in the open space of multiple formal and informal activities, its objective being to complement previous school education or to compensate for its gaps and shortcomings.

Pre-school education

In 1997 a new law was ratified: Law 5/97 on Pre-school Education of 10 February 1997 declares this phase of education to be the first stage of basic education, incorporating the participating role of the family as well as the strategies to be developed by the government, local authorities and private institutions of a cooperative and social character. Pre-school education is optional for children between age three and the age of entry to basic school, recognizing that it is for the family, by natural and constitutional right, to play an essential role in the process of pre-school education and upbringing.

School and tertiary-level education

This unfolds at three levels, each with its own objectives, priorities and organizational characteristics:

- the first level: nine years of basic education, which is universal, compulsory and free for all children between the ages of 6 and 15;
- the second level: three years of secondary, non-compulsory education for pupils between the ages of 15 and 17 in possesion of a certificate of completion of basic education;
- the third level: higher education, either at university or polytechnic, for students with a secondary school certificate or an equivalent qualification, or for people over the age of 25 without that qualification who have succeeded in a special test.

Higher education students are aged between 18 and 25 years. The length of higher education courses depends on what academic degree they lead to. The bachelor degree obtained in a polytechnic requires three years and a university degree between four and six years of full-time study.

Basic education consists of three stages:

- the first stage (*1° ciclo*) – four years of school education – is a general education provided by one single teacher sometimes supported by another for specific areas of the curriculum;
- the second stage (*2° ciclo*) – two years of school education – is organized in multidisciplinary areas of basic education with one or more teachers responsible for each;
- the third stage (*3° ciclo*) – three years of school education – is organized in a wide range of common subjects for all, with several integrated vocational areas with one teacher responsible for each subject or group of subjects.

Secondary education encompasses the tenth, eleventh and twelfth years of schooling and in the regular system of education it is made up of a number of courses with different curricular organization depending on whether it prepares pupils for working life – technological courses – or for further and tertiary education – advanced general education courses.

Higher education comprises university and polytechnic study. The former ensures a good scientific and academic preparation together with the technical experience necessary for future professional careers and profiting from the cultural activities available, and develops the skills of inquiry, innovation and critical analysis. The latter aims at providing a good general as well as specialist technological education developing innovation and critical analysis skills. Both impart theoretical and practical scientific knowledge necessary for careers in the scientific and engineering professions, though not exclusively in these.

The curriculum

The options available through the curricular organization of basic and secondary education arise from the following five general aims:

- Increased importance given to the teaching and learning of the Portuguese language.
- Emphasis given to pupils' personal and social development. This is intended to ensure young people's civic and moral development through the curricular area of personal and social training. Besides getting support in all school-based subjects and in extra-curricular activities, the so-called School Area (*Area-escola*) and other complementary components of the curriculum, it also includes the topic of personal and social development as an alternative to the subject of moral and religious education, either Catholic or that of other religions.
- Adoption of an interdisciplinary integrating approach. This emphasizes the integration of knowledge and skills acquired in each subject, as opposed to the traditional separation that had been the practice in delivering curricula in the past.
- Inclusion of complementary curricular activities. These are mainly artistic and cultural options, the aim of which is to fill pupils' leisure time with creative, educational activities.
- Adoption of an evaluation system. With two models corresponding to the curricular differences between basic and secondary education, its objective is to use evaluation to promote the success of all pupils by stimulating their self-esteem and taking into consideration their different rhythms of development and progression.

The details of the main curricular innovations follow.

Transdisciplinary education

This ensures that, besides the objectives already mentioned, the basic and secondary education curriculum includes extra-curricular activities which address pupils' personal and social development in their upbringing and that there is provision for helping young people to improve their command of their mother tongue.

All basic and secondary education syllabuses must make a systematic contribution to the aim of developing pupils' critical minds and promoting their spiritual, aesthetic, moral and civic values. To this purpose there is provision of a subject-free curricular area, specially orientated towards enabling pupils' general maturity by instilling specific attitudes and competences by means of integrating the teaching results of the other subjects of the curriculum and applying them in fostering pupils' personal and social education.

Area-escola (School Area)

Area-escola is a compulsory curricular area, not a school subject, taught during the several years of basic and secondary schooling. Its aim is to make full use of all the knowledge and skills acquired at school through encouraging the use of interdisciplinary activities, such as linking the school with its environment as well as pupils' personal and social education. This requires devising projects that involve pupils as well as teachers and other members of the school community, namely parents, those responsible for the pupils' receiving an education and representatives of the local authorities and of the social, cultural, scientific and professional interests of the area. Projects are expected to address the common objectives of all the subjects or subject areas of the curriculum, drawing on their methods and merging with their syllabus contents and applying them to undertake tasks which are relevant in the community.

The School Area is an important component given over to the curricular implementation of the programmes constructed and providing guidance to pupils' educational activities. School Areas are expected to be sufficiently varied so as to be a concrete expression of the schools' pedagogical autonomy.

Complementary curricular activities

These aim at making a substantial contribution to promoting pupils' personal fulfilment as well as their readiness to be members of their community, achieved through the development of their personality and character and the acquisition of citizenship skills. A balanced physical growth is an integral part of the programme. Complementary activities are non-curricular activities organized at national, regional or local levels, focused directly on cultural and civic development, physical education and sports, artistic education and working for the integration of pupils in the community. As they are activities aiming at creative and educational pursuits during pupils' leisure time, the activities are optional and carried out outside school time.

Education other than compulsory regular schooling

This covers such activities as special education, vocational education, adults' recurrent education, distance teaching and Portuguese teaching abroad:

- Special education seeks to adapt teaching conditions for those pupils whose learning needs in the basic and secondary state schools require individual attention.
- Vocational education aims at a dynamic integration into the working world by providing professional knowledge and skills. This education lasts three years and is offered by vocational schools attended by young pupils who have completed the third stage of basic education and prefer this alternative type of preparation to the regular general education system. Measures have been taken to boost vocational training by improving vocational schools and rearranging existing funding methods.
- Adults' recurrent education is part of a scheme to enable men and women past normal school age to obtain education at levels they may require. Recurrent education can be attended by people over the ages of 15 and 18 at basic and secondary education stages.
- Distance teaching consists of approaches, methods and technologies to provide tuition which does not require attendance in person because of its use of written media teaching materials and regular exchanges of written information between the students and the agency responsible for the teaching. It is used mainly in recurrent education, also in both in-service postgraduate training and in-service initial training of teachers as well as education offered outside school. The main institution responsible for distance teaching is the Open University.
- There is also another subsystem, alternative to the regular second stage of basic school education which uses new information technology in geo-graphically remote, sparsely populated areas without a network of state and private schools to bring education to the people.

Education outside the school is part of a concept of permanent education and continuous training enabling people to extend their knowledge and potential, complementary to school education or remedial of the gaps and omissions caused by the lack of it, comprising in particular: teaching adults basic literacy; organizing activities of professional retraining or improvement; developing technological skills and technical know-how; and promoting creative free time activities:

- Teaching of Portuguese abroad aims at promoting the study of the Portuguese language and culture on an intercultural basis through several actions and means, including introducing its study in the curricula of the upper (third) stage of basic and secondary education in other countries.
- Artistic education: steps are being taken towards closer cooperation of the

departments of culture and education that may invigorate general and specialized artistic education.
- Initial professional education of youth: the definition of an integrated policy on young people's initial professional education is being undertaken.

The structure, means and locations enabling non-school education are several but it is central government that is mainly responsible for support and initiative as well as supervision of this sector.

Progress achieved with the Comprehensive Law

Much has been achieved to secure implementation of the aims of the Comprehensive Law of the Education System in Portugal, in particular including:

- development of a national network of state pre-school education;
- restructuring and organizing basic and secondary education;
- revising curricula;
- reinforcing and diversifying technological and vocational education.

This has been matched by improving teachers' professional preparation and their working conditions referred to later. An important feature has been the transfer of some responsibilities at the levels of pre-school and basic education to the local authorities as part of a policy to decentralize the administration of the entire education system. This involves restructuring the organization and management of the basic and secondary schools and some of their teaching activities, as mentioned.

European links between schools and teachers

Exchanges between Portuguese schools and teachers and their European counterparts take place either through direct personal contacts or by means of bilateral and multilateral programmes. They also occur on the basis of programmes and projects of international organizations, especially those fostered by the European Union, the Council of Europe and UNESCO.

In the European Union Arion (for educational fact-finding visits and research), TEX (Teacher Exchange Schemes) and Erasmus, currently Socrates study and exchange programme, have made a significant contribution to European collaboration. Projects and activities organized by the Council of Europe, as well as the cooperation CDCC scholarship system for practising teachers and in-service teachers' training programmes have been helpful. The exchanges which have been taking place and the participation of teachers and experts of the Ministry of Education in seminars and international conferences could not but help adjust the Portuguese reality to a number of European models through study and analysis.

The European Dimension in Education programme, as organized in Portugal, was essential in raising a sense of European awareness by means of the creation of the so-called European Clubs (*Clubes Europeus*) and by intensifying links and exchanges between schools and teachers. This programme has now been integrated in a new structure created in the Ministry of Education: the Coordinating Unit of European Clubs (*Unidade de Coordenação dos Clubes Europeus*).

Clubs Europeus: *European Clubs*

An interdisciplinary project complemented by out-of-school activities is a collective undertaking. Whether it relates to an educational exchange, the organisation of a sporting or theatrical event, editing a newspaper or mounting an exhibition, teachers, pupils, and parents as a whole are involved in it. Some projects may attract participation from other interest groups both close to and far from the school.

The establishment of European Clubs in Portugal is a good example of this. They meet outside school hours and permit all those participating in the life of the school to take part and become involved in a project which obviously affects everyone in the local community. Interaction is gradually established between classwork and the peripheral activities organised in the club. The existing borderlines between the various activities become blurred, giving way quite naturally to group work on a common project.[1]

To introduce the European dimension into the schools, Portugal chose in 1986 a distinctive way: the European Clubs, aimed at encouraging the development of a European awareness. The European Clubs are centres set up by teachers and pupils or older students, free to plan their own activities which are designed to enhance the European dimension in education within the general activities of the school. Membership is voluntary. In basic schools they are wholly integrated into the curricular activities; at secondary level the Clubs' series of activities considered appropriate are discussed in school planning committees and incorporated in relevant projects. Programmes are mostly inter- and multidisciplinary, being developed in a variety of contexts according to the approach adopted by the Club's coordinator. They appeal to the creative sense of teachers, pupils and students as well as parents and are an important tool for the creation of a European presence in school life and for the development of the responsibilities of European citizenship.

The aims and objectives of European Clubs are stated as follows:

1 to instil a truly European spirit, to be disseminated among all members of the community as Europeans;
2 to promote, with the support of competent institutions, activities that may provide better information about:

(a) Europe, its geographical, historical, cultural, economic and other features;
(b) European institutions, their aims, structure and functions;
(c) member states of the European Union and of the Council of Europe, raising an awareness of European politics and European social and cultural life;
(d) European heritage, nature as well as culture;
(e) European issues that must be faced by contemporary Europeans together with an understanding of the objectives of European integration and the role of Europe in the world;

3   to contribute towards a comprehension of pluralism – similarities and differences;
4   to contribute towards mutual understanding and tolerance;
5   to promote awareness of European global interdependence and the steps required for cooperation;
6   to imbue pupils and young people with a sense of responsibility as European citizens, especially with regard to peace, human rights and the preservation of the natural environment and the cultural heritage; and, while giving people a greater sense of their national identity, to cultivate a sense of European identity.

How keen are young Portuguese on Europe?

From the activities organized by the European Clubs in schools excellent outcomes have been identified as regards the interest of young Portuguese in European matters. Over 600 European Clubs exist at present in schools at all levels – from primary (basic) to the end of secondary – and some are even being set up in nursery schools. The idea is that the sooner children start learning about Europe the easier it is to build on what has been learned during the earlier years of schooling so as to achieve a European objective which is of the utmost necessity for achieving a united Europe.

The different activities promoted by the clubs according to the age group of the children, the involvement of hundreds of teachers and pupils in the planned tasks, the impact on the families and on whole neighbourhoods, indicate a movement which has been spreading in Portugal since 1987 with gratifying results. Awareness of the impact that the different structures of a united Europe may have on everyone – individual, local, regional, national and worldwide – will only be achieved through direct contact of the young with all aspects of Europe, be they geographic, cultural or political.

The fundamental aim, which is to educate pupils for Europe, can be achieved by working for the creation of a new mentality, new attitudes, different approaches and perspectives, not confined to the Europe of the fifteen. This involves the European Clubs in the following main tasks:

- the dissemination of values, such as solidarity and respect for differences and for human rights;

- the search for the common roots of all European peoples while getting acquainted with the role of Europe in the world;
- the preparation of the young for life in a democratic society;
- teaching youth how to live in communities – such as schools, be they local, national and international;
- and how to take decisions by consensus and to cooperate in working life.

The following are some of the tasks undertaken in the European Clubs to carry out their objectives, grouped into three activity areas:

1   developing group and project work;
2   collecting documentation and updating information:
    (a) researching and using documentation;
    (b) exchanging information and documentation among national clubs and other member states' clubs or schools;
    (c) sharing information about and participating in activities which may contribute to the introduction of the European dimension in education, particularly 'Europe at School';
3   organizing meetings, colloquia, conferences attended by students, teachers, parents, and members of the local community:
    (a) organizing and participating in cultural activities, competitions and exhibitions for the purpose of improving knowledge of European realities;
    (b) organizing 'Europe Week' and 'Member States Week' events, dedicated to member states of the European Union and the Council of Europe;
    (c) organizing visits to European Clubs or schools in Portugal or in the other member states of the Union.

Each European Club may make its own regulations provided that they fit into this general conception. Each Club may also devise its own badge as well as its own motto.

The Coordinating Unit of European Clubs has developed a specific programme that involves, among others, the following activities:

- support for the setting up of European Clubs in Portuguese schools;
- orientation and coordination of the International Network of European Clubs and the organization of 'Europe at School' activities;
- launching of or participation in projects with the aim of enhancing the European dimension in education;
- production of suitable teaching materials and the diffusion of information and documentation;
- training teachers responsible for European Clubs, who will act as multipliers in their respective schools;
- motivation of teachers, pupils and students, parents, authorities, and the local community.

Special emphasis has been given to putting into practice measures envisaged in the Resolutions and Recommendations on the European Dimension in Education drawn up by both the European Community and the Council of Europe, and by the Portuguese National Council of Education which advises the Minister (Recommendation no. 2/92 on the European Dimension of Education).

The International Network of European Clubs

The Portuguese initiative has found interest in many countries, in 17 of which European Clubs have been established. They are Austria, Belgium, Bulgaria, France, Germany, Hungary, Ireland, Italy, Lithuania, Luxembourg, Netherlands, Norway, Poland, Spain, Sweden, the United Kingdom, and Portugal acting as coordinator of the Network. Over 1,000 European Clubs exist in Portugal and Poland alone.

The Network aims at promoting an ever-increasing commitment from all concerned to allow the European Clubs to achieve their objectives by means of joint projects involving exchange of experiences in the production of teaching materials; and strategies making the schools more dynamic in their European approaches through developing sub-networks in the different countries and training teachers for working with the Clubs.

The Portuguese Recommendation on the European Dimension of Education

> What we should keep in mind is a continental Europe, a source of influences yet ready in turn to accept contributions from other civilizations and cultures. The fact is that the European citizen should not be looked upon as just a participant in a uniform Europe but as a subject of a heterogeneous history where different influences are brought together – thereby implying the existence of a pluralistic community of shared destinies and values. That complex reality characterized by diversity and based on pluralism has undoubtedly far reaching effects on the organization of education systems and the daily life of schools.

Recommendation no. 2/92 of the Portuguese National Council of Education on the 'European Dimension of Education', from which the above extract has been taken, is unique in the European Union for its explicitness of aims and the specificity of its educational objectives. It is a fundamental text, stressing the important fact of 'how to be European at the beginning of the twenty-first century'. This encourages the pursuit in education of such topics as:

- multilingualism and multiculturalism: identities and diversities in a Europe of cultures;
- past and present – perspectives of European history;
- dialogue of civilizations versus Eurocentrism;

- science as culture – the encounter of different branches of knowledge;
- ethics and values – 'between happiness and justice';
- mobility: free circulation and communication;
- European citizenship and education;

which can be discussed within the context of most school subjects, but especially so in the social sciences and the arts.

Europa na Escola: *Europe at School*

'Europe at School' is a competitive activity sponsored jointly by the Council of Europe, the European Commission, the European Parliament and the European Cultural Foundation, designed to promote the European dimension in education. It aims at arousing the interest of the young, particularly as regards those aspects which will enable them to live and work comfortably in the European Union, bearing in mind the unity and diversity of the European cultural heritage and present-day European reality examined with the need for productive cooperation between European countries, the challenges facing contemporary Europe arising from the role and responsibility of Europe in an interdependent world, and the involvement of all Europeans in the processes.

The competition fulfils its objectives through organizing an annual contest of artistic and literary productions, specific programmes about European education, seminars for teachers and international gatherings of competition prizewinners. The subjects proposed are generally wide-ranging issues of international impact that might illustrate the European component of the questions raised. At the same time, basic knowledge of the functions and structures of the European institutions are expected of all participants.

The gatherings are an excellent opportunity for raising young people's awareness of studying, living and working in the cultural unity and simultaneous diversity of the European countries. Ten gatherings have already been held in Portugal, organized by the Portuguese committee.

The suggested type and themes of gatherings, workshops and guided visits or debates on important European matters are subject to common general guidelines which accord with the objectives of 'Europe at School'. Results have confirmed the great interest activated. In fact, the multicultural meetings establish links of friendship and solidarity between the participants, and favour contacts between cultures and peoples different but united by common interests and affinities. They provide a convenient opportunity for exchanging impressions and views on important themes and problems of Europe: a relevant contribution to the creation of a true European spirit.

Higher education

The right to higher education enshrined in the Constitution of the Portuguese Republic is laid down in the Comprehensive Law on the Education System, Head

4, Article 12: 'The State must establish the conditions which guarantee citizens the opportunity of access to higher education so as to lessen the discriminatory effects arising from economic and regional social disadvantages.'

The immediate socio-educational objectives arising tend to aim at:

- balancing out the existing disparities in the distribution of students in regional institutions by taking into account the density of the young population in each district;
- promoting short-cycle polytechnic education geared to working life but guaranteeing permeability between courses both with regard to field of study and level of training so as to leave open the possibility of further study;
- changing the access to higher education so as to establish a more efficient and fairer system to be applied in higher education in general: university (state and private) and polytechnic education.

University education

University education is designed to ensure a sound scientific and cultural background and also to provide the necessary specialist education equipping people to carry out and administer professional and educational activities at the highest level of expertise, furthering the development of comprehensive innovation and critical analysis.

Portuguese universities award the following degrees:

- first degree (*licenciatura*): four-, five- or six-year courses;
- master's degree (*mestrado*): for postgraduates (two-year courses and a thesis);
- doctor's degree (*doutoramento*): for postgraduates, requiring the submission of high level, original scientific work.

Universities enjoy scientific, pedagogical, administrative, financial and disciplinary autonomy. The growth of university education is part of a policy of diversifying higher education intent on promoting the development of the regions where the new universities are located.

Polytechnic education

Polytechnic education is designed to provide a sound tertiary-level general and technological education and to develop a capacity for innovation and critical analysis as well as to impart theoretical scientific knowledge and practical expertise qualifying for taking up professional activities. In polytechnic education the title *bacharel* (bachelor) is awarded as a first degree after specialized training and study lasting three years. However, if the student so wishes, he or she may apply for entry to university courses after obtaining an equivalent certificate to continue their studies in greater depth.

The polytechnic institutions network includes colleges specializing in a professional education with teacher training colleges, higher schools of technology and agriculture, and colleges of arts and engineering. In addition there are also accountancy and administration and business studies institutes.

Expansion of higher education

The present growth of university, polytechnic and other tertiary-level education is also evident in the private and cooperative higher education sector. The Portuguese Catholic University was created in 1971 within the framework of the Concordat between Portugal and the Vatican. The diversification of university education through the setting up of new courses in universities, as well as polytechnics, has brought about a significant increase of student rolls. With regard to the postgraduate master's degree courses, a remarkable increase is likewise worth mentioning. Social assistance is available to students, especially the provision of accommodation in halls of residence free of charge or at reduced rates.

Teacher preparation

Initial training

The average length of an initial training course for teachers is four years including at least one year's practical teaching and professional study. Courses are organized as follows:

- the training of all pre-school educators and teachers of the first, second and third stage of basic education takes place at a higher education level teacher training college or at university;
- teachers for secondary education are trained at university;
- the training of pre-school and kindergarten instructors is carried out in higher education colleges and lasts three years.

In-service training

Pre-school kindergarten as well as basic and secondary education teachers are entitled to in-service training regarded not only as a means to improve their teaching quality but also as a means of their career advancement.

Institutions responsible for training

The higher education institutions providing teacher training are those concerned with educational and specialized pedagogical sciences. The school partners involved are training centres set up by school consortia. In addition teachers' professional associations and both central and local administration authorities and various interest groups maintain training centres especially for the in-service training sector.

With the main objective of promoting a concept of in-service training that may help the integration of teachers in their own schools and educational catchment areas and thus to contribute to improving teaching quality and expediting pupils' learning in given areas, the rules of the system called FOCO (*Formação Continua de Professores e Responsaveis pela Administração Escolar*: In-service training of teachers and those responsible for school administration) within the scope of Measure 2 of the PRODEP (*Programa de Desenvolvimento Educativo para Portugal*: Programme of Educational Development for Portugal) were changed. The emphasis is now on:

- defining teachers' careers and access to posts – promotion to higher posts;
- teachers' salary increases;
- new in-service training programmes for teachers.

In particular, the development of a national network of state pre-school education has involved a substantial increase in the number of suitably trained teachers required to teach in the pre-schools, entailing a new evaluation system for kindergarten, basic and secondary education teachers and changes in the qualifications necessary for admission to the different professional categories of teachers working in basic and secondary schools.

Training in the European dimension in education

The concern with European awareness among the young is another factor affecting teacher supply and training. Clearly the large-scale mobilization and training actions involving a large number of schools (from basic to end of secondary education) and teachers responsible for initial teacher training affecting their professions could not be achieved all at once and has led to local shortages.

A decision was made some 13 years ago to organize seminars designed to motivate teachers and Ministry of Education officials for European awareness. The Centre for European Education provided back-up, and occasionally foreign specialists could be found who worked with national educationists on international projects and were willing to collaborate to spread awareness throughout the system. At the same time, an information campaign was launched in the schools aided by the Information Bureau of the Commission of the European Communities in Lisbon.

The training action has been considerably reinforced, and is now carried out by means of training seminars organized by the Coordinating Unit of European Clubs of the Ministry of Education for all teachers with responsibility for the European Clubs. This action has proved eminently successful.

Language teaching

The growing interest in the acquisition of language skills in Portugal has prompted changes in provision of language education. It is possible to start learning (or teaching) a first foreign language in the first stage (*ciclo*) of basic education. In the second stage a foreign language is compulsory. A second foreign language is not compulsory in the third stage, but all schools are due to offer it as an option. Furthermore, all pupils who choose to proceed to secondary education must learn a second language if they have not studied it in one of the previous stages. Oral and recreational methods in the early basic education years have been introduced. The most popular foreign language now is English, followed by French and German. Language teaching is a particular priority of the European dimension.

Inspection and administration of education

General inspection of education

Inspection is carried out on a regular basis at local, regional and national levels of education. The legal basis for the responsibilities of the system of general inspection of education was changed to achieve a better definition of its duties, and to enable the creation of an appropriate structure of the system and suitable training of high status personnel adequately prepared to undertake their inspection activities. The reorganization emphasizes the role of observation and the competencies necessary for a department that controls the quality of education. The education of immigrant workers' children is subject to the same rigorous inspection as that of native children.

Administration

The administration of the education system is ensured at four levels, ranging from central government policies down to local practice. Central government is responsible for designing, planning and setting up standards for the entire education system, the overall coordination and evaluation of education policy and the curriculum to be implemented. A separate central responsibility operates in the autonomous regions of the Azores and Madeira, which have their own governments and may pursue their own educational policies suited to their own needs. Regional, that is second-level responsibility in Continental Portugal, operates in the five regional directorates of education: North, Centre, Lisbon, Alentejo and Algarve. The decentralized structures are responsible for the more detailed coordination, support and management of the human as well as financial and material resources at their disposal.

The regional directorates of education deal with four areas: management of the teaching and non-teaching staffs; administration of school welfare services; counselling and pedagogic support; and educational equipment.

The local, third tier is taken to mean that the municipalities have a specific responsibility at this level. The competences which are already theirs are being extended and reinforced, namely in matters affecting school transport, school maintenance, provision of educational equipment and the administration of school subsidies. This is part of government policy for more devolvement.

Towards increased local responsibility

A number of administrative procedures have been changed to provide increased local responsibility. They include support for individual school projects enabling schools to organize their own alternative curricular activities, setting up educational zones as priority action areas where different stage schools can link up in consortia in order to develop a common educational project. A new regime of autonomy and management of basic and secondary schools which will result in schools acquiring their own administration and management boards is currently the subject of public debate.

Future provision

Pacto Educativo para o Futuro: *The Education Pact for the Future*

The negotiation of an educational pact currently being conducted is one of the steps considered essential by government for its improvement of education programme. The Education Pact for the Future was presented in May 1996 and its guidelines and options have been the theme of wide debate carried out at local level looking into the problems of decentralization and the subject for negotiations and agreement among all the parties involved in the education process. The objectives of the Pact for the Future are targeted in particular at:

- the involvement of parents;
- the improvement of the image and role of the school;
- the development, autonomy and responsibility of the schools;

constituting a debate in which the status and careers of teachers and other school staff and parental support for school activities are frequently invoked.

Several strategies, in which decentralizing trends can be recognized, are actively pursued, for example, promoting the participation of society in the development of the educational system, a process in which up-dating and reorganizing the administration of the educational system on a regional basis is an essential factor. There is active development of the means of strategic information and widening the communication network with a view to promoting education and training as a permanent life-long process. In order to enhance literacy, policies are actively being adopted regarding the use of books by professionals, for example for improving teaching methods and organizing wider reading activities by school pupils and the general public.

In the context of this global strategy, the Education Pact for the Future represents the government's commitment to eight points of action, indicative of its determination to improve the quality of education to meet the challenges of the future:

- to decentralize educational policies and to transfer some decisions to the local authorities, making the school the main area of policy;
- to set up a national network of pre-school education;
- to ensure education and training are permanent life-long processes;
- to ensure training for active life acknowledging the link between education and training for employment;
- to promote and enhance the role and status of teachers and educators;
- to ensure equality of the systems for funding education and social welfare;
- to secure a balanced development of higher education;
- to promote the image and the role of private and cooperative schools in the educational system.

The law of university autonomy, the increased provision of private, co-operative schools and the new building programme represent the government's commitment to education which is borne out by new construction, including sport centres, libraries and public reading networks, and the expansion of higher education and improving its facilities.

Conclusion

The Comprehensive Law on the Education System of 1986 was designed and is being implemented to help the Portuguese to feel at home in Europe while prepared to face the problems and challenges of European society in the future. The interest in new technologies and their development, not only as teaching aids but foremost as an area of educational specialization, ensures improved qualifications for forthcoming generations.

The development of European awareness among all school pupils and students, through European Clubs and European teacher training activities, makes it possible to predict that Portuguese citizens will become more European and at the same time more Portuguese – within the European Union.

These priorities bode well that the Portuguese education system will never be static. It has its own dynamic which will allow it to address the cultural and professional needs of the future along with other European states. Many of its own creative features will, it is hoped, make a contribution to European Union policies affecting education.

Note

1 Extract from Recommendation no. 2/92 on the European Dimension in Education, approved by the National Council of Education, Portugal.

Reference

Barthélémy, D., R. Ryba, C. Bîrzéa and Jean Michel Leclercq (1997) *The European Dimension in Secondary Education*, Strasbourg: Council of Europe Publishing.

Barreto, António (1996) *A Situação Social em Portugal, 1960–1995*, Lisbon: Instituto de Ciências Sociais da Universidade de Lisboa (statistics and comments on many social and cultural issues in Portugal between 1960 and 1995, including data on education).

Conselho Nacional de Educação (1998) *Educação: Memórias e Testemunhos*, Lisbon: Gradiva (with a preface by the current President of the Republic, a series of essays on education).

Delgado-Martins, Maria Raquel, Rocheta, Maria Isabel and Pereira, Dilia Ramos (1996) *Formar Professores de Português, Hoje*, Lisbon: Colibri (an anthology of texts about teachers of Portuguese language training; authors are linguists concerned with pedagogy).

Mattoso, José (1998) *A Identidade Nacional*, Lisbon: Fundação Mário Soares – Gradiva (a booklet about Portuguese national identity from origins to today).

Proença, Maria Cândida (1998) *O Sistema de Ensino em Portugal, Séculos XIX–XX*, Lisbon: Colibri (anthology of texts on Portuguese education).

13 Spain

Antonia Ruiz Esturla

Political and historical approaches to the education system

As in most European countries, the national education system in Spain is the outcome of a political and historical process which has its initial point of reference in eighteenth-century Europe. Three main phases are identified by historians of Spanish education: the liberal, the authoritarian and the democratic education systems.

The liberal education system

The Constitution of Cadiz (1812) can be considered the starting point of the liberal education system in Spain. Despite several difficulties and hold-ups the system was consolidated in the nineteenth century and its main features remained for quite a long time in the twentieth century.

In the eighteenth century in Europe, education was the Church's monopoly in each country, and only when the bourgeoisie arose with new expectations from education was this situation seriously questioned. While in France the bourgeoisie tried to replace the ecclesiastical monopoly with a system under the new national state, and in England it created its own network of schools to teach the new knowledge that its interests demanded, in Spain the bourgeoisie tried to create a national education system which co-existed with that of the Catholic Church.

This double network of schools in Spain was based, on the one hand, on the principle of freedom of teaching, which was accepted by the bourgeoisie, and, on the other, on the fact that the state tried to secularize education and at the same time to come to an agreement with tradition and the Church, recognizing the Catholic religion as the national religion. Mainly because the Church in Spain has been anti-liberal almost up to the present day, conflicts between Church and State lasted for a long time. The teaching of religion in the schools is still a clear example of disagreement between these two institutional powers in Spain.

The liberal education system was characterized by a centralized organization of provision and also by its uniformity; two principles which reinforced the liberal state. The institutional structure of the education system was formed by: a primary sector which only became compulsory in 1857 by virtue of the Moyano Law, although it was initially conceived as universal; a secondary sector; and a university sector. What happened in practical terms, as in other European countries, was that primary schools serviced a large number of people from the popular classes while secondary education and universities were reserved for the elites.

These features of the liberal education system remained entrenched in the Spanish education system until they were drastically interrupted by the Civil War of 1936–9.

The authoritarian education system

In the first post-war years the Church was in conflict with the state about control over education. After some years of struggle, the Church's position was enforced by the acceptance of a law, in 1945, of the principle of subsidiarity. The education system in the 1940s was characterized by the Church's monopoly in education, a rigid institutional structure, and by an extreme uniformity and centralization.

The 1950s were years of change in Spain, the beginning of economic liberalism, and also years of change in education. The state initiated a slow intervention in the education system which was accelerated in the 1960s to respond to the new demands from education that the years of economic growth required. The General Law of Education in 1970 (the *Educación General Básica* as it was called) favoured the process of secularization of education and reformed the traditional institutional structure with great benefits for basic education, which was extended from six to fourteen years, and was compulsory and free.

The democratic education system

The process of transition from an authoritarian regime to a democratic political system has produced dramatic changes in Spanish society. In the 1970s Spain initiated an overall process of modernization which affected all sectors of society. The ultimate aim of the Socialist Party (PSOE) when it came to power in 1982 was to modernize the country, a task which was politically linked to Spain's entry into the European Community in 1986. Spain has since been one of the most committed supporters of European integration and political and economic union.

In education this process of modernization has been activated so as to achieve the level of provision, freedom and autonomy already experienced by some other European systems.

Statutory provision

The Spanish Constitution provides the basic guidelines governing all legislation in the education sector. Article 27 guarantees the right to education as well as the cost-free and compulsory nature of basic education. The Constitution also stipulates the right to autonomy at local, regional and autonomous community levels. Other Articles of the Constitution contain basic rights related to education: equality (Article 14); freedom of teaching (Article 20 1.c); ideological and religious freedom (Article 16); the right to local cultural expression (Article 44); and human rights in general.

The right to education

The LODE (*Ley orgánica 8/1985 reguladora del derecho a la educación*: Right to Education Act) was the outcome of the need to put the general framework of Article 27 into a legal context. It excludes paragraph 10, which relates to university education.

The preliminary title of the LODE specifies the right of all Spaniards to a basic education. It includes a statement of the general aims of education together with the rights of teachers, pupils and parents as members of the school community, which comprises:

1 the freedom of teaching for teachers: this principle allows teachers to teach without the ideological, religious and political constraints which existed during the pre-democratic years;
2 the right of pupils to obtain an education that ensures the full development of their personality: they are given the right to an objective evaluation of their achievement; to respect for their personal convictions; to receive special assistance to compensate for family, economic or socio-cultural deprivation; to social protection if it is needed; and to the right of association;
3 the right of parents to obtain an education for their children; to choose a school; to obtain religious and moral education for their children; and to freedom of association.

State and private schools

In order to meet the social demand for education, the first fundamental proposition of the LODE is to create a combined network of state and grant-aided private schools. Private schools wishing to be funded by the state have to accept the freedom of ideology principle and to follow the other regulations of the state. Non-agreed private schools can enjoy total autonomy. A dual system of education is formed based on the 'freedom of teaching'. It is worthwhile to note that state schools represent approximately 72 per cent of pupils in Spain. The objective is to achieve a rational planning of resources and an agreed system of operation for all schools which are supported by the system.

This change is of great importance, particularly since it has taken place within the context of difficult relations between Church and state. The Catholic Church, as described above, has a long history of dominance in Spanish education. It was not until the 1979 state–Church agreements that the idea of an official religion was rejected and Spain was declared a pluralist society.

It must be emphasized that progress continues to be made, and relations are better than before as both sides are learning that the only way forward is through compromise. The present secular state system is no longer at variance with the systems of other European countries.

The schools in Spain can be classified in the following ways:

- *state schools* owned by the central administration, by the autonomous communities or by local councils;
- *private schools* owned by private institutions or individuals. These are further classified as grant-aided or non-grant-aided, according to whether or not they are state-maintained.

Both state and private schools can be classified by their level of teaching as follows:

- *Centros de educación infantil* (infant schools);
- *Centros de educación primaria* (primary schools);
- *Institutos de educación secundaria* (secondary schools).

There are other types of schools which teach music, drama and various artistic activities as well as languages.

Participation in education

The second fundamental proposition of the Constitution is that of participation: the essence of any democratic system. This was a controversial step at the time and revealed the socialist government's commitment to develop a democratic process in education. The law provides for the creation of a board of education at school, local, regional and national levels.

At school level, the *Consejo Escolar del Centro* (school board) is the body through which all members of the school community participate in the life of the school. This body is formed by representatives of teachers, parents, pupils (over 12 years old), non-teaching staff, and the local council of the catchment area, or the owner in the case of agreed private schools. The *Consejo* meets at least once each school term and is chaired by the head of the school, assisted by the secretary of the school.

The powers conferred by the law to the *Consejo* can be summarized as follows: to elect the head of the school as well as his or her team and to propose the head's resignation; to decide on pupil admission procedures and on disciplinary matters; to approve the school budget; and to approve and evaluate a general annual plan of school activities.

The other school governing body is the *Claustro*, which is made up of teaching staff. This has power over teaching programmes, the coordination of teaching activities, pupil evaluation and tutorials.

At national level, the *Consejo Escolar del Estado* (State Board of Education) coordinates all the sectors affected by general educational programming. It was created by the LODE and is regulated by Royal Decree 2378/1985. This national body comprises: the chairman (appointed by the Ministry of Education (MEC)); the deputy chairman (elected by board members); the secretary-general (appointed by the Ministry); and 80 board members allocated as follows: 20 teachers (12 from state schools and eight from private schools); 12 parents; eight pupils; four representatives from the administrative personnel of education; four private school owners; four state school representatives; eight senior representatives from the Ministry of Education (MEC), four representatives from universities; and 12 people of recognized prestige in the field of education who are appointed directly by the Secretary of State for Education.

As a consultative body the *Consejo Escolar del Estado* must be involved in issues relating to the general programming of education, to the basic norms and regulations of developing Article 27 of the Constitution, and to the regulation of the general education system. The *Consejo* has to approve and publicize an annual report on the state of the education system which is produced by its permanent commission. It also has to approve and deliver to the Ministry of Education proposals on the issues indicated above.

Other bodies of participation which have been created include: *El Consejo General de la Formación Profesional* (the General Council for Vocational Training). This is defined as a consultative body which serves to advise the government on issues relating to vocational education: *El Consejo de Universidades* (the University Council) arranges, coordinates, makes proposals and advises on issues relating to higher education.

The LODE also provides a board of education for each autonomous community. Other boards are created at district, provincial and local levels.

A decentralized education structure

Article 2 of the Constitution, later developed by Chapter III of Title VIII, states the right to autonomy at local, regional and autonomous community levels. Recognized and guaranteed by the Constitution, this right is regulated by the Statutes of Autonomy which serve to balance political influence in education as between the central state and the autonomous communities.

After almost two centuries of a centralized administrative system in Spain, the change represented by the introduction of the *Estado de las Autónomias* (state of autonomies) is considered a change of considerable historical importance. Moves to realign the political and administrative process in favour of the regions and nationalities which form the Spanish state have implied dramatic changes in the administrative system of education. This decentralized system has also affected the uniformity of education in Spain.

Under the mandates of the Constitution, the Spanish state is divided into 17 autonomous communities. Seven of them, Andalucia, the Basque Country, the Canary Islands, Catalonia, Galicia, Navarre and Valencia, have assumed full powers in education. Four of these communities, the Basque Country, Catalonia, Galicia and Valencia, have their own language which is co-official with Spanish (*castellano*).

Autonomous communities with full powers in education can regulate and administer education in all facets, levels and grades, forms and specializations, with no limits other than those which are reserved to the state. Those autonomous communities that have not assumed full powers, although they have their own education departments, are under the power of the Ministry of Education. These autonomies may come to assume equal powers in education in the future.

Under the provisions of the Constitution and according to the Statutes of Autonomy, the state has to ensure the 'basic unity' of education and guarantee equal conditions for all in the exercise of their rights. To guarantee this unity the state has power on those issues which are part of the *Reserva Competencial del Estado* (the state-reserved powers). The areas of education controlled by the central state are:

1   the power to regulate conditions to obtain, issue and homologate academic and professional degrees;
2   to promulgate the legal norms to develop Article 27 of the Constitution;
3   the general arrangement of the system of education;
4   the basic norms and minimum requirements for schools;
5   the power to regulate the basic teaching of Spanish language;
6   the higher inspectorate system;
7   student grant policy;
8   the ownership and administration of Spanish schools abroad;
9   international, bilateral and multilateral cooperation in the education sector.

Three mechanisms have been created to guarantee the required levels of cooperation and coordination between central, autonomous and local administrations: (a) the *Conferencia de Consejeros Titulares de Educación*, a body formed by the heads of the Departments of Education of each autonomous community and the Secretary for Education; (b) the Agreements of Cooperation through which it is attempted to clarify the mechanisms by which the shared areas of each administration are to be administered; (c) the Higher Inspectorate of the state, which is accountable for the implementation of all norms related to state powers in education.

While allowing for regions and communities to add their own characteristics, the basic provision of education should be of an equal minimum standard throughout the country.

Education reforms in progress

The current position of the education system in Spain is somewhat special. The *Ley General de Educación* (LGE: General Education Act) was passed in August 1970. It represented a great potential for developing those sectors that would overcome some of the shortcomings of the education system so that it could face the economic and social changes of Spain at that time. It would also guarantee that school curricula responded to truly scientific criteria. The model, however, emphasized a knowledge-orientated approach more engaged in the promotion of intellectual and cultural values than in the personal development of individuals and the values of diversity. Consequently, those pupils who did not adapt to the system were left in an underprivileged situation with little or no alternative. Soon after the implementation of the LGE some of its flaws became apparent and different institutions started to promote new areas of research and development that culminated in the new *Ley de Ordenación General del Sistema Educativo* (LOGSE), the General Structure of the Education System Act. The LOGSE came into force in 1992 and will replace some out-of-date aspects of the LGE by the year 2000. However, it seems necessary to explain here how both LGE and LOGSE systems work to fully understand the present education spectrum in Spain.

Ley General de Educación: *the old system*

The LGE established compulsory and free education for pupils between 6 and 14 years of age. This applied to both state and private schools. It also introduced pre-school education into the system for the first time. Although it was not compulsory, 100 per cent of 5–6-year-olds attend school. There was a noticeable difference in the quality of pre-school education between the various regions of the country.

Educación General Básica: *primary education*

Primary education (EGB) 'shall be compulsory, free and equal for all'. Compulsory education lasted from 6 to 14 years old. This level was divided into three stages:

1   *ciclo inicial* (6–8), years 1 and 2 (lower cycle);
2   *ciclo medio* (8–11), years 3, 4 and 5 (intermediate cycle);
3   *ciclo superior* (11–14), years 6, 7 and 8 (upper cycle).

Whilst offering many of the subjects available in other European countries, the Spanish primary school curriculum tended to be more academically orientated than most. The subjects studied included the following: official first language, mathematics, art, physical education, social sciences, natural sciences and religious or ethical studies (parents could choose between the two). The study of a foreign language as a compulsory subject was introduced in year 6, although many schools offered it before then.

The content was decided by the Ministry of Education in Madrid for the whole country. In the first two stages, work was organized around topics. The last stage concentrated more on specific subjects.

EGB was taught by qualified teachers with a diploma from an *Escuela Universitaria de Formación del Profesorado* (University Teacher Training School). The last stage, however, was usually delivered by teachers who had a university degree as well as the teaching diploma.

Pupils progressed from one year to the next following continuous assessment. At the end of each term a written statement about levels of achievement reached in the different subjects was issued to parents. Those pupils who did not achieve the required standards in June had to retake examinations in September. If at the end of the stage they failed more than two subjects they had to repeat the year.

At the end of year 8, successful candidates were awarded the title of *Graduado Escolar*, which enabled them to go on to study for the *Bachillerato* (academic secondary education). Those who did not obtain adequate grades were awarded a *Certificado de Escolaridad*. This qualification enabled pupils to study *Formación Profesional* (vocational training). In the academic year 1987–8, 76.8 per cent obtained the *Graduado Escolar*. This determined that 23.2 per cent of pupils only received the *Certificado de Escolaridad*, a percentage which was considered far too high. Moreover, the dual qualification system was socially divisive as it clearly placed vocational education as the inferior option.

EGB has now been replaced by the new system.

Enseñanzas Medias: *secondary education*

Secondary education in Spain was usually referred to as *Enseñanzas Medias* and it was probably the least satisfactory area. For the academic year 1997–8 the estimated number of pupils following this type of course was 904,145, which represented approximately 25 per cent of the total number of students in secondary level.

The LGE established two different kinds of non-compulsory secondary education:

- *Bachillerato Unificado y Polivalente* (BUP). This course caters for the most academically able pupils, who have the title of *Graduado Escolar*. It lasts three years and is followed by an additional one-year pre-university course, *Curso de Orientación Universitaria* (COU);
- *Formación Profesional* (FP). This vocational course mainly attracts those who do not qualify for BUP. It is divided into two stages: FP1, which is a two-year course; and FP2, which lasts for two or three years.

Bachillerato Unificado y Polivalente: *academic secondary education*

The purpose of the three years of *bachillerato* is to prepare pupils for higher education as well as for work induction. It has both a humanistic and a scientific approach with some vocational training. Although there is room for some specialization, the idea is that pupils should not specialize too soon.

The curriculum for BUP includes the following core subjects: sciences, history, geography, Spanish language and literature, foreign languages, mathematics, music, art, Latin, physical education, religious or ethical studies and philosophy. These subjects are covered over a period of one to three years. In 1978 the study of the language of the autonomous community was introduced as a compulsory subject. Since then, the vernacular languages (Basque, Catalan and Galician) have been replacing Spanish as the means of instruction in those autonomous communities in which they are official languages, and at present in many parts of Catalonia and the Balearic Islands, for example, it is no longer possible to follow BUP and COU in Spanish, although it can be studied as a subject.

In the third year, pupils can follow a science course which includes literature, as well as mathematics, natural sciences, physics and chemistry or they can opt for a more literary and humanistic course which includes literature, Latin and classical Greek. Technical-vocational studies include such subjects as computer studies, graphic design, photography, arts and crafts and home economics.

Students are assessed continuously by the individual teacher. As in EGB, reports are sent to the parents at least once a term. A specific mark is given for each subject. The LGE emphasizes the continuous nature of assessment, but with up to as many as 40 pupils per class, individual assessment is clearly very difficult in practice. In most cases, therefore, pupils have to be assessed by internal examinations throughout the year. It should be explained that there are no external examinations in Spain, the *Prueba de Acceso a la Universidad* (university entrance examination) being the only exception. Those who fail a given subject in June have a chance to retake it in September. If pupils fail more than two subjects, they are required to repeat the whole year. The number of *repetidores*, pupils who retake the year, is said to be higher in state schools. Some argue that this is so because the private sector unloads its weak pupils on to the public system.

Pupils who compete the three years successfully obtain the title of *Bachiller*, which enables them to enrol for COU or FP2.

Curso de Orientación Universitaria: *university orientation course*

This is intended as a transitional year, linking school and university. Since 1988–9 the following subjects have been offered: Spanish and the language of the autonomous community, foreign languages and philosophy. Additionally there are four different options; each consisting of two compulsory subjects and two others to be chosen from a choice of four (the percentage of students following each option for the academic year 1995–6 is indicated in brackets):

- Option A: science and technology (32.5 per cent);
- Option B: *Biosanitaria* (biological and health studies) (25.2 per cent);
- Option C: social sciences (28.3 per cent);
- Option D: languages and humanities (14.0 per cent).

Assessment follows the same pattern as in BUP. If pupils fail more than three subjects in September, they have to retake the whole year. Those who intend to enrol for a university course have to pass the *Pruba de Acceso a la Universidad* (university entrance examination), more commonly known as *Selectividad*. Although it is set independently by each university, the examination must comply with the regulations laid down for the whole country.

The COU is another particularly unsatisfactory element of secondary education. Intended to bridge the gap between school and university, the COU has not fulfilled its purpose. It offers few, if any, links with university and has come to be regarded as an extension of secondary school study.

Formación Profesional: *vocational education*

The *Formación Profesional* caters for those students who leave school at 14, with or without the title of *Graduado Escolar*. According to the LGE, it was intended to enable students to start working life as well as to continue their education.

The curriculum includes some academic studies taught by teachers with a university degree. It also includes technical subjects taught by qualified specialist instructors.

The common core subjects are Spanish and the language of the autonomous community, foreign languages, social sciences and religious or ethical studies. Among the areas of specialization are included business studies, farming, art and design, motor engineering, building studies, home economics, travel and tourism, child care, film technique, woodwork, metalwork, fishing, mining, fashion and design and dress-making, hairdressing and beauty treatment, leather work, electrical studies, electronics, nursing and auxiliary work, textiles, stained-glass work and pottery. According to the area of specialization, specific additional subjects are also studied. These include mathematics, physics and chemistry and natural sciences or information technology.

Students who finish the first two years successfully obtain the title of *Técnico Auxiliar* (technical assistant), which gives access to both BUP and FP2, with some extra qualifications needed for the former. Those who fail to achieve the grade obtain a *Certificado de Escolaridad* (school-leaving certificate).

There are two different approaches in FP2: the so-called *General*, a two-year course, and the *Especializada*, a three-year course. Students with the title of *Bachiller* or *Técnico Auxiliar* can enrol for this stage. The law also makes provision to include pupils who, for whatever reasons, do not qualify under the general criteriá. On the successful completion of FP2, the title of *Técnico Especialista* (qualified technician) is awarded. Pupils may then study COU or enrol at an *Escuela Universitaria* (university school).

There is a special programme of work experience for FP2 students. The main objectives are:

- to provide students with first-hand experience of working life;
- to make it easier for students to find a job after their training;
- to promote the exchange of information between FP schools and companies.

Schools and companies sign an agreement of collaboration. A tutor is then appointed and made responsible for the scheme of work. Both schools and companies receive financial support for as long as the agreement exists. A committee is set up at provincial and national level to evaluate the experience. Financing for this programme comes directly from the Ministry of Education and the European Social Fund.

However, vocational training is still seen as second best. The estimated figure of those doing FP for the academic year 1997–8 is 488,702 as opposed to 904,145 doing BUP and COU. As the BUP is not geared to meeting the needs of the economy, it is not surprising that FP has often been chosen by poorer families; when proposals for reform were announced, the FP sector expected to benefit.

Ley Orgánica de Ordenación General del Sistema Educativo: the new system

The flaws in the LGE system indicated a pressing need for educational reform. The structure and curriculum of education at the various levels needed to be reformed in order to reduce the high level of *fracaso escolar* (school failure). As the basis for the modernization of Spanish society, education had to respond to the requirements of the economy and the world of work. Spain had to adapt the system not only to the social values of a democratic Spain but also to the values of its European counterparts. The system had to provide equality of opportunity in every region in the country; the double qualification at the end of the EGB had to be modified to prevent social division; the secondary sector had to be adjusted to avoid discrepancy between the end of compulsory education at 14 and a minimum working age of 16.

The socialist government at the time recognized the need to reform several areas of the system, and years of experimentation and discussion followed before the LOGSE was passed in October 1990.

In the school year 1983–4, schools began experimenting with the *reforma*. The new curriculum was laid down in terms of general aims and particular objectives. Learner-centred approaches to teaching were introduced, with special emphasis being given to diversity and the process of assessment and evaluation. Teams of curriculum support teachers emerged and materials were designed to help teachers implement the new curriculum.

In 1987 the *Proyecto para la Reforma Educativa: Propuesta para Debate* (Project for the Reform of Education: Proposal for Debate) was presented. This was completed in 1988, with a detailed document on vocational training. For almost two years educational authorities, trade unions, professional groups, political parties, religious organizations and the various sectors of the educational community could present their views.

An overall consensus regarding the results of the experimentation was difficult to obtain. An important sector of teachers felt that the *reforma* was not reducing the level of *fracaso escolar*. Although the results in some FP institutions were encouraging, this was not the case in the more traditional academic BUP institutions.

Despite the controversy, the various contributions led to a much better understanding of the *reforma*. Discussions between the Ministry of Education and the education authorities of the autonomous communities took place to determine which aspects of the curriculum were to be controlled by the state and which by each autonomous community.

The structure and operation of the new system

The new system is structured in terms of levels, stages and grades:

1 *Educación infantil* (infant education) 0–6 years of age, in two stages of equal length, 0–3 and 3–6.
2 *Educación primaria* (primary education) 6–12 years of age, in three stages of equal length, 6–8, 8–10 and 10–12.
3 *Educación secundaria* (secondary education) 12–18 years of age, which includes:
    (a) *educación secundaria obligatoria* (compulsory secondary education), 12–16 years of age, in two stages, 12–14 and 14–16.
    (b) *educación secundaria post-obligatoria* (post-compulsory secondary education), 16–18 years of age, offering two possibilities: *Bachillerato* or *Formación Profesional de Grado Medio* (vocational training).
4 *Formación Profesional de Grado Superior* (higher vocational training).

The law also makes provision for distance learning, adult education and compensatory education. There is also scope for specialized teaching of music, dance, singing, drama and foreign languages.

Educación infantil: *infant education*

Infant education is voluntary, but education authorities have to ensure that there are enough places for those children who may require it. In the school year 1995–6, 61.2 per cent of all 3-year-olds attended school and 100.0 per cent of all 4- and 5-year-olds. State schools catered for 68.2 per cent of the total number of pupils.

Infant education is taught by qualified infant teachers, although in the first stage it may be delivered by qualified staff who do not necessarily have a teaching diploma. Its aims are to help children to get to know their own body; to establish contact with others; to acquire autonomy in their daily routine. Consequently, the curriculum for this level is organized around three main areas: personal identity; discovery of the physical and social environment; and communication.

The law also makes provision for *pre-escolar en casa* (pre-school at home) delivered by peripatetic teachers, intended to help families in remote areas. This addresses the question of equal opportunities and is aimed at providing a common standard of pre-school education in every region.

Educación primaria: *primary school*

This is the first level of compulsory free education. Its fundamental aim is to provide children with a common education that will enable them to acquire basic cultural elements as well as to increase useful independence within their personal context. There are attainment targets to be reached at the end of this level which are directly related to this general principle.

The curriculum is organized around the following areas:

1   knowledge of the cultural, social and physical environments;
2   Spanish language and the language of the autonomous community;
3   one foreign language, to be taught from the age of 8;
4   mathematics.

Emphasis is laid on an integrative and cross-curricular approach to teaching. There is a maximum of 25 pupils per class. Every school should have a specialist teacher for music, for physical education and for modern languages. This, however, is not always the case, especially in rural areas.

Pupils progress from one stage to the next following continuous assessment. Those who do not achieve the main attainment targets may remain in the same stage for an extra year.

Enseñanza secundaria: *secondary education*

Enseñanza secundaria obligatoria

Compulsory secondary education is from 12 to 16 years of age. This represents a radical change from the previous system. It takes on the last two years of EGB and the first two years of BUP or FP. Its purpose is to provide comprehensive education for all pupils in that age group regardless of ability, with a view to preparing them for the world of work or further study (*formación profesional específica de grado medio* or *bachillerato*). The general aims are not purely academic but geared to developing pupils' abilities to solve problems and to encourage positive social attitudes through cooperative learning.

The curriculum laid down in 1991 states the general aims and programmes of studies for each of the areas, as well as the assessment criteria. There is a *tronco común* (common core) of compulsory subjects: natural sciences, social sciences, history and geography, foreign languages, Spanish and the language of the autonomous community, mathematics, information technology, physical education and music. Each of these subjects has a minimum of contact hours per week, leaving some timetable room for the Minister of Education and the autonomous communities to introduce their own adjustments to the core.

There is limited specialization towards the end of the second stage, which offers pupils some choice. Educational authorities, for example, must ensure that, at least, classical studies and a second foreign language are offered in the school curriculum.

The maximum number of pupils per class is 30. Pupils may progress from one stage to the next following continuous assessment. Each school, in its curricular project, must lay down exactly the criteria for progression from one stage to the next, but it is always possible for a pupil to repeat the last year of each stage. The number of *repetidores* (pupils who remain in the same year) varies from school to school, and in some it can represent up to 20 per cent of the total number of pupils. This is worrying, since one of the aims of the new system was to reduce the so-called *fracaso escolar*. To face this problem the school must offer a diversified curriculum for pupils with learning difficulties. It must include at least three areas from the ordinary curriculum and it can be followed in one or two years, depending on the pupil.

All pupils, regardless of their marks, will receive a certificate from their school stating the number of years they have attended and their examination results. Those who successfully complete the last stage will obtain the certificate of *Graduado de Educación Secundaria*. This will enable them to go on to *Bachillerato* or *Formación Profesional Específica de Grado Medio*. Programmes of *garantia social* (youth training) are being launched to provide young people without this certificate with some basic vocational training.

Bachillerato

This is a two-year stage of education (16–18 years of age) and it constitutes a non-compulsory tier of secondary education open to pupils with the Secondary Education Graduate Certificate. Its purpose is to prepare them for higher education as well as for work. As from 1998–9, it will replace the last year of BUP and COU, although it is already being offered by some schools.

The LOGSE establishes a maximum number of 35 pupils per class and four different programmes of studies for *bachillerato* (the percentage of pupils following each one in the school year 1995–6 is shown in brackets): art (5.7 per cent), health and natural sciences (36.9 per cent), humanities and social sciences (43.5 per cent), and science and technology (13.9 per cent). The curriculum turns, first, on general requisites which address pupils' overall education and pursue the reinforcement of the value of *bachillerato* as the final stage in the educational process; second, on subject areas specific to each programme of studies; and third, on optional subjects intended to enhance pupils' understanding of the programme chosen. Core subjects, common to all programmes, are: Spanish language and literature and that of the autonomous community, one foreign language, history, philosophy and physical education. Languages are studied throughout the two years, physical education and philosophy in the first year and history in the second. Pupils have to study four or five other specific and optional subjects each year.

Pupils' assessment in the *bachillerato* is continuous and performed on a subject-by-subject basis against the aims and objectives and assessment criteria set by each educational authority. Grades are given on a scale of 1 to 10, with 5 or over being considered a pass grade. Academic standards for *bachillerato* stipulate that pupils who fail more than two subjects at the end of the first year have to retake the year's course entirely. Those with more than three fail grades in the second year must repeat that year's course entirely. Pupils who fail three subject areas or less need only repeat the subjects in which they have a fail grade.

Pupils who pass all subjects are awarded the *bachillerato* diploma, which specifies the programme of studies taken and the average grade obtained. This diploma enables them to enrol on advanced vocational training. Those wishing to enrol at university must pass a university entrance examination. Provisionally the examination set up is similar in structure to that for COU.

Formación profesional: *vocational training*

At present, apart from the FP1 and FP2 already referred to, there are experimental vocational modules, instituted as a result of the experimental reform in secondary education. All of these will be phased out by the new intermediate and advanced vocational training established under the LOGSE. The law draws a distinction between basic and specific vocational training. The former is intended to provide vocational training as a component within compulsory education. This represents a radical change from the old system. On the one hand, it adds a more practical approach to the most traditional subjects. On the other hand, it will make the transition from school to working life easier. This is also in accordance with the different programmes established by the European Union, which recommend closer contact between school and work.

Specific vocational training, in turn, is intended to prepare students for a given trade. It comprises a series of training stages leading to the award of intermediate and advanced training certificates. The occupational profile underlying each training stage is defined by experts in the vocation in conjunction with representative employers' organizations, trade unions and professional associations in the sector or industry concerned. In the school year 1995–6, 61.8 per cent of students were following courses related to the service sector, 34.7 per cent to the industrial sector, as opposed to 0.9 per cent following courses related to the building sector and 2.6 per cent to the primary sector.

Intermediate vocational training certificates attest to the skills required of a 'technician' and, from the standpoint of equivalence in Europe, constitute second-level training, backed by a certificate. Students with this certificate, or the diploma of *Bachiller*, may enrol for advanced vocational training.

Advanced vocational training diplomas attest to skills required of higher level technicians and, from the standpoint of equivalence in Europe, constitute third-level training, backed by a diploma.

As in any other LOGSE-regulated schooling, assessment is continuous. Promotion calls for a pass grade in all the modules comprising the training cycle in question. The person appointed by the educational establishment to supervise on-the-job training participates in assessing students' progress in that area.

Although both the technician's certificate and the diploma are primarily meant to mark the end of formal education and inclusion in the working world, they make it possible for students to be assessed in certain other kinds of studies provided that certain prerequisites are met.

Initial and in-service teacher training

The structure of initial training is the same nationwide, while the requirements differ depending on the educational level attempted. The LOGSE specifies the new degrees required to teach at non-university level while the LRU (*Ley de Reforma Universitaria*: University Reform Act) prescribes the ones needed to teach at university level.

Infant and primary education teachers must have a Teacher's Diploma, a first-cycle university degree obtained after three years of higher education. This diploma may be obtained for various kinds of specialization: infant education, primary education, foreign language, physical education, musical education, special education and speech therapy. The institutions responsible for providing this professional training are the teacher training university schools. A full university degree as well as teaching qualifications are required to teach at secondary level. In order to acquire the status of qualified teacher, prospective teachers must follow a 300-hour course which includes teaching practice in school. These courses are run by the *Institutos de Ciencias de la Educación* (ICEs), in conjunction with school departments.

Teachers wishing to work in state schools, regardless of level, take a competitive examination, known as *oposiciones*, which is set by the Ministry of Education or the autonomous communities. This grants the status of *funcionario* (civil servant) and gives security of tenure in the job. Mobility within the same autonomous community is relatively easy, but between different autonomous communities, especially one with its own vernacular language, a certificate of language competence may be required. Since 1993 Spanish nationality has no longer been a prerequisite to enter any of the competitive examinations set by the central and regional governments in order to acquire the status of qualified teacher in the public sector. This means, at least in theory, that any European Union national could stand as a candidate, providing that he/she has enough knowledge of the language to carry out the job. This system of selection, however, does not seem to attract significant numbers of foreign candidates and the natural trend appears to be that once someone has settled in the country, he/she might consider this option as a way of improving salary and working conditions. Private schools may, in principle, be a better alternative since no examination is required, especially for modern language teachers.

The LOGSE stipulates that continuing education is both a right and an obligation for all teaching staff, who are expected to update their scientific, educational or professional expertise from time to time. The 1995 *Ley Orgánica de la participación y el gobierno de los centros docentes* (LOPEGCE) urges education authorities to plan the necessary activities to make such training possible and available to teachers free of charge. Teachers may also apply for financial support to the Ministry of Education or the autonomous communities to follow the courses of their choice anywhere in Spain or abroad. The institutions recently involved in in-service training are teachers' centres as well as ICEs and professional associations of teachers.

Higher education

University education caters for 95 per cent of all students in higher education. The other 5 per cent is shared among other types of studies which are not delivered by universities but institutions with equivalent academic status (for example, military academies) or higher vocational or artistic training. During the Franco dictatorship the university was the centre of much anti-authoritarian feeling. In recent years, universities have been recognized as self-governing institutions, a major transformation from the extreme central control of previous years. The *Ley de Reforma Universitaria* 9/1983 (LRU: University Reform Act) recognized this right to autonomy at the same time as it created the University Council, a body responsible for the coordination, planning and advice on higher education matters. Its members include representatives from the Ministry of Education, regional authorities and vice-chancellors of all the universities.

Higher education is provided by university faculties, higher technical schools (HT), university schools and university institutes. Faculties, HT schools and university schools are responsible for the planning and organization of appropriate degree courses. University institutes are primarily devoted to scientific and technological research together with teacher training courses. University education is supplied by state or private institutions. At present there are 45 public universities and 10 private ones.

In order to qualify for a university place students must pass the *Prueba de Acceso a la Universidad* (university entrance examination), which is administered by each university for the students of its so-called 'district'. This examination is not required for university schools. Criteria for admittance are similar throughout the country. Universities give priority to students who have attended COU or the two-year stage of *bachillerato* in an educational establishment attached to the university they are applying for. In other words, priority is given to students from the university district and to those students who apply for courses which are not offered in their district. Students who pass the examination in June take preference over those who pass in September. Places are then awarded on the basis of such priorities and, for students assigned to the same priority bracket, on the basis of their grades in the university entrance examination and their average grade in *bachillerato* or BUP and COU. Universities reserve a certain number of places to meet specific needs such as foreign students from non-European Union member states (5 per cent), university graduates (5 per cent) and students from other districts (5 per cent).

Since the mid-1970s the number of students who have gained access to university has continued to rise. In the academic year 1975–6 there were 539,002 university students, compared to 1,505,611 in the academic year 1994–5, of whom over 52 per cent were women. The proportion of women varies from course to course and there are still some predominantly attended by women. In humanities and medical sciences two in three students are women; in technical courses, on the other hand, women represent only 23 per cent of the total number. This increase in numbers is indeed very encouraging; however, it has led to problems of overcrowding and high demand for specific courses. Consequently, only students who manage to obtain high grades in the entrance examination are able to enrol in the most popular courses. Each year more and more students are forced to follow their second or third choice of course. University fees range from the equivalent of £300 to £600 per year depending on the course. Science and technology degree courses tend to be more expensive. There is a system of grants and scholarships with allocation based on parental income and examination results.

University education is organized in cycles with specific educational objectives and separate academic accreditations. Its organizational model may be broken down as follows:

- *First cycle education* is vocational in nature, with no associated second cycle. It involves three academic years of study and a total of 180 to 270 credits, after which a diploma (*Diplomatura*) is awarded.
- *Dual cycle education* lasts for four or five years and studies are organized in two cycles but no degree or diploma is awarded after the first cycle; 300 to 450 credits are needed. A degree (*Licenciatura*) is awarded upon completion of the two cycles.
- *Dual cycle education with an intermediate degree* is structured in the same way as the previous one but a degree is awarded upon completion of the first cycle.
- *Second cycle education only* These are two-year courses, for which specific first-cycle studies or degrees are a prerequisite to admission.
- *Third cycle education* studies are intended for university graduates. A doctoral thesis must be completed after five years and part-time seminar attendance which normally runs for two years.

Credits are defined as units for evaluating student performance and correspond to ten hours of classroom attendance; they constitute a substantial change in the organization of this aspect of university training.

Universities enjoy full autonomy to design different curricula leading to any given official degree. The course content covered under each curriculum is grouped into subjects, some of which are core subjects, compulsory nationwide, some are defined by each university and may be optional or compulsory and some subjects are chosen freely by students from any kind of degree or even from other universities in Spain or abroad. This allows for study in languages other than Spanish.

The European dimension in education

It can be argued that a European dimension has always been present in the Spanish curricula in primary and secondary education. Spain has a traditional humanistic approach to education and has played a particularly important role in the history of Europe. Moreover, in subjects like history and geography, aspects of Europe and its history feature prominently.

Since joining the European Union, Spain has been keen to promote the European dimension in education. In line with Action 3 of the EC Resolution of 1988, the LOGSE has proposed including a European dimension as a cross-curricular theme. Other themes of this kind are co-education, health education, environmental education and education for peace.

Exchanges with schools and colleges in other European countries, together with teacher exchanges, are encouraged. Each year the Ministry of Education and the autonomous communities publish regulations for the funding of these exchanges.

A number of sets of material have been published by the Ministry which are intended to promote European awareness among young people. The most relevant are: *Europa sin Fronteras* (Europe without Frontiers), a set of 17 didactic games used in primary schools to explore Europe; *Cuadernos Educativos*, a multimedia pack of materials to incorporate the European dimension as a cross-curricular theme in secondary schools; and *Carpeta Europa* (European Folder), a folder on Europe for secondary schools. Similar materials have been published by the autonomous communities.

The European dimension in higher education

The European dimension is also incorporated into higher education. University students can take advantage of various programmes, such as the Erasmus scheme offered by the European Community to encourage scientific and cultural exchanges. Some private institutions offer combined degrees to enable students to spend half their academic time at another European university.

It is increasingly popular to enrol for MA courses, known as *Masters*. These courses are studied both in Spanish institutions and abroad. It is also possible to obtain a university degree by distance learning. This is done through the *Universidad Nacional de Educación a Distancia* (UNED: National University of Distance Learning).

Spain's universities are faced with the problem of overcrowding which has led to a shortage of resources. This problem of funding and shortage of resources is common in many European countries but is particularly acute in Spanish higher education. In an attempt to modernize the system, the structure of higher education is undergoing a profound change. University schools and faculties are being brought together to form a departmental structure, based on subject areas. Moreover, Spanish entry into the European Community called for a drastic review of university courses. Most of the courses on offer were of a narrowly academic nature with no relevance to the world of work. As a result, university courses are being adjusted to meet the needs of a modern economy. New professional subjects have been introduced alongside the more traditional academic subject areas. The effects of the new reforms on higher education will take time to become evident and will be liable to evaluation.

The issue of language

Since the Constitution of 1978, education authorities have made provisions to ensure that all children learn the official language of the state, *castellano*, and the official language of each autonomous community (Basque, Catalan or Galician). This is achieved by different bilingual/immersion programmes or through the study of the language as part of the curriculum, with encouraging results.

The government recognized the need positively to encourage and diversify the study of foreign languages if Spain is to take full advantage of its membership of a Single Europe. The study of a foreign language is therefore introduced in the third year of primary school (at 8 years of age) and is compulsory throughout the whole system. In secondary education a second foreign language is offered as an optional subject at the age of 12. English is still in great demand, very much at the expense of French. As a result, the government is introducing measures to ensure that French is offered as well as English by all schools.

The teaching and learning of Spanish abroad, as a foreign or second language, is taken into account. The *Consejerías de Educación* of the embassies provide resources and support to both the Spanish community resident in the host country and the teaching/learning of Spanish as a foreign language within the educational system. Recently, the *Instituto Cervantes* came into existence. It is an autonomous body, attached to the *Ministerio de Asuntos Exteriores* (Ministry of Foreign Affairs). The function of this body is to promote Spanish language and culture throughout the world.

Education for the future

Spain's commitment to Europe is reflected in the nature of the government's commitment to the improvement of Spanish education. In this sector, the process of modernization has been addressed to achieve the levels of provision, freedom and autonomy that are features of the education systems of other European countries. Indeed, it can be no coincidence that the new reforms came into force in the same year that Spain became a full member of the European Community. These aim to provide a high level of education which is geared to the needs of the economy. Moreover, the radical change in the structure of the system reveals a positive response to the implications of a Europe *sans frontières*. By moving the education system to a structure that is more in line with other European systems, Spain is in a better position to offer qualifications and a standard of education that are comparable with those of its European partners. It is hoped that the new system will eradicate existing flaws and strengthen Spain's position within a united Europe, as well as facilitating increased mobility.

Young Spaniards, and students in particular, are becoming increasingly conscious about raising the international visibility and status of Spain. Consequently, they appreciate and participate in the new opportunities provided by increased internal flexibility in Spanish education as well as the international schemes operated by the European Community. The youth of Spain in general see these opportunities in a genuinely European dimension rather than merely as a better means of individual advancement. They and the majority of their families are enthusiastic about the 'Single Europe', and especially the increased and varied educational experiences that will inevitably follow.

This generation of young Spaniards is possibly one of the best prepared and most widely travelled in Spanish history. Programmes like Erasmus, Leonardo and Socrates have contributed enormously to this. As a whole, young people are well informed about their European neighbours, manifest great interest and curiosity in all European issues and are committed to a united Europe, despite some discrepancies over those readjustments that affect traditional sectors in the Spanish economy, like mining, shipbuilding or agriculture. Eager as they are to travel, they do not appear to be interested in a more permanent move to other countries. In general, and despite high unemployment, they seem relatively confident about their future in their own country.

Conclusion

The rapid transformation of Spanish society in the last few decades has been closely related to changes in education in such a way that it has produced continuous feedback between society and the education system. Education has become a key factor in the extraordinary social permeability existing in present-day Spain, which in itself is an entirely new phenomenon in Spanish history. Full schooling from 6 to 16 years of age, over 80 per cent of 16-year-olds and 73 per cent of 17-year-olds attending school, has had a remarkable effect in the number of university students. Even though it is clear that the population has never enjoyed these levels of educational development before, tensions brought up by social and economic changes are also noticeable. Such tensions are reflected in particular problems which are a top priority for the country at the end of the second millennium. Perhaps some of the most important ones are the overcrowding of university education, the unpopularity of vocational education and the lack of a clear connection between the education system as a whole and the world of commerce and industry. Finally, as an exponent of the new state of autonomous communities, the conflict that has recently arisen over the teaching of humanities is a sign of the tensions between a more centralized versus a decentralized vision of the country. Tensions would seem to be unavoidable outcomes of the changes undergone in the space of one generation, which have taken Spaniards themselves by surprise.

For a long time, education in Spain followed a continental pattern which reflected a deductive approach and favoured a methodology in which the teacher was a key figure. The education reform in progress has meant a change in the direction of a more pragmatic and inductive focus where predominance is given to a learner-centred curriculum.

In general terms, one could safely say that there has been a switch from a French influence to a British one. In fact, a kind of synthesis is taking place at the moment. Advantages and disadvantages of both approaches are being brought to light and schools are faced with the challenge of how to deliver, with limited resources and within a comprehensive framework, a curriculum which incorporates traditional subjects like philosophy, Latin or physics, to name but a few, with new ones like environmental studies or information technology; how to keep a right balance between core and optional subjects to ensure similar education for all but with the maximum degree of flexibility to cater for different abilities and learning styles; and finally, how to achieve this while giving enough scope for the cultural and language diversity of the country as a whole.

Bibliography

Centro de Investigación, Documentación y Evaluación (1991). *El Sistema Educativo Español*. Madrid: Centro de Publicaciones del Ministerio de Educación y Ciencia.

Delgado Agudo, J. (1993). *Centro escolar y acción directiva*. Madrid: Servicio de Publicaciones del Ministerio de Educación y Ciencia.

Fernandez, D. *et al.* (1994). *Proyecto curricular de Educación Secundaria Obligatoria*. Madrid: Ed. Escuela Española.

Gimeno Sacristan, J. (1988). *El curriculum: Una reflexión sobre la practica*. Madrid: Ed. Morata.

Manzano, Jesus (1996). *El sistema educativo y las salidas profesionales*. Madrid: Aguilar.

Ministerio de Educación y Cultura (1989). *Diseno Curricular Base. Educación Secundaria Obligatoria (I, II)*. Madrid: Servicio de Publicaciones del Ministerio de Educación y Cultura.

Ministerio de Educación y Cultura (1991). *Bachillerato: Estructura y contenidos*. Madrid: Centro de Publicaciones del Ministerio de Educación y Ciencia.

Ministerio de Educación y Cultura (1996). *El acceso a la Universidad desde las Enseñanzas Medias*. Madrid: Servicio de Publicaciones del Ministerio de Educación y Cultura.

Ministerio de Educación y Cultura (1997). *Curso Escolar (1997–98). Datos y cifras*. Madrid.

Ministerio de Educación y Cultura, Organizacion de Estados Iberoamericanos para la Educación, la Ciencia y la Cultura (OEI) (1997). *Sistemas Educativos Nacionales: España*. Madrid: Centro de Publicaciones del Ministerio de Educación y Cultura.

Moya Otero, J. (1993). *Reforma Educativa y Curriculo Escolar*. Las Palmas: Ed. Nogal.

Nieto, J. (1992). *De la LOGSE al Proyecto Curricular de Centro. Esquemas para Educadores*. Madrid: Ed. C.C.S.

Ramos, Z. and Rodriguez Carreno, M. (1997). *Guia de organización de los institutos de educación secundaria*. Madrid: Ed. Escuela Española.

Secretariado de la Escuela Cristiana de Cataluña (1989). *El curriculo escolar: que es, que pretende, de que consta y como se aplica (I, II, III y IV)*. Barcelona: Secretariado de la Escuela Cristiana de Cataluña.

14 Sweden

*Sven Salin and Chris Waterman**

Background

Sweden covers a total area of 450,000 square kilometres and has a population of 8.8 million. The national language is Swedish. For many centuries, Sweden was ethnically and linguistically very homogeneous with two exceptions: the Finnish-speaking population of the north-east and the Sami (Lapps) in the north of the country. Today, approximately one million of Sweden's total population are immigrants or have at least one immigrant parent. 'Immigrant' includes citizens of other Nordic countries.

Sweden is a constitutional monarchy with a parliamentary form of government. The formal power of the government decision rests with the Cabinet. Parliament (the one-chamber *Riksdag*) is the country's highest decision making body.

With the exception of six years of non-socialist rule (1976–82), the Social Democrats were in power from 1932 to 1991, either alone or in coalition with other parties. In the 1991 elections, the non-socialist parties together won a majority and ruled for three years. After the 1994 elections, the Social Democrats were back in power, a situation which changed again in 1998 when their majority was cut, and the ministers for education and schools were replaced.

Local government has two tiers: there are 23 county councils (*landstingen*) and 290 municipalities (*kommunerna*). County councils are responsible for health and medical care – practically all the hospitals, dental health services and services for mentally handicapped people; they are also responsible for the training of nurses and upper secondary education in agriculture, forestry, horticulture and certain social care occupations. County councils are the responsible authority for approximately 50 folk high schools (*folkhögskolor*).

Municipalities are responsible for child daycare, education at all levels except university, social welfare and care services for the elderly, for energy, water and sewage services, as well as refuse collection and disposal.

In January 1998, the unemployment rate was 7.6 per cent.

---

* Translated into English by Brenda Bennett.

Education and the European Union

Since 1988–9 the Swedish education system has been going through a process of radical reform. Both the compulsory school (*grundskolan*), for pupils aged from 6 or 7 to 16, and the upper secondary school (*gymnasieskolan*), for pupils over the age of 16, have adopted a new curriculum, course plan and assessment system. At the moment, the question of integrating the pre-school (*förskolan*), for children up to age 6, with the compulsory school is under discussion. Adult education is expanding. A commission to look into teacher training has been set up.

The current curricula for compulsory schools (*grundskolor*), upper secondary schools (*gymnasieskolor*) and adult education (*vuxenutbildningen*) were drawn up and adopted in 1994, before Sweden became a member of the European Union. Europe does not, therefore, play a prominent part in these documents. Preparatory documents[1] do, however, take up the rapid changes which have taken place in the world since 1989 and the ongoing process of internationalization. The Swedish curricula emphasize both the Nordic and the global perspective, in which the European identity plays a part. Taking into consideration the number of immigrants who have made Sweden their home since the 1950s the Swedish curricula put great emphasis on ethnic diversity and a multicultural perspective. Against this background it is important to increase awareness of national identity. It is probably correct to state that so far Sweden's membership of the European Union has not had much influence on central government policy for schools.

Sweden has, however, been actively involved in two of the educational programmes within the European Union, Socrates and Leonardo. Before membership, Swedish students took an active part in the Erasmus student exchange programme, within the framework of an EEC agreement. Although unable to influence the programmes, Swedes were very interested in taking part, especially in Lingua and Comenius. At the moment, Swedish schools are taking part in a large number of European projects and act as coordinator for quite a few. There has also been a large number of teacher and pupil exchanges with schools in Europe. Although contacts with the south of Europe were rare when Sweden entered the European Union, a considerable number of cooperation projects have now been established – thanks, to a great extent, to the excellent work of the Swedish European Union programme office.

Sweden also took a very active part in the European Year of Lifelong Learning 1996. More than 50 courses, conferences and cooperation projects backed by European Union grants were organized, and more than 100 with only Swedish backing but with a European hallmark. By taking part in European Union projects, conferences and exchanges a considerable number of Swedish schools, teachers and pupils have made good contacts in Europe. These contacts have created an awareness of a European identity, resulting in education being more influenced at a local level by Swedish membership in the European Union than appears in the central policy documents.

An intensive debate went on in Sweden during 1996, about the White Paper *Teaching and Learning: Towards the Learning Society* of the Commission of the European Communities.[2] Much irritation was caused by the fact that neither the member countries nor the European Union institutions concerned were given the opportunity of influencing the contents as the Commission chose not to publish a preparatory Green Paper as is usual. The then Swedish Minister for Schools, Ylva Johansson, decided, therefore, to publish her own Green Paper,[3] based on the Commission's White Paper. This paper included Sweden's points of view and Sweden's attitude towards the Commission's suggestions. In her introduction Ylva Johansson writes:

> Cooperation within the European Union in the field of education is built, to a very large extent, on voluntary agreements and on decisions which the member countries themselves are responsible for implementing in ways they find suitable. Educational policy is and should remain to a great extent a national concern. I consider this to be a sound starting point.

There is wide support in Sweden for the statements made in the introduction to the White Paper about the way in which society is changing and the demands these changes make on educational policy. Education is one of the foremost means of combating unemployment and social maladjustment. The education system must also be flexible enough and of a high enough standard to cope with the rate of change and the demands which tomorrow's society will make on it.

The Swedish government also agrees in principle with the five general objectives stated in the White Paper:

- to promote the acquisition of new knowledge;
- to bring schools and business enterprises closer together;
- to combat societal maladjustment;
- to give competence in three European Union languages;
- to invest in education.

The Swedish government, however, does not agree with the ways suggested to achieve these aims. They are considered either too bureaucratic or impractical or they encroach on national educational policy. Ylva Johansson sums up by saying:

> Sweden has decentralized its schools. Instead of central control and top-down direction, schools are directed by their own aims and results, which gives a greater opportunity for local influence. This is a question of both democracy and efficiency. In the same way, I consider that the members of the European Union ought to strive towards educational cooperation where the Council of Ministers sets down clear political aims and priorities but where the execution of these aims is allowed to vary from country to country. This means that prioritizing must be clearer than is the case at present and

that aims must concern questions within the competence of the Commission and not the educational policies of the member countries.

(Ibid.)

Finally, Ylva Johansson takes up three areas where she feels European cooperation is important, namely adult education, vocational training and multicultural and integration questions. Sweden has valuable experience in these areas which can be shared with other member states within the framework of European cooperation. These areas are of vital importance for the future development of society.

In 1996 the European Commission's Green Paper, *Education – Training – Research: The Obstacles to Transnational Mobility*,[4] was also discussed. Sweden finds the question of free mobility of great importance and supports the Commission's opinion that existing Community legislation must be respected. In general, however, Sweden has less legislation in this area than other countries. Sweden has also taken various steps to facilitate free mobility for Swedish students, researchers and others. Sweden's general viewpoint is that it is not necessary to harmonize legislation and examinations, but that member countries should recognize each others' qualifying examinations. Sweden agrees that there is a need for better information and knowledge about study and work opportunities in other countries and about different cultural and social conditions. It would be of advantage if information of this kind were available on the Internet.

The current discussion in Sweden concerning the European Union, within the framework of the intergovernmental conference and before the European Union's expected expansion, is directed towards matters other than educational policy. In its continuing cooperation with the European Union, Sweden has chosen to give priority to growth and employment, the environment and open government and measures aimed at increasing citizens' trust in the Union, an area where Sweden wishes to emphasize the consumer perspective. When it comes to expansion, Sweden puts special emphasis on cooperation in matters concerning the Baltic Sea area and with the Baltic States themselves. Swedish public opinion is very critical of, not to say negative towards, several current European Union policies: among others, European Monetary Union, increased bureaucracy and the lack of influence that small countries have within the European Union. Many people also think that the European Union, to a much too great extent, involves itself in Sweden's internal affairs, such as the state alcohol monopoly. If these matters are not handled carefully, there is a risk that negative opinions will spread and could even affect the area of educational policy where, until now, cooperation has worked very well. The younger generation, however, see themselves very much as citizens of Europe.

Developments in the Swedish education system

Since the end of the 1980s, the Swedish education system has undergone an extensive programme of change and reform, characterized by the following three aims:

- deregulation;
- decentralization;
- using goal-setting and monitoring of outcomes as planning tools.

The government adopted these principles for the development of the Swedish school system in three government bills, which were all approved by Parliament, namely:

- the development and management of the school (Act (*proposition*) 1988/89: 4);
- the educational role of the municipality (*kommun*) as the authority responsible for the work of headteachers, teachers, directors of studies and vocational guidance officers (Act (*proposition*) 1989/90: 41);
- responsibility for the school (Act (*proposition*) 1990/91: 18).

As a result of these three parliamentary Acts, the Swedish school system, which had been very strictly regulated and centrally directed, was deregulated and decentralized. The state, government and Parliament set up aims for schools and then monitor and evaluate the results of the teaching. Municipalities (*kommunerna*) were given full responsibility for carrying out the teaching with help from the National Agency for Education (*skolverket*) set up in 1991 under the Ministry of Education.

The National Agency's three main tasks include:

- school development: the preparation of national curriculum guidelines and help with their implementation by informing teachers and commissioning appropriate research;
- teaching assessment: by commissioning national tests in Swedish, English and mathematics, and test banks in German and French, physics and chemistry;
- monitoring decisions passed by Parliament.

Municipalities were given complete responsibility for employing school personnel, including headteachers, teachers, directors of studies and vocational guidance officers. These posts are no longer regulated by the state; it is the municipalities which decide the terms of employment and salary level after negotiations with the unions involved. The only state regulation which remains in force concerns qualification requirements. Municipalities are obliged, when appointing permanent teachers, to employ persons who are qualified to teach the main subject they will be teaching. The 1997 edition of the regularly updated Education Act (*skollagen*) (first published in 1985) guarantees a link between the state teacher training system with examinations recognized by the state and the teaching posts created by the municipalities, in order to ensure uniformity.

Under the new regulations the state no longer controls the development of schools through the grant system and other financial means. To begin with, a sector grant was fixed for education in each municipality. This was based, in principle, on the division of costs between the state and the municipality which had existed previously. The state paid for almost half of the total costs (mainly the salaries of headteachers, teachers, directors of studies and vocational guidance officers) while the municipality was responsible for the other costs, including school buildings, teaching materials and equipment. During the first year the municipalities had the right to reapportion costs between different types of schools. The sector grant has, however, now been abolished and education is financed within the framework of a central government grant to the municipalities, which receive a lump sum to cover child care, education and care of the elderly. This grant is based mainly on demographic factors, such as the number of inhabitants and the distribution of age groups. Other characteristics of the municipality are also taken into account: whether it is in a rural or a built-up area, and the revenue from local tax. This grant must cover all the municipality's costs for the education of its inhabitants except university colleges and universities, adult education which is not organized or commissioned by the municipality, and employment training for the unemployed or disabled. If a municipality does not provide upper secondary education or adult education corresponding to the education available to young people in school, it must pay an inter-municipal fee to the municipality where its young people or adults receive their education.

These proposals were put forward by a Social Democratic government and passed between 1989 and 1991 by a parliament with a Social Democratic majority. The non-socialist parties came into power after the election in 1991 and formed a coalition government. In spite of protests against some of the proposals which had been put forward by the Social Democratic government, especially the one concerning municipality responsibility for headteachers, teachers, directors of studies and vocational guidance officers, no important changes were made to decisions previously taken. After some relatively minor directives, two inquiries concerning the curriculum and the assessment system were completed, both groups presenting their reports in 1992: *School for Education* (SOU 1992a: 94) and *A New Assessment System* (SOU 1992b: 86). It was, however, the non-socialist coalition government which presented 'A new curriculum and a new assessment system for the compulsory school' (Act (*proposition*) 1992/93: 220) and 'A new curriculum and a new assessment system for the upper secondary school and upper secondary adult education' (*komvux*) (Act (*proposition*) 1992/93: 250).

In the main, the school curricula which were later agreed by Parliament, *Curriculum for Compulsory Schools* (Lpo 94) and *Curriculum for the Non-*

compulsory School System (Lpf 94), still apply (see note 8). Only small changes were made by the Social Democratic government which was returned to power in 1994.

Each curriculum comprises two parts. Part 1 covers the basic values and tasks of the school (which will be discussed later in this chapter); and Part 2 deals with goals and guidelines. In this section there are, among others, the following six sub-headings:

- knowledge: the goals to be aimed at and the goals to be attained;
- norms and values;
- responsibility and role of pupils within schools;
- choice of education – work and civic life;
- assessment;
- responsibility of the headteacher.

The curricula do not say anything about how the teaching should be planned and organized, nor about its content or teaching methods. This is left entirely to the professionals in the schools – the headteachers and teachers. Only the goals are stated in the curricula, a document which runs to only 37 pages for the entire Swedish school system.

In accordance with the new system, which covers the entire Swedish education system, each municipality draws up its own plan which states the municipality's aims and expectations for the development of education in its area. Each school has its own local work plan (*lokal arbetsplan*) drawn up by the school staff and approved by the headteacher.

The new system gives municipalities a much greater influence over the education system. In some municipalities local politicians and civil servants have delegated this responsibility to the local schools, making them responsible for their own budgets and financial management. As a result headteachers and teachers also have much greater influence and responsibility, a responsibility for which they have not always been prepared, especially since it has often also been associated with substantial budget reductions.

At the beginning of the 1990s, the Swedish economy went through a period of considerably lower growth than was the case in other comparable countries. Unemployment increased sharply, which led to an increase in the national debt. It was, therefore, necessary both at national and municipal levels to make cuts in the public sector. Municipalities did not receive compensation from the state for the increase in the number of pupils or for inflation. They were also obliged to make cuts in their spending, which hit education, special education, and study and vocational guidance especially hard. Pupil welfare was also affected. Many people blamed these cuts on the new, decentralized system and felt that municipalities had failed in their responsibility towards schools. Others are of the opinion that cuts would have been necessary even if the old system had continued. It is, however, questionable whether it is possible, in present circumstances, to maintain an education system which can provide education of the same high standard throughout the whole country. The government's National Development Plan for the School System (*nationellt utvecklingsplan för skolväsendet*),[5] which was presented in the spring of 1997, and the ensuing bill presented to Parliament on 15 April 1997 concerning increased grants to municipalities, show that the government had taken action as a result of the negative developments mentioned above.

A five-year agreement between the teachers' unions and their employers' organization, the Swedish Association of Local Authorities (*Svenskakommunförbundet*), plays a significant part in the process of change and development within the school system. The agreement comprises two parts: (a) school development, which is summarized in the booklet *En satsning till tvåtusen* (On the Threshold of the Twenty-first Century); and (b) regulations concerning salaries and working hours for teachers, which can be found in *Avtal 2000* (Agreement 2000).[6] In this agreement the teachers' unions take responsibility for participating in changing and developing the organization of work and the methods of work used in schools, taking into consideration, among other things, the social changes taking place and the new technology which is increasingly being used in teaching. The agreement changes the role of the teacher, who becomes more of a mentor, an organizer, inspirer and leader of the pupils' learning.

The teachers' unions also share the responsibility for developing ethical rules for the teaching profession and assisting in the professional development of teachers in various fields, including teacher training, professional development and research. Teaching hours are no longer synonymous with working hours, but now, as in other professions, include related work, such as contact with pupils and parents, competence development, union business and preparation and follow-up work. Salaries are differentiated and individually set. During the five-year period, the agreement gives teachers in the maintained school system some 10 per cent more in salary increases than other employees in the public sector.

By means of this five-year school development agreement the teachers' unions aim to increase their influence over the decentralized, school-directed system. Decentralization must not stop at the municipal level, with responsibility resting with local government politicians, chief education officers or headteachers. It must spread further until it reaches individual schools and every teacher, allowing teachers to share responsibility for change and development within their schools.

In accordance with the policy documents mentioned previously, the government has to make a report every third year (in future, every second year) stating its basic views on the state of the education system and which matters are to be given priority during the coming period. This takes the form of a written report to Parliament in which the government states its political plans and its intentions concerning change and development.

The March 1997 National Development Plan for pre-school, school and adult education gave priority to raising the standard of education and achieving equality of standards throughout the whole of the country. Only a brief report on the relationship between the state and local authorities, and central policy and evaluation will be given here. The government's intentions concerning change and development in the sections about the respective school forms will be dealt with later.

The division of responsibility between the state and local authorities remains unchanged, although the government expressed anxiety about the financial cuts made in education during the last year. These have hit hardest those pupils in need of extra help and support. A lack of resources has led to a reduction in special teaching and support teaching. There are indications that an increased number of pupils are failing to attain the required standard. Providing equivalent education seems, therefore, to be in danger. Local authorities have not succeeded in following up and evaluating the results and quality of school activities. The state will, therefore, make greater demands on municipalities concerning evaluation and the reporting of results. This will involve greater powers being given to the National Agency for Education (*skolverket*) and clarification of its tasks. Special school inspectors, attached to the Agency, will be introduced to follow up and evaluate the results and standards of education. The government will draw up guidelines for continuous quality control at national level. This monitoring will be carried out and reported on in such a way that it provides a basis for assessing the situation of the school system as a whole and can also be used as an instrument to support quality development at a local level.

From the autumn of 1997 and for the next few years, the state will provide additional resources to municipalities to be used, among other things, to improve educational standards.[7] The National Development Plan, the five-year school development agreement and additional resources combine to create the conditions needed for quality development of the education system. The latest National Development Plan[8] presented in May 1999 has integrated the pre-school into the school system.

Basic principles of the Swedish education system

One fundamental principle of the Swedish education system is that all children and young people aged 7–20 years must have access to equivalent education facilities regardless of their sex, ethnic and social background and place of residence. This right is combined with a choice: children and young people or their parents can choose a school other than the one nearest to their place of residence. This applies to both maintained schools and independent schools. If the desired course is not available in the home municipality (*hemkommun*), post-16 upper secondary education must be offered in another municipality. If this is the case, the home municipality is required to pay the other municipality for the services.

Adults also have the right to adult education corresponding to that provided in the compulsory school, up to and including year nine. There is currently a discussion in Sweden as to whether adults should also have a right to upper secondary education and whether municipalities should be required to provide upper secondary education either in the home municipality or ensure that it is available in another municipality.

There is now a relatively clear division of responsibility between the state and local authorities when it comes to the education system. The state, through government and Parliament, has the overall responsibility for education and for defining its objectives. Municipalities are charged with providing and financing all education up to and including the upper secondary level: pre-school, primary, lower secondary and upper secondary education. The state is responsible for providing and financing education at university or university college (tertiary – *högskola*) level. The regional public authorities, the county councils (*landstingen*), are still responsible for some parts of upper secondary education (agriculture, forestry and certain caring occupations) and some university colleges of health science. There are about 140 folk high schools (*folkhögskolor*) with grants paid by the Ministry of Culture; slightly more than half of them are under the supervision of county councils, the others are operated by the 11 voluntary adult education associations (*studieförbunden*) affiliated to political parties, churches of various denominations, trade unions or non-profit-making organizations following particular philosophies of education but independent of them, and financed by the state and the municipalities.

There are only two types of education below tertiary (university college: *högskolor*) level which are under the direct supervision of the state. These are the two schools which arrange distance courses for adults and special schools for the disabled. There is also a grey area of various courses which build on upper secondary education or a corresponding level, but which are not classed as university college courses. This involves qualified vocational training or complementary education of different kinds. Such courses can be arranged by local authorities, university colleges or private institutions.

Legislation concerning education is passed by Parliament which also lays down the aims and guidelines. The government – the Ministry of Education (*utbildningsdepartementet*) – issues the ordinances and prepares the curricula. There are various central authorities subordinate to the Ministry which are responsible for different sectors of the education system. The National Agency for Education (*skolverket*) is responsible for development, supervision, monitoring and evaluation of the compulsory school, the upper secondary school and municipal adult education – also for the pre-school from January 1998. The National Agency for Higher Education (*högskolverket*) is responsible for monitoring, evaluation, coordination and information at university (*universitet*) and university college (*högskola*) level. The Council for Popular Adult Education (*folkbildningsrådet*) is responsible for the allocation of funds between the folk high schools and the adult education associations and for the evaluation of their work. The National Board of Student Aid is responsible for grant support to pupils and students at all levels.

In addition to responsibility for the various levels of education, there are also several ministries responsible for the different sectors. The University of Agricultural Sciences comes under the Ministry (*departement*) of Agriculture, employment training comes under the Ministry of Employment and all other education under the Ministry of Education (*Utbildningsdepartementet*).

An overwhelming percentage of education in Sweden is provided in the maintained sector. Only about 2 per cent of pupils studying at the primary, elementary, lower and upper secondary levels attend private so-called independent schools. Most private schools at the compulsory level are very small and are run by parent cooperatives or foundations and have a specific pedagogical orientation. Private schools at the upper secondary level are run either by individual companies or organizations. All private schools which are recognized by the National Agency for Education are entitled to a grant from the pupils' home municipality. There are only three private educational institutions within higher education, namely the Stockholm School of Economics (*Handelshögskola*), Chalmers University of Technology (*Tekniska Högskola*) and the University College (*Högskola*) of Jönköping.

An important principle of the Swedish education system is that all tuition should be free. In the compulsory school teaching materials and school meals are also free. This also applies, in the majority of municipalities, to the upper secondary school. Municipal adult education and tuition at universities and tertiary (university) colleges is also free of charge but students have to pay for teaching materials. Private schools which receive a grant are not allowed to charge for tuition but other activities may be financed by pupil contributions.

The compulsory school, the upper secondary school and municipal adult education are financed jointly by the state and the municipalities. State subsidies take the form of a topping-up equalization grant paid to each municipality which is based, among other things, on demographic factors. Each municipality meets the remaining costs from tax revenues. It also decides on the size of the budget for each type of school and educational institution and the finance for each individual school. The municipality is also responsible for paying for students who study in another municipality or in a recognized private school.

Higher education is financed entirely by state grants. Institutions receive a lump sum based on the number of students and fulfilment of the education task, the contract for which runs for a three-year period. The size of the grant is affected by the results achieved, measured by the number of credit points earned by the students at the institution.

Both the Education Act (*skollagen*) and the curricula (*läroplaner*) stipulate that all school activities shall be carried out in accordance with fundamental democratic values. All teaching must develop the pupils' ability and desire to take personal responsibility and an active part in the community.

The opening paragraphs of the curricula state that the school shall encourage respect for the intrinsic value of each person and the environment shared by all, and that the school has the important task of imparting, instilling and forming in pupils those values on which Swedish society is based:

> The inviolability of human life, individual freedom and integrity, the equal value of all people, equality between women and men and solidarity with the

weak and vulnerable are all values that the school shall represent and impart. In accordance with the ethics borne by Christian tradition and Western humanism, this is achieved by fostering in the individual a sense of justice, generosity of spirit, tolerance and responsibility.

. . .

Teaching in public schools shall be non-denominational. The school shall be open to different ideas and encourage their expression. Education shall be unbiased and encompass a range of different approaches.[9]

The international perspective is emphasized in the curricula in the following way:

The internationalization of Swedish society and increasing cross-border mobility place great demands on people's ability to live together and appreciate the values that are to be found in cultural diversity. The school is a cultural and social meeting place with both the opportunity and the obligation to strengthen this ability among all who work there.

An international perspective in education is important for making it possible to see one's own reality in a global context, for creating international cohesion and preparing pupils for a society with more and closer contacts which cross national and cultural borders.

A secure identity and consciousness of one's own cultural heritage strengthens the ability to understand and empathize with others and their value systems. The school shall contribute to people developing an identity which can be related to and encompass not just Swedish values but also those that are Nordic, European and global.

(Ibid.)

Pre-school education and child care services

Since 1995 municipalities have been obliged to offer all children aged 1–12, whose parents are gainfully employed or studying, a place in a care centre provided by the local authority or privately. Children aged 1 to 5 years are offered a place in a day care centre, 6-year-olds who do not attend school a place in a pre-school and children who attend school a place in an after-school centre, until they are 12 years old. Parents can choose whether or not to use these facilities but local authorities must meet the demand for them. In addition there are a number of private facilities run by churches or other organizations. Nearly all 6-year-olds who do not attend school take part in some kind of pre-school activity.

There are three kinds of personnel working within child care services and pre-school education: child care attendants, pre-school teachers and recreation instructors. Child care attendants are trained in special three-year programmes in upper secondary schools while pre-school teachers and recreation instructors take a three-year diploma course at a university college.

Until January 1998, child care, pre-schools and after-school centres were under the supervision of the Ministry of Health and Social Affairs (*Socialdepartementet och Socialstyrelsen*) and the National Board of Health and Welfare. This responsibility has now been transferred to the Ministry of Education and the National Agency for Education. The revised curriculum for compulsory schools includes pre-school activities. In 1997 the Ministry of Education proposed the introduction of a special school class for 6-year-olds, the so-called pre-school class.[10] In accordance with the 1999 National Development Plan, central government has given pre-school an added importance as the foundation stone of the education system. The pedagogical role of the pre-school ought, therefore, to be strengthened and made clearer. By integrating pre-schools, schools and child care services, all pedagogical activities concerning children and young people will form one unit. This will, it is hoped, improve the standard of work in this area.

In December 1997 Parliament made a decision about this. The opposition parties are, on the whole, positive towards increasing the importance of the role of the pre-school. They suggest that compulsory school should begin at the age of 6 and should be for a period of ten years.

The compulsory school and its curriculum

The nine-year compulsory, integrated comprehensive school, a model for comprehensive reorganization elsewhere in Europe, was decreed by Parliament in 1962 and established throughout the whole country by the end of the school year 1972–3. School attendance is compulsory for all children aged 7 to 16; however, since 1991, local authorities have been obliged to provide places for those children who wish to start school at 6. As a result, 8 per cent of children now start school one year earlier. Parents also have the choice of letting their children spend their compulsory school years at a recognized private school or at a school other than that nearest in their municipality, or even, in some circumstances, at a school in another municipality.

In 1993 Parliament legislated on a new structure, a new curriculum, new course plans, a new time allocation and a new assessment system for the compulsory school. These policy documents were introduced for years 1 to 7 in the school year 1995–6 and for the whole nine years in 1997–8.

Unlike previous curricula, the new curriculum and course plans state only the general goals which each pupil should attain at the end of year 5 and year 9. The time allocation gives only the total number of teaching hours for each subject or group of subjects for the whole nine years of the compulsory school.[11] Appendix A gives the figures.

The teachers themselves decide how the hours will be apportioned in the different years, taking into account the goals to be achieved at the end of year 5. Teachers have considerable freedom to decide both the content of their teaching and the working methods they use. Every school decides in which year to begin the teaching of English. As a rule it is in school year 3 or 4 but some schools begin in year 1.

Particularly noteworthy in the new curriculum is the freedom that the municipalities, schools and teachers have, which allows local conditions and needs to influence the planning and organization of the teaching. The time plan allocates 410 hours in the nine years of schooling to local issues. Also, all pupils are allocated 470 hours in this timetable to spend either on extra teaching in one of their subjects or on an extra subject chosen from those on the time plan.

The time allocation does not prescribe the length of lessons or how lessons are distributed in any given week or school year. The timetable which states the total number of hours, that is 60 minutes, for the whole of the compulsory school, specifies the total of hours for all natural sciences and the social sciences respectively. It does not state how these hours should be divided among the different subjects within each block. This means that schools can decide themselves whether to treat each subject separately or to teach subjects in blocks.

Language teaching has been given greater weight in the new compulsory school. Pupils can now choose a second foreign language in year 6 and local authorities are obliged to offer German, French and Spanish as alternatives. This means that in school year 7 or 8 pupils can choose a third foreign language within the framework of the free choice of an extra subject mentioned above.

Assessment

The new compulsory school has also introduced a new assessment system linked to the achievement goals set up for each subject and to centrally stipulated assessment criteria. Marks are given in years 8 and 9 on a three-point scale: pass, pass with credit and pass with distinction. Pupils who are in danger of not reaching the pass level are offered remedial teaching or guidance. If, in spite of this, they do not qualify for a pass they will leave compulsory school without a final mark in the subject or subjects concerned. In order to guarantee equivalency and comparability throughout the whole country, the National Agency for Education has been given responsibility for setting national tests in Swedish, English and mathematics for pupils in year 9. These tests are mostly of the essay or problem-solving type, answers to questions or filling in blanks. It is recommended that the schools themselves should set tests in other subjects. All pupils receive a leaving certificate at the end of compulsory schooling.

Issues under discussion at the moment concerning the compulsory school are, among others, the results achieved and the standard of education at this level. According to international comparisons, Swedish pupils are not very good at mathematics and natural sciences; on the other hand, they are considerably better at reading and languages. There is also concern that the financial cuts made during the last few years have hit hardest those pupils most in need of extra support or special teaching. According to reports from the National Agency for Education, about 5 per cent of pupils run the risk of leaving compulsory school without a pass mark in all subjects. The government has, therefore, decided priority measures to improve the standard of teaching. The suggestion, mentioned previously, concerning the coordination of schools and child care services is part of this work. A government commission, the School Committee (*skolkommittén*), which had been looking into these questions presented a report in the autumn of 1997. As already suggested, the National Development Plan emphasizes the importance of local authorities taking much greater responsibility via their local plans for the monitoring and evaluation of the results of education.

School management

The internal working of the school, the prevention, or at least reduction, of harassment, bullying and violence is also being widely discussed. The school must be a safe place of work for both staff and pupils. Schools are cooperating in this matter with child ombudsmen and social authorities. The government is expected to report back to Parliament.

A third topic of debate is how children and parents can be given more influence in the school: not only concerning the teaching but also the use of the school's resources. In 1995–6 Parliament initiated an experiment with parent-dominated school boards.[12] Every local authority is free to start such an experiment in its schools, to appoint a board and to define in which areas the board has authority to make decisions. The headteacher is a member of the board and the staff must be represented but parents must be in the majority.

The School Committee has also been asked to see whether there are still some central rules and regulations which are impeding school development, for example the structure of the time plan and the rules concerning the length of the school year. Suggestions concerning further deregulation can certainly be expected within the next few years.

As can be seen, there is a great deal of change and development currently taking place in the compulsory school, some of which is connected with the five-year development agreement. In this context the use of computers, information technology and the Internet plays an important role. The Swedish, Nordic and European school computer network has created opportunities for both national and international contacts between schools. It is also speeding up the continuing process of internationalization.

Non-compulsory education: upper secondary schools

Sweden has a three-year upper secondary school (*gymnasieskola*) designed to accommodate all young adults. It offers both theoretical education, as a preparation for higher education, and vocational education, as a preparation for working life. It is not compulsory, but about 98 per cent of young people attend an upper secondary school after leaving the compulsory school at age 16 and local authorities are obliged to offer a place to all young people up to the age of 20. All compulsory school education, irrespective of the foreign languages studied and the optional subjects taken, qualifies pupils to attend upper secondary school. Pupils are required, however, to have pass grades in Swedish, English and mathematics from the compulsory school before being admitted.

A reform of the structure of the upper secondary school was approved by Parliament in 1991 and introduced in the school year 1992–3. The first cohort of young people to complete a full three-year course in the new *gymnasieskolan* left school at the end of the spring term 1997. The reform is being monitored and evaluated by a government committee and by the National Agency for Education.

Municipalities are responsible for most of upper secondary education; however, those municipalities which do not provide their own upper secondary schooling pay a fee to another municipality where their young people attend such a school. Studies in agriculture, forestry, horticulture and certain social care occupations, however, are provided in schools run by the county councils. There are also a few private upper secondary schools, mainly for vocational education, managed by individual companies. All upper secondary schooling is co-educational and free of charge.

Upper secondary curriculum

Upper secondary education is organized in 16 study programmes taught throughout the country.[13] Appendix B gives the various options. Many of the 16 programmes are divided into sub-branches for the second and third year of schooling. In addition, it is possible to offer specially designed individual programmes and apprentice schemes. Municipalities may choose to adapt programmes to local needs and conditions.

A characteristic of Swedish upper secondary education is that it is made up of a number of courses, which gives pupils a great deal of freedom of choice. Every subject is divided into a number of courses each with its own goals. Within the framework of a particular programme, which provides the main direction for the studies, pupils can choose courses from other programmes or local courses. All national programmes and special programmes must, however, include eight core subjects: Swedish or Swedish as a second language, English, mathematics, social studies, sports and health studies, science, religious knowledge and aesthetic activities. There is a recommended number of hours for each course which can, however, be changed depending on the pupils' needs and capacity. The schools and the teachers decide themselves how the courses will be organized, either as short concentrated courses or spread out over a number of terms. Teachers also decide, with reference to the attainment goals set for each course, the course content and the methods of work used.

A problem which arises when attempting to compare Swedish upper secondary education with that in other countries is that it is difficult to differentiate between general and vocational education in the Swedish system. Of the 16 national programmes, three are mainly theoretical, namely: social science and humanities; natural sciences and technology; and aesthetics. But even within these programmes pupils can choose courses with a vocational orientation. The other 13 programmes are mainly vocational in orientation but they also include a fairly high proportion of general education subjects. In addition to the eight core subjects pupils can also choose other theoretical subjects, for example modern or classical languages. This makes it difficult for Swedish pupils to take part in such European Union programmes as Leonardo and Socrates.

Language teaching is extensive in Swedish upper secondary schools. All pupils have to study English as a core subject. In addition many pupils, also those in vocational programmes, choose another foreign language, usually German, French or Spanish. Pupils in theoretical programmes also have the opportunity of choosing Portuguese, Italian, Russian, Latin or Greek. In addition, English teaching is often reinforced by the fact that a considerable number of upper secondary schools offer bilingual education, with various subjects taught through the medium of English.

The system of assessment for the upper secondary school is similar to the one for the compulsory school. There are four different grades: fail, pass, pass with credit, pass with distinction. For every course there are centrally stipulated assessment criteria for the grades pass and pass with credit linked to the attainment goals stated in the course plan. In order to facilitate the task of grading and to guarantee consistency and comparability, the National Agency for Education is responsible for setting national tests in Swedish, English and mathematics. Similar tests in physics, German and French are under discussion.

A leaving certificate from the upper secondary school will contain a record of grades obtained for all the courses studied during the three years. A leaving certificate from all three-year programmes meets the general requirements for access to institutions of higher education, providing the pupil has studied all the core subjects and has at least a pass grade in 90 per cent of the courses studied.

There has been a lively discussion recently about the reform of the upper secondary school. The topics which have received most attention are all centred on the fact that the vast majority of young people – 98 per cent – go on to study in the upper secondary school after completing the compulsory school. Upper secondary education – even the vocational programmes – has become increasingly theoretical. The same demands are made on all pupils in terms of knowledge and skills in the core subjects, despite the fact that a large number of pupils have difficulties in achieving the stated goals. Against this background, the government have given notice, in the National Development Plan, that certain changes will be made and a Ministry of Education working group has recently made some proposals.

One such change concerns adapting the course plans of the core subjects so that they are better suited to the special character of vocational education programmes. The government is also considering cutting down the number of compulsory core subjects and the introduction of a completely new, modern type of apprentice scheme, in the light of the positive experiences which other European Union countries have had with such schemes. Upper secondary school work experience and apprentice schemes should lead to an examination including work skills (*yrkesexamen*).

Within the framework of individual programmes, the government also wants to make it possible to offer the opportunity of combining teaching in certain compulsory school courses with upper secondary school courses and work experience, especially for pupils with large gaps in their knowledge and skills at the compulsory school level, linking the two sectors of education. Work experience for these pupils would be more extensive than that offered in the present programmes, which is a minimum of 15 weeks. Apart from this, the government wants to make the educational programmes even more flexible, giving pupils a wider choice.

Adult education

The Ministry of Education is responsible for two different kinds of adult education: municipal adult education and national distance education for adults. The Ministry of Culture is responsible for popular adult education in the *folkhögskolor* and adult education associations (*studieförbund*). The Ministry of Employment is responsible for vocational training.

There are three levels of adult education provided by the municipalities: basic adult education which corresponds to the nine-year compulsory school and gives the same qualification; upper secondary adult education which corresponds to the *gymnasieskolan* and gives the same qualification as the latter; and supplementary education which is a vocationally orientated education and qualification which builds on a three-year upper secondary education or corresponding knowledge and skills.

Adults who do not have the knowledge and skills equal to those gained in the compulsory school are entitled to basic adult education, and local authorities are obliged to provide this. Local authorities must also make an effort to provide upper secondary education and supplementary education to meet the demand and any individual needs which may arise. All municipal adult education is free of charge for students and there are no special entry requirements or examinations. The same assessment system is used in municipal adult education as in the regular schools.

Local authorities must also offer all adult immigrants instruction in Swedish as a foreign language within three months of their arrival. This instruction – on average 525 hours – should give not only a basic knowledge of the Swedish language but also of Swedish society. Local authorities can choose whether to arrange this teaching within the framework of municipal adult education or whether to commission another provider such as an adult education association (*studieförbund*). Local authorities are also responsible for offering mentally disabled adults an education which corresponds to that given to mentally disabled young people.

There are two national schools for adults, one in Norrköping and the other in Härnösand, whose task is to offer adults in the whole country, especially those living in remote rural areas, the same education and qualifications as can be obtained from municipal adult education in the form of distance education. Students study at home and communicate with their teachers by letter, telephone or computer. Videoconference techniques are also used.

The oldest form of adult education in Sweden is so-called Popular Education, provided by folk high schools (*folkhögskolor*) and adult education associations (*studieförbund*). The 136 folk high schools are spread out over the whole of Sweden, as are the 11 adult education associations which organize study circles all over the country. Folk high schools arrange both long courses – usually residential, which give an education corresponding to the compulsory school or the upper secondary school, and short courses of about 2–5 days. Tuition is free of charge but pupils have to pay for their own board and lodging. Folk high schools are free to plan the content of their own courses.

Adult education associations also enjoy great freedom of choice concerning the subjects in which they organize study circles. Aesthetic subjects and social studies dominate. Adult education associations receive state grants and also as a rule municipal grants, but participants in study circles usually have to pay a fee.

In view of the high level of unemployment, the government and Parliament have suggested a considerable expansion of the adult education sector during the coming Five-year Plan which covers the years 1997 to 2001.[14] The rapid changes in society and working life and the development towards an ever-more knowledge-intensive society make it important to ensure that the adult population has a broad knowledge base. The government and Parliament are willing to invest 3 billion Swedish kronor in adult education during each year of the five-year period in order to reduce unemployment and to improve the general level of skills. This gives local authorities the possibility of offering education to over 100,000 adults a year. The aim is that all adults without upper secondary school qualifications should have the opportunity of receiving an education – both theoretical and vocational – which corresponds to the three-year upper secondary school study. Local authorities will be given the responsibility for closing the 'knowledge gap', but they can choose between arranging it themselves or collaborating with other course organizers, such as the folk high schools, adult education associations, organizers of employment training or individual companies.

It is important that the education offered is adapted to each individual adult's capacity and needs and that the needs of the local labour market are taken into account. Unemployed adults who choose to study will be allowed to retain their unemployment benefits and others will receive a generous study grant. The whole of this educational investment is being financed by the state. One of the aims is that it should lead to closer cooperation between different providers of adult education and to a reform of the entire adult education system. A government commission responsible for following up and evaluating this educational investment began work in July 1995 and will continue for five years.

The investment in the adult education programme can be seen as an example of how Sweden wants to tackle employment within the European Union and use education as a means of reducing unemployment and creating economic growth.

Higher education

In Sweden, the term higher education applies to all education which builds on the three-year upper secondary education. Since 1997 all higher education has been brought under the single heading *högskola*, which covers both university (*universitet*) and university college (*högskolor*) education. Some complementary vocational training or qualified vocational education is offered by private upper secondary schools or local authorities.

The state is responsible for all higher education except that provided by certain university colleges of health science. It is financed by the state and is free of charge to students.

There are three kinds of institutes of higher education in Sweden:

- *Universities* These are institutions which provide education in several different faculties and carry out their own research on a regular basis. The traditional universities are Uppsala, Lund, Stockholm, Göteborg, Umeå and Linköping. There are two other institutions which count as universities: Sweden's University of Agricultural Sciences and Luleå's University College of Technology, which has recently been granted university status;
- *sixteen regional university colleges* As a rule these institutions provide education in several faculties but do not carry out research on a regular basis and therefore have no postgraduate research students. There is a discussion going on at the moment about coordinating the activities of some of these university colleges in order to raise them to university status;
- *single-faculty institutions* These include the Karolinska Institute (Medicine), the Royal Institute of Technology, the Royal University College of Music, the Stockholm Institute of Education, and the University College of Physical Education and Sports.

As well as the state institutions of higher education, there are 19 *högskolor* of health sciences run by the county councils. As mentioned, the county councils are also responsible for certain upper secondary education in this field. The merits of transferring the teaching of health science at university college level to the state *högskolan* are under discussion.

In accordance with the current Higher Education Act, which came into effect on 1 July 1993, each institution has considerable independence, is given an educational task and a budget for a three-year period and, in principle, freedom to decide within this framework what courses it will arrange and how many students it will admit. Basic higher education is of two different kinds, leading to a professional or a general degree.

Educational programmes leading to a professional degree are similar in all universities and university colleges. The aims and lengths of these programmes are regulated by a special ordinance. This applies for example to degrees in medicine, education or the law. The length of the programmes can vary between two and five and a half years.

There are three kinds of general degrees:

- university college diploma (*Högskoleexamen*) involving at least two years of study;
- bachelor's degree (*Kandidatexamen*) involving at least three years of study, including at least three terms in the major subject, and a thesis;
- master's degree (*Magisterexamen*) involving no fewer than four years of study, including at least two years in the major subject, and a thesis representing at least one term's work or two theses each representing half a term's work.

The general entry requirements to higher education are the same for all universities and university colleges. Also the special entry requirements for studying professional programmes are the same for all universities and university colleges in Sweden. The standard competence required is usually obtained by following either the social science or the natural sciences programme in the upper secondary school. Each institution is free to determine the entry requirement for single-subject courses. All responsibility for admission and selection rests with the institutions themselves. If the number of applicants exceeds the number of places, selection is usually based on the following criteria: upper secondary school marks, results in the university aptitude test (a national, non-compulsory test), a special aptitude test or interview.

The Higher Education Act also allows each institution considerable freedom to determine the range of courses on offer, their content and organization. Certain goals are, however, stipulated for educational programmes leading to a professional degree. Apart from this, students are able to choose their own study route and to combine different subject courses into a degree. Details of educational programmes and course plans and the organization of teaching in the form of lectures, seminars, group or laboratory work can be decided by each institution. A number of study programmes such as medicine and education include practical training in relevant areas.

As from the academic year 1993–4, each university and university college can decide on the establishment of chairs and the appointment of staff. The teaching staff are grouped in three main categories: professors, senior lecturers and lecturers. Both professors and senior lecturers are required to have a doctorate and the posts involve research, teaching, study and vocational guidance and administration. The lecturers' duties are teaching and study and vocational guidance. Restructuring teaching posts at universities and university colleges is at present being discussed.[15]

The number of students attending universities and university colleges has increased steadily since the beginning of the 1990s and in the academic year 1994–5 there were about 270,000 full-time students. This figure has continued to increase during the last few years due to the difficulty of finding employment. Unemployment among certain groups of academics, including architects, sociologists and psychologists, is lower than among groups who have only a compulsory school or an upper secondary school education. Government and

Parliament have recently decided to find resources for 30,000 more university and university college places mainly in the fields of natural sciences and technology.

Whether it will be possible to find enough lecturers to cope with this increase and whether it will be possible to maintain the standard of teaching are questions being discussed. The idea is that it is easier for people with an academic education to make a contribution to economic growth and in so doing create job opportunities and reduce unemployment. This extra investment is linked with the government's policy to reduce unemployment by 50 per cent by the year 2000.

Teacher preparation

Initial training

Responsibility for teacher training is divided between the universities and tertiary colleges which provide the general education in teaching subjects, and the teacher training colleges or relevant university departments which teach methodology, pedagogics, school curriculum studies and also arrange practical teaching experience. Teacher training has not yet been adapted to fit in with the reforms in the school system which have been carried out within the last few years. The government has, therefore, recently appointed a commission to look into teacher training for all school forms and to suggest necessary changes.

The present system of training compulsory school teachers was introduced in 1988–9. There are three different educational programmes which lead to three different qualifications:

- training of teachers for school years 1 to 7, in either mathematics and natural sciences or Swedish and social science. It is also possible to choose an additional subject such as English, music, art, sports and health science;
- training of teachers for school years 4 to 9, specializing in different subject areas, such as modern languages or Swedish in combination with modern languages, social science, natural sciences or natural sciences and mathematics;
- training of teachers in aesthetic and practical subjects, such as domestic science, art, music, sports and health science. Prospective teachers can also combine these subjects with another subject taught in the compulsory school to obtain a broader qualification.

All these educational programmes are run by university colleges. The length varies between three and a half and four and a half years. Programmes include a course in practical pedagogy, including teaching practice, lasting on average one year. The course in practical pedagogy is usually integrated with the compulsory theoretical studies part.

In the academic year 1992–3, an alternative educational programme was introduced for teachers to teach in school years 4 to 9. This programme makes it possible to choose different subject combinations more freely. After the theoretical courses have been completed the students take a one-year course in practical pedagogy which includes teaching practice in conjunction with a teacher training college. Remedial teachers working in compulsory schools must, as a rule, be in possession of a basic teaching qualification followed by a year-long course in remedial teaching.

Most of the teachers now working in the compulsory school who completed their teacher training before the new training system was introduced fall into one of the four following categories:

- class teachers trained to teach in all subjects in years 1 to 3 (junior school teachers);
- class teachers trained to teach in all subjects in years 4 to 6 (middle school teachers);
- teachers trained to teach in different combinations of subjects in years 7 to 9 – usually two or three subjects. These are secondary school teachers or teachers of special subjects;
- teachers such as sports teachers, music teachers, art teachers, trained to teach practical or aesthetic subjects in school years 1 to 9.

Teachers of general subjects in the upper secondary *gymnasieskola* have a university degree, comprising two or three subjects, achieved after at least four and a half years of study. Courses in modern languages, Swedish, social science and practical or aesthetic subjects must comprise at least two years' study and the practical pedagogy course, including teaching practice, of no less than one year. In the *gymnasieskola* there are also senior teachers with a doctorate or a licentiate degree. Teachers of economics, technology or vocational subjects will have studied economics or technology at university level, have a vocational degree and have taken a course in practical pedagogy. They are also expected to have considerable practical work experience in their respective fields.

Teachers working in the municipal adult education system have the same qualifications as teachers in the compulsory school and the *gymnasieskola*. There is a one-term complementary course for teachers engaged in basic adult education but this is voluntary. Teachers of Swedish for adult immigrants are usually required to have studied Swedish as a second language or to have considerable experience in this field. The only special education programme for teachers of adults is the folk high school line at the University of Linköping. The possibility of introducing a special course in adult pedagogy is under discussion at the moment and is one of the directives addressed to the commission looking into teacher training.[16] Pre-school educators must have a higher education preparation. Care staff are trained in a specialized upper secondary school.

In-service teacher training

The changes which have taken place in all types of schools during the last few years have led to a great demand for in-service training. The introduction of new curricula, new course plans and new systems of assessment would not have been possible if teachers had not acquainted themselves with the policy documents and, using them as a starting point, drawn up local plans of work. The introduction and use of new information technology has also put added demands on in-service training and the professional development of teachers.

The state together with the employers, in most cases municipalities or county councils, share responsibility for teachers' professional development. The state has overall responsibility for providing in-service training – usually through university colleges. The National Agency for Education also has certain responsibilities for seeing that particular types of in-service training courses are available, especially in unusual subjects and for small target groups, but also in fields seen as government priorities.

The employers' obligations are regulated by the Education Act (*skollagen*) which states:

> Each Local Authority and County Council shall see to it that in-service training is arranged for personnel in charge of education. Local Authorities and County Councils shall make every effort to plan the in-service training of their personnel.

The extent of this training is regulated by the school development agreement entered into by the teachers' unions and the Swedish Association of Local Authorities. This agreement states that, on average, 104 hours per teacher per year shall be put aside for professional development.[17] Some of these hours are used at the start of the school year for planning and others at the end for evaluation. Most of the time is spent attending courses arranged by the local authority, the National Agency for Education, one of the university colleges or another organization or local company. Courses abroad are also arranged for teachers of modern languages and other subjects. Teachers who wish to take part in long in-service training courses exceeding the allocated 104 hours can reach a special agreement with their school headteacher and use up several years' allocation in one year. Each local authority and, in principle, each school can decide how much time and money is to be spent on in-service training within the framework of the school's agreed budget. The National Agency for Education is responsible for ensuring that in-service training is also provided for teachers working in isolated areas, either by subsidising their travel expenses or by means of distance learning courses.

As well as the introduction of new curricula, course plans and assessment systems, the following topics have been dominant in in-service training during the last few years:

- the introduction and use of information technology. The National Agency for Education, local authorities, the KK Foundation (a private research foundation) and individual companies such as Telia have contributed large sums of money for equipping schools with computers and for the further training of teachers;
- in-service training of language teachers within the framework of the Council of Europe language projects and the Commission of European Communities' programmes, Comenius and Lingua;
- development work and in-service training within the framework of the Five-year School Development Plan. Projects designed to change methods of work and the way the work of the school is organized are in progress in many local authorities and individual schools. In projects of this kind teachers themselves take a great deal of responsibility for their own professional development;
- Swedish schools and teachers have taken part in a considerable number of projects and exchanges with other countries, both teachers of modern languages and teachers of other subjects, not least vocational subjects. These exchanges and contacts have, perhaps, contributed most to creating an awareness of Europe and of other countries' cultures and social conditions.

Teacher employment conditions: mobility

Unemployment among teachers at about 4 per cent is relatively low compared with other occupations. It is most prevalent in university towns and is often a question of part-time unemployment. There is a shortage of qualified teachers in the north of Sweden, especially of teachers of natural sciences and technology. A shortage of teachers is anticipated at the turn of the century, due partly to an increase in the number of pupils, first in the compulsory school and then in the upper secondary school; and also because a large number of teachers are due to retire at this time. More teachers will also be needed in adult education to cope with the expansion during the next five years.

Mobility is limited both within Sweden and internationally. This is due to the fact that most teachers – about 70 per cent – are women married to men with other occupations and are tied to a certain district. International mobility is made difficult by the fact that in most European Union countries teachers are civil servants which means that special conditions are attached to their employment status; it is not just a question of language proficiency. This makes it difficult, not to say impossible, for Swedish teachers to get a permanent job in another European Union country. In Sweden teachers are not employed by the state but by local authorities, and each municipality decides if applicants are qualified for the post they are seeking. Local authorities can even waive the requirement concerning knowledge of Swedish if it is a question of bilingual education. Only a very few senior Swedish teachers have the opportunity of getting a temporary post teaching Swedish at a European university.

During the next ten years, it seems that there will be good job prospects for those wishing to be teachers in Sweden, especially in mathematics, natural sciences and technology and in modern languages. The prospects for pre-school teachers and recreation and care instructors are not so good, however, as the number of children in pre-school and child care will decrease in the next five years. A number of pre-school teachers and recreation instructors are taking a complementary course in order to be able to qualify for a post as a teacher in the compulsory school.

Administration and evaluation

The Ministry of Education, the highest public authority responsible for the education system, is led by a head of department who is also the Minister of Education and responsible within the department for universities and university colleges. The school section and the adult education section are led by the Minister for Schools. The National Agency for Higher Education (*högskoleverket*) is responsible, under the Ministry of Education, for coordination and information concerning universities and university colleges. The National Agency for Education (*skolverket*) is responsible for the development, supervision, monitoring and evaluation of the compulsory school, the non-compulsory school and municipal adult education. It also draws up course plans and assessment criteria and produces different types of information material, as well as collecting statistics from schools and evaluating educational standards. The Council for Popular Adult Education (*folkbildningsrådet*) is the coordinating authority for the folk high schools and adult education associations.

The 290 municipalities (*primärkommunerna*) are responsible for providing the bulk of education services. In each municipality there are one or more committees (*politiska nämnder*) responsible for schools and adult education. Each municipality decides how these committees are organized. The two most usual forms are either a joint committee for all forms of education, that is, the compulsory school, *gymnasieskolan* and municipal adult education, or one committee for child care services and the compulsory school and a separate one for *gymnasieskolan*, municipal adult education and employment training. Some municipalities are divided according to their different responsibilities; in these cases, compulsory school, child care services and care of the aged usually come under the respective district committee while the *gymnasieskolan* and municipal adult education come under a central committee. Each municipality is obliged to draw up a municipal school plan for all types of education. This plan is adopted by the municipal council and includes a statement of aims which sets the direction for local education.

County councils (*landstingen*) are responsible for upper secondary school education in agriculture, forestry, horticulture and social care occupations, also courses provided by university colleges for the caring occupations. They are also responsible for a large number of folk high schools. Other such schools are organized by the adult education associations operated by political parties, religious organizations, trade unions or voluntary help organizations. There are about 350 private schools, most of them very small. They also have to abide by the Education Act *skollagen* and the central curricula and are assessed by the National Agency for Education. Most universities and university colleges are independent, publicly maintained institutions directly under the Ministry of Education.

University-level education is evaluated by the *Universitetskanslern*, a national authority of principals and top administrators responsible for the standards of all universities, and by the National Agency for Higher Education. Each municipality is obliged to assess its own education programme; national tests, however, in year 9 of the compulsory schools and at various levels in the upper secondary school are set by the National Agency for Education. The National Development Plan indicates that the role of the National Agency for Education is to be strengthened in the fields of monitoring and evaluation, with the introduction of special school inspectors to monitor the results of education. There are no common examinations either at the upper secondary or the university levels. An examination for the upper secondary school has been proposed. The suggested introduction of such an examination and of inspectors to evaluate it has certainly been inspired by what happens in other countries.

The question of language

Sweden is a relatively small language area and Swedish is spoken by only about nine million people. Although about 20 million people in the Nordic countries can understand Swedish it is still a relatively small linguistic group. This is a handicap and makes European cooperation more difficult. There are always considerably more Swedes who wish to study or work elsewhere in the European Union than there are other Europeans who want to come to Sweden. The fact that the Union protects small languages is very much appreciated in Sweden.

Education is carried out mainly in Swedish, even if there are a few independent schools where teaching is carried out in English, German, French, Finnish, Estonian or Sami. An increasing number of upper secondary schools conduct the teaching of various subjects in English. In the few bilingual schools, all subjects are taught in English. Teaching in universities and university colleges is carried out mainly in Swedish, even though course books are often in English and sometimes in German or French. The large universities and university colleges also provide alternative courses taught in English in order to enable exchanges within the framework of Erasmus.

Sweden realized at an early stage the importance of learning other languages in order to be able to make contact and exchanges with other countries. English was introduced as an integral subject in the compulsory school as early as the 1940s, and German and French and more recently Spanish are optional subjects. The number of languages offered in the upper secondary school has also increased. A relatively large number of pupils following vocational programmes in the upper secondary school now study a second foreign language. Their motivation is, naturally, reinforced by the possibility of contacts or exchanges with schools in other European Union countries and, later, jobs.

More than 10 per cent of the total number of pupils studying in Sweden have an immigrant background. Since immigrants are often concentrated in certain suburbs of large towns and, therefore, in certain municipalities, the percentage of immigrants in some schools can be extremely high – sometimes over 80 per cent. In Sweden immigrants have the right to instruction in Swedish as a second language and in what used to be called their home language but is now called their mother tongue. The idea behind this is that immigrants will develop both languages and become truly bilingual. A great deal is said about immigrants as a resource in Swedish working life and society; however, their knowledge of languages and of different cultures and social conditions in other countries has not been used nearly enough. Unemployment is still greater among immigrants than among native Swedes. This is certainly due to the fact that many immigrants have not a sufficient command of Swedish.

The most recent reform of the compulsory school has given the teaching of modern languages a more prominent position. Pupils begin studying a second foreign language as early as year 6 which makes it possible to choose a third foreign language in the upper years of the compulsory school. So far, the effect of this on the upper secondary school has not been seen but it can be expected that more pupils will have a better chance of managing both English and another foreign language. Swedish people in general have a positive attitude to learning foreign languages, and also to make contacts and exchanges with other European Union countries. As early as the second year of Sweden's membership of the European Union, there were not enough grants available to meet the demands made by Swedish schools, pupils and teachers who wanted to participate in the European Union programmes Comenius and Lingua. The number of applicants will certainly increase.

Conclusion

Despite the recent comprehensive reform of the entire education system there is a feeling of anxiety that the changes have only affected the structural framework of the education system and not the school's working methods and quality. The previous government's motto was to create 'The best school in Europe'; the last but one government talked about achieving 'a school which can compete with any in the world'. Although Sweden invests a higher percentage of its GNP in education than any other OECD country this has not led to the best results. The mediocre results in mathematics and natural sciences, compared with other countries, worry both politicians and decision makers, especially as Sweden is in competition with other countries both in European and world markets.

Because of the cuts in the Swedish school budget in the 1990s, local authorities have not received additional resources for the increased number of pupils in the compulsory school, nor has allowance been made for inflation. Indeed, the entire education budget has been cut in real terms due to the need to make reductions in the public sector in order to restore the Swedish economy to health and to reduce the negative balance of payments. This is causing considerable anxiety among headteachers, teachers, pupils and parents. There are clear indications that pupils are not receiving the help they need to achieve the stated educational attainment goals.

The relatively high cost of education in Sweden in relation to the GNP is due to several factors. Sweden is a sparsely populated country with many small schools and many small classes, leading inevitably to a relatively high, and costly, teacher–pupil ratio. Sweden has also, to a very great extent, integrated disabled pupils and pupils with special problems into the regular school system, creating additional demands on the provision of special teaching and additional personal assistance. The right of the many immigrants to instruction both in Swedish as a second language and in their own mother tongue has also led to an increase in the teacher–pupil ratio. The Swedish school had relatively good support services: a school health service, school doctors, nurses and psychologists and school welfare officers. Furthermore, the state has also borne the cost of teaching materials, school dinners, school buses/transport to and from school, which in other countries have been met by the pupils or their parents. During the last few years pupil care, teaching, educational and vocational guidance, special teaching and support teaching have suffered as a result of reductions in expenditure.

A problem which Sweden shares with many other European countries, and which is a source of anxiety to many, is the high rate of unemployment amongst young people. Many are asking if the fault lies within the education system which does not educate for employment. The Swedish upper secondary school has perhaps become too theoretical, with its integrated vocational and theoretical courses and its eight core subjects. It has been shown that pupils who attend independent, so-called industrial upper secondary schools, which have adapted their vocational training needs, are more successful in finding jobs. Sweden's decision to introduce a new sort of apprentice scheme has been inspired mainly by Germany and Austria. The vocational colleges and technical colleges found in other countries, for example, Germany and Finland, have also influenced Sweden's educational policy. At the moment certain experimental, vocationally orientated courses are being run for students who have completed a three-year upper secondary course, following the European Union's recommendation to establish closer cooperation between the educational system and the world of industry and commerce. These courses vary in length between one and three years and one-third of the time is given to work experience.

European influence on Swedish educational policy can also be seen in other areas. An argument used in favour of introducing an upper secondary school examination is that Sweden is the only country in the European Union which does not have a qualifying examination at the end of the upper secondary school. This is also because students often pursue part of their studies at a foreign university, usually within the framework of the Erasmus programme or other exchange programmes. Exchanges are also quite frequent among teachers, researchers or visiting professors, but international activities are still relatively unusual at the upper secondary school level, apart from short exchanges and cooperation projects of various kinds.

Research has, of course, always been international, but in preparation for a possible expansion of the European Union, Sweden has given priority to contacts with the Baltic States, Russia and Poland, within the framework of cooperation concerning the Baltic Sea. Sweden has well-established contacts with these countries and wishes to see them involved in educational cooperation. Sweden supports Poland's and the Baltic States' applications to become members of the European Union.

During the last few years there has been a growing understanding within the European Union, including Sweden, of the importance of education for the part it plays in creating economic growth and in this way reducing unemployment. This means that greater demands are being made on educational standards, which in turn means that the teaching profession and teachers assume a central role in educational policy. During the last 50 years, the status of the teaching profession in Sweden has fallen, but it now seems to be subject to reappraisal. The decentralization of schools and the five-year school development agreement have given teachers an increased influence over the development of the school and, at the same time, an increased responsibility for its development. The Swedish school system is at present going through a period of change but it is too early to say what results will be seen after the turn of the century. European teachers' organizations have combined in the European Trade Union Committee for Education (ETUCE) in order to influence the European Union's educational policy. This work will also hopefully contribute to the internationalization of education and a strengthening of the European dimension.

Appendix A: Time allocations

Time allocation for the compulsory school, showing the total number of teaching hours for each subject, or block of subjects, during the nine-year course.

Art	230
Domestic science	118
Sports and health studies	460
Music	230
Handicraft	282
Swedish	1,490
English	480
Mathematics	900
Geography History Religious knowledge Social studies	885

Biology Physics Chemistry Technology	}	800

Second foreign language	320
Pupil's free choice	470

Total hours (guaranteed)	6,665
School's free choice	410

In order to accommodate the hours envisaged for the school's free choice, the total hours allocated to each subject or block of subjects can be reduced by a maximum of 15 per cent. The hours allocated to Swedish, English, mathematics, a second foreign language and the pupils' free choice may not be reduced.

Appendix B: national programmes

Arts programme	Broad basic education: for work with art-related professions
Business and administrative programme	For work in commerce and administration in private business and public administration
Child recreation programme	For work in child care, after-school and recreational activities, health care, sports and libraries
Construction programme	For work in the construction industry, building and civil engineering
Electrical engineering programme	For work on installation, repair and maintenance of electrical, telecommunications and electronic equipment
Energy programme	For work in, for example, electricity and power stations, heating, ventilation and sanitation installations as well as related work on board ships
Food programme	For work with food processing, sales and distribution
Handicraft programme	For work with different handicraft and trade professions with a large part of the education located in the workplace
Health care programme	For work within the health, dental care and support service sectors

Hotel, restaurant and catering programme	For work as, for example, receptionist, conference organizer, waiter or chef
Industry programme	For work within industrial production, including programming and operating computer-controlled machines and processes
Media programme	For work within advertising, various forms of design and production and graphic media
Natural resource use programme	For work in agriculture, forestry, horticulture and animal husbandry
Natural science programme	Directed towards further studies in mathematics, science subjects and technology
Social science programme	Directed towards further studies in social sciences, economics and languages
Vehicle engineering programme	For work in the repair and maintenance of cars, lorries and machines

Notes

1 *Läroplanskommitténs slutbetäkande 'Skola för bildning'* (Statens offentliga utredningar – SOU 1992:94) Utbildningsdepartementet (Report by the School Curriculum Committee 'School for Education'), Stockholm: Ministry of Education, 1992.

2 *Teaching and Learning: Towards a Learning Society*, White Paper on Education and Training, Brussels: European Commission, 1995.

3 *Utbildningsdepartementets grönbok* (Green Paper), Stockholm: Ministry of Education, 1996.

4 *Education, Training, Research: The Obstacles to Transnational Mobility*, Green Paper, Brussels: European Commission, 1996.

5 Regeringens skrivelse till riksdagen 1996/97:112 *'Utvecklingsplan för förskola, skola och vuxenutbildning – kvalitet och likvärdighet'* (Government Paper 1996/97: 112 'Development plan for pre-school, school and adult education – quality and equivalence', Stockholm: Ministry of Education, 1997.

6 *Avtal 2000 'En satsning till tvåtusen'* (Svenska Kommunförbundet 1996) (School agreement 'On the Threshold of the 21st Century'), Swedish Association of Local Authorities, 1996.

7 *1997 års ekonomiska vårproposition* (Prop 1996/97:150) (Government Economic Bill 1997, Stockholm: Ministry of Finance, 1997.

8 Regeringens skrivelse 1998/99: 121 *'Utvecklingsplan för förskola, skola och vuxenutbildning – samverkan, ansvar och utveckling'* (Government Paper 1998/99: 121 'Development plan for pre-school, school and adult education – cooperation, responsibliity and development', Stockholm: Ministry of Education, 1999 addresses the fundamental norms and values of education, and emphasizes problem solving and creativity.

9 *Läroplaner för det obligatoriska skolväsendet och de frivilliga skolformerna – Lpo 94, Lpf 94* (Curricula for Compulsory Schools and for the Non-Compulsory School System), Stockholm: Ministry of Education, 1994.

10 *Utredningsbetänkande 'Samverkan för utveckling. Om förskolan, skolan och skolbarnsomsorgen'* (Departmentsskrivelse – Ds 1997:10) (Committee Report 'Cooperation for

Development: About Pre-school, School and Child Care'), Stockholm: Ministry of Education, 1997.

11 *Timplan för grundskolan – utbildningens omfattning i grundskolan i timmar om 60 minuter för ämnen och ämnesgrupper samt totalt (Skollagen, bilaga 1 – bifogas)* (Time Plan for the compulsory school, number of hours – sixty minutes – for subjects and groups of subjects and total number of hours) (School Act, see Appendix A to this chapter), 1993. See also Note 8.

12 *Regeringens proposition 'Lokala styrelser med föräldramajoritet i skolan'* (Prop 1995/96:157 (Government Bill 'Local School Boards with Parents in the Majority'), Stockholm: Ministry of Education, 1996.

13 *Nationella program i gymnasieskolan (Skollagen, bilaga 2 – bifogas)* (National Programmes in the Upper Secondary School) (School Act, see Appendix B to this chapter).

14 *Regeringens vuxenutbildningssatsning 'Kunskapslyftet'* (Delegationen för Kunskaplyftet, 'The Adult Education Initiative') Stockholm: Delegation for Adult Education Initiative. Ministry of Education, 1997.

15 Regeringens proposition *'Högskolans ledning, lärare och organisation'* (Prop 1996/97:141) (Government Bill 'The Administration, Organization and Teachers of Universities and University Colleges'), Stockholm: Ministry of Education, 1997.

16 *Lärarutbildningsutredningen* (Direktiv 1997:54) (Commission on Teacher Training: Terms of Reference 1997:54).

17 *Avtal 2000* (Svenska Kommunförbundet 1996) (Agreement 2000 between the Teachers' Unions and the Swedish Association of Local Authorities 1996).

Bibliography

Education in Sweden 1997, Stockholm: Statistika Centralbyrän (SCB), 1998.

Ministry of Education, *The 1994 Curriculum for Compulsory Schools*, Stockholm: Ministry of Education, 1994.

——, *The 1994 Curriculum for Non-Compulsory Schools*, Stockholm: Ministry of Education, 1994.

National Agency for Education, *The Adult Education Initiative*, Stockholm: National Agency for Education, 1998.

OECD, *Economic Survey: Sweden*, Paris: OECD, 1998.

A School for the Future, Stockholm: Liber, 1998.

Special features: education, training and labour market reform.

Statens Offlentiga Utredningar (SOU) (1992a) *School for Education*, Stockholm: SOU.

—— (1992b) *A New Assessment System*, Stockholm: SOU.

Swedish Institute, *Compulsory Schooling in Sweden*, Fact Sheet, Stockholm: Swedish Institute, 1998.

——, *Upper Secondary and Adult Education in Sweden*, Fact Sheet, Stockholm: Swedish Institute, 1998.

——, *Higher Education in Sweden*, Fact Sheet, Stockholm: Swedish Institute, 1998.

15 The United Kingdom

*Andrew Convey and Anthony Merritt**

Any examination of the state of education in the United Kingdom (UK) in the late 1990s must acknowledge the importance of the key themes which pervade the reforms of educational provision and organization taking place at every level of the system. The intentions of recent reforms include:

- the improvement of quality across the education service in relation to the needs of the economy, international comparisons of pupil performance and the need to tackle the consequences of under-performance and under-achievement;
- the eradication of variations in performance which continue to exist between the best and worst performing schools, colleges and local education authorities with adverse consequences in terms of individual entitlement and the effect on society and the economy as a whole;
- the promotion of the capacity of the education system to manage change in a society in which technological progress and development in communications makes modernization of education essential;
- the identification of the most appropriate ways to combine the benefits of school autonomy, diversity of provision in a competitive environment and local responses to identified needs with a national framework of curriculum organization, regulation of standards and requirement for rigorous inspection and accountability.

Educational reform

The 1988 Education Reform Act (ERA) unleashed a flow of legislation which has changed the education system of England and Wales almost beyond recognition. Few democratic societies in recent time have undertaken such a comprehensive transformation, with consequences that will continue well into

---

* The authors of this chapter in the second edition are greatly indebted to Robert Blackledge, who wrote the United Kingdom chapter in the first edition. Wherever possible, they have retained his work in this updated and rewritten version.

the twenty-first century. Key changes resulting from ERA were the introduction of:

- a compulsory national curriculum (set out as an entitlement) for all pupils in state schools from ages 5 to 16 specified in subject terms in more prescriptive detail than the curriculum of most other countries;
- national tests of pupils' achievement at ages 7, 11, 14 and 16 years;
- a system of local management of schools (LMS), with funding of schools according to a pupil admission formula;
- parents' right to vote for schools to opt out of existing local education authority control and become grant-maintained schools (GMS), directly funded by the Schools Funding Agency, a government appointed committee which works independently of government and with no control by the electorate;
- open school enrolment, with parents able to send their child to the school of their choice, providing there is physical space in that school;

During the years between the end of the Second World War and 1988 there was a general consensus to build upon the principles established by the previous 1944 (Butler) Education Act. This had created a national system of education, locally administered, in which elementary schools gave way to primary schools for pupils between the ages of 5 and 11 and secondary schools for pupils between 11 and 14 years of age. The system was administered by local government education authorities (LEAs). The 1944 Act imposed a duty on the parents of every child of compulsory school age to cause him or her to receive efficient full-time education suitable to the child's age, ability and aptitude. A tripartite system of secondary schools was created to enable pupils to be educated in grammar, technical or secondary modern schools. The age of transfer from primary to secondary education was set at usually the age of 11. Psychometric 'intelligence' tests, the so-called 11-plus, now considered to be flawed and simplistic, were the instruments by which children were selected and routed through the secondary stage of education. The 1944 Education Act made hardly any reference to the curriculum to be taught in schools, the only prescribed subject being religious education. In the years which followed, streaming of children by ability and selection at 11-plus gave way to mixed ability teaching and, following government circular 10/65 in 1965 (DES, 1965), selective schools were replaced in most parts of the country by comprehensive schools catering for all abilities.

In the primary sector, the Plowden Report of 1967 (DES, 1967) was influential in changing teaching practice from formal whole class methods, including rote learning and drill, to child-centred, informal activity-based group learning approaches, later to be disparaged in certain political circles as progressive education. Released from the constraint to prepare pupils for an examination at the age of 11 to select them for admission to grammar and technical schools, primary schools were free to experiment, and a proliferation of curriculum organization and teaching styles was introduced. In the later years of secondary education the demands of external examinations regulated the school syllabuses but an excessive proportion of pupils were leaving secondary school without gaining formal qualifications. At the same time the diversity of regional examination boards and their requirements gave credence to suggestions that standards were inconsistent in the performance of those pupils who did attain qualifications after the completion of secondary education at the ages of 16 or 18.

Following the publication of the Warnock Report of 1978 (DES, 1978), a radical review of educational provision for children with special educational needs was undertaken in the 1981 Education Act. This legislation promoted the integration of most children with special needs into mainstream schools and imposed upon LEAs an obligation to make provision for those children whose needs were assessed as requiring the protection of a 'statement' of special need.

During the 1960s and 1970s a feeling was developing that the whole education system might have begun to ossify, that standards of achievement had become depressed at every level of the system, and that schools and higher education institutions were failing to meet the needs demanded by employers. Progressive education, together with an alleged decline in standards of teacher preparation and the deliberate policy of expanding access to further and higher education, were held to be responsible for a perceived educational 'crisis'.

It was in this context that the then Labour Prime Minister, James Callaghan, in a speech to Ruskin College, Oxford, in 1976, asserted his government's intention to intervene in the secret garden of the curriculum and quoted Richard Tawney who had said: 'What wise parents would wish for their children, so the state must wish for all its children' (Callaghan, 1976). A White Paper, *Better Schools* published in 1985 (DES, 1985), stressed the government's intention to introduce a national curriculum to raise standards in schools and to improve the efficiency and accountability of the education system in its use of resources. The Ruskin College speech and the *Better Schools* White Paper initiated a sequence of developments which in 1988 culminated in the previously mentioned ERA: 'a revolutionary Act brought in and then implemented at a revolutionary speed' (Baker, M., 1994). Indeed, it was left to the Thatcher government, re-elected in 1987, to legislate for a national curriculum. The Prime Minister, with some perspicacity, wanted a simple national curriculum, concentrating on English, mathematics and science and absorbing no more than 20 per cent of the school timetable. In the event, its principal architect, the then Secretary of State for Education Kenneth Baker, set up subject groups which recommended an overburdening ten-subject curriculum taking up some 90 per cent of the school timetable.

The National Curriculum

The 1988 Education Reform Act requires maintained schools in England and Wales to provide all pupils with a curriculum which is balanced and broadly based; which promotes spiritual, moral, cultural, mental and physical development and which prepares them for adult life (NCC, 1992). The National

Curriculum is a statutory entitlement for all pupils aged 5–16 years (the leaving age was raised in 1972) which aims to 'raise educational standards by setting demanding but achievable targets for pupils' learning'. It consists of three core subjects: English (or Welsh in those schools in Wales which are Welsh-speaking), mathematics and science, and of seven foundation subjects, technology (including design technology and information technology), history, geography, art, music, physical education and, in secondary schools, a modern foreign language. Welsh is a foundation subject in those schools in Wales which are not Welsh-speaking. The content of each National Curriculum subject is defined by a Statutory Order and consists of a programme of study (PoS) setting out the minimum entitlement of knowledge, understanding and skills for the subject and attainment targets (ATs) which define the expected levels of performance in terms of level descriptions which apply to the four Key Stages of compulsory schooling. The Key Stages define the time-frame of the compulsory National Curriculum: so Key Stage 1 includes school years 1 and 2 (pupils 5–7 years); Key Stage 2, school years 3, 4, 5 and 6 (pupils 7–11 years); Key Stage 3, school years 7, 8 and 9 (pupils 11–14 years); and Key Stage 4, school years 10 and 11 (pupils aged 14–16 years).

Whilst the PoS sets out the content of each subject as a basis for teachers' formulation of units of work and specifies objectives and outcomes for learning and assessment, attainment targets define the expected standards of pupil performance at the end of each Key Stage. In each subject, eight hierarchical-level descriptions have been defined for each AT, except for art, music and physical education which have 'end of Key Stage descriptions' instead. Teachers are expected to use these descriptions to make judgements about the performance of individual pupils against the attainment target. Most pupils are expected to achieve Level 2 around the age of 7 years, Level 4 by age 11, and Levels 5 or 6 by the age of 14 years, the chronological ages corresponding to the end of Key Stages 1, 2 and 3 respectively. Assessment is integral to the National Curriculum and consists of on-going teacher assessments related to subject-level descriptions and Key Stage descriptions, together with end of Key Stage standardized assessment tests and tasks, using external standardized test materials. Thus, at reporting ages 7, 11 and 14, and then at 16 when most pupils sit General Certificate of Secondary Education (GCSE) examinations, all pupils are required to undertake tests which assess their level of achievement in specific aspects of the curriculum. Aggregated test results are then published nationally as School Performance Tables (Dearing, 1993).

The advent of the National Curriculum and its associated arrangements for assessment and testing has effected a revolution in UK classrooms and has brought about a great increase in the workload of teachers as they assimilate the voluminous literature produced by the controlling body, the Qualifications and Curriculum Authority (QCA). A nine-subject curriculum in primary schools has imposed rigorous demands upon the subject knowledge of primary school teachers and has identified additional needs for their in-service education and training (INSET). Objections raised to the formulation of an early years curriculum (Key Stage 1) were to its delivery in terms of discrete subjects rather than areas of experience.

The initial designation of technology as a compulsory subject from 5–16 years and its later development as part of the extended core, has imposed considerable demands upon teachers but has also achieved a breakdown of the traditional gender-stereotyping of practical subjects. The inclusion of technology has also pointed the way to valuing academic and vocational skills equally and, through its emphasis on information and communication technology (ICT), has encouraged innovative pedagogical teaching and learning styles. However, curriculum overload became inevitable in Key Stage 4, where the full ten-subject National Curriculum plus compulsory religious education was continued into the 14–16 years age phase, in which many pupils would be tested by the GCSE examinations in all ten subjects. Many pupils were unable to cope with the burden of the demands made on them, while schools still had to find time to introduce subjects outside the compulsory National Curriculum, such as a second modern foreign language, the classics, geology or economics.

There is broad agreement that the introduction of the National Curriculum has improved the quality of learning in classrooms. However, an influential report on *Curriculum Organization and Classroom Practice in Primary Schools* (Alexander *et al.*, 1992) urged that extensive changes were essential to class-room organization, teaching methods and classroom practice if the National Curriculum was to continue to be successfully implemented at Key Stage 2. Responding to the widespread concerns of teachers, articulated by their profes-sional associations, as well as to the accumulating evidence that there was a need for review, Sir Ron Dearing was appointed in 1993 to undertake a major revision and attempt a 'slimming down' of the National Curriculum. The resulting revised subject orders for Key Stages were introduced in 1995, together with detailed advice and evidence about the planning processes which schools should adopt to ensure successful implementation of a revised version of the National Curriculum (SCAA, 1996). Following the Dearing review, each National Curriculum subject continued to be taught in the first three Key Stages, but in Key Stage 4, history and geography ceased to be mandatory subjects as a response to concerns about 'overload'. Continuing concerns that standards of achievement in basic subjects (especially in mathematics and English) were not improving despite the investment represented by the National Curriculum, led the newly elected Labour Government to set out, in 1998, proposals to legislate for a suspension of requirements to teach the detailed PoS in art, music, physical education, design and technology, history and geography in primary schools, in order to enable a dedicated hour to be set aside each day for developing the skills of literacy and numeracy. At the same time, the status of ICT (information and communications technology) was elevated with the establishment of a National Grid for Learning which combines both a database on best practice and a Virtual Teachers' Centre to support INSET, the necessary in-service education and training activities.

OfSTED and school performance tables

Apart from the National Curriculum itself, further changes to the educational landscape of England and Wales have been implemented through the increased accountability of teachers and schools brought about by the setting up in 1992 of the Office for Standards in Education (OfSTED) and by the subsequent introduction of a requirement for schools to provide information on test and examination results for publication in the School Performance Tables mentioned earlier. Prior to the establishment of OfSTED, schools were subject to occasional inspection by the national inspectorate, Her Majesty's Inspectors of Schools (HMI), and by local authority inspectors, whose main role was to assist schools in the appointment of newly qualified teachers (NQTs), support their induction, contribute to schools' INSET provision and participate as members of teams periodically inspecting and reporting on the work of schools to their employing LEA. From 1992 the work of HMI was augmented by a new and privatized inspection agency in which freelance teams of qualified and trained Registered and Additional Inspectors are contracted to undertake school inspections according to a rigorously defined framework. The OfSTED framework is intended to ensure that judgements about the quality and standards achieved by schools are solidly based on evidence and that teams of inspectors are consistent in their evaluations of school performance (OfSTED, 1995b). Initially, it was intended that schools should be inspected every four years, with more frequent supplementary inspections of schools which were found to be unsatisfactory. The timescale has now been relaxed to, normally, once in six years.

The impact of OfSTED has been dramatic and controversial. Conceived by a government which was determined to overcome the prevailing education establishment (the said establishment perceived by that government to be responsible for low expectations and poor standards of achievement), the OfSTED agency was intended to empower consumers of education in a drive to 'improve standards through inspection'. Consequently, inspection teams include a 'lay inspector', a person who has not previously been professionally involved in schools. Each inspection process commences with a meeting of the parents of pupils attending the school, from which school staff and governors are excluded unless they are also parents of enrolled children. The outcome of the inspection is published in full and a summary must be sent to all parents of pupils attending the school. Prior to the visit of an inspection team, a school must present the registered inspector with substantial documentation, including: the school development plan; curriculum policies and units of work; policy documents for school organization and management; the previous annual report to parents; completed headteacher's form and statement; a staff handbook; and other documentation. During inspections, each inspector observes a sample of lessons taught by all members of the teaching staff and including all areas of the curriculum. The quality of teaching is judged on a seven-point scale from 1 (very good) to 7 (unsatisfactory). This is set within the context of a very comprehensive analysis of every aspect of the life of the school and its partnership links with the local community. The report also includes an overall judgement about whether or not the school is 'efficient, effective and provides good value for money'. After the publication of the school inspection report, the school governors are responsible for drawing up an Action Plan (which must be circulated to parents) setting out the actions which the school intends to take to respond to the issues or concerns contained in the inspection report. Schools which 'fail' the OfSTED inspection are deemed to be 'in need of special measures' if, in the judgement of the inspection team, many pupils are under-attaining and not receiving the education to which they are entitled, or if pupils are at a serious physical or emotional risk from adults in the school or from other pupils (OfSTED, 1995b). If, despite attempts to improve standards, a school continues to be reported as being in need of special measures, the school's governing body may be disqualified by the Secretary of State and the management of the school passed to an action team appointed by the LEA or the Secretary of State in the case of the opted-out direct grant-maintained schools. Private finance can become involved or indeed the school may even be closed.

OfSTED is also responsible for the inspection of all courses of initial teacher training whether taking place in partnerships between higher education institutions (HEIs) and schools or in recently developed School-Centred Initial Teacher Training (SCITT) schemes. From 1997, OfSTED was also made responsible for inspecting the performance of local education authorities in their function of providing support to state-maintained schools and in securing improvement in the schools controlled by the authority (OfSTED, 1997). OfSTED is not restricted to reporting upon individual schools; it may also undertake systematic surveys such as the controversial report on *The Teaching of Reading in 45 Inner London Primary Schools* (OfSTED, 1996). The agency also undertakes scrutiny of education systems in certain other countries for comparative purposes. It is beyond dispute that the work undertaken by OfSTED between 1992 and 1998 has accumulated an evidence base relating to standards of achievement and quality of performance in the education system of England and Wales which must be unique. The commentaries contained in the *Annual Report* of Her Majesty's Chief Inspector (OfSTED, 1992 onwards) are essential reading for anyone who wishes to chart the progress which has been made towards the government's aims of improving standards in education to meet the requirements of the twenty-first century.

The 1992 legislation also contains a requirement that all maintained primary and secondary schools should provide data to enable the publication of comprehensive performance tables which depict the proportion of pupils who have reached expected levels of performance at the end of Key Stages 1, 2 and 3 and in terms of GCSE and of the Advanced Level secondary school examinations which are usually taken some two years later. These performance league tables have been phased in gradually since 1992, and it is intended that parents should consult them to inform and guide their choice of school and to be better prepared to exert consumer pressure, if necessary, for school improvement. As with the data obtained by OfSTED, annual performance tables amass a large amount of data relating to variations in standards of performance in schools and consequential variations in pupil achievement. Parents have been able to consult the tables to compare the performance of schools within localities and in relation to national average standards.

The development of performance tables has also imposed huge stresses and demands upon teachers' time in developing, piloting, marking, moderating and standardizing the tests. The scale of concern was so great in 1993 that the majority of schools supported a teacher unions' national boycott of tests at 7 and 14 years. There remains great concern that the tests ignore the value-added dimension of the school's general contribution to pupils' education, prompting the present government to attempt to develop such value-added indicators, by the inclusion of data on the previous level of pupils' performance. Schools are also being required to set and publish annual targets for pupils' performance against which future progress may be compared.

Developments in Scotland and Northern Ireland

The National Curriculum in Northern Ireland (NI) differs from that for England and Wales in some respects. It has the same ten-level grading scale for measuring children's progress through the four Key Stages of their education but NI National Curriculum subjects are grouped into six broad areas of study. Primary school children in Key Stages 1 and 2 study five compulsory subjects: English, mathematics, science and technology, environment and society (comprising geography and history), and creative and expressive studies (which includes art and design, music and physical education). Irish is compulsory in Irish-speaking schools. Children in Key Stage 3 in the first three years of secondary school continue with all five areas of study and in addition study a modern foreign language or Irish. Pupils in Key Stage 4 continue to study English, mathematics and science, some study technology and a modern foreign language or Irish. They also have to undertake some study of history or geography, or both. Physical education remains compulsory, while pupils must also continue some study of art and design, music, drama or media studies. Religious education, based upon a core syllabus drawn up by the four main churches in Northern Ireland, is compulsory for all pupils from 5 to 16 years. Children are tested at ages 8, 11 and (by GCSE examinations) at 16, but tests are based on teacher assessment with externally set tests limited to a few schools in order to sample the quality of test materials and arrangements. Schools then report the results to parents, using the national ten-level grading scale.

Scotland is preparing its own national curriculum, which is expected to be more flexible and less comprehensive than the equivalent in England and Wales. It covers the ages 5–14 years and also establishes a system of national tests in reading, writing and mathematics. The Scottish curriculum covers five areas: English language, mathematics, environmental studies (including history and geography), expressive arts, and religious and moral education. Each of these areas is divided into 'attainment outcomes', which outline the skills and knowledge to be covered within each area and within which further sub-division occurs into subject 'strands'. In each strand the minimum competences expected of children at each stage of education are defined as attainment targets which are grouped into five levels (A–E), through which children progress from 5 to 14 years. Whereas in England and Wales national tests take place at fixed ages and dates, in Scotland tests will be taken 'when a teacher considers that a child has generally completed the work at one level and is ready to move on to the next'. Each level takes about two years to complete, though some children will progress more rapidly. The results of tests are confidential to parents and the school and enable parents to know how their child is performing in relation to the national benchmarks.

The four main sectors of educational provision

Pre-school education and primary schools

Children in the UK commence compulsory education in the year in which they reach the age of 5. Whilst successive governments have claimed to prioritize investment in the early childhood years, nursery and other forms of pre-school education still lack a clearly stated national policy underpinned by legislation and administered by a statutory body. Pre-school education provision is under-taken by a mixture of agencies, some privately owned and fee-paying, others maintained by LEAs or by the Departments of Health and Social Services. There is a correspondingly high variation in the quality of pre-school provision and in the ratio of places to demand, which often has the consequence of the inverse care law, with less provision in disadvantaged areas or sections of the community (such as those whose first language is not English), whose needs for early childhood education are greatest. An initiative by the previous (Conservative) government to promote expansion in nursery school places by the provision of vouchers (worth £1,000), which parents of 4–5-year-old children would exchange for the provision of a free place in an LEA nursery or school reception class or 'top up' to purchase a place in a nursery, was cancelled by the incoming new Labour government in 1997. LEAs have been anxious for the additional funding to remain in the maintained sector rather than be diverted to private agencies – and parents were often anxious to secure a place for their child in the primary school of their choice through the device of nursery or reception class enrolment. The issue of structural arrangements and funding of pre-school provision has, unfortunately, distracted attention from issues such as the training of nursery school teachers and the range of experiences and appropriate resources which should be provided to 3–4-year-old children (SCAA, 1997a).

From 1998, the new government has introduced a baseline assessment of children entering primary school in reception (or Year 1) classes. There are two stated purposes: to provide information to help teachers to plan effectively in order to meet the child's individual learning needs; and to measure children's attainment so that the outcomes can be used subsequently in 'value-added' analyses of children's progress as measured by teacher assessments and tests at the end of each Key Stage. The baseline assessment is accompanied by Desirable Outcomes for children's learning when entering compulsory education, which are intended to provide a foundation for later learning across the subjects of the National Curriculum (SCAA, 1997b). Six areas of learning have been identified: personal and social development; language and literacy; mathematics; knowledge and understanding of the world; physical development; and creative development. A range of activities is proposed to enable 4–5-year-old children to obtain experiences and opportunities which enable them to achieve the intended learning which promotes their progress towards the Desirable Outcomes. Schools will be able to choose from a range of available baseline assessment schemes approved by the Qualifications and Curriculum Authority (QCA). All schemes must cover the first three listed components, whilst the others are optional.

The introduction of the National Curriculum led primary schools to review the process and structure of their curriculum planning, in particular to move away from a 'topic' approach for organizing and delivering the curriculum to one in which there is much greater emphasis upon subject teaching with a greater use of direct, whole class teaching. The Dearing reform of the National Curriculum in 1995 has been welcomed, but there are still concerns that curriculum over-load leads towards superficial teaching, in which depth of learning is being sacrificed in pursuit of breadth, with the added consequence that lack of rigour and challenge is not resulting in the necessary improvement of standards. The government is concerned by evidence such as that contained in the Third International Mathematics and Science Study (TIMSS, 1997) which demonstrates that pupils in the UK lag well behind children in other countries in their performance in mathematics and science. To improve standards, schools are urged both to undertake more direct teaching and to devote much more time to the teaching of English and mathematics in primary schools.

Comparative studies of performance have shown that countries which achieved higher standards of performance in language and mathematics also devoted more time to their study. For example, in mathematics 16.5 per cent of time at Key Stage 1 and 14.9 per cent of time at Key Stage 2 was devoted to mathematics teaching, compared with 19–20 per cent of time in countries with more successful outcomes (Straker, 1997). In response to this evidence, the government first established National Numeracy and National Literacy Projects in 1996 to pilot a new approach to the organization and teaching of these subjects, including a designated literacy and numeracy hour each day and a highly structured and teacher-directed approach to planning and teaching, using guidelines developed by the national project. Early evidence of successes achieved by the projects encouraged the Secretary of State for Education and Employment to announce that, from September 1998, all primary schools would be expected to set aside a dedicated hour for the teaching of structured lessons in English and mathematics. To make this possible, schools would be freed from the demand to teach the full Programmes of Study contained in the Statutory Orders setting out the National Curriculum. Schools would still have a requirement to teach these subjects but would be allowed much greater flexibility in doing so (QCA, 1998).

Target setting is seen to be a vital strategy for the improvement of standards in literacy and numeracy, both at national level and school level. National targets have been set for 80 per cent of children to attain level 4 in English and 75 per cent the same level in mathematics by the year 2002 (DfEE, 1998b). Each primary school is now required to set its own achievement targets related to its own circumstances but keyed-in to the government's national targets aimed especially at raising standards in under-performing schools. In Key Stage 2, schools are urged to move away from reliance upon generalist whole class teaching, often organized in the form of children working in groups on topic-defined themes, towards a greater use of whole class teaching methods. Provision of subject teaching throughout the Key Stage by 'subject specialists' with particular expertise in one or more subjects is being encouraged. In turn, this has imposed considerable demands for INSET and Continued Professional Development (CPD) as teachers have sought to develop their skills and knowledge in subject specialisms which are often defined by the needs of the school rather than by the subject in which teachers may have specialized during their initial teacher training.

Secondary and vocational education

In the secondary sector of education it is hoped that more effective use of Key Stage 2 test results and improved liaison between secondary and feeder primary schools will contribute to the improvement of standards in Key Stage 3. The government is especially concerned to reduce the variation between standards of achievement at Key Stages 3 and 4 between different schools, especially as many high-performing schools secure good results despite being located in areas of relative disadvantage. At Key Stage 4 and in the 16–19 curriculum considerable attempts have been made to develop a coherent and balanced curriculum which continues to develop knowledge and skills in key subject areas but is flexible in permitting students to develop vocational and occupational competences. To reflect the broadening of curriculum provision in Key Stage 4, new syllabuses have been devised for National Curriculum and other subjects by GCSE examining bodies and for some vocational courses. General National Vocational Qualifications (GNVQs) have been developed by the National Council for Vocational Qualifications (NCVQ), established in 1986 to reform the vocational qualification system of England, Wales and Northern Ireland.

Proliferation of qualifications, together with the sheer diversity of course provision from 16–19 years, a concern to increase participation and achievement in education and training post-16, and a perceived lack of confidence in some examination standards, led the government (in 1995) to request its 'trouble shooter' Sir Ron Dearing to undertake a comprehensive review of the framework of 16–19 age range qualifications. Essential to the purpose of this review was the provision of support to new National Targets for Education and Training with their aim of 'providing a highly-educated, well-trained workforce able to meet the international competitive challenge through high levels of skill and adaptability to change' (Dearing, 1996). The key recommendations of this review are that a single, clear national framework of qualifications should include improved GCE Advanced Level, GCSE, GNVQ, NVQ and a new style 'Advanced Supplementary' (AS) qualifications; improved youth training for 16–19-year-olds through modern apprenticeships, which link work experience to NVQ qualifications; a reinvigoration of National Records of Achievement (NRA) to encourage young people's skills in planning and managing their own learning and for use as the foundation for life-long learning. In proposing a national framework for qualifications, the Dearing Review acknowledges that GCSE and GCE Advanced Level, on one side, and GNVQ and NVQ qualifications, on the other, have developed in response to distinctive needs for alternative approaches to learning but that transfers between pathways should be facilitated to reduce wastage.

The concern to promote increased links between education, commerce and industry and, in particular, to enhance the qualifications and skills of new entrants at every level of employment has galvanized other initiatives. The 1988 ERA permitted the establishment of City Technology Colleges (CTCs), sponsored and part-funded by commercial organizations to act as beacons of excellence in promoting a technologically based curriculum. The Technical, Vocational and Educational Initiative (TVEI) launched in England and Wales in 1983 and Scotland in 1984 was a deliberate attempt by the Conservative government to create a business model for delivery of a utilitarian and vocational model for the curriculum, in which LEAs and schools contracted to provide a work-related enterprise ethos curriculum to equip 14–18-year-olds for the demands of working life. The initiative was funded and organized by the Department for Employment, presaging the subsequent merger of the two government departments of Education and Employment to create, in 1995, a Department for Education and Employment (DfEE). The TVEI initiative also finds echoes in the more recent provision of government grants to enable secondary schools to become specialist colleges in activities such as modern foreign languages, technology, creative arts or physical education. In 1998 (Barber, 1998), the government announced the creation of Education Action Zones (EAZs), to involve a partnership of businesses, community organizations and schools, and which will be jointly funded by government and business to develop innovative plans for raising standards. EAZs will, if they choose, be able to alter radically the National Curriculum and teachers' pay and conditions.

The central role assumed since 1944 by LEAs in the organization of educational provision is challenged in the setting up of EAZs by the new policy that organizations other than LEAs might be responsible for their management. Another example is the setting up of Training and Enterprise Councils (TECs), which are regionally based and have responsibility for development and delivery of youth training in educational establishments and in the workplace. Decline in the role of LEAs has also been evidenced by the 'incorporation' (that is, self-governance) of sixth form and further education colleges (FECs), which provide a broad range of academic, vocational and recreational courses for 16–19-year-olds who continue their education beyond the minimum school-leaving age and also for mature students. Sixth form colleges traditionally focus their provision upon full-time 16–19-year-old students but FECs provide for students of varying degrees of maturity who may be continuing or returning to education to obtain vocational or non-vocational qualifications or simply to undertake leisure and hobby-related activities.

Incorporation of FECs and sixth form colleges was meant to enable college managements to diversify course provision, for which there was aggressive marketing to attract full-time and part-time students. However, as participation rates increased, influenced also by recession in the economy, competition between college providers became intense, leading to 'franchising' arrangements for course delivery and the use of 'outreach' centres by successful institutions. The whole sector has experienced a severe reduction in resources for funding the growth of student numbers, and the consequences have been widespread teacher redundancies, increased contact hours, larger classes, increased staff workloads and a greater extent of casualization through increased use of part-time staff. The issue of widening participation in FE was the subject of a 1997 Report of the Further Education Funding Council chaired by Helena Kennedy (FEFC, 1997), which highlighted the funding bias towards schools and universities rather than FE. In response, the new Labour government committed itself to an expansion of student numbers in full-time sub-degree (higher national diploma) courses and to increasing the participation of groups underrepresented in further and higher education, including people with disabilities, young people from semi-skilled and unskilled backgrounds, and those from economically disadvantaged areas.

Higher education

In the higher education sector, universities and other degree-awarding institutions, the Robbins Report of 1963 (DES, 1963) planned an increase from 8 per cent to 17 per cent in the proportion of young people going into higher education. As student numbers grew in response to a bi-party commitment to the principle that there should be no limit to the proportions of young people who could benefit themselves and the economy from participation in higher education, new universities were created, polytechnics were granted university status and colleges of higher education achieved 'university college' status. However, concern in some quarters about erosion in standards led to the development of much more rigorous systems of quality assessment of course provision in the form of published course reviews undertaken by the Quality Assurance Group of the Higher Education Quality Council (HEQC).

Growing recognition that access to university study, issues of institutional and student funding as well as maintenance of academic standards have interacted to produce a state of crisis in higher education led to cross-party agreement for an inquiry headed by the ubiquitous Sir Ron Dearing. The recommendations of the

Dearing Report on Higher Education (Dearing, 1997), which were slightly modified by the government in respect of proposals for the introduction of new student loans for tuition fees, pave the way to lifting the 'cap' on further expansion of the higher education sector imposed by the previous Conservative administration. The latest government proposals for FE and HE are contained in a 1998 Green Paper *Lifelong Learning*, which envisages a 'learning revolution' expected to have as much impact as the nineteenth-century industrial revolution. FE and HE systems are set to become more flexible in delivery. Higher professional standards will be promoted by a new Institute of Learning and at the heart of the Green Paper is a proposal for a University for Industry (UFI), intended to make contact with those who want to learn by offering 'individual learning accounts' which will link the individual, state and employer in new learning pacts (SOEID, 1998). The new Labour government sees the UFI as significantly extending higher education opportunities to learning centres in the community and the workplace (DfEE, 1995).

Teacher education

Since 1994 responsibility for initial teacher training (ITT) and the continuing professional development of teachers (CPD) has been invested in the Teacher Training Agency (TTA) which was set up to improve the quality and standards of teacher education and training and to promote teaching as a profession (DfE, 1993). In setting up the TTA, it was recognized that the introduction of the National Curriculum would not itself be sufficient to 'drive up standards'. The recruitment, retention and continuing professional development of a highly skilled and well-motivated teaching profession was seen as vital to the achievement of educational policy (DfEE, 1998a). DfEE funding to providers of ITT is distributed by the TTA on the basis of providers 'bidding' for student allocations at fee bands fixed by the TTA according to the type of course. The TTA is charged with improving quality by increasing over time the proportion of trainees allocated to high-quality providers. The 'quality' of ITT courses is determined by regular OfSTED inspection and by the TTA's own monitoring of the performance of ITT providers (TTA, 1997a). A significant development to improve simultaneously the TTA's ability to monitor quality whilst also contributing to induction and professional development of new entrants has been the requirement that all newly qualified teachers (NQTs) be provided with a Career Entry Profile (CEP) by their training institution. In 1998 the TTA commenced publication of 'performance tables' to exert further pressure for quality improvement through encouragement of recruits to ITT to apply to best-quality providers (DfEE, 1997).

Inevitably, reforms of the ITT sector being introduced by the government have encountered resistance from the traditional ITT providers, university departments of education (UDEs) and other higher education institutions (HEIs). There is concern that the methodology of course inspection undertaken by OfSTED may itself be flawed. Criteria against which courses are assessed have been applied to training courses that were not designed and validated to meet their specification. If an OfSTED inspection reveals that an ITT course is 'non-compliant' with the standards specified in the relevant government circular and the DfEE/TTA Framework for Assessment of Quality and Standards, the TTA may withdraw 'accreditation' from the institution concerned. The course will close and existing students and future applicants will be directed to other providers. Institutions 'rewarded' for the quality of their provision may find that additional student numbers are not funded sufficiently to enable staff and other resources, including physical resources, to be enhanced so as to maintain the 'quality' which triggered the higher target intake allocation in the first place. Increased ITT training allocations are also unwelcome if it proves impossible to obtain the additional school placements essential to the school-based training element of ITT courses. Indeed, there remains a continuing anomaly in that there is a statutory requirement for ITT courses to include school-based training but no corresponding obligation imposed upon schools to provide the placements needed, nor any requirement in teachers' pay and conditions of service contracts to provide training to trainees.

Diversification of the range and type of providers of ITT and of the training 'routes' to qualified teacher status (QTS) has also been central to recent government policy. Whilst UDEs and HEIs remain the most established providers of courses for graduate students and of longer courses for undergraduate students (BA/BSc or BEd with QTS) which combine subject studies to degree level with their professional training, the Open University and school-centred initial teacher-training (SCITT) schemes now compete for potential entrants to teacher training. The government encourages, via financial inducements, the most 'successful' primary and secondary schools to become increasingly responsible for teacher training. Alternative routes to QTS status, such as the graduate and registered teacher employment-based schemes extend access to ITT for mature students and potential recruits from other areas of employment and from abroad, whilst exerting a competitive pressure upon traditional UDE and HEI providers. There is no doubt that the agenda for such initiatives has been set by continuing dissatisfaction with the perceived low quality and uncritical methodology of at least some existing courses of training which, it is alleged, have had detrimental consequences for standards of teaching and learning in school classrooms.

Since 1992 the government has required that all courses of ITT offered by UDEs and HEIs should be developed in partnership with schools (OfSTED, 1995a) and that both college-based and school-based training should be focused upon defined statements of competence which NQTs should have acquired as the outcomes of their training. In 1997 these statements of competence were augmented and re-formulated as standards of performance which should be manifest: some as the standards required of training, with others as the standards of practice requisite for successful course completion and the award of QTS. OfSTED inspections evaluate ITT courses in relation to these standards and grade them on a scale from 1 to 4, on which grade 4 is 'non-compliant with statutory requirements'. The NQT's performance is then monitored during the first year of teaching so that QTS which is provisionally awarded on completion of the course of training is subsequently confirmed to the DfEE by the newly trained teacher's first appointment school. Whilst the structure of ITT has been subject to considerable reform, the government has, until recently, refrained from intervening to influence the subject content of training courses or to specify peda-gogical methods. However, just as the introduction of the National Curriculum has had a profound effect upon the processes of education in British schools, so the Labour government has recently determined to influence both subject content and pedagogy by introducing a National Curriculum for ITT. The rationale for doing so is consistent with the overall thrust of national policy:

> Raising the standards expected of new teachers . . . is central to the delivery of the Government's commitment to raising pupil performance across the education system. I am confident that these documents will ensure that new teachers have a clear understanding of best classroom practice and sound subject knowledge before they enter teaching. I also believe that they will prove indispensable to serving teachers.
>
> (Millet, 1997)

The ITT National Curriculum for primary mathematics and English was introduced with statutory effect from September 1997. That for secondary English, mathematics, science and primary science, together with the use of ICT for all trainees, took statutory effect from September 1998. At the time of writing there is no stated intention to extend the ITT National Curriculum to foundation subjects and it may be consistent with the government's overall policy framework to desist from doing so at least until a review of the school National Curriculum occurs in 2000.

Already, a tension exists between those who see the emergence of a National Curriculum for ITT as essential to the achievement of high standards of teaching, and hence to an improvement of the status of teaching as a profession, and those who deplore the initiative as a further erosion of teachers' professional autonomy in an undesirable 'aping' of a subject-based school National Curriculum, which may be both overloaded in content and inappropriate to the learning needs of the future citizens of the twenty-first century.

There is little doubt that the overall effect of government reforms of teacher education has been the achievement of higher standards of training and trainees' preparation for their future career. However, persistent difficulties of recruitment to teacher training courses, especially in secondary mathematics, music and modern foreign languages, science and technology, have impeded the realization of intentions to improve the quality of teaching in schools. Even in those subjects and age-ranges in which a higher ratio of applications per place pertains, the academic qualifications of potential entrants are often lower, both at under-graduate and postgraduate level, than for applicants to higher education courses in areas other than ITT. Government has responded by setting advisory standards for entry to ITT providers: a minimum lower second (II(2)) degree for PGCE courses and C grades (on a scale A to E) at GCE Advanced Level for undergraduate training. However, the TTA's preoccupation with issues of course quality and funding, in which it was able to establish a 'controlling' role, may have deflected some of its energies from its role to promote teaching as a career. Consequently, there has been little to counteract the frequently negative, even disparaging, portrayals of teachers and the state of the education system which sometimes appear in the media and, together with a perception of low pay and poor conditions of work, still deter many more able candidates from applying for initial teacher training (TTA, 1997b).

Developing a European dimension in UK curricula

The subject of 'Europe' has figured in curricula in the UK throughout the twentieth century and indeed before that. Textbooks in geography and history written before the First World War were much concerned with the UK's near neighbours in Europe, often approached from a geopolitical point of view, and European history (as opposed to specifically 'British' history) has been a constant feature of history syllabuses. This situation continued without much change until the mid-1970s, governed largely by the dictates of public examination syllabuses and by individual teachers' enthusiasms. However, with the accession in 1973 of the United Kingdom to the then European Economic Community, followed ten years later by the move towards a National Curriculum, the situation changed somewhat. In the first place, it was felt that as the UK was now a member, any study of Europe should be influenced by the fact that the UK was no longer on the outside looking in. It was at this stage that the UK Centre for European Education was set up to advise teachers and curriculum developers on how they might proceed. A few years later it became quite clear, as the discussions towards a National Curriculum progressed, that the resultant curricula to be followed would be quite prescriptive, thus reducing the amount of teacher freedom to make decisions about the content and presentation of syllabus material, including 'Europe'.

The National Curriculum Council (NCC), which had been set up to develop and deliver the new National Curriculum, had appointed a committee to decide what exactly might be meant by a European dimension in the National Curriculum, both within subject areas and as a cross-curricular theme. This body reported to the Minister in 1990, and the NCC was then able to produce its own definition of what it understood by the term 'a European Dimension':

> The major purpose of a European Dimension is to strengthen pupils' sense of European identity; to prepare them to take part in the economic and social development of the Community following upon the Single European Act; to improve their knowledge of the European Community and of its member states; and to inform them of the significance of the cooperation between those states and the other countries of Europe and of the World. The

> European Dimension in Education should enable pupils to live and work with a degree of competence in other European countries, to reflect critically on experiences in them so as to give an informed understanding of the predicaments and aspirations of other Europeans in order to accept or challenge existing perceptions.
>
> (NCC, 1990)

The NCC went on to produce proposed aims and objectives for working with the European dimension, which are broadly those which had been adopted by the then Department of Education and Science (DES). The NCC's identification of the place of the European dimension in education in schools subsequently appeared in many of its subject documents. At the time it was possible, for example, to see the progression from an early English subject document which stated hopefully that 'English should be regarded as part of the family of European Languages', to a later geography subject document which featured 'The Study of the UK within the European Community' as a major attainment target. While there was a certain amount of attrition as the documents went through the discussion and implementation processes, there remained a degree of encouragement to work with other European countries, as for example within the cross-curricular theme of 'Citizenship'.

It was evident that British teachers operating within this framework were going to be made progressively much more aware of a European dimension in what they were doing, and that at least some were likely to look for in-service and other forms of advice on the topic. The European dimension might seem ideally suited to the sector of the National Curriculum which is given over to cross-curricular themes, and cross-curricular terminology was originally used in DES documents referring to the European dimension in education. However, a 'European Dimension' did not specifically appear amongst those cross-curricular themes which were formally approved for development within the National Curriculum. It is not quite clear why, given the positive ministerial statements about it, though it is possible that the 1988 Resolution from the Council of the European Communities on developing a European dimension in education (Council, 1988), agreed by all Ministers of Education from the member states, came too late to be included in the original structural thinking about the design of the overall National Curriculum. It is also possible that the idea of a European dimension in UK schools was just too much for certain political interests to swallow. Notwithstanding this, a situation existed where the UK government subscribed to the EC 1988 Resolution and had prescribed that all educational institutions should take account of it, even though a European dimension did not figure formally in the National Curriculum.

Teachers, teacher trainers and lecturers were given further guidance in these fields in 1992. Given the perceived need to refocus attention upon European events, the then newly formed Department for Education (DfE) produced its *Policy Models* (DfE, 1992), which made fairly specific suggestions about how a European dimension might be developed within schools and colleges and within certain subject areas. This was helpful to teachers in many respects, but in terms of detailed advice from central government, it was not followed up until January 1998 with the issue by the Department for Education and Employment (DfEE, 1998c) of *Partners in Europe*, a much more detailed document, produced to commemorate the British presidency of the European Union in the first half of 1998.

A number of schools and teacher education institutions have taken up these challenges. A crucial question regarding the European dimension in teacher education is of course one of the availability of time. There are not many teachers who do not see the point of including work on the European dimension in their course structure, but the majority who wanted to proceed were still asking, 'How do we fit it in?', in addition to 'How do we do it?'. In a pilot study undertaken under the auspices of the UK Centre for European Education, and based upon direct experience in their own institutions, Welch and Porter (1992) had put forward guiding principles for institutions aiming to set up policies and practice concerning the European dimension in teacher education. They also went so far as to suggest a form of 'audit checklist' which may be used within a given institution to see to what extent these or other appropriate guidelines were being followed, and in turn to what extent the delivery of a European dimension is being achieved.

With the recent changes in the pattern of teacher education described above, trainee teachers now spend a larger percentage of their course time being trained in schools, which leads to a consideration of how many opportunities to develop a European dimension will realistically continue to be available to student teachers, or indeed to the teachers who are helping to train them? The increased emphasis upon school-based initial teacher education means that partner schools and higher education institutions which provide the educational background to complement the classroom experience exercise a joint responsibility for the planning and management of courses and the selection, education and assessment of student-teachers. Schools have an increased responsibility for preparing students to teach their specialist subjects and to manage classes, and for supervising student-teachers and assessing their competence in these respects. HEIs retain a responsibility for ensuring that courses meet the requirements of academic validation, presenting courses for accreditation, awarding qualifications to successful students and arranging student placements in all schools. Concern has been expressed that the omission of explicit reference to the European dimension as an element for inclusion in ITT courses will have adverse consequences for new entrants in this field.

Meanwhile, the Scottish Office Education Department (SOED, 1994) produced its own statement of policy relating to the position of Europe in the curriculum. Within the overall UK framework of policy, the SOED priorities have been confidently expressed as follows:

- to encourage and support initiatives at regional and institutional levels aimed at developing a European dimension;
- to increase the number of learners of modern European languages;

- to promote the development and dissemination of teaching materials relating to the promotion of European and wider international awareness and understanding;
- to advise on and support teacher training initiatives related to the introduction of the European dimension;
- to encourage the establishment of partnerships between similar institutions in different member states of the EU;
- to establish and develop effective communication points and information networks dealing with the European dimension in education;
- to encourage the development of action plans for short- and long-term implementation of the European dimension in all sectors;
- to establish an effective organizational arrangement within the SOED and other agencies.

(SOED, 1994)

Scottish educationalists accompanied this policy statement with their detailed publication, *Thinking European* (SCCC, 1993), which provided teachers and teacher trainers with many models concerning the introduction of a European dimension into their teaching.

The more recent *Partners in Europe* from the Department for Education and Employment (DfEE, 1998c), to be followed by a sequel, *Europe in the Primary School*, states that 'in some National Curriculum subjects, notably Geography, History, Art, Music and Modern Foreign Languages, the programmes of study ensure that a European Dimension is included', but there is still no specific statement that such a dimension must be included, and of course an 'awareness' of Europe goes beyond 'knowing' about Europe. A key purpose of including a European dimension in education is to develop pupils' understanding of cultural diversity and to refine their attitudes and perceptions about other countries, partly through increasing their self-awareness and partly through challenging their ideas and judgements, so that they feel confident and comfortable in a European context: 'Crucially, a European Dimension can help to demystify the unfamiliar and to enrich the learning process in linguistic, subject-specific and cross-curricular ways.'

Including a European dimension in the school curriculum therefore aims to help all pupils to:

- develop awareness and understanding of their position as active citizens within Europe and in the wider interdependent world and of the opportunities, rights and responsibilities this involves;
- develop a healthy, positive national and international identity and an appreciation of diversity;
- develop the knowledge and skills necessary to feel at ease in a different community, deepen their understanding of other countries and change their perceptions of both their own and other people's communities;
- appreciate different languages and cultures;

- become tolerant and understanding and be friendly, courteous, curious and assured in the company of people from other cultural backgrounds;
- deal with the rapidly accelerating pace of change in today's world and feel secure in the knowledge that their skills, training, qualifications and potential contributions will be recognized and valued across international boundaries.

(DfEE, 1998c)

In addition, a suggested schema of audit, policy development, implementation and evaluation to assist in the management of such programmes is provided. Even so, a European dimension in education is still not an explicit part of the inspection framework. However, an inspector will make judgements on a school's work in promoting the spiritual, moral, cultural and social development of its pupils and in preparing them for adult life. It is assumed that schools which have been including a European dimension in the education of all pupils 'will wish to draw this to the attention of the inspector'.

Under 'Opportunities for Developing a European Dimension' at each of the four main key stages of the National Curriculum, the same DfEE package draws specific attention to:

- examples of opportunities available in National Curriculum Orders to use European examples, context or data and to go with these opportunities; and
- examples of teaching and learning activities and wider experiences;

and it provides many fully worked out models as guidance for teachers. This is a big step forward from all previous situations, making a clear and repeated link between the National Curriculum Order and the 'opportunity'. In Wales, the appropriate Order is even more prescriptive in favour of developing a European dimension.

The extensive role of the Central Bureau for Educational Visits and Exchanges (CBEVE) remains highly significant. It has developed a network of 18 regional European Resource Centres throughout England and Wales, under the slogan: *Europe – it's closer than you think!* It also directs the European Commission's Comenius Programme for the UK, producing major Comenius documentation for schools and colleges, with different editions for England and Wales, Scotland and Northern Ireland. The BBC's *Windows on the World* series (BBC, 1998) 'School Linking and the Internet' promotes contacts between schools throughout the world and has the support of the European Commission. This will be followed by further TV broadcasts on 'European Awareness in Primary Schools', 'Schools across Europe' and 'Bringing Languages Alive'.

The year 1996, proclaimed by the European Union as the European Year of Lifelong Learning, aimed to promote the 'personal development of individuals and their integration into working life and society through lifelong learning'. The UK selected the following areas for top priority for funding from this programme:

- adults in work and adult education: especially in small and medium-sized enterprises (SMEs) and links between SMEs and further education colleges;
- higher education: especially for the development of part-time courses, non-traditional entry routes into universities, and links between higher education and SMEs;
- information, advice and guidance: including more advice on the Training and Enterprise Councils (TECs), continuing education, careers education, partnerships with libraries, non-governmental organizations (NGOs) and others;
- young people (14–19) preparing for work: especially for initial vocational education, modern apprenticeships and SME-linked business projects.

Business education

During the run-up to the Single European Market (SEM) in 1992, a number of studies were undertaken in the UK regarding the degree of preparedness of British business for the new market situation (for example, Department of Employment, 1992; Clarke *et al.*, 1991). The aims of most of these studies were to assess the needs of business and industry with respect to the SEM and to make recommendations as to how higher education institutions might assist businesses in meeting these needs.

In general, studies such as these found that a considerable mismatch existed between the levels of Europe-related activity which had been developed within most institutions of higher education and the comparative lack of interest shown in going in similar directions which characterized much of industry, and especially the SMEs. At this stage, a tendency towards short-termism in many businesses operated against the longer-term strategic thinking which was implied by the onset of the SEM. At the same time, many businesses did not seem prepared to regard the developing SEM as in any way separate from the whole global market.

These reports all recommended a higher level of cooperation between business and higher education institutions, both in respect of the provision of those new graduate skills which business said it was looking for, and in the provision of in-service training within business and industry. Such levels of cooperation are now considerably higher than they were in 1992 and there is good reason to say that all the parties concerned are benefiting from this.

Language skills

One question which always arises at an early stage in a discussion of the European dimension in the UK, and indeed elsewhere in Europe, is that of modern European language competence. The National Curricula in the four parts of the UK all specify fairly clearly how much time should be spent on language learning in schools. Also, with official government encouragement, many teacher education institutions in the United Kingdom have put into practice 'Languages for All' programmes. While there has been a temptation to regard language competence as the prerogative of language students and teachers, clearly at least some form of language 'awareness' should become much more widespread in the UK than is presently the case. A number of individuals and institutions have already shown ways in which non-specialists can make very considerable progress in the field of language (Moulds, 1992).

Progress is of course made easier if pupils and students, language specialists or otherwise, can spend periods of time in another European country, but the need for institutions to develop programmes which lead towards forms of language competence among language non-specialists who cannot for one reason or another spend time in another country remains very important. At the same time, the DES in its *Policy Models* (DES, 1992) and later in *Partners in Europe* (DfEE, 1998c), again supports the important role which teacher education courses and opportunities play in this field.

The learning of one foreign language is compulsory from ages 11 to 16 in England, Wales and Northern Ireland, and in Scotland from 12–16 although this is preceded by language learning in primary schools from 10–12 years (European Commission, 1996). A second language is always optional in UK secondary schools. The picture in primary schools is less clear. Outside Scotland, 'pilot schemes' are available in some places from ages 5 to 11 in England and Wales and from 4 to 11 in Northern Ireland.

Thorogood (1998) has pointed out that there appears to be a new 'language barrier' building up in British students and suggests that 'insularity and complacency are leading youngsters to reject learning foreign tongues, raising problems for the future'. It is not clear why this is now the case, as more optimism was being shown in the early 1980s. Could a decade of apparent public 'anti-Europeanism' in the press and to some extent in government have had its effect? Of crucial importance is the fact that: 'the take-up for modern foreign language GCE Advanced Level [the public examinations taken at age 18] has dropped sharply in the past five years, despite a general increase in student numbers and a larger pool of school pupils studying French in their early teens' (Thorogood, 1998).

As there is already a serious shortage of qualified modern foreign language teachers in British schools, these reduced numbers of students will clearly be insufficient to replenish the already inadequate supply of language teachers. As a consequence, perhaps, the UK has a lower percentage of young people pursuing their higher education in another member state of the EU than any other member state (that is, 0.6 per cent), though only Luxembourg, Greece, Ireland, Austria and Portugal send more than 1.5 per cent abroad.

Education for citizenship

Important issues concerning an understanding of a European dimension in education are raised by the significant cross-curricular theme of 'Citizenship'. Though there is nothing especially new about the existence of what the French call *l'éducation civique* in certain parts of the curriculum in schools and colleges in the United Kingdom, it is really only in the last few years that more general public attention has been drawn to what is now being called 'Education for Citizenship'. Educationalists in the UK have been aware of the implications for teaching programmes of the need to give renewed attention to this matter, and it is notable that great progress in these fields was made during the 1970s and 1980s in curriculum development for intercultural education.

The 1990s saw the appearance of two major developments in the area of citizenship and related curricular matters. The first was the formation by the Speaker of the House of Commons at the beginning of 1989 of the Commission on Citizenship which reported in 1990 (Speaker's Commission, 1990), and the second the adoption by the National Curriculum Council of the subject of 'Citizenship' as one of the formal cross-curricular themes in the original National Curriculum. A glance at some of the features of these initiatives is instructive where the European dimension in education is concerned.

The Report of the Speaker's Commission alerted both government and the educational world to the newly emerging question of 'European citizenship', as outlined in the Fontainebleau Declaration of 1984. It stated that 'Citizenship, whatever it means, is a cultural achievement, a gift of history, which can be lost or destroyed.' The Report made a number of further recommendations which were directed specifically at the educational world, including making 'the experience of citizenship' available as part of young people's education across the curriculum and providing training 'on the entitlement and duties of citizens' to members of the judiciary, teaching, medical, police, armed forces and government civil service professions (Tulasiewicz, 1994).

The Report urges further that a major objective of educational establishments should be to make sure that young people leave school with some confidence in their own ability to participate in their society, and that this will involve the development while in school or college of skills such as 'the capacity to debate, argue and present a coherent point of view; participating in elections; taking responsibility for representing others (e.g. on a School Council); working collaboratively; playing as a member of a team; protesting (e.g. by writing to a newspaper)'.

Such skills would also be useful in developing European awareness amongst pupils. In the event, the National Curriculum Council rejected the creation of a new 'subject' called Citizenship, but maintained the position that a cross-curricular approach is likely to be more effective with pupils and students, as all subject teachers would then be required to consider how they might approach the theme, and develop a 'Whole-School Policy on Education for Citizenship'. It is notable also that recommended approaches to the European dimension in education in the United Kingdom are very similar to this.

The National Curriculum Council's recommended framework for its *Education for Citizenship* is based upon the three elements: objectives, content and activities. There is clearly a close relationship between the successful development of a European dimension in educational programmes and a good comprehension of what is meant and is implied by the concept of citizenship. Is it possible to be a citizen 'of the world' or of a part of the world such as Europe, or must the idea of citizenship be forever confined within existing national boundaries?

These two Reports spoke positively about forms of 'European' citizenship, and were followed, in March 1998, with a newly commissioned Advisory Group Report from the government which recommends that lessons in modern citizenship should become a compulsory 5 per cent of all secondary schools' teaching timetable in the UK (*The Independent*, 1998). Pilot schemes have already been instituted with 11,000 pupils in London-based schools. The results of these current and future developments are therefore certain to have a bearing on how education for citizenship is seen in the future, and on how an appreciation of European citizenship and a European dimension in education grows in the increasingly multicultural schools across the United Kingdom.

Bibliography

Alexander, R.J., Rose, A.J. and Woodhead, C. (1992) *Curriculum Organisation and Classroom Practice in Primary Schools*, a discussion paper, London: Department for Education and Science.

Baker, M. (1994) *Who Rules Our Schools?*, London: Hodder and Stoughton.

Barber, M. (1998) 'Creating a World Class Education Service', text of address to the North of England Education Conference, Bradford, 6 January.

BBC (1998) *Windows on the World: School Linking and the Internet*, Learning Zone, BBC2, March (Online. http://www.wotw.org.uk).

Callaghan, J. (1976) Ruskin College speech, *The Times Educational Supplement*, 15 October.

Clarke, G., Convey, A.L. and Stillwell, J. (1991) *Business Expansion in Europe: a Survey of Information and Training Needs*, University of Leeds.

Council of the European Communities (1988) 'Resolution of the Council and the ministers of education meeting within the Council on the European Dimension on Education', paper from the Council, General Secretariat, 24 May 1988, Brussels: European Educational Policy Statements.

Dearing, R. (1993) *The National Curriculum and its Assessment*, London: School Curriculum and Assessment Authority.

Dearing, R. (1996) *Review of Qualifications for 16–19 Year Olds*, London: School Curriculum and Assessment Authority.

Dearing, R. (1997) *Higher Education in the Learning Society*, London: National Council for Institutes of Higher Education.

Department of Education and Science (DES) (1963) *Report of the Committee on Higher Education* (Robbins Report), London: HMSO.

Department of Education and Science (DES) (1965) *The Organisation of Secondary Education*, Circular 10/65, London: HMSO.

Department of Education and Science (DES) (1967) *Report of the Central Advisory Council on Children and Their Primary Schools* (Plowden Report), London: HMSO.

Department of Education and Science (DES) (1978) *Report of the Committee on Special Educational Needs* (Warnock Report), London: HMSO.

Department of Education and Science (DES) (1985) *Better Schools*, White Paper, London: HMSO.

Department for Education (DfE) (1992) *Policy Models: A Guide to Developing and Implementing European Dimension Policies in LEAs, Schools and Colleges*, London: HMSO.

Department for Education (DfE) (1993) *The Government's Proposals for the Reform of Initial Teacher Training*, London: HMSO.

Department for Education and Employment (DfEE) (1995) *1996 European Year of Lifelong Learning*, London: HMSO.

Department for Education and Employment (DfEE) (1997) *Primary and Secondary School Performance Tables, 1997*, London: HMSO (published annually).

Department for Education and Employment (DfEE) (1998a) *Teaching: High Status, High Standards*, Circular 4/98, London: HMSO.

Department for Education and Employment (DfEE) (1998b) *From Targets to Action: Guidance to Support Effective Target-setting in Schools*, London: DfEE Standards and Effectiveness Unit.

Department for Education and Employment (DfEE) (1998c) *Partners in Europe*, London: DfEE. Online. http://www.dfee.gov.uk.

Department of Employment (1992) *Integrating European Competencies into Higher Education Curriculum Studies: Interim Report*, London: DOE.

European Commission (1996) *Key Data on Education in the European Union*, Brussels/Luxembourg: DGXXII Education, Training and Youth.

Further Education Funding Council (1997) *Learning Works: Widening Participation in Further Education: Report* (chair: Helena Kennedy), London: FEFC.

The Independent (1998) Pupils face 'good citizen' class, *The Independent*, 15 March.

Millett, A. (1997) Bringing a new professionalism into teaching, *Education*, March.

Moulds, D. (1992) 'The Language Element in ERASMUS Exchanges for Trainee Teachers', in *Approaches to the European Dimension in Teacher Education*, Convey, A.L. (ed.), UKCEE/CBEVE, August.

National Curriculum Council (NCC) (1990). Quoted in *Approaches to the European Dimension in Teacher Education*, Convey, A.L. (ed.), UKCEE/CBEVE, August 1992, p. 8.

National Curriculum Council (NCC) (1992) *Starting Out with the National Curriculum*, London: HMSO.

Office for Standards in Education (OfSTED) (1992) *Education in England 1990–91: The Annual Report of Her Majesty's Chief Inspector of Schools*, London: HMSO (published annually).

Office for Standards in Education (OfSTED) (1995a) *School-centred Initial Teacher Training (1993–94)*, London: HMSO.

Office for Standards in Education (OfSTED) (1995b) *Guidance on the Inspection of Nursery and Primary Schools; Guidance on the Inspection of Secondary Schools; Guidance on the Inspection of Special Schools* (3 vols), London: HMSO.

Office for Standards in Education (OfSTED) (1996) *The Teaching of Reading in 45 Inner London Primary Schools*, London: HMSO.

Office for Standards in Education (OfSTED) (1997) *A Framework for the Inspection of Local Education Authorities*. London: HMSO.

Qualifications and Curriculum Authority (QCA) (1998) *The National Curriculum in Primary Schools*, letter of consultation on 'new arrangements for curriculum flexibility' to headteachers of KS1 and KS2 schools in England, London: QCA.

School Curriculum and Assessment Authority (SCAA) (1996) *A Guide to the National Curriculum*, London: SCAA Publications.

School Curriculum and Assessment Authority (SCAA) (1997a) *Looking at Children's Learning: Desirable Outcomes for Children's Learning on Entering Compulsory Education*, London: SCAA Publications.

School Curriculum and Assessment Authority (SCAA) (1997b) *The National Framework for Baseline Assessment*, London: SCAA Publications.

Scottish Consultative Council on the Curriculum (SCCC) (1993) *Thinking European: Ideas for Integrating a European Dimension into the Curriculum*, Dundee: SCCC.

Scottish Office Education Department (SOED) (1994) *Scottish Education and the European Community: Policy, Strategy and Practice*, Edinburgh: SOED.

Scottish Office Education and Information Department (SOEID) (1998) Green Paper: *Opportunity Scotland: a Paper on Lifelong Learning*, Edinburgh: The Stationery Office.

Speakers Commission (1990) *Encouraging Citizenship; Report of the Commission on Citizenship*, London: HMSO.

Straker, A. (1997) 'Developing the primary school curriculum', in *Developing the Primary School Curriculum*, London: SCAA Publications.

Teacher Training Agency (TTA) (1997a) *TTA: Annual Review*

Teacher Training Agency (TTA) (1997b) *Career Entry Profile for Newly Qualified Teachers*

Third International Mathematics and Science Study (TIMSS) (1997) *Patterns of Mathematics and Science Teaching in Lower Secondary Schools in England and Ten Other Countries: Second National Report, Part 2*, by W. Keys, S. Harris and C. Fernandes, Slough: National Foundation for Educational Research.

Thorogood, J. (1998) British students build new language barrier, *The Times*, 3 January.

Tulasiewicz, W. (1994) 'Education for citizenship: school life and society: British–European comparisons', in W. Tulasiewicz and G. Strowbridge (eds), *Education and the Law*, London: Routledge.

Welch, G. and Porter, I. (1992) 'Implementing the European Dimension in Initial Teacher Training: a Pilot Study', in *Approaches to the European Dimension in Teacher Education*, Convey, A.L. (ed.), UKCEE/CBEVE, August 1992, pp. 9–13.

Index